William Tans'ur

The Psalm-Singer's Jewel

Or, useful companion to the singing-psalms. Being, a new exposition on all the one hundred and fifty. With poetical precepts to every Psalm.

William Tans'ur

The Psalm-Singer's Jewel
Or, useful companion to the singing-psalms. Being, a new exposition on all the one hundred and fifty. With poetical precepts to every Psalm.

ISBN/EAN: 9783337149512

Printed in Europe, USA, Canada, Australia, Japan

Cover: Foto ©Lupo / pixelio.de

More available books at **www.hansebooks.com**

THE
Pſalm-Singer's Jewel:
OR,
Uſeful COMPANION
TO THE
Singing-Pſalms.
BEING, A NEW
EXPOSITION
ON
All the One Hundred and Fifty:
With Poetical PRECEPTS to every *Pſalm*.

The whole are faithfully explained from *Sacred Hiſtory*, from *Verſe* to *Verſe*, for the *Uſe* of all Lovers of PSALMODY in general: With *Expoſitional Notes*, referring to all concording Parts of the *Scripture*.—Alſo, An Alphabetical DESCRIPTION of *Perſons*, of *Places*, and of *Things* mentioned in the *Old* and *New* Teſtament; and of *CHRIST*, Poetically.—With a general CALENDAR for the Adapting of *Pſalms* to all Occaſions: And a *New* Set of PSALM-TUNES, in *Three* and *Four* Parts.—With ſelect HYMNS, and DOXOLOGIES: And a general KEY to the whole; for the Uſe of all *Chriſtian* Families, &c. &c. &c.

By WILLIAM TANS'UR, SENIOR.—*Muſico-Theorico*.
AUTHOR of *The New Royal* MELODY; and *The New Muſical* GRAMMAR, and DICTIONARY, &c. &c.

{ Let ev'ry Soul their *Voices* raiſe,—With *Underſtanding* ſing:
 Be not aſham'd the LORD to *Praiſe*,—Who is Our GOD and KING. }
(ECCLUS. li. 29.—1 COR. xiv. 15.)

LONDON: Printed for *S. Crowder*, at the *Looking Glaſs*, over-againſt *St. Magnus*'s Church, *London-Bridge*: Alſo ſold by the AUTHOR, and by his SON, late *Choriſter* of *Trinity-College, Cambridge*; Who TEACH all Manner of *Church-Muſick*, in the *Neweſt*, and *Beſt* Method. M.DCC.LX.

[Price Bound Three Shillings and Six-pence.]

THE
PREFACE:

To all *Lovers* of PSALMODY, &c.

AS PRAISE, and *Thanksgiving* unto GOD, was even as early as the *Creation*, when *the Morning Stars sang together, and the Sons of* GOD *shouted for Joy*[a]; so it is our bounden Duty to *praise* Him, and return our most hearty Thanks for all the *Graces, Mercies,* and *Benefits* we receive at His most gracious Hands: And more, particularly, for that inestimable LOVE of our *Redemption*; by His only SON, *JESUS CHRIST*; under Whose *Gospel* we may have eternal Salvation, &c. &c. &c.

THE Excellent, and most *Glorious,* BOOK of PSALMS was written, by *Inspiration,* for our *Learning* and *Instruction*; by several devout and holy Men, in past Ages; it being a BOOK of *Sacred Songs, Divine Praises, Prayers,* and *Meditations* for every Condition of Human Life: So

---

[a] Vide *Job* xxxviii. 7. and *Preface* to my *Royal Melody*.

that a PSALM, is a *Song* of *Praise*, a musical *Prayer*, or a pious *Meditation*, &c.

THE BOOK of *Psalms* is mentioned sixty-four Times in the *Old Testament*, and three Times in the *New* [b]; in which ten principal *Authors* are put to the old *Titles* [c]: Which *Psalms* are said to be collected into one BOOK by *Ezra*, or *Esdras*, though all called *David's* Psalms [d]: But the Best *Expositors* and *Commentators* thereon are said to be *Musculus*, *Molerus*, *Muis*, *Calvin*, and *Ford*.

THE PSALMS in general, are the very *Marrow* of the holy *Scriptures*; being the extracted *Word* of GOD, in all its choicest Parts; and are as well used by the *Jews* in their Synagogues, as by the *Christians* in Churches; and even the very *Turks* themselves swear as often by the BOOK of *Psalms* as they do by their Book called the *Alcoran*.

ST. *Basil* says, "That if all the rest of the *Scriptures* were to perish, there remains enough in the Book of *Psalms* to supply all:" By Reason, therein are contained the most selected *Promises*, *Threats*, *Instructions*, and *Comforts*: Some of which having, (in their old *Translations*,) the most worthy *Inscriptions* or *Titles*; being therein called JEWELS, and *Golden* PSALMS, &c. from their being formerly written in *Letters* of *Gold*; and ornamented with the most curious *Decorations* in various Colours: Especially those *Psalms* which contained the most *Precious Matter* of the Holy *Scriptures*. GOD hath often shewed Himself to take great Delight in this *Part of Divine Worship* [e]; it being a singular *Means* in his *Service* [f]: So that all the Reformed *Churches* used to *Begin*, and *End* their *Divine Service* with a PSALM or HYMN, &c. in order, that the People might be the better acquainted with Them [g]; and use

---

[b] *Luke* xx. 42. xxiv. 44. *Acts* i. 20. — [c] Viz. *David, Solomon, Moses, Asaph, Ethan, Heman, Jeduthun*, and the three *Sons of Corah*. — [d] Vide *Acts* iv. 25. Read *Ecclus*. xlvii. 5. 8. 9. 10. 13. 17.—Vide also *Ecclus*. li. 23. — [e] 2 *Chron*. v. 13. and xx. 22.—[f] *Eph*. v. 18. 19. and *Acts* xvi. 25.—[g] *Psal*. cxviii. 15.—Vide *Jam*. v. 13. and *Col*. iii. 16. — Read *Ecclus*. xliv. 1. &c. ver. 5. 7. and to the End.—Also *Ecclus*. xxxii. 3. 5.—Also *Ecclas*. xl. 20. 21.

such

To all Lovers *of* Pſalmody.

ſuch *Pſalms, Hymns,* &c. in their Private *Families:* A PSALM, or HYMN, being a ſtrict *Compoſition* of *Words,* in *Meaſure,* and *Number*; fitted to be ſung to a muſical TUNE, agreeable thereunto; and uttered by a *tuneable* VOICE; either *alone,* or with an Artificial *Inſtrument.*

To *ſing* a PSALM, or HYMN, well, and as it ought to be, is one of the hardeſt *Exerciſes* in all our *Chriſtian Religion*; by Reaſon, it requires our greateſt *Attention,* and *Affection* to GOD, to Whom We do ſing; and ſhould lay hold on our grandeſt Affections.—We muſt do it alſo with *Underſtanding* [h], and with *Feeling* [i]: Lifting up Our *Voices* unto the LORD, with a due Reverence, with *Grace* in our Hearts [k]; and in ſuch a decent Manner, obſerving both *Tune,* and *Words,* that the whole *Congregation* may join either with *Voice,* or in *Thought,* as one Man; with one *Heart* and one Soul, in that moſt noble *Part* of *Divine Service*; all STANDING, with the greateſt *Attention*, both of *Body* and *Soul* [l], and not with Oſtentation, or Vain-Glory.—But to be more particular.

Firſt. THE BOOK of *Pſalms,* (as I ſaid in [m] another *Treatiſe*) is *A Compendiary of the whole Scriptures* in general; and was formerly called *The Leſſer Bible,* and were divided into *Five Books*: Containing Divine *Laws, Precepts, Precedents, Politicks, Proverbs, Parables,* and *Prophecies*; and under *Them,* both *CHRIST,* and the *Goſpel.*

Secondly. IT alſo contains the very *Anatomy of the Soul:* And diſcovers all its inmoſt *Sentiments*; wherein all its *Affections, Griefs, Joys, Hopes, Fears, Doubts, Cares,* and *Anxieties,* are ſo ſenſibly touched, as to make *Us* think *We, Ourſelves,* are the very *Parties* concerned; *viz.* The *Penitents,* in the Penitential; the *Petitioners,* in thoſe of

---

[h] *Pſal.* xlvii. 7. 1 *Cor.* xiv. 15. — [i] *Col.* iii. 16. — [k] *Eph.* v. 19. — [l] *Matt.* xxviii. 30. *James* v. 13. *Acts* xvi. 25. *Mark* xiv. 26. — [m] My *Royal* MELODY, 2d Edit. *&c.* Vide *Eccluſ.* xl. 21.

Prayer;

The PREFACE:

Prayer; and the Joyful *Addreſſers*, in PSALMS of *Praiſe* and *Thankſgiving*.

Thirdly. THAT precious BOOK, is alſo *The Soul's Divinity School*: Or, A choice *Directory* of Our ſeveral *Duties* to GOD, Ourſelves, and to our Neighbours; being the very *Seat* of religious *Diſcipline*; viz. To Mortify the *Proud*; to Advance the *Humble*; to Inform the *Ignorant* ⁿ; and to Improve the *Skilful*, the Willing, and the Ingenious.

Fourthly. IT is likewiſe *The Soul's Diſpenſatory*, of all *Medicines*: Wherein are *Lenitives* for tender Wounds; *Corroſives* for Inveterate; *Cures* for the Infected; *Preſervatives* for the Sound; *Cordials* for the Weak; and *Reſtoratives* for the Relapſed º.

Fifthly. IT is *A Treaſury*, or, *Magazine of all Accommodations*: For every Circumſtance of Human *Life*; whether in *Sickneſs*, in *Health*, in *Youth*, Old-*Age*, *Day*, *Night*, *Plenty*, *Poverty*, *Safety*, *Danger*, *Peace*, *War*, *Society*, *Solitude*, *Liberty*, *Confinement*, *Exile*, on *Land*, or *Sea* ᵖ.

Sixthly. IT is *An Infallible Oracle*: And may be conſulted in all *Caſes* whatſoever, by all Sorts of People in general; viz. By *Princes*, by *Prieſts*, *Magiſtrates*, *Rulers*, or *Families*; *High* or *Low*, *Rich* or *Poor*; one with another; even from the *Throne*, down to the *Cottage* ᵠ.

Seventhly. IT is *The Church's Oeconomy*, Militant, and Triumphant: Containing, *A Common Oratory* of *Prayers*, *Praiſes*, and *Thankſgivings*, ſuitable to every Circumſtance of *Life*, &c. keeping up the Glorious *Correſpondence* between *Men* and *Angels*; *Earth*, and *Heaven* ʳ.

Eighthly. This BOOK is alſo, *A true Proſpect of Nature*, and a *Mirror* of the whole UNIVERSE in general: Wherein is a Beautiful Diſplay of *Animals*, *Elements*, *Earth*, *Sea*, and *Sky*, &c. the *Corporeal*, and *Incorporeal World*, from the *Creature* to the CREATOR; with all

---

ⁿ *Pſal.* xix. 8. — º *Pſal.* li. — ᵖ *Pſal.* cvii. — ᵠ *Pſal.* xxix. — ʳ *Pſal.* cxlv.

To all Lovers *of* Pſalmody. vii

His Divine *Attributes*, and Perfections: And all *Theſe* are Invited to *Praiſe the* LORD ˢ.

Ninthly. It is alſo, *The Soul's Paradiſe of Spiritual Recreations:* And affords the Body ſweet *Refreſhments* after hard *Labour*, and *Study*; it ſweetens the ſeverer Exerciſes of religious *Duties*, it recruits the exhauſted Spirits with freſh Supplies of *Devotion*; and gives Wings to *Praiſe*, and *Fervency* to Prayer; by the reſiſtleſs Charms of Divine *Rhetorick*, Seraphick *Eloquence*, and *Solemn* Harmony ᵗ, *&c.*

Tenthly. In that *glorious* Book We are alſo exhorted to Three *Theological Virtues*, viz. To *Faith* ᵘ, to *Hope* ʷ, and to *Charity* ˣ; and unto *Three* Kinds of *Good Works*, viz. To *Faſting* ʸ, to *Prayer* ᶻ, and to *Alms-Deeds* ᵃ: Which proceed from the *Seven* Gifts of the *Spirit*, viz. From the Spirit of *Wiſdom* ᵇ, the Spirit of *Underſtanding* ᶜ, the Spirit of *Counſel* ᵈ, the Spirit of *Spiritual Strength* ᵉ, the Spirit of *Knowledge* ᶠ, the Spirit of *Piety* ᵍ, and the Spirit of *Holy-Fear* ʰ.

Eleventhly. Therein are alſo ſhewed the *Twelve* Fruits of the Holy *Spirit* of GOD, *viz.* The Fruits of Love ⁱ, the Fruits of *Joy* ᵏ, the Fruits of *Peace* ˡ, the Fruits of *Patience* ᵐ, the Fruits of *Mercy* ⁿ, the Fruits of *Goodneſs* ᵒ, the Fruits of *Long-Suffering* ᵖ, the Fruits of *Meekneſs* ᑫ, the Fruits of *Faith* ʳ, the Fruits of *Modeſty* ˢ, the Fruits of *Shame-facedneſs* ᵗ, and the Fruits of *Sobriety* ᵘ, *&c.*

Twelfthly. We are alſo therein called to the *Seven* Spiritual *Works* of *Mercy*, viz. To *Inſtruct* the Ignorant ʷ, to

---

ˢ *Pſal.* cxlviii. and cl.—Vide *Pſal.* l. ver ult. and *Col.* iii. 16. — ᵗ *Pſal.* xcii. — ᵘ *Pſal.* cxxv. — ʷ *Pſal.* cxxxvi. — ˣ *Pſal.* cxii. Vide 1 *Cor.* xiii. — ʸ 1 *Cor.* vii. 5. — ᶻ *Pſal.* cii. 17. *Matt.* xxi. 22. — ᵃ *Pſal.* xli. — ᵇ *Pſal.* cxi. 10. — *Exod.* xxxi. 6. *Prov.* ii. 6. — ᶜ *Pſal.* cxix. and civ. — ᵈ *Pſal.* xxxiii. 11. — ᵉ *Pſal.* lxviii. 35. — ᶠ *Pſal.* ix. 10. *Prov.* ii. 10. — ᵍ *Pſal.* i. 2 *Tim.* iv. 8. — ʰ *Pſal.* ii. *Deut.* vi 24. — ⁱ *Pſal.* xci. — ᵏ *Pſal.* xcviii. — ˡ *Pſal.* xxxvii. — ᵐ *Pſal.* xxvii. — ⁿ *Pſal.* xxxvi. — ᵒ *Pſal.* ciii. — ᵖ *Pſal.* xliii. — ᑫ *Pſal.* xxxvii. 11. — ʳ *Pſal.* xci. and cxxv. — ˢ 1 *Tim.* ii. 9. — ᵗ 1 *Tim.* ii. 9. *Ecclus.* xxvi. 26. — ᵘ *Tit.* ii. 12. — ʷ *Pſal.* xix. *Matt.* xviii. —

Correct

Correct Offenders [x], to *Counsel* the Doubtful [y], to *Comfort* the Afflicted [z], to *Suffer* Wrongs patiently [a], to *Forgive* all Offenders [b], and to *Pray* for others [c] : And also to *Six* other *Works* of *Mercy*, viz. To *Feed* the Hungry [d], to *Cloath* the Naked [e], to *Entertain* the Stranger, and the Needy [f], to *Minister* to Prisoners, and Captives [g], to *Visit* the Sick [h], and to *Bury* the Dead [i].

Thirteenthly. IN like Manner, We are therein greatly cautioned utterly to avoid these *Seven* deadly *Sins*, viz. To avoid the Sin of *Pride*, and *Vain-Glory* [k], the Sin of *Covetousness* [l], the Sin of *Luxury* [m], the Sin of *Anger*, and *Wrath* [n], the Sin of *Gluttony*, and *Intemperance* [o], the Sin of *Envy*, and *Malice* [p], and the Sin of *Sloth*, and *Idleness* [q].

Fourteenthly. IF We would be Eternally *Happy* in the next *Life*, We must have a strict Observance to the *Seven* following Pious *Virtues*, viz. To *Humility* [r], to *Liberality* [s], to *Charity* [t], to *Gentleness* [u], to *Temperance* [w], to *Patience* [x], and to the *Fear of* GOD, and Love of His SON *JESUS CHRIST* [y]; and Daily *meditate* on the *Four last Things*, viz. On *Death* [z], on *Judgment* [a], on Heaven [b], and on *Hell* [c], &c. &c.

Precept. { In ev'ry Act, to Foe, or Friend,
  May All *remember* This :
  To have in Mind *their* latter End,
  And they'll ne'er Do amiss [d]. } *W. T.*

---

[x] *Psal.* xxxix. 11. *Jam.* v.— [y] *Psal.* xxxiii. 11. *Gal.* vi.— [z] *Psal.* xli. *Prov.* xxvii. *Ecclus.* vii. 33.— [a] *Psal.* xxxvii. *Ecclus* v.— [b] *Psal.* lxviii. 5. *Rom.* xv.— [c] *Psal.* cxxii. *Mark* xi — [d] *Rom.* xii 20. *Matt.* xv.— [e] *Jam.* ii. 15. *Matt.* xxv. — [f] *Eph.* ii 9. *Tobit* ii.— [g] *Psal.* lxxix. *Tob.* ii.— [h] *Psal.* xvii. 3. *Ecclus.* vii. 35. *Isa.* lviii. — [i] *Matt.* viii. 22. *Ecclus.* xxxviii. 16.— [k] *Psal.* lii. and ci. *Prov.* viii. 13.— [l] *Psal.* lii. *Ecclus.* xxxii. 24. — [m] *Prov.* xi. 2. *Ezek.* xvi. 49. — [n] *Psal.* xxxvii. 8. — [o] *Prov.* xxiii. 21.— [p] *Psal.* cxl — [q] *Prov.* xii. 4. *Rom.* xii. 11.— [r] *Psal.* cxxxi. — [s] *Psal.* xli. *Prov.* xi — [t] *Psal.* cxii.— [u] *Psal.* cxix.— [w] *Psal.* cxix. [x] *Psal.* xxxvii. 7.— [y] *Psal.* xix. 9.— [z] *Psal.* xxxix. and xc.— [a] *Psal.* l.— [b] *Psal.* xvi.— [c] *Psal.* xi.— [d] Vide my *Poetical* MEDITATIONS on the Four *last Things:* And *Ecclus.* vii. ver. ult.—*Psal.* v. 5. vi. 5.—*Psal.* xi. 6.—xiii. 15.—*Matt.* xxv. 35.—*Ecclus.* xxxiii. 21. *Ecclus.* xxxvii. 15. 16.

Fifteenthly.

To all Lovers *of* Pfalmody.   ix

Fifteenthly. IF we do but well confider the Beautiful *Style* of the PSALMS, (whether in *Profe*, or in *Verfe,*) they cannot but have a great Influence over Us, efpecially if we apply them to a *right Ufe*; and not prophane them; but perform them with DAVID's Heart. (But, alas! Holy DAVID's *Spirit* is almoft loft, in this Drunken, Ungrateful, degenerate Age!)—What can be more charming, to a *Godly Mind*, than the Variety of the *Style* of the prophetical *Pen-Men* of thofe *Sacred* SONGS! even from the *Majeftick, Sublime, Magnificent, Triumphant,* and *Exultory*; down to the moft *Mournful, Condoling, Commiferating, Pathetical,* and *Expoftulatory!* all regularly, and wifely adapted to their refpective *Subjects*; in which confifts the very *Soul* of *Divine Poetry:* And he that has the true KEY of *Them*, may, with great Eafe, unlock all other *Secrets* in the holy *Scriptures:* Which is the very *Subject* of this fmall TREATISE. For, *Behold! I have not laboured for Myfelf only, but for all fuch as would feek Knowledge*; and SING *with Underftanding* [e] *:* In compiling of which, I have confulted [f] the beft *Writers*, on this Subject, both *Ancient*, and *Modern*; which, I hope, will make the WORK the more approved.

[I fhall not in this BOOK infert any Thing touching the Ground-Work of MUSICK, By Reafon I have treated very largely on that *Head* in [g] feveral other former TREATISES, which I publifhed intirely on that *Subject*, and for the Ufe of *Churches:* In which *Prefaces* I have fhewed *the Beauty and Excellency of* CHURCH-MUSICK, and of the feveral Abufes thereof, *&c. &c.*]

---

[e] *Ecclus.* xxiv. 39. 1 *Cor.* xiv. 15. [f] St. *Gregory*, St. *Auguftine*, St. *Bafil*, St. *Athanafius*, St. *Ambrofe*, Venerable *Bede*, *Plutarchus*, *Beza*, *Gilby*, *Tremellius*, *Ainfworth*, *Mayer*, *Patrick*, *Ofterwald*, *Chamberlayn*, *Leigh*, and others, too tedious to mention.—[g] My New *Mufical* GRAMMAR, 3d Edit. and *Royal* MELODY, 2d Edit. And my PROVERBS of *Solomon*, in *Verfe*, and fet to *Mufick*, &c. Read *Ecclus.* xxxiv. 7. 8.

The

The PREFACE:

The *Reader* is herein defired to take Notice, that, in the primitive Ages, the *Pfalms* were generally fung in *Profe*, to *Tunes* called *Chants*, viz. the *Gregorian-Chant*, the *Ambrofian-Chant*, &c. fo called from the *Authors* who firft compofed them; in which State Pfalmody continued, for many Centuries, before any of them were put into Rhyming *Verfe*, or *Metre*.

In the Reign of King *Edward the Sixth*, 1552, one Mr. *Thomas Sternhold*, Groom of his Majefty's Privy Chamber, compofed thirty-feven of the Psalms of David into *Englifh Verfe*, as an Example for others to do the reft, for the Eafe and Ufe of *Churches*, &c. and greatly encouraged Mr. *John Hopkins*, and others, to compleat the reft; which were done in a little Time after, and Printed with the *firft Letters* of their *Names* over the *Pfalms*; which *Letters* are ftill continued, and whofe *Pfalms* are called the *Old Verfion*: But that *Verfion* has undergone great Amendments, fince their firft Publication, and ftill want more [h]. Their 137th Pfalm begins thus:

𝔚𝔥𝔢𝔫 𝔞𝔰 𝔴𝔢 𝔣𝔞𝔱𝔢 𝔦𝔫 𝔅𝔞𝔟𝔶𝔩𝔬𝔫,
  𝔱𝔥𝔢 ℜ𝔦𝔟𝔢𝔯𝔰 𝔯𝔬𝔲𝔫𝔡 𝔞𝔟𝔬𝔲𝔱:
𝔄𝔫𝔡 𝔦𝔫 ℜ𝔢𝔪𝔢𝔪𝔟𝔯𝔞𝔫𝔠𝔢 𝔬𝔣 𝔖𝔦𝔬𝔫,
  𝔱𝔥𝔢 𝔗𝔢𝔞𝔯𝔰 𝔣𝔬𝔯 𝔊𝔯𝔦𝔢𝔣 𝔟𝔲𝔯𝔰𝔱 𝔬𝔲𝔱.   *W. W.*

About the fame Time the old *Latin* Hymns were turned into Metre, fuch as *Te Deum*, *Veni Creator*, &c. and printed before the *Pfalms*; alfo feveral *New Hymns* were added after the *Pfalms*, fuch as the *Lamentation* of a Sinner, &c. and bound up with *Sternhold*'s Verfion; to be ufed in *publick* Service, and in *private* Families; even from the Beginning of the *Reformation* of the Church of *England*, to its *Eftablifhment*, under Queen *Elizabeth*; which are ftill continued: But, I cannot learn that any of

---

[h] Vide the Hift. of *Oxford* Writers, and *Sternhold*'s Pfalms.

the

To all Lovers *of* Pſalmody. xi

the *Reformed Churches*, abroad, take ſo much Liberty, in this Point as we do in *England*.

I HAVE now in my *Library* an old Quarto *Treatiſe*, containing fifty *Pſalms*, in very odd *Poetry*, and *old Spelling*, put into *Engliſh Verſe* by one *Robert Taylour*; and was printed in 1615. They are ſet to *Muſick* in *Five Parts*, to the *Viole*, *Lute*, or *Orph-arion*, in old muſical *Characters*, very unintelligible. His 137th *Pſalm* begins thus:

> By *Babel* Streams, exil'd from Contri deer,
> As doun we ſate, a ſad diſmaied Crue;
> Ah, *Sions* Wrongs to penſive Mynds appear,
> *Sions*, whom now our Eys no more ſhould vieu.—*R. T.*

ABOUT the Year 1682, Dr. *Patrick*, Biſhop of *Ely*, compoſed 100 of the PSALMS of DAVID into *Verſe*, for the Uſe of the *Charter-Houſe* in *London*; whoſe 8th *Pſalm* begins thus:

> O Lord, our Governor, on Earth
> Thy Name is excellent:
> Thy Glory is exalted far
> Above the Firmament. — *J. P.*

In 1696, *Nicholas Brady*, D. D. and *Nahum Tate*, Eſq; and *Poet-Laureat* to his Majeſty King *William the Third*, compoſed a *New Verſion* of the PSALMS, which were printed for the Uſe of *Churches*; and called the *New Verſion*: Whoſe 137th *Pſalms* begins thus:

> When we our weary Limbs to reſt,
> Sat down by proud *Euphrates*' Stream,
> We wept, with doleful Thoughts oppreſt,
> And *Sion* was our mournful Theam.—*N. B.*

THESE *Verſes* I have *copied* only to ſhew what Improvement is now made in *Poetry*[1]: Not having Room

---

[1] Vide *Sternhold's*, *Patrick's*, *Tate's*, and *Watts's* Pſalms, &c.

to insert a *Verse* from every *Author* I have seen, who have composed *Versions* on the BOOK of *Psalms*, or *Hymns*, from other *Scriptures*[k], &c. many of whose *Works* I have often perused with great Pleasure, as well as Profit.

The Result of near forty Years *Practice*, and *Study*, at most vacant Hours, hath given Birth to this small TREATISE, (as my former BOOKS will testify, from the Sale of many Thousands:) In compiling of which I have consulted all *Authors* I could meet with, on this *Subject*; having, by an *Itinerant Life*, had the greatest Opportunities in reading the Best *Authors*; which many well-disposed Gentlemen have favoured me with, from their several Libraries.

A WORK of this Kind has been long wanting, to restore PSALMODY to its wonted *Esteem*; and prevent it from being shamefully *prophaned*. To this EXPOSITION I have added 100 *Poetical* PRECEPTS, as precious *Motives* to a godly Life; being very *Useful* for *Schools*, and *Instructive* to *Youth*. I have also added, a short DESCRIPTION of *Persons*, of *Places*, and of *Things* mentioned in the *Old* and *New Testament*, and of *CHRIST, Poetically:* With a general CALENDAR, for the adapting of *Psalms* to *Divine-Service*, concordant to the *Collect, Epistle*, and *Gospel* of the *Day*, and Church-*Services*; and to all other *Conditions* and *Vicissitudes* of Human Life. With a *New* Set of TUNES, to several PSALMS, both *Old* and *New Versions*, in *Three* and *Four* musical *Parts*, in *Score:* With select HYMNS; and DOXOLOGIES; and a general KEY, or *Index* to the whole BOOK of *Psalms*; for the Use of all Christian *Families*, &c. &c.

[☞ In the following TREATISE, the *Reader* is therein to take Notice, *That*, (as the BOOK of *Psalms* has under-

---

[k] Sir *Philip Sydney*, King *James* I, *Sands, Ainsworth, Barton, Milbourn, Roberts*, Bishop *Hall*, Lord *Bacon, Taylour, Mason, Herbert, Vincent, Boyse, Stennet, Brown, Pope, Addison*, &c. &c.—Read *Ecclus.* xxxviii. 24. 25.—xxxix. 1. 2. 3. 5. 8. 9. 10. 11. Also *Ecclus.* xxxiv. 9. 10. 11. 12. 14.

gone

To all Lovers *of* Pſalmody.   xiii

gone many *Tranſlations*, and *Verſions*, (as I before hinted) which has tranſpoſed or altered many of the *Verſes*, to other *Numbers*, &c.) *The Figures in this* Book *refer to the Verſes of the Original* Psalms, *as they are commonly now printed in* Prose: So that it will be no great Difficulty to find any particular *Matter* therein pointed at; in any *Tranſlation*, *Paraphraſe*, or *Verſion* whatſoever; though the *Numbers* of the *Verſes* ſhould vary in the *Pſalms* in *Metre*, from thoſe *Pſalms* in *Proſe* [1].]

Finally, I heartily recommend this Work, (as my *laſt Legacy)* to all Perſons in general, but more particularly to my *Pupils*, for their farther Improvement in Psalmody, whereby every One may truly know the real *Matter* that is *ſung*; that, that moſt *glorious* and *laſting Part* of *Divine-Worſhip* may not be ſhamefully prophaned; but be done *Reverently*, and in *Good Order*; with my beſt *Wiſhes* to their *Endeavours*: Hoping it may be as generally *Uſeful*, as it is intended; and may G O D alone have all the *Glory*.

May all Our pious *Performances* reach even to the very *Heavens*, where lieth a ſure *Reward* for the *Righteous*, at the *Laſt Day*, from G O D the Father, and from His Son *JESUS CHRIST*.—Which that We may all *enjoy*, G O D of His infinite *Mercy* grant: To whom all *Might*, *Majeſty*, *Power*, *Honour*, *Glory*, *Dominion*, and *Praiſe*, be given, *now*, and for evermore.—Amen.—Amen.

I *am* Gentlemen,

Your moſt Affectionate,

Harmonious, and

{ From the Ancient *Univerſity of Stamford, May* the 29th, A. D. 1759. }

Humble Servant,

William Tans'ur, Senior.

---

[1] See the old *Bible*-Pſalms; the *Pointed* Pſalms in the *Common Prayer*, for Chanting; and *Sternhold*'s, and *Brady*'s Pſalms in *Verſe*, &c.

A New

A New KEY *to the* Principal Paſſages *contained in the* Book *of* PSALMS: *Temporal, Spiritual,* and *Prophetical. For all Chriſtian Families.*

By WILLIAM TANS'UR, Senior.

☞ N. B. That as Holy DAVID's *Battles* were chiefly to *Uſher in,* and *Defend* the CHURCH, and GOSPEL of *CHRIST* to *come*; That *Royal Prophetical* PRINCE, and *Soldier* of *CHRIST* here, in *Figure*, repreſenteth them *Both:* So that, in Effect, DAVID, *CHRIST,* and his CHURCH, are (in moſt Caſes) meant as but *One,* though of *Three* ſeveral Denominations.

Proſe-Pſalms.	*Proſe.Verſes.*
I.—THE *Bleſſedneſs* of the *Godly* foretold	1
The endleſs *Miſery* of the Wicked	5
II.—*CHRIST*'s vain Conſpirators defeated	1
KING's, and *Rulers* to obey *CHRIST*	10
III.—DAVID's Enemies increaſed	1
CHRIST ſleeping by *Death,* and riſing again	5
Salvation only from *CHRIST*	8
IV.—Juſt Men's *Prayers* heard, and they delivered	1
V.—Sacrifice to GOD accepted	7
VI.—*Prayer* for Sins in general	1
Succeſs of *Prayer,* cometh by *Patience*	8
VII.—Confidence in GOD preſerveth from Evil	
GOD's *Arms* againſt the Wicked	12
VIII.—GOD's Providence and Liberality	1
CHRIST's Glorification by *Children*	2
CHRIST over all Things, and how	5
IX.—*Praiſe* to GOD for Victories	1
Spiritual Enemies ſubdued by *CHRIST*'s Death	13
X.—GOD's Help is deſired by the *Godly*	1
CHRIST's Enemies deſtroyed	14
The *Fatherleſs* and Poor defended	16
XI.—Godly Men's Conſtancy diſplayed	1
GOD's Judgments on the Wicked	7
GOD's eternal *Love* to the Righteous	8
XII.—Decay of Chriſtian *Piety* lamented	1
GOD's *Word* recommended to preſerve all	7
XIII.—GOD helpeth the Juſt in all Afflictions	1
GOD's *Mercy* rejoiceth and bringeth *Salvation*	5
XIV.—Goſpel *Scoffers,* and *Atheiſts* deſcribed	1
Salvation to *Iſrael,* and all the *Faithful*	11

XV. Righteous

A New Key to the Book of Psalms.

Profe-Pfalms.	Profe-Verfes.
XV.—Righteous Men are *Citizens* of Heaven	1
Slanderers, Extortioners, and *Ufurers,* condemned	3
XVI.—DAVID's Prayer, by Faith	1
GOD's Goodnefs to the *Faithful*	6
CHRIST's Refurrection foretold	9
XVII.—A *Prayer* againft wicked Perfons	1
Fleeing to GOD for Succour	5
XVIII.—Calling on GOD is a fure Safeguard	1
Righteous are defended by GOD's *Power*	16
GOD giveth *Victory* to defend His *Church*	34
A Thankfgiving for *Victory*	49
XIX.—GOD's Power fhewed to all the World by His *Works*	1
GOD's *Laws, Precepts,* and *Fear,* excelleth all Things	7
All Men have *Faults,* none perfect	12
XX.—*Prayers* heard of People, *Church, King,* or *CHRIST*	9
XXI.—A Song of *Victory,* when *Church* Enemies are defeated	1
XXII.—*CHRIST* perfonated on the *Crofs*	1
Praying the Night before his *Paffion*	2
No Man fo much *defpifed* as He	6
Scribes, Priefts, and *Pharifees,* as Bulls or Dogs	12
CHRIST's Hands and Feet pierced	17
Of his *Refurrection* foretold	21
His *Body* eaten, as in the *Sacrament,* and *Alms* given	26
He fhall be *ferved* and *honoured* throughout all Generations	27
XXIII.—On the holy *Sacrament* of the LORD JESUS	1
XXIV.—*Converfion* of the *Gentiles* foretold	1
Juft Men fhall enjoy Heaven	3
CHRIST's Afcenfion into Heaven foretold	7
XXV.—A *Prayer* for *Forgivenefs* of Sins, and Deliverance	1
XXVI.—*Innocency* avowed, and *Rewarded*	1
Other Men's Sins not to hinder Us from Godlinefs	5
XXVII.—GOD is our only Shield to deftroy the Wicked	1
XXVIII.—A *Prayer* for GOD's Defence againft Enemies	1
A Song of *Praife* for Deliverance	7
XXIX.—Great Men to *Praife* GOD	1
Thunder, &c. to caufe Men to *fear,* and know GOD	3
All Men to fing, *Glory be to the Father,* &c. in the Church	8
XXX.—A Dedication-*Song* for *Churches,* and *Houfes* New, GOD's *Mercies,* &c.	1
Good Men fhould take no *Sufferings* Ill, and Why	12
XXXI.—Confidence in GOD, and *Meditation,* our only Safeguard	1
Vanity to truft in Wordly Things	7
GOD's Goodnefs is laid up for them that *fear* him	21
XXXII.—None *Bleffed* without *Redemption*	1
Inftructions to the *Fear* of GOD	9

XXXIII. Righ-

A New Key *to the* Book *of* Psalms.

Prose-Psalms.	Prose-Verses.

XXXIII.—Righteous Men to *Rejoice*, and *sing* to GOD with *Instruments* — — — — 1
    GOD's *Mercy* always delivereth the Righteous — 18
XXXIV.—A Song of *Praise* for Deliverance — — 1
    The *Angels* assist the Righteous in Battle — 7
XXXV.—GOD defends the *Just* Man's Cause, and destroys the Wicked — — — — 1
XXXVI.—Wicked Works, shew a Wicked Heart — 4
    GOD's *Mercy* is above all Things to the Righteous 7
XXXVII.—None to fret at wicked Men's Prosperity — 1
    A little to the *Righteous*, is better than much to the Wicked — — — — 16
    The Righteous are never forsaken, nor hurt by Charity 28
    Upright Men have *Peace*, but the Wicked cut off 38
XXXVIII.—A *Prayer* for Sins in general — — 1
XXXIX.—*Afflictions* must be borne with *Patience* — 1
    Our *last End* necessary to be thought of — 5
    Faith, and *Senses*, always ought to be prayed for 11
XL.—GOD's Goodness in converting the *Gentiles* — 2
    CHRIST is the *New Song*, and our only Salvation 3
XLI.—*CHRIST*, and His *Faithful*, here called *Poor* — 1
    DAVID's or *CHRIST*'s Enemies not taken into Glory 8
XLII.—A good Heart desireth to Worship GOD — 1
    GOD's *Judgments*, as *Water-pipes*, break out unawares 9
    Yet, the *Righteous* are saved by *Faith* — 15
XLIII.—The LORD's *Table* is our only Place of Comfort 4
XLIV.—GOD's former *Mercies* always to be remembered 1
    GOD knoweth the *Secrets* of all Hearts — 21
    GOD our only *Succour* and *Redeemer* — 26
XLV.—Of Solomon's, and *CHRIST*'s Kingdom — 2
XLVI.—A *Thanksgiving* Song for Deliverance — 1
    CHRIST, and His *Spirit* foretold — 4
    Of the universal *Peace* that *CHRIST* should bring 9
XLVII.—All are to be Joyful in *CHRIST*, chosen for us 4
    CHRIST's *Ascension* figured — — 5
    To *sing* with *Zeal*, and *Understanding* — 6
XLVIII.—The City of *Jerusalem praised*, where GOD is worshipped 1
XLIX.—Riches cannot *Redeem* the Wicked, but *CHRIST* 1
L.—A Prophecy of the *Gospel* going from *Sion* — 1
    CHRIST's coming to *Judgment* foretold — 3
    The *Jews* called *Saints*, for being in *Covenant* with GOD 5
LI.—A general *Prayer* for Forgiveness of Sins — 1
    How the *Soul*, or GOD's *Grace* cometh to Children 5
    GOD loves not outward *Sacrifices*; but of the Heart 16
LII.—*Tyrants* and *Lyars* are destroyed, and *Godly* preserved 1

LIII.—Gospel

A New Key to the Book of Psalms.

Prose-Psalms.	Prose-Verses.
LIII.—Gospel *Scoffers*, and *Atheists* described — —	1
Salvation to *Israel* prayed for — — —	6
LIV.—Sinners are punished, as *Strangers* to GOD — —	3
Praise given to GOD for Deliverance —. —	6
LV.—By familiar Deceivers, CHRIST and *Judas* foretold	3
Prayer three Times a Day heard —. — —	18
Men lose *half* their *Days* by their *Wickedness* —	25
LVI.—DAVID's Confidence *figureth* the Continuance of CHRIST and His *Church* — — — — —	4
LVII.—DAVID's *Faith* sheweth the *Conversion* of the *Gentiles*	2
GOD *praised* for *Mercy* and Deliverance —	8
LVIII.—Malicious Men are like *Adders*, in *Words* and *Deeds* —	4
CHRIST's Enemies are destroyed; and *Faithful* preserved	9
LIX.—DAVID's Enemies as *Dogs*; figured to CHRIST's	6
LX.—DAVID rejoicing in his *Kingdom*, cheareth the *Faithful*	6
LXI.—DAVID's *Success* sheweth the *Continuance* of CHRIST's Kingdom — — — — —	6
LXII.—*Patience* and *Meditation* bring *Salvation* — —	5
LXIII.—A *Thanksgiving* for Deliverance in general — —	4
LXIV.—A *Prayer* against false Enemies — — —	2
Wicked Men's *Destruction rejoices* the *Righteous* —	8
LXV.—GOD to be *Praised* in the *Church* — —	1
GOD's *Blessing* on the *Faithful*, over all the World	4
Water and Corn, the *Gospel* of CHRIST — —	9
Sheep, the *Faithful* in CHRIST, to rejoice —	14
LXVI.—The Rejoicing of the *Gentiles* foretold — —	1
Martyrs *Sufferings* foretold, to *Convert* the People —	11
GOD heareth the *Prayers* of the Righteous —	18
LXVII.—The Church's *Prayer*; or, all are *Blessed* in CHRIST	1
LXVIII.—CHRIST's *Resurrection* foretold — — —	1
Of Gospel *Preachers*, &c. — — — —	11
The *Sufferings* and *Deliverance* of the *Church* —	13
The Rejoicings of CHRIST's *Birth* foretold; and Apostles, &c. — — — — —	25
LXIX.—DAVID personateth CHRIST's *Passion*, by his own Complaints — — — — —	1
None to *fear Death* for Righteousness Sake —	17
The *Faithful* are delivered from the Wicked —	36
LXX.—Wicked Men destroyed; but, *Godly* seek *Comfort* —	1
LXXI.—DAVID's *Faith*, shews CHRIST's *Resurrection* —	1
DAVID's *Prayer* in his *old Age* — — —	8
His *Song* of *Praise* and *Thanksgiving* — —	20
LXXII.—DAVID's last *Charge*, and *Prayer* for his Son *Solomon*	1
Praying in the Name of CHRIST — —	8
DAVID's last *Blessing*; meaning also CHRIST's Kingdom — — — — —	17

B LXXIII.—Wicked

A New Key to the Book of Pfalms.

Profe-Pfalms.		Profe-Verfes.
LXXIII.—	Wicked Men's *Profperity* not to move our *Faith* —	2
	Wicked Men are to be *defpifed* at the Day of *Judgment*	20
	Godly *Worfhip* is preferable to all Things — —	25
LXXIV.—	Deftruction of the *Temple* foretold — —	1
	A *Prayer* for the *Faithful* in general — —	20
LXXV.—	*CHRIST*'s coming to *Judgment* foretold —	2
	Wickednefs and *Pride* bring *Deftruction* —	8
LXXVI.—	*GOD* known, and *Worfhipped* in the *Tabernacle*	1
LXXVII.—	A Godly *Meditation* on *GOD*'s *Mercy* and *Works*	12
LXXVIII.—	*GOD*'s Wonders in *Egypt* reminded, &c. —	1
	Enemies fubdued to the *Gofpel* — —	65
	Temple built; and DAVID ruled — —	69
LXXIX.—	*Ifrael*'s Complaints to GOD; with *Faith* —	4
LXXX.—	The *Church's Prayer* to GOD, in Diftrefs —	14
LXXXI.—	A *Feftival-Song*; *Ifrael*'s Deliverance hinted —	5
LXXXII.—	*Judges* exhorted to do *Juftice* — — —	3
LXXXIII.—	*Ifrael* prays for Deliverance at Home or Abroad —	2
	Prayer againft turning GOD's *Houfe* to prophane Ufes	12
LXXXIV.—	A *Longing* for GOD's *Publick Worfhip* — —	2
	Godly *Company* preferable to Worldly Men's —	10
LXXXV.—	A Rememberance of GOD's *Mercy* to *Ifrael* —	1
	Righteoufnefs and *Peace* are infeparable — —	10
LXXXVI.—	A *Prayer* for Deliverance — — —	1
	A *Thankfgiving* for Mercy — — —	12
LXXXVII.—	*Reftoration* of the afflicted *Church* promifed —	2
	The *Birth* of *CHRIST*; and *Chriftians* foretold	4
LXXXVIII.—	To *Pray* to GOD in our *Afflictions* — —	1
	No *Prayers*, nor *Praifes* in the *Grave* —	11
LXXXIX.—	GOD's *Mercy* and *Power*; or, *CHRIST*'s Kingdom foretold — — — — —	6
XC.—	The *Brevity* of Man's *Life*; and *Prayer* for *Mercy* and *Comfort* — — — — —	10
XCI.—	GOD our only *Shelter*, in all Dangers — —	1
	GOD's *Angels* guard the *Faithful*; *CHRIST*'s *Temptation* foretold — — —	11
XCII.—	Pfalm for the *Sabbath-Day*, of *Joy* and *Meditation*	1
XCIII.—	*CHRIST*'s Reigning on *Earth* foretold —	2
XCIV.—	*Vengeance* only belongeth to GOD — —	1
	GOD knoweth the *Hearts* of all Men —	11
XCV.—	An Exhortation to *Praife* GOD — —	1
XCVI.—	*CHRIST*'s *Firft*, and *Second* Coming foretold	10
XCVII.—	Repetition of the former. GOD preferves His *Saints*	10
XCVIII.—	All Things to *Praife* GOD; with *Faith* in *CHRIST*	6
XCIX.—	Concerning *CHRIST*'s Coming, &c. —	1
C.—	All to *Praife* GOD, for being made *New*, by *CHRIST*	1
CI.—	DAVID's *Rule* of *Government*, to be Ours —	2

CII.—*Prayer*

A New Key *to the* Book *of* Psalms.

Prose-Psalms.	Prose-Verses.
CII.—*Prayer of the Faithful*, in Captivity — —	1
GOD's *Word*, and *People* endure for ever —	25
CIII.—*Prayer to* GOD for *Pardon*, and *Deliverance* —	1
He pitieth such as *fear* Him — — —	13
Angels, and Men, to *Praise* GOD — —	20
CIV.—GOD is *Praised* for His *Works*, and *Creation* —	1
Angels created, left out in *Genesis* — — —	4
Glory to GOD *for ever*, &c. — — —	31
CV.—GOD is *Praised* by *Israel*, for past *Mercies* —	1
CVI.—GOD's *Goodness magnified*, concerning *Israel* —	1
CVII.—All the *Redeemed* to *Praise* GOD for *Mercy* —	2
CVIII.—GOD is *Praised* for His *Promise*, and Deliverance	1
CIX.—*CHRIST*, and *Judas* foretold, by DAVID's own Usage	1
CX.—*CHRIST's Power*, and *Kingdom* foretold —	1
CHRIST's Sufferings foretold by *Drinking* —	7
CXI.—*Thanksgiving* to GOD, for *Mercy* to His *Church* —	1
Redemption to His People by *fearing* Him —	8
CXII.—GOD's *Providence* on the *Merciful* and *Charitable*	1
CXIII.—GOD to be *Praised* for His *Humility* and *Mercy* —	6
CXIV.—GOD's *Mercy*, and *Wonders* in *Egypt* — —	1
CXV.—GOD only to have all *Praise* and *Glory* — —	1
Idols, not accepted of GOD — — —	4
The *Blessedness* of such as *fear* GOD — —	13
CXVI.—GOD's *Mercy* magnified — — —	1
Sacramental Sacrifice must be offered to GOD —	15
CXVII.—All *Gentiles* to *Praise* GOD; eternal *Life* by *CHRIST*	2
CXVIII.—GOD to be *Praised* for His *Mercy* by all Men —	1
CHRIST the only *Gate* to Heaven — —	20
The *Feast* of *CHRIST's Nativity* foretold —	24
CXIX.—*Precious Motives* to a *Godly Life*, &c. &c. &c. —	All
CXX.—*Lyars* hated of GOD, to their own Destruction —	2
CXXI.—GOD preserves the *Righteous* at all Times —	3
CXXII.—All to rejoice in *CHRIST's Church* — —	1
CXXIII.—A *Prayer* of the *Faithful*, for Deliverance —	1
CXXIV.—GOD the only *Defender* of the *Just*, from the Wicked	1
CXXV.—Confidence in GOD never fails the Righteous —	1
CXXVI.—*Israel's* joyful *Deliverance* repeated — —	1
CXXVII.—GOD the *Prosperity*, and *Safeguard* of all —	2
Spiritual *Children*, the *Blessings* of Heaven — —	4
CXXVIII.—GOD's *Blessings* appertain to all that *fear* Him —	1
CXXIX.—The Righteous are *Saved*; and Wicked Destroyed —	4
CXXX.—GOD must be *Prayed* to, from the Depth of the Heart	1
All must *Wait* and *Trust* on GOD for *Redemption*	5
CXXXI.—All must be *Humble*, and *Wait* with *Patience* on GOD	1
CXXXII.—GOD's *Promise* to DAVID, desired by the *Faithful*	2

B 2 CXXXII—Nothing

A New Key *to the* Book *of* Pſalms.

Proſe-Pſalms.   *Proſe-Verſes.*

CXXXII.—Nothing is finiſhed but in *CHRIST*; and on what Terms — — — — — 12

              CHRIST, the *Light* of the *Gentiles,* foretold — 17

CXXXIII.—Brotherly *Love* commended; *Temporal* and *Spiritual* 1

CXXXIV.—GOD muſt be *Praiſed* with *Sincerity,* to be accepted 1

CXXXV.—GOD to be *Praiſed* for His *Mercy* and wonderous *Works* — — — — — 3

CXXXVI.—GOD to be *Praiſed* for His *Government, Liberality,* and *Mercy* — — — — — 1

CXXXVII.—*Iſrael*'s Moan for the *Decay* of Chriſtian *Piety* — 1

             Babylon's Deſtruction foretold — — — 7

CXXXVIII.—All Nations to *Praiſe* GOD in His *Church* — 2

CXXXIX.—GOD's Eye is over all, at all *Times,* and in all *Places* 2

             GOD's *Mercy, Counſel,* and *Wiſdom* endleſs — 17

CXL.—A *Prayer* againſt cruel *Backbiting* Enemies — 1

CXLI.—To be watchful of our *Words* in *Prayer,* with *Patience* 3

CXLII.—A *Prayer* when in Diſtreſs — — — 1

CXLIII.—A *Prayer* for *Remiſſion* of Sins; and GOD's *Guidance* 7

CXLIV.—A *Thankſgiving* Song for *Victories* obtained — 1

CXLV.—GOD is *Praiſed* for His *Juſtice, Mercy, Works,* and *Providence* — — — — — 3

CXLVI.—GOD to be *Praiſed* for ſundry *Mercies* and *Benefits* 1

CXLVII.—GOD to be *Praiſed,* for many great *Cauſes* — 1

CXLVIII.—*Angels,* and all *Creatures* to *Praiſe* GOD for the *Goſpel* 2

CXLIX.—All People, *High* or *low,* to *Rejoice* in *CHRIST*'s Kingdom — — — — — 3

CL.—All *Inſtruments,* and Breathing *Things* to *Praiſe* GOD, &c.

HALLELUJAH.

Amen.

A NEW

A NEW
EXPOSITION
ON THE
One Hundred and Fifty PSALMS.

By WILLIAM TANS'UR, SENIOR.

On PSALM I.

THIS PSALM is set in the Manner of a PREFACE to all the rest; and, in order to exhort all Men to *Study*, and *Meditate* on *Divine* and *Heavenly Wisdom*; according to the Holy *Scriptures:* Shewing, ¹ That all such are truly *Blessed* as take Delight therein.—And, on the contrary, ⁴ that all prophane and wicked *Contemners* thereof, and of GOD, shall surely be miserable in the End.

(—Vide *Deut.* vi. 3.—*Jer.* xvii. 8.—*Josh.* i. 8. and *Prov.* vi. 22.—)

Herein are precious *Motives* to a *Holy Life*, shewing the different *Fate* of the *Righteous* and the *Wicked*, in this World, and in that which is to come; from whence we may infer, that when once a *Wicked Man* has given himself up to *Evil Counsel, Bad Company, Concupiscence,* and the like; (which are the very first Steps to *Ruin)* he so far forgets himself in his Sins, that he falls under GOD'*s Anger,* and *Contempt* ; and is then said *to sit in the Seat of the Scornful.*—On the contrary, all *Good, Holy,* and *Devout Men,* that fear GOD's Holy *Name,* delight in His *Word*; and do His blessed *Will,* so far as they are able; are (as it were) moistened with his *Grace* for ever: So that their *Works* shall surely tend to their own *Salvation* at the *last Day*.—And though the *Wicked* may seem to flourish, and prosper for a while, in this World; yet the LORD will so drive them down, that they shall not be able to stand, at the *Last Day,* in *Company* of the *Righteous:* But, they shall surely tremble, when they feel GOD's *Wrath,* and fiery *Judgment:* For it is He alone, that knoweth the *Secrets* of all *Hearts*, and will bring every *Work* into *Judgment,* whether it be *Good* or *Evil. — Matt.* xvi. 27.

The PRECEPT.

{ *Thus, they are* Blest, *that never go astray,*
By false Advice, but serve GOD *Night and Day :*
For, GOD *approves the Ways the* Righteous *tread,*
But, sinful Paths *to sure* Destruction *lead.* }

N. B. *That some* Commentators *say, this* Psalm *was first composed by* Esdras; *who is said to be the Man that first collected the* Psalms *together into* one Book : *But whether he was, or not, it is not very material.*

On PSALM II.

1047. IN this *Pfalm*,¹ the *Prophet*, Holy DAVID, rejoiceth, with a ſtrong *Faith*, that GOD will continue his *Kingdom* for ever and ever, though his Enemies conſpire, rage, and murmur ever ſo much againſt it. He alſo ¹⁰ exhorteth all *Kings* and *Rulers*, humbly to ſubmit under GOD's Yoke, by Reaſon, all Reſiſtance is vain againſt the *Will* and *Power* of the ALMIGHTY.

* (—Vide 2 *Sam.* viii.—*Acts* iv. Ver. 25.—*Prov.* i. 26.—*Rom.* vii. 23.—*Matt.* xviii.—*Hoſ.* xiii. 2.—*Luke* xvii. 27.—)

Herein is figured the *Kingdom* of our LORD and *Saviour*, JESUS CHRIST; which neither the Conſpiracy of the *Gentiles*, the Murmuring of the *Jews*, nor the Power of *Kings* could prevail againſt. And though the Wicked ſhould ſay, *We will caſt off the Yoke of* GOD, *and of* CHRIST, yet the LORD declares, That in reſiſting CHRIST, they fight againſt *Him*. Holy DAVID alſo ſhews, *Ver.* 7. &c. That his Vocation to the *Kingdom*, is of GOD: This being the firſt Time he appeared to be *elected* of GOD; and is applied to CHRIST on His firſt Coming, and Manifeſtation to the World, whether *Jew*, or *Gentile*, &c. He alſo exhorteth all *Rulers* to repent in Time, as well as others; and to *homage* the LORD of Life: Leſt, when the Wicked ſhall ſay, *Peace and Reſt*, and are in the Middle of their wicked Purpoſes, a ſudden Deſtruction falls upon them, to their eternal Ruin. Of this, the *Righteous* are no way in Fear of, by Reaſon, the *Bleſſing* of GOD is herein promiſed to all ſuch as truſt in Him.

(—See *Acts* xiii. 23, 33.—*Heb.* i. 5.—*Rev.* ii. 27.—1 *Theſ.* v. 3.—)

The PRECEPT.

{
Spurn not at CHRIST (*as* Jews) *to be undone*,
But, love the LORD, *and honour* CHRIST, *His Son:*
All, High and Low, on JESUS *muſt depend*,
For, diff'rent Faith *will ſure in Ruin End*.
}

N. B. Holy DAVID probably wrote this *Pſalm* on his being refuſed to build the Temple, and driven to War with other Nations; that *Solomon* might rule in Peace: Being transferred to CHRIST, of whom both He, and Solomon were Types. *

On PSALM III.

1023. THIS was a *Pſalm* of Holy DAVID, when he fled from his Son *Abſalom*; and being driven from his *Kingdom*, was greatly tormented in his Mind for his Sins againſt GOD:

And

A New Exposition *on the* Book *of* Psalms, &c.

⁴ And calling earnestly on GOD, grew much more the bolder through His gracious *Promises* against the Railing, and Terrors of his Enemies; nay, even of Death itself, which he then seemingly saw before his Eyes, &c. Lastly, ⁷ he greatly rejoiced for the good *Success* that GOD gave him, and all the *Church.*

* (—See 2 *Sam.* xv. 15.—*Psal.* iv. 5.—)

Here we have a perfect *View* of the great *Security* of GOD's Divine *Protection*, to such as faithfully confide in Him. Herein is also shewed by our Holy *Author*, that in all his Troubles, his *Faith* was firm and unmoveable; and had always an earnest Recourse to GOD, and confided in His *Promises*; and trying the same, *Experience* the more increased his *Faith*, &c. — From which we may learn, That be our Troubles, in this World, ever so many, or our Dangers ever so great, if we but faithfully *Trust* in GOD, He will assuredly afford us Means of Deliverance, and eternal *Salvation* in the End.

(—See *Psal.* xxvii. 3.—*Isa.* xliii. 11.—*Hos.* xiii. 3.—*Matt.* xxi. 7.—)

ʳ The Word, *Selah,* (after the second and last Verses of this *Psalm,* in the old *Translation,)* signifies, sometimes *for ever,* or *Amen,* or to *lift up the Voice* with a louder Tone, that we also consider the *Sentence* of great Importance; as more to be observed, &c. *Selah*, is an *Hebrew* Word, and is used seventy-three Times in the old *Psalms,* and twice in the Book of *Habakkuk.*

The PRECEPT.

{ *Grieve not, though Sinners* Godly *Men despise,*
Nor fearful be, though Thousands on you rise:
Rely on CHRIST, *let nothing you dismay,*
Such Hope *will save you at the* Judgment-Day. }

N. B. This *Psalm* was written on *Absalom's* Rebellion, and *David's* Fright, &c. see the *Scriptures* above quoted. *

※※※※※※※※※※※※※※※※※※※※※※※※※※※※※※

On PSALM IV.

THIS was a *Psalm* of Holy DAVID, when *Saul* persecuted him; wherein he first ¹ called upon GOD for Audience: And trusting most assuredly in His Promise, he boldly ² reproveth his Enemies, who ⁶ confidently resisted his *Dominion.* Lastly, He ⁷ greatly preferring the *Favour* of GOD before all worldly Treasures, ⁸ lieth down in *Peace,* trusting that GOD is his *only Safeguard* in the greatest of Dangers.

(—Vide *Psalm* l. 14.—1 *Chron.* xv. 21.—*Eph.* iv. 26.—*Luke* ii. 32.—)

Here Holy DAVID heartily begs that GOD would hear his Petition; and, exhorting his Enemies, shews, that Man's *Happiness* intirely depends on GOD's

Mercy

4   The Psalm-Singer's Jewel: Or,

Mercy and *Favour*, &c.—This *Psalm* he directed, or inscribed, *To the chief Musician that excelleth on the* Neginoth; (an *Instrument* of eight Strings, to *beat* on as a *Dulcimer*;) i. e. To the *Overseer*, or *Best Player*, it being then customary with them to *direct* who, amongst his *Company* of *Singers*, and *Players*, should have the Charge to *begin*, and carry on each *Psalm*, and with what Kind of *Instruments*; and sometimes the *Tune* was called by the same Name as the *Instrument*, &c. Herein DAVID also shews, That GOD is the only *Judge* of every Cause, and the sole *Defender* of both Body and Soul, at all Events: and though *worldly wise Men* crave only for the Riches of this Life, yet GOD's *Blessing*, and *Favour*, is preferable to all: For if worldly Men's Enterprises please them ever so well, yet GOD alone is able to bring them all to nought, and to be of none Effect; whilst they who have *Felicity* in GOD's *Favour* are secure from all Dangers, &c. thereby signifying, that he could dwell more joyfully *alone*, than if many were about him; because the LORD was always with him, and *directed* all his Goings.

The PRECEPT.

> *When in Distress to* GOD *address thy* Pray'r,
> *And He thy righteous* Cause *will surely hear:*
> *From cruel* Foes *he'll be thy only* Guard,
> *And give thee* Heav'n, *at last, for thy* Reward.

(—See *Psalm* I. *Ver.* 15, 16, 17.—)

On PSALM V.

THIS was a *Psalm* of Holy DAVID, when the Cruelty of his Enemies grievously oppressed him; and fearing greater Dangers might then come, he [1] *earnestly prayeth* to GOD for Succour; shewing how greatly necessary and requisite it is that GOD should punish them for their Malice.—Afterwards, being assured of *prosperous Success*, he [7] greatly feeleth *Comfort* from GOD; concluding [12] that when GOD should deliver him, others also should be Partakers of the same *Mercies*, *Blessings*, and the like.

(—See *Psal.* cxxx. *Ver.* 6.—*Isai.* xliv. 25.—)

This our Holy *Author* inscribed *To him that excelleth on the* Nehiloth, (a Wind *Instrument* so called,) that he, whoever he was, should be the chief *Master*, and *Manager* of both *Singers*, and *Instruments*, in order to perform it. *Isai.* v. 12. Hence we may learn, with what *Ardency* he *prayed*, and with what *Patience* he waited till he was heard, and that GOD will surely punish the Wicked, and never forget the Righteous who *faint not*, and stedfastly trust in Him.—He also shews, that in the greatest of all his Temptations, his *Trust* was alone in GOD, who brought all the vile Designs of the Wicked to no Effect; and that GOD's *Favour* and *Love* to him, confirmed the *Faith* of others: From which we may infer,

A New Exposition *on the* Book *of* Psalms, &c.

infer, that they who *patiently*, and *faithfully trust* in GOD, shall surely be safe from all Dangers.

(—See *Psal.* xli. *Ver.* 2.—*Rom.* iii. *Ver.* 13.—)

The PRECEPT.

⎰*When wicked Men thee wrongfully oppress,*⎱
⎰*On* GOD *rely, for* Help, *in all Distress:*⎰
⎱*Their vile Designs upon themselves shall fall,*⎰
⎱Almighty AID *shall keep thee out of all.*⎰

N. B. This *Psalm* was probably wrote on *Saul's* promising *Merab*; and giving *Michal* to be a Snare to him. See 1 *Sam.* xviii. 17, &c.

On PSALM VI.

THIS was one of the *Penitential Psalms* of DAVID, when he, by his grievous Sins, had sorely provoked GOD's Wrath and Anger against him. And feeling GOD's Hand sorely upon him, and conceiving the Horrors of everlasting Death, he [1] greatly desireth *Pardon* and Forgiveness. — Then [6] greatly bewailing, that if GOD took him away in his Indignation and Wrath, he should inevitably lack that Occasion to *Praise* Him as he had always used to do whilst he was amongst Men. — Then [9] suddenly feeling GOD's *Mercy* and loving Kindness to him again, he very sharply rebuketh his Enemies that had rejoiced at his Sorrow and Affliction.

(—See *Jer.* x. *Ver.* 24.—*Psal.* xxvi. 1.—xxx. 10.—)

This *Psalm David* inscribed *To him that excelleth upon the* Neginoth, (an *Instrument* so called,) upon the *Eighth Tune*; which was, doubtless, a very *mournful* Piece of *Musick*, and well adapted to express the *Passion* and *Sense* of so grave a Subject: Wherein he shews, that though his Sins had deserved utter Destruction, yet he trusted that GOD would in Mercy *pity* his *Frailty*; by Reason his *Repentance* was unfeigned, his Tears had watered his Couch, and his Conscience was touched to the Quick, for Fear of GOD's Judgment; his Strength was abated, and he sorely lamented that he could not *Praise* GOD in the Congregation as he had wont to do.—Lastly, GOD sendeth him Comfort in the Midst of his Sorrows and Afflictions, shewing, that by *Faith*, and unfeigned *Repentance*, we may boldly triumph over our Enemies; and that when the Wicked rejoice, and hope the Righteous will perish, GOD suddenly delivers them, and destroys the Wicked in their Stead. Oh! that we could but *Repent* as Holy DAVID did! But alas, the old Proverb is still too true, that is, "*Many can Sin with* DAVID, *but few can* Repent *with him*."

(—See *Psal.* cxv. 17. — cxviii. 17. — xxxviii. 18. — *Mat.* vii. 23. and xxv. 4.— *Luke* xiii. 27.—)

The

> *Have* Mercy, LORD, *for cruel Foes oppress,*
> *My Sins* forgive, *and help me in Distress:*
> *Restore my* Soul, *that I with chearful* Voice,
> *May* Praise *Thy Name, and evermore rejoice.*

N. B. This *Psalm* was written on the same *Occasion* as *Psalm* xxxii. and xxxv. which see.

On PSALM VII.

HOLY DAVID being very falsly accused by *Cush*, (who was one of *Saul*'s Kinsmen,) he ¹ greatly calleth upon GOD to be his Defender; unto whom he ³ commendeth his Innocency.—And then shewing ⁹ that his *Conscience* no ways accused him of any Evil towards *Saul*; he ¹⁰ next thought it was to GOD's *Glory*, to award Sentence against the Wicked. —Then ¹² entering into a deep Consideration of GOD's *Mercies*, and *Promises*, he boldly derideth the vain Enterprises of his Enemies; threatening, ¹⁶ that, that Mischief should fall on their own Heads, which they maliciously had purposed for others.

(—See 1 *Sam.* xvi. 7.—*Psal.* xviii. 19.—1 *Chron.* xxviii. 9—*Psal.* cxxxix. 1.— *Jer.* xi. 19, 20. and xvii. 10. and xx. 12.—*Hab.* iii. 1.)

This *Shigaion*, or *Psalm* of Delight, (or *Tune* so called,) of DAVID, which he sung to the LORD, concerning the false Accusation of *Cush*, the Son of *Jemini*, the *Benjamite*, shews how greatly he trusted, and called on GOD to deliver him from the Hands of cruel *Saul*, who was then so bitter against him.— And as he was intirely *innocent* of what *Cush* had charged him with, to confirm the same, he did not only wish that *Death* might fall on him, if he was guilty, but that his *Name* might afterwards be dishonoured for ever.—And touching his Behaviour towards *Saul*, though his Enemies pretended they had a just Cause against him, yet he firmly trusted that GOD would judge their Falshood in the End; who seldom come to any *Repentance*, but by some *Signs* of GOD's *Judgments*.— And DAVID knowing that *Saul* had great Store of *Men* and *Weapons*, he thought he must inevitably die, unless *Saul* changed his Mind.—Thus, considering the great Danger he was in, he wholly trusted in GOD, and magnified His *Name*, for his great, and gracious Deliverance: From which we may infer, that if we are ever so *falsly accused* by our Enemies, if we trust but in GOD, and His Mercies, He never fails in Rewarding us according to our *Righteousness* and *Innocency*; either in this World, or in a future one, which is more preferable.

(—See *Job* xv. 35.—*Isa.* lix. 4.—*Jam.* i. 15.—*Psal.* ix. 15. and x. 2.— *Prov.* v. 22.—)

The

A New Exposition *on the Book of* Psalms, *&c.* 7

The PRECEPT.

Though Foes engage, in GOD *the* LORD *I trust,*
His Mercy's *sure, His* Promise *is most just:*
From cruel Men, that causeless would devour,
Save me, my GOD, *with Thy great* Arm *and Power.*

N. B. The *Cup* that is herein mentioned was probably *Saul* himself, and also those his Words. See 1 *Sam.* xx. 30, 31.—xxii. 7, 8.

On PSALM VIII.

IN this *Psalm* Holy DAVID ¹ greatly meditates on the excellent *Liberality* of Almighty GOD, by his fatherly *Providence* towards Men; whom he hath so beautifully made, and to be as ⁵ an earthly *Governor* over all other Creatures, *&c.* For which, he doth not only give to GOD his greatest *Thanks*, but ⁹ is also astonished with the Admiration of the same: As counting nothing able to compass such great and manifold *Works, Mercies,* &c.

(—See *Mat.* xxi. 16.—*Job* vii. 17.—*Psal.* cxliv. 3.—2 *Sam.* vi.—1 *Tim.* vi. 9.—*Eph.* i. 21.—)

Herein the Holy *Prophet,* DAVID, shews, how greatly GOD's *Glory* is manifested by His *Works*; and also shews His wonderful *Love* to Men. (Which *Psalm* he inscribed *To him that excelleth upon the* Gittith, or to him that best performed on that *Harp-like Instrument,* &c.) And though the wicked Contemners of GOD, and his *Works*, endeavour all they can to eclipse His *Glory*, and *Praise*; yet, the very Babes are sufficient Witnesses of the same: His *Glory* being evident enough by the *wonderful Works* of the *heavenly Canopy* of moveable *Orbs*, had he not thought fit to come so low as earthly Man, which is but Dust; and our other *earthly Creation.*—And as GOD hath been so bountiful as to make Man *Lord* over all *Beasts, Fishes, Birds,* &c. how much the more is it our bounden Duty, seriously to consider the great *Benefits* which we have by His *Regeneration* through *JESUS CHRIST:* And to magnify His great and *Glorious Name* for his *Divine Providence,* Blessings, and *Mercies*; Who is every Moment our chief Support; and without Whose *Mercies*, and *Favours*, our Lives are no more than the smallest of His Creatures; though he hath fashioned us in His own *Image*, and crowned us with His loving Kindness. A true *Contemplation* of this *Psalm*, is sufficient to convince the most obdurate *Atheist* in the World.

(—See *Heb.* ii. 6.—1 *Cor.* xv. 27.—*Gen.* i. 26.—*Psal.* ciii. 4.—)

The PRECEPT.

How manifold, LORD, *are Thy Works Abroad!*
The least I see declares that Thou art GOD;
LORD, *let Thy Works teach me* Thee *to adore,*
And Live *to* Thee, *and* CHRIST *for evermore.*

N. B.

8   *The* Pfalm-Singer's Jewel: *Or,*

N. B. This *Pfalm* is alfo a Confideration of the State of the *firft Adam,* Gen. i. 28 or, of the *fecond Adam* by Redemption, *Mat.* xxviii. 18. and *Phil.* xxix. 10. Holy DAVID's Conquefts being as a *Type* of CHRIST's, which was then to come; foretold in HIM by the *Spirit* of *Prophecy.*

On PSALM IX.

1018. THIS *Pfalm* Holy DAVID directed to him that could beft perform on the *Muth-labben,* (an *Inftrument,* or *Tune* fo called) wherein he greatly giveth *Thanks* to GOD for fundry *Victories,* as that over *Goliab,* &c. and affures himfelf of the like *Succefs* for the Future, from the very fame *Juftice:* Shewing, ¹⁰ from his great and manifold *Experience,* how ready GOD was always to affift him in his greateft *Troubles.* He then being in *Danger* of new Enemies, ¹³ defireth GOD to help him as He was wont; that he might deftroy all the malicious Defigns of the Wicked.

* (—Vide 2 *Sam.* vi. 12 —2 *Sam.* viii.—)

From this we may *infer,* that GOD is not fully *Praifed* unlefs the WHOLE GLORY is given to Him alone. Likewife, however fo prevalent an Enemy may feem to be, for a little Time, yet GOD will affuredly defend the *juft Man's Caufe,* in the Midft of Danger. And though the Wicked make a Derifion of GOD's People, and daily ftrive to work the Deftruction of *CHRIST's Church,* yet GOD will furely deliver them; for He always confiders the *Poor Man's Caufe,* and His *Mercy* is over all His *Saints,* in CHRIST JESUS. And though he does not haftily *revenge* the Wrongs done to the *Righteous,* yet He will never fuffer the Wicked to go unpunifhed; for He has an Eye over all their wicked *Defigns,* and Enterprifes, though they think themfelves ever fo fly and *fecret;* and will bring every WORK into *Judgment,* whether they be Good or Evil.

(—Vide 2 *Sam.* xxii. 1.— *Pfal.* xcii. 3.—)

The PRECEPT.

{ *Moft mighty* LORD! *Thy* Judgments *all are juft,*
Thy Mercy's *great, to fuch as in Thee truft:*
The juft Man's Caufe *Thou always doft defend;*
Due Thanks, *and* Praife *can never, to* THEE, *End.* }

N. B. This *Pfalm* was penned after the *Ark* was feated in *Sion;* and in Midft of thofe *Victories,* mentioned in the *Scriptures,* before quoted. *

On

On PSALM X.

IN this *Psalm* our *Royal Author* DAVID ¹ greatly complains ² of the *Fraud, Rapine,* and *tyrannous* Wrongs which *worldly wise Men* in their great Prosperity, impose on GOD's People: They ⁴ setting apart all Godly *Fear* and *Reverence*; do as they list, without Controul; and persist in their own vain and careless Security, till their own wicked Enterprises come all to nought: For, GOD will never forsake His People, nor suffer their Enemies to go unpunished. Therefore, ¹² DAVID earnestly calls upon GOD to send them a speedy *Remedy* against their desperate Evils; and ¹⁶ greatly comforts himself with the Hope thereof; and of the *Success* of a speedy *Deliverance,* &c. &c.

(—Vide *Psal.* ix.—)

Hence we may learn, that although the *Church,* and GOD's People are often held in Derision by the wealthy Wicked, and are deemed as *Poor,* in the Goods of this Life, yet GOD never failed to help them, in His own due Time: For which Reason, whensoever we fall under any Troubles and Afflictions, we must always wait with *Patience,* till His good Time of Delivery. And although *wordly wise Men* boast of their Prosperity, *Riches,* and *Wit,* blaspheme their Maker, and think themselves secure in all Events; because they never had any Troubles; they, being in great *Power* and *Authority,* screen all their Villainies with *Hypocrisy*; devour the *Poor,* and despise both GOD and Man; and so run on, till *Justice* overtakes them, with utter Destruction. But, and to our great Comfort, the LORD helpeth the *Just,* when the Help of Man faileth; and their *Faith,* Hope, and *Good Works,* will bring them Peace at the *last,* when *Time* shall be *Eternity.*

(—Vide *Psal.* xxix. 11.—*Rom.* xv. 33.—)

The PRECEPT.

> *Save me,* O LORD, *for Trouble is at Hand,*
> *That I may all my haughty Foes withstand:*
> *Thou dost relieve the* Poor, *and* Fatherless,
> *In Thee I trust;* LORD *help me in Distress.*

On PSALM XI.

THIS *Psalm* ¹ sheweth Holy DAVID's firm *Confidence* in GOD's *Protection*; although ² the Wicked, by their Strength, and Subtlety, endeavour to persuade him to the Contrary.

The Psalm-Singer's Jewel: Or,

trary. He + also greatly rejoiceth in the *Succour* which GOD sent him, in his greatest Necessity: And *s* truly shews the *Justice* of GOD's *Judgments*, both on the Righteous, and on the Wicked, &c.

* (—Vide 1 Sam. xix. 2.—xx. 13. 41.—xx. 1.—xxiii. 24.—*Prov.* xxvii. 8.—)

Herein is shewed how hardly the Assaults of *Temptations* are sustained, and also what *Anguish* of Mind DAVID was in, when persecuted; for his wicked *Companions*, under Colour, and Pretence of Friendship, strove to baffle his *Confidence* in GOD; by telling him he would be slain by *Saul*; and that GOD's Residence was above taking Notice of him; or that his Hopes of His *Promises* and *Protection* were of none Effect, &c. The *Godly*, in this World, are here compared to *Birds*, who are compelled to fly from Place to Place, to hide themselves from the Snares of the Fowler; being destitute of any certain Habitation. But, the *End* always declares itself, and shews the *Mercy* and *Providence* of GOD over all His *Works*; for he never forsakes those that firmly *Trust* in Him, at all Events; nor lets the Wicked go unpunished, that despise him: Like those of *Sodom* and *Gomorrah*, which drink the very Dregs of his Indignation, as a Reward for their Wickedness. *Ezek.* xxiii. 34.

The PRECEPT.

$\left\{\begin{array}{l}\text{LORD, give us Grace our precious }Time\text{ to spend}\\ In\text{ all }Thy\text{ Laws and Precepts to the End:}\\ To\text{ live in }Love,\text{ and bear a godly }Mind,\\ That\text{ we, with }Thee,\text{ in }Heav'n\text{ may Glory find.}\end{array}\right\}$

N. B. It is very probable this *Psalm* was penned when *Jonathan* bad DAVID fly, and hide himself; when he was forced to fly from *Najoth*. See the Scriptures before quoted. *

※※※※※※※※※※※※※※※※※※※※※※※※※※

On PSALM XII.

IN this *Psalm* the *Royal Prophet*, DAVID, ¹ greatly lamenteth the miserable Estate of the People; and shews the great Decay of good *Order*, and *Christian Piety*; chiefly occasioned by *Flattery*: And desireth GOD would speedily send them such Succour, as to work a *Reformation*. Then ⁷ comforting himself, and others, with the Assurance of GOD's speedy *Help*; he commendeth the constant *Verity* that GOD always observed in keeping His holy *Promise*.

* (—Vide 1 *Sam.* xxii. — xxv.—)

We are taught, from this *Psalm*, always to call upon GOD with a sure *Confidence*, if we would persevere in our *Desires*; for He will always defend the *Truth*, and will shew *Mercy* to all such as are wrongfully oppressed. DAVID also

A New Exposition *of the* Book *of* Psalms, &c.   11

also shews that *Flatterers,* at *Court,* often do more Harm with their *Tongues,* than the many *Weapons*; by Reason, they think they are able to persuade Men to *comply* with whatsoever they take in Hand ; be their Designs ever so *pernicious* to the People. But let all such *observe,* that GOD is always *moved* with the *Complaints,* and *Sighs* of His People; and will, in His due Time, *deliver* them from the Snares, and Dangers of the Wicked : Because His *Word* is true, and His *Promise* is unchangeable. He will preserve the *Poor* from the wicked Generation, who strive to suppress the *Godly*; and destroy the Wicked : For the LORD knoweth the *Secrets* of all *Hearts,* and of every *Scheme,* and Disguise.

The PRECEPT.

{ *From flattering Tongues,* O LORD, *do thou defend*
 And keep me safe; *'tis hard to find one Friend :*
 Thy Words *are pure,* O LORD, *thou canst destroy*
 The Double Heart, that would my Soul annoy. }

N. B. Probably this *Psalm* was penned on the *Notice* of the *Priests* that were slain by *Doeg*'s Advancement; and on *Samuel*'s Death, &c. See the *Scriptures* before cited.

✱✱✱✱✱✱✱✱✱✱✱✱✱✱✱✱✱✱✱✱✱✱✱✱✱✱✱✱✱✱✱✱✱✱✱✱✱✱

On PSALM XIII.

HOLY DAVID, in this *Psalm,* being a little *dispirited* with sundry *Afflictions,* ¹ fleeth to GOD; and expostulateth with Him about the Length of their Continuance ; and ³ begs earnestly of Him, for a speedy *Deliverance.* And being encouraged through GOD's *Promises* of *Success*; he ⁵ puts his whole Confidence in Him; and, at last, *sings* of His *Mercy,* and loving Kindness, in dealing so favourably with him.

(—Vide *Psalm* lxxxix. 1. 15. 16. 29. 32, 33.—)

From this we are instructed, that although our *Afflictions* continue a long Time, yet we ought not to *faint* in our *Faith*; but to trust in GOD, and to bear all *patiently* that he lays upon us, until it is His good Time to *deliver* us ; lest the great *Enemy* overcome us, we *die* without *Hope,* and undergo the *second Death.* But, as the *Mercy* of GOD is our eternal *Salvation,* both by his Mercies *past,* as well as by those to *come* ; we should always *pray* the most earnestly, when our *State* and *Condition* is most *desperate*; and have a full Confidence in GOD, for our Deliverance : For as much as we know, that the *Prayers* of *CHRIST*'s *Church,* and *Saints,* will never be in vain in the LORD.

(—Vide 1 *Cor.* xv. 58.—*John* xi.—*Acts* xvi.—*Rom.* v. 1.—)

The PRECEPT.

{ *Leave me not,* LORD, *for boundless is thy* Grace,
 Let not my Foes *prevail in any Case :*
 In Thee *I trust* ; *I'll of Thy* Mercy *sing,*
 And praise *Thee Daily,* O *my* GOD, *and King.* }

N. B.

12   *The* Psalm-Singer's Jewel: *Or,*

N. B. This *Psalm* was probably wrote when DAVID was in *Despair* of the Safety of *Israel*; and was forced to fly unto *Gath*.—1 Sam. xxvii. 1. 5.

On PSALM XIV.

OUR Royal *Author,* in this *Psalm,* (and the next) describeth ¹ the perverse *Nature* of licentious wicked Men, whose Sins are grown to such a Height, as to forget GOD, and *despise* His People; whereby they ⁵ brought themselves under His utter Contempt. And although DAVID was greatly grieved for them, he was still persuaded that GOD would send them some Remedy: Of which *Hope* he hath comforted himself and others: And ⁷ *prayeth* for the whole *Church,* &c.

(—Vide *Rom.* iii. 10. 11.—*Job* xxi. 15.—*Rom.* xi. 26.—*Eph.* iv. 8.—)

Here we have a true *Comparison* between the *Faithful,* and the *Reprobate*; although St. *Paul* mentions the same, in some Measure, to be the *Nature* of all Men, before *Regeneration*; which is the Corruption of both the *Understanding,* and the *Will,* which doth chiefly utter itself into *Atheism,* and *Hatred* against the *Church*; as it hath been from the Beginning of the World: From which, our Royal *Prophet* bids *Israel* be of good *Courage,* and rest on the *Hope* of the Comming of our LORD JESUS. And since CHRIST is *now come,* how much the more ought we to be of Comfort, since he hath *fulfilled* the Mystery of our *Salvation!* Whereby we should rest with a stedfast, and unshaken *Belief* of His *second Coming,* to Judge both Quick and Dead, and *Reward* all Men, according to their *Works.*

Observe, That the 5th, 6th, and 7th *Verses* of this *Psalm,* (which are put into *new Translations,*) are not in the *old Translations,* nor in the *Hebrew*; but they are rather put into the *new,* more to express the *Nature* of wicked Men; being gathered out of *Psalm* the 5th, the 140th, the 10th, the 59th, and the 59th of *Isaiah*; all of which are alledged by St. *Paul,* and placed together in the 3d *Chapter* of *Romans.*

The PRECEPT.

$\left\{\begin{array}{l}\text{How blind must Atheists be, who do deny}\\\text{The Works of GOD; and all His Pow'r defy!}\\\text{The heav'nly Orbs, and great terrestrial Ball,}\\\text{Shews one Supreme, and one GOD governs all.}\end{array}\right\}$

N. B. This *Psalm,* and the 53d, seem to be wrote on the People's *Defection,* under wicked *Absolom:* By the last *Verses* of each.

On PSALM XV.

AS the foregoing *Pfalm* fhewed the perverfe Nature of *Reprobates, Atheifts*, &c. this *Pfalm*, on the contrary, defcribes ² the Nature of the *Faithful* and *Holy*; alfo what Manner of Perfons the People of CHRIST's *Church* ought to be, in their *Lives* and *Converfations*; and what *Vices* they ought to fhun, to become *Citizens* of the Kingdom of *Heaven*.

(—Vide *Rom*. ii —*Levit*. xix. 16.—*Prov*. vi. 24.—)

In this precious *Pfalm*, our holy *Author*, DAVID, fhews on what *Terms* GOD chofe the *Jews* for His peculiar People; and why he placed his *Temple* among them: which was, that their *godly* and *upright Lives* might be as a *Mark* to witnefs that they were His holy and *chofen People*. From this *we* may infer, that our *Behaviour* in this Life muft be as becomes the *Church* of CHRIST: i. e. To live *honeftly*, without Guile; and *ferve* GOD in *Sincerity*, and in *Truth*. To fpeak *Evil* of no Man, nor *wound* any one's *Character*, publickly or privately; nor encourage, or connive with, fuch as do. To *flatter* no Man, but to fpeak the very *Truth* according to the beft of our Knowledge; nor be a *falfe Witnefs* againft any one, left his Blood cry out againft us. Not to grind the *Poor*, nor take an *Advantage* of their *Neceffity*, in making them pay Extortion for what we *lend*, or *fell* them; nor hinder your Neighbour's honeft *Advantage* when Opportunity offereth; but, do by all Men as we would they fhould do unto us, both in *Thought*, in *Word*, and in *Deed*: for GOD will *judge* both the *Deceitful*, and the *Hypocrite*; and the honeft SINCERE MAN fhall find PEACE at the laft.

(—Vide 1 *Chron*. xxii. 1.—2 *Chron*. iii. 1.—2 *Sam*. vi. 6. 9.—) *

The PRECEPT.

{ *Be to thy* Neighbour *juft and innocent,*
Free from all Guile, *all* Words *thy Heart's Intent*;
No Envy *bear, nor injur'ous* Tales *regard,*
And thou in Heav'n, *with* CHRIST, *fhalt find* Reward. }

N. B. This *Pfalm* was wrote in Oppofition to the xivth, and on fome Occafion alluding to the *prefent* Tabernacling of the *Ark of Sion*; and the *future* Place of it in *Mount Moriah*: Or poffibly on the *Breach* made on *Uzzah*. *

On PSALM XVI.

IN this *Michtam* or *Golden Pfalm* of holy DAVID, he ¹ earneftly *prays* to GOD for *Succour*, not for his *Works*, but for his *Faith*: And ⁺ fhews his utter Abhorrence to all Kinds of *Idolatry*. Then, [6] rejoicing in his own *State*, he [s] shews his *Faith* in G O D, [10] by *C H R I S T*'s *Resurrection* ; and wholly relies thereon as his greatest *Felicity* and Comfort.

(—Vide *Acts* ii. 25.—Heb. v. 7.—*Acts* xiii. 34, 35, &c.—*Psal.* xxiv. 4.— *Job* xiv. 13.—)

This *Psalm*, (amongst many others) was *wrote* by holy DAVID, intirely from the Power of *Faith*, and Spirit of *Prophecy*; by Reason, the *Prophet*, being ravished in Spirit, sheweth from his *Faith*, and *contented State*, what *present Trust* he had then on G O D, and His *Promises*, in the future Coming of *C H R I S T* the *Messiah*; by whose *Death* and *Resurrection*, he should be made a Partaker of the *Joys* of *Heaven*.—This is the very *Sum* of the whole *Doctrine* of the *Gospel* of *C H R I S T*, and should be the perfect *Pattern* and *Ground-work* of all our *present Comfort*, in this World, and all our *future Hope* of *eternal Felicity* in the next: For as the *Prophecy* of DAVID is now made manifest according to the *Promise* of G O D, by the *Coming* of *C H R I S T*; we should, with an unshaken *Hope*, now trust on his *second Coming*, to *judge* the whole World; and endeavour, by our *Faith* and *good Works*, to *die* from all Manner of Sin, and *rise* again to a *new Life* of Righteousness, while we are in this World; so that our *Faith* may not only *lay* us down in Peace in our *Graves*, but also *raise* us again at the *last* Day of *Judgment*, to receive the joyful *Sentence* of COME YE BLESSED! in whose *Presence* there is Fulness of JOY, and at whose Right-Hand there are *Pleasures* for *evermore*. Amen. Amen.

The PRECEPT.

{
L O R D, keep my Heart in good and pious *Frame*,
That *I* obey, and love *thy mighty Name*:
For well I know, my Saviour *has in Store*
For me a Crown, in Heav'n, for evermore.
}

On PSALM XVII.

THIS *Psalm* is a *Prayer* of DAVID, wherein he greatly complaineth of the cruel *Pride*, *Arrogance*, and causeless *Wrongs* of *Saul*, and other Enemies; and [2] earnestly *prays* to G O D to judge his Innocency, [8] defend him, [13] revenge his Cause, and deliver him : [15] whereby he was not ashamed to face the L O R D in Righteousness, which was his greatest Felicity and Comfort.

(—Vide *Jer.* vii. 11.—1 *Sam.* xxiii. 26.—) *

We are *taught* from this *Psalm*, that whensoever cruel *Tyrants* oppress and persecute either *us*, or our *Religion* of *C H R I S T*, that we should alway keep a safe and good *Conscience*, void of Offence both to G O D and *Man*; and, with

A New Exposition *on the* Book *of* Psalms, *&c.* 15

a firm *Hope*, earnestly *pray* to GOD for Deliverance according to our Innocency: For GOD will assuredly bring down their Pride, stop their Rage, and confound their wicked *Designs* and *Allegations* in the End. And though the *Proud*, (like rich *Dives*, the Glutton,) fare sumptuously for many Days in this World, and despise and grind the *Poor*, and make them, (like *Lazarus*,) undergo all the *Miseries* and *Hardships* of this World, yet, the LORD will revenge their *Cause*, and take them into His Bosom in the End; whilst their wicked Enemies feed on nothing but endless Misery, in the *Torments* of *Hell:* for the LORD knoweth, and *loveth* the *Righteous*, and will bring down the Wicked to a *Death* of endless Misery.

The PRECEPT.

{ GOD *will preserve the Man of upright Heart,*
But, wicked Men he surely will subvert:
Shield me, O LORD, *for, whilst I trust in Thee,*
I need not fear what Foes can do to me. }

N. B. This *Psalm* was probably wrote when *Saul* thought he had surely ensnared DAVID. See the xxiiid of 1 *Sam.* as above cited *.

※※※※※※※※※※※§※※※※※※※※※※※

On PSALM XVIII.

OUR Princely *Prophet*, holy DAVID, set forth this excellent *Psalm* on the Day the LORD delivered him from the Hands of his Enemies, and from the Hands of *Saul:* Wherein he ¹ highly extolleth and *praiseth* GOD for His *Mercies*, in so graciously *defending* him, *&c.* Also he ¹² setteth forth the very *Image* of CHRIST's Kingdom, by his own, by which the *Faithful* may be well assured that CHRIST will surely overcome and conquer *all*, by the unspeakable *Power* of the FATHER, *&c.*

* (—Vide 2 *Sam.* vii.—2 *Sam.* xxii.—)

This *Psalm* is the Beginning of holy DAVID's *Gratulation* and *Thanksgiving* in the entering into his *Kingdom*, wherein he declares, he not only reigns for his *own Cause*, but for the GLORY OF GOD; and that he taketh no *Praise* at all to himself; whose *Kingdom* only figures out to the *Faithful*, that the MESSIAH should come from his Loins; and that ALL the *Earth* should receive *Him* for their KING. See *Rom.* xv. 9, 10, 11, 12. In the *Beginning*, he useth divers *Names* for the *Power* of GOD, in Order to shew, that as the W:cked have many Ways to *hurt*, GOD has, in like Manner, many Ways to *help* and *save:* which none can receive unless they *faithfully* join in His *Glory* and *Petition*. He also shews the *Wrath* of GOD against His Enemies, and how horrible His *Judgments* will be on the Wicked, by *Darkness, Thunder, Lightning, Hail, Bottomless Pits,*
&c.

The Pfalm-Singer's Jewel: Or,

&c. and, on the contrary, what *Favour* He has to the *Faithful*, in *bearing* their *Complaints*, and mercifully *delivering* them out of their Troubles, &c. &c. &c.

(—Vide 2 Sam. xxii.—*Pfal.* civ.—*Rom.* xv. 9.

The PRECEPT.

{ *From cruel Foes, Thou,* LORD, *haft set me free,*
Great was Thy Love *and Favour unto me!*
Of thy Deliv'rance, LORD, *I'll ever sing,*
And daily love *Thee, O my* GOD *and* King! }

N. B. This *Pfalm* was uttered after all his Enemies in *Canaan* were fubdued, and he in full *Tranquillity*; and, from his Purpofe to build the *Temple*, was driven to the *Wars* abroad, in all which he promifeth himfelf *Succefs*, and had it accordingly. See the *Scriptures* above or before quoted.

※※※※※※※※※※※※※※※※※※※※※※

On PSALM XIX.

HOLY DAVID, in this *Pfalm*, [1] moveth the *Faithful* to *glorify* GOD by the vifible and exquifite *Workmanfhip, Proportion*, and glorious *Ornaments* of *Heaven*, as the *Sun, Moon*, and *Stars:* And then [7] calleth them to the *Law*, which GOD has fo familiarly revealed to his chofen People: Shewing, by its feveral *Names*, its Divine *Nature*, its gracious *Effects*, [10] its *Precioufnefs*, and [11] its *Profitablenefs*. He then [13] prays for *Purification*, and *Prefervation* from all Sin; and [14] for GOD's favourable *Acceptance* of his Duty, &c.

(—Vide *Rom.* x. 18.—*Gal.* iv. 21.—2 *Tim.* iii. 16.—*Exod.* xx. 5.—)

This glorious *Pfalm*, or Morning *Meditation*, teacheth us the whole *Sum* of all true DIVINITY, whereby we may know both GOD himfelf, and the *Worfhip* due to Him, fo as to attain everlafting Life. The *Glory* and *Worfhip* due to GOD is manifefted by the Works of the *Heavens*, which is as a *Schoolmafter* to every Nation of the World, or as a *Line* of large Capital *Letters*, to fhew His Magnificence and *Glory*; fo that none can pretend to be ignorant thereof, be they ever fo barbarous, when they behold the orderly *Changes* of *Days, Nights, Seafons,* and *Years*; and more efpecially of the glorious SUN, which *warmeth* and *fhineth* over the whole Earth, and cometh forth in his Courfe, as a *Bride* and *Bridegroom* in great So'emnity, from the Veil of Darknefs, rejoicing the whole *Affembly*, both of HEAVEN and *Earth*.

The *Honour* and *Worfhip* due to Him is here fet forth at large by the *Law*, which we fhould have fo *printed* in our Hearts, as to *teach* us, that true *Wifdom* is not in *Words* alone, but in *Deeds* alfo; whereby we may have Forgivenefs of Sins, which, in DAVID's Time was only fhadowed by the Law; but *now*, fince CHRIST, it is expounded by the *Gofpel*, and uttered to us moft fully, and manifeftly, both by CHRIST himfelf; and by the *Writings* of His holy
infpired

A New Exposition *on the* Book *of* Psalms, *&c.* 17

infpired *Apoſtles:* Which Belief, with Practice, will bring us to Life everlaſting. Amen. Amen.

The PRECEPT.

$\left\{\begin{array}{l}\textit{The Sun, the Moon, and Stars do plainly ſhow}\\\textit{GOD's Handy-Works, to Mortals here below:}\\\textit{His Laws and Precepts ſo in Glory ſhine,}\\\textit{To guide our Souls to laſting Joy, Divine.}\end{array}\right\}$

(—Vide Rom. i. 10.—*Acts* xvii. 27.—1 *Cor.* i. 21.—)

On PSALM XX.

THIS *Pſalm* or *Prayer* of DAVID was compoſed for his People to join with *him*, before he went to Battle againſt the *Ammonites*; *viz.* 1 That GOD would pleaſe to hear both *him*, and his *People*, and receive the *Prayers* they offered unto Him: 7 Declaring, that, (though the *Heathen* put all their Truſt in their *Chariots*, *Horſes*, and their *King*,) they truſted only in GOD, to give them a compleat *Victory:* Whereby one ſhould *fall*, and the other ſhould *ſtand*.

(—Vide 2 *Sam.* x. 1.—1 *Kings* xix. 2.—)

From this *Pſalm* we are taught that *Kings*, *Potentates*, and *Magiſtrates*, ſhould *join* with the meaner *People* to call upon GOD, in Time of *War*, and other *Dangers*; to preſerve every *Subject*, as well as themſelves: for the *Hands* cannot ſay to the *Legs*, I have no Need of ye.—We alſo may gather, from this *Pſalm*, four principal *Points* of *Doctrine*. 1. That, *at ſome* Times, a Warfare is neceſſary to a *Commonwealth*, to allay *Pride*, and promote *Godlineſs*. 2. That there is a wide Difference between the *Confidence* of the Wicked, and of the *Righteous*; for one *falleth*, and the other *ſtandeth*. 3. That all prudent *Policies* are eſtabliſhed when GOD's Help is conſulted; and not by mere *Fortune*. And 4. That as GOD is the *Author*, and Preſerver of all *good Policies*, in like Manner He will aſſiſt in all *Laws* wherein His mighty Power is conſulted; and will *preſerve* the *Righteous* in all *Perils* and *Dangers*, be their Enemies ever ſo, ſeemingly, powerful.

The PRECEPT.

$\left\{\begin{array}{l}\textit{In Time of War, truſt in the LORD of Might,}\\\textit{'Tis He alone that does your Battle fight:}\\\textit{Princes and Subjects muſt on GOD depend,}\\\textit{Without His Aid, all muſt in Ruin end.}\end{array}\right\}$

N. B. Probably this *Pſalm* was left with the *Levites* and People, as a Form to pray for the *King* in his *Atchievements* abroad; as thoſe in 2 *Sam.* viii. and x.

On PSALM XXI.

AS the foregoing *Pfalm* was a *Prayer* for *Succefs*, this is a *Thankfgiving* for *Victory*; wherein Holy DAVID, (in the Perfon of the People,) ¹ greatly *praifeth* GOD for his *Succeffes*; which ³ he wholly attributed to His *Divine Providence*, and bountiful *Clemency*; and ⁷ not to the *Strength* and *Number* of his *Men*. This alfo hinteth, ⁸ that the *Holy Ghoft* will direct the Faithful to *CHRIST*, notwithftanding all their Enemies; and that they ¹³ fhall furely know the full *Perfection* of His Kingdom in the End.

* (—Vide 2 *Sam*. viii. and x.—)

By this *Triumphant Song* we are taught the wonderful *Effects* of PRAYER, and *Duty* of GRATITUDE; for as DAVID *prayed*, and trufted in GOD for *fuccefs*, before he went into *Battle*, he, in like Manner, made as grateful an Acknowledgment, by giving *Thanks* for Victory at his Return. It fhews alfo, that the Enterprizes, and Defigns of the Wicked, are of none Effect, when GOD ftands by the *Righteous*. And though the Wicked daily ftrive againft *CHRIST*, and the *Faithful*, we fhould bear all patiently, till GOD, in his good Time, fhall think fit to deftroy them; when we fhall have ample Occafion to *Praife* His Name, and SING of His *Power*. From hence, for every *Supply* of Life, we fhould always feek to GOD for it by *Prayer*; and for all *Mercies* and *Benefits* received, we fhould return a grateful *Thankfgiving*: For His *Mercy* is over all His WORKS, He is the bountiful *Giver* of all good Things; *and, it becometh well the Juft to be thankful*. Pfal. xxxiii. 1.

The PRECEPT.

{ *If* PRINCE *and* People *on the* LORD *depend,*
The Battle's *fafe*; *Foes do in vain contend:*
When virtuous Princes *do with* Juftice *rule,*
He that rebels, *muft be both Knave and Fool.* }

N. B. This *Pfalm* feems to be left with the *Levites*, and People, as a *Form* to pray for the *King*, in his *Atchievements* abroad; as mentioned in the above *Scriptures*. *

On PSALM XXII.

THIS *Pfalm* fhews the *Sufferings* and *Victory* of *CHRIST*, although written by holy DAVID fo many Years before His Coming: In which the Royal *Prophet, perfonating* Him,

¹ mourn-

A New Exposition *on the* Book *of* Psalms, *&c.* 19

1 mournfully complaineth over His *Passion*, 7 His *Scorns*, 16 His *Piercings*, 19 His *Prayers*, and 20 even the very *Agonies* of *Death*. He then 22 praiseth GOD for hearing him; and 27 foretelleth the glorious *Enlargement* of the *Church* thereby.

(—Vide *Matt.* xxvii. 43.—*Psal.* xxxv. 17. xxv. 16.—*Heb.* ii. 13.—)

This *Psalm* holy DAVID inscribed *To him that excelleth on* Aijeleth-Shahar, (or a *Tune* so called:) And must needs be wrote purely from the *Spirit* of *Prophecy*, wherein we may plainly behold both how horrible it is to fall into the Hands of GOD our *Judge*; and also how great His *Mercy* is towards His *Church*, &c.—Surely this precious *Psalm* ought to be wrote in *Letters* of *Gold*, and never out of our Hands, or Memories; if we but consider, that on this *Battle* of *CHRIST*, all our Victory dependeth. It is here so painted to the Life, that we may, as it were, behold his *Accusing*, his *Hanging* on the *Cross*, and hear his sorrowful *Sighs* and *Sobs* in that Conflict with *Satan*, our *Sins*, and with *Death*; as if He were struggling with the very Bottom of Hell itself. We also may see, as it were, the very *Victory* of His *Resurrection*; and that everlasting *Office*, which he shall exercise to the End of the World; by whose *Ambassadors* he shall gather His *Church* from every Nation, and preserve it from Age to Age. This you'll find interpreted by the *Four Evangelists* in their *History* of His *Passion*; and by the Apostle, in his Epistle to the *Hebrews*. All of which see, read, mark, and learn.

The PRECEPT.

{ Our Fathers *old, did on the* LORD *depend,*
Not vain their Trust, *for He did* Succour *send;*
Let me, O LORD, *on* JESUS *now rely,*
That, by His Blood, *my Soul may never die.* }

✿✿✿✿✿✿✿✿✿✿✿✿✿✿✿✿✿✿✿✿✿✿✿✿✿✿✿✿✿✿

On PSALM XXIII.

THIS is a *Psalm* of COMFORT.—DAVID, the Royal *Prophet*, having often tried the manifold *Mercies* of GOD several Ways, in this *Psalm* 1 he, by *Faith*, promiseth himself that GOD will not forsake Him all the Days of His Life: But that 6 He will continue His *Goodness* to him for ever.

(—Vide *Isai.* xl. 11.—*Jer.* xxiii. 5.—*Ezek.* xxxiv. 5.—*John* x. 11.—1 *Pet.* ii. 25.—)

Although this sweet and *grateful Lesson* of *Humility*, was wrote by the *Royal* Hand of DAVID after he had settled the *Ark*, and was in full *Tranquillity* *, yet he was not puffed up like the *Epicureans*, who think all they have comes by *Fortune*, or by their own *Industry*, and so turn all good Things into Filthiness: No, he attributed all he had, and enjoyed, to the *Liberality* of a good and *merciful* GOD. And though now a KING, in *Splendor*, he thought it no Disgrace to own he had been a *Shepherd*; for which Reason he probably used these two *Similitudes*

litudes in his Writing, *viz. one*, of a *Shepherd* that carefuly provideth for his Flock; and the *other*, for the *Sheep* that are fed and guarded by him: From the which, all *Kings* are admonished to feed and guard the People, and use *Hospitality* and *Liberality* amongst them. He also sheweth that all Things, of this Life, come to us from GOD, and are *sanctified* unto us by His holy WORD; for which Reason we should not intirely set our Affections on the Things of *this* transitory *Life*, but should raise our Thoughts on His everlasting and heavenly *Being*; since we have, (by our Hope, and good Works,) His most gracious *Promise* of being *Blessed* both in this World, and in that which is to come.

* (—Vide 2 *Sam.* vii. 1.—)

The PRECEPT.

{ *A stedfast Heart need never dread or fear,*
For why? a loving SAVIOUR'*s always near:*
CHRIST will support, and be his greatest Friend,
And safely guide him to his Journey's End. }

N. B. This *Psalm* was wrote after the Ark was settled, when he was in full Tranquillity. *

On PSALM XXIV.

1017. FROM this *Psalm* of DAVID, we may learn, [1] that as GOD *created all*, He is even LORD over *all*, and [2] *governeth all*, and *preserveth all*; and [3] that His gracious *Goodness* most appears to His *chosen People*, that [4] are true *Worshippers* of Him; whom [5] He hath appointed for His eternal *Glory* in *Heaven*, as willingly as they would be *Members* of His *Church* on Earth. He then, by the Spirit of *Prophecy*, speaking of the *Building* of the *Temple*, desireth [7] that the *Gates* and *Doors* thereof might be opened, that the *Glory* of GOD might enter in; according to the *Promise* in *Psalm* cxxxii. ver. 14, *&c.*

* (—Vide 2 *Sam.* vi. 9 —2 *Sam.* vi. 12. 20.—)

It is herein declared, that the true *Members* of the Church are known unto GOD by their good Works; for GOD knows the Hearts of all, at all Times, and in all Places. The Word *Mount* or *Hill*, herein means the *Place* whereon the *Temple* was to be built: Which earthly *Temple* figures out to us the *everlasting Temple* of GOD, His eternal and heavenly *Residence*: Whereunto all His faithful *Worshippers* of the earthly *Church* shall be taken after this Life (and enjoy the full Fruition, and *Presence* of GOD, and *CHRIST*, for evermore. Amen. Amen.

The

A New Exposition *on the* Book *of* Psalms, *&c.*

The PRECEPT.

{ LORD, *let thy Precepts be my Rule and Guide,*
That I from Thee, and CHRIST *may never slide:*
In Mercy, LORD, *count me among the* Blest,
And guide my Soul to Thy eternal Rest. }

N. B. This *Psalm* was *written*, probably, while the Ark tarried with *Obed-Edom*; respecting the Breach made on *Uzzah*; and the Preparations for the removing the *Ark* to *Sion*. See the above Scriptures. *

On PSALM XXV.

IN this *Psalm* of *Prayer*, holy DAVID being greatly grieved at the *Malice* of his *Enemies*, and for his own *Sins*, especially for those of his *Youth*, ¹ by his *Hope* in GOD, he ⁴ earnestly *prays* for His *Safeguard*, ⁶ *Direction*, and ¹⁴ *Remission* of Sins; and also for his *own*, and the *Church*'s Deliverance out of all Afflictions, *&c.*

(—Vide *Isai*. xxviii. 26.—*Rom*. x. 9, 10, 11.—)

This excellent *Psalm* is full of Affections to GOD, and answers to *three Petitions* contained in the LORD's *Prayer*, 1. That we may have a free *Forgiveness* of our Trespasses, and *Sins*. 2. That the *Will* of GOD may be *done*, by our being *guided* and *governed* by His *Holy Spirit*. And 3. That we may be defended, and *delivered* from the *Evil*, and Injuries of all our Enemies, *&c.* This *Psalm* being a very proper *Form* of *Prayer*, to be used by our whole *Church*, in public; and for all godly *Families*, in private, *&c.*

* (—Vide 2 *Sam*. xviii. 1. 6.—)

The PRECEPT.

{ *Defend me,* LORD,-*in* Thee *I put my Trust,*
Guide Thou my Soul, to do Thy Will *most just:*
Confound my Foes, *let none my Soul destroy,*
Forgive my Sins, and I shall never die. }

N. B. This *Psalm* was probably wrote just after his *Sin* with *Bathsheba*; when GOD visited him for it with many *Troubles* of Heart, as well as with many unjust, and cruel Enemies. See ver. 11, 17, 18, 19, 21.

As *Psalm* iii. 1. was wrote on *Absalom*'s Insurrection, this, the xxvth; was probably composed when he had dispatched his Army out against those *Rebels*: As also was *Psalm* lxxi. See the Scriptures above quoted. *

On

On PSALM XXVI.

DAVID, being greatly oppressed with many cruel Enemies, and Injuries, and finding but very little Help in the World; ¹ *appeals*, from his own *Conscience*, unto GOD to judge his *Cause*, according to his *Innocency*; and *prays* for Deliverance: Desiring ⁸ to be again in *Company* with the *Faithful*, in the *Church* of GOD; though *Saul* had banished him. He also ¹¹ promiseth himself that GOD will *preserve* and keep him, for his *Faith*, *Piety*, and *Integrity*, that he ¹² might again *worship* and *praise* Him in the Congregation, as he was wont to do.

(—Vide 2 *Sam.* xx. 30, 31.—xii. 7, 8.—*Psal.* cxxxix.—)

From this *Psalm* we are taught that GOD is the best *Judge* in every Cause, and that there is but very little *Equity* amongst Men. Also how hard a Thing it is in *Court* to retain true *Religion*, *Uprightness* of Life, and godly Conversation; especially when wicked Men reign, *Flatterers* rage, and open *Violence* is used by false *Accusations*: Or, when Persons will frame their *Wits* only to serve the Turns of the Wicked for every Purpose, (even as the *Polypus Fishes* change their Colour to be the same as every Stone they stick to;) to their own private Ends, though they destroy the *Commonwealth*. But *David's Case* was quite contrary to this, for though his State was no better in the *Court* of *Saul*, yet he persevered in his *Place* and *Vocation*; and frequented all holy *Assemblies* that were not polluted with *Idolatry*; though he was driven from them by Violence; for he was always the same Man, and committed his *Cause* to GOD, living an upright and pure Life: And, as GOD had preserved him by His mighty *Power*, he would not fail to *Praise* Him openly for it.

The PRECEPT.

{ *Great* GOD! my Judge, *to whom my* Heart *is known*,
 Let me not be by Evil overthrown :
 LORD, *let Thy* Church *be all my Soul's Delight*,
 And Precepts *guide me ev'ry Day and Night*. }

N. B. This *Psalm* was wrote when DAVID was first accused and *persecuted* by *Saul*, as a *Conspirator* against him. *

On PSALM XXVII.

IN this *Pſalm*, holy DAVID, being delivered from many Perils and Dangers, ſheweth, ¹ from many Experiences, his undaunted *Faith* in GOD; and ⁴ *prays* to be admitted again into the *Temple*, to *Praiſe* GOD, as he was wont. He alſo ⁷ *prays* to GOD for *Audience*, ¹¹ for His *Direction*, and ¹² *Deliverance* from falſe *Witneſſes*: And ¹⁴ greatly encourageth in the *Succeſs* thereof, to the *End* that he might *Praiſe* GOD in the *Congregation*, to his eternal Comfort.

* (—Vide 2 *Sam.* xxvi. 21. 25.—*Pſal.* xxviii. 3,—)

We have here laid open to us, That whenſoever Things ſeem to us moſt *deſperate*, we ſhould, *firſt*, take hold of the *Power* of GOD by *Faith*; and ſtrongly oppoſe all the *Brags* and *Aſſaults* of our Enemies. *Secondly*, we ſhould always have an unſhaken *Deſire* of the *Glory* of GOD, keeping a ſafe, and good *Conſcience*, and uſe a diligent Means whereby our *Faith* may be confirmed; by hearing the *Word* of GOD preached, uſing His *Sacraments*, and performing His *Praiſes*; and by *meditating* always on them. *Thirdly*, to be earneſt in *Prayer*, with *Faith* and PATIENCE, till GOD's good Time of *Deliverance*: which are the never-failing *Springs* to afford us *Comfort* in our greateſt Troubles and Afflictions.

The PRECEPT.

{ *If* GOD *aſſiſts, why ſhould I fear to try*
A dangerous Combat, *ſince my* Guardian's *nigh?*
My heav'nly PRINCE *can* Armies *put to Flight,*
And turn their Day into eternal Night. }

N. B. This *Pſalm* was probably wrote on Occaſion of *Saul's* Perſecution, after many Deliverances from him; when DAVID's *Friends* could yield him no Succour; he being rather fain to get Sanctuary for them in *Moab*, and go again to *Judea*. It agreeing to the ſame Time. See the *Scriptures* before quoted. *

On PSALM XXVIII.

ROYAL DAVID, in this *Pſalm*, ¹ being in great *Fear* and Heavineſs of Heart, to ſee how GOD was *diſhonoured*, ² deſires that his *Petition* may be heard; and ³ that GOD would take him away from among them. He alſo ⁴ prays that

that GOD will *reward* them according to their wicked *Inventions, Malice,* and *Deceitfulness*; and ⁶ *praiseth* GOD that He hath heard his *Petitions:* Shewing, that He is his only *Safeguard,* at all Events; and hath mercifully saved both him and his People; for whom he *prays,* as well as for himself; and ⁷ joyfully *sings* of GOD's Mercy and Loving-kindness.

(—Vide *Malachi* i. 4.—)

Herein holy DAVID behaves not only as a *private* Man, but even as a KING appointed by GOD; praying both for himself, and GOD's People; and undoubtedly by the *Spirit* of *Prophecy,* concerning such as would wilfully persecute the *Church.* He counted himself but as a dead Man till GOD had granted his *Petitions*; and begged that GOD would not destroy the *Good* with the Bad; (meaning *himself* and his *Soldiers*) being well assured that GOD would punish all the Enemies of His *Church*; and would *save, feed, bless* and *exalt him* and his People for ever.

* (—Vide 1 Sam. xxiv. 16. 22.—xxvi. 21. 25.—)

The PRECEPT.

{ *Hear me,* O LORD, *when unto* Thee *I cry,*
With the Ungodly do not me destroy:
Thou art my Shield, *I'll sing of Thy Renown,*
Thy tender Love *will me with* Glory *crown.* }

N. B. This *Psalm* was wrote after DAVID was anointed; on Occasion of some of *Saul's* Distresses, deceitful Tears, and *Promises,* &c. See the *Scriptures* above quoted. *

On PSALM XXIX.

IN this *Psalm,* holy DAVID, ¹ exhorteth all *Kings, Potentates,* and *Rulers* of the Earth, to be subdued by the *Power* of GOD, from His ruling the ¹ *Waters, Tempests, Winds, Thunder, Lightning,* and ⁹ increasing the Earth: Seeing that ¹⁰ He *governeth* all, and ¹¹ *blesseth* the People. That they shall also submit to His great and mighty Name; and ² *Praise* Him with all *Honour,* and *Glory,* as well as meaner People.

(—Vide 2 Sam. viii.—)

From this *Psalm* all *Rulers* are admonished not to be proud, nor puffed up, although they are put into High Places; but, that there is a GOD more *mighty* than they. But alas! the greatest Part that are in any *Power* too often think there is *no* GOD, or at least take little or no Notice of His Divine *Precepts* or *Praises*; thinking such Things too mean for them to take Notice of. No, they

want

want even themselves to be honoured as *Gods* by all that are under them; and distress the meaner People, that they may be the more subservient to their private Ends: They would have none *thrive* but themselves, and very seldom encourage the *Industrious*, unless their own *Interest* is concerned; and then they are accounted *virtuous*.—On the contrary, those that *rule* with *Justice*, love to see the People *thrive*; they *honour* GOD, *promote* His GLORY, and suppress Indolence, and Vice; they trust in His Divine Providence, obey His *Will*, and receive all good Things from Him, with *Thanksgiving*. Their *Lives* are as *Patterns* to the People; they love their *Subjects*, and their *Subjects* love and *honour* them; they live all in *Peace* and *Unity* in this World; and have a perfect *Hope* of the *Joys* of that which is to come.

(—Vide *Psal.* cxxxiii.—)

The PRECEPT.

{ Thunder *and* Tempests *are at* GOD's *Command,*
 At which the Heathens *do affrighted stand:*
 Great Men of Might their Praises *ne'er should cease,*
 To honour GOD, *and* CHRIST, *their lasting* Peace. }

N. B. Probably this *Psalm* was composed in the Midst of the *Wars* with foreign Princes, as also were *Psal.* xciii. xcvi. xcvii.

On PSALM XXX.

1042. THIS *Psa'm* was a *Song* of DAVID when he *cleansed* and *dedicated* his *House* again to GOD, after it had been *polluted* with the filthy *Incest* of his Son *Absalom*; and when he was delivered from many dangerous Enemies: Wherein ¹ he renders *Thanks* to GOD, and ⁴ exhorts others to do the like; and to learn, by his *Example*, that ⁵ GOD is always more *merciful* to His Children, than He is *rigorous*, and severe in punishing them. He also sheweth ⁶ that the Fall from *Prosperity*, to *Adversity*, is often very sudden; and ⁸ then returneth to *Prayer*, promising ¹² to *Praise* GOD for ever.

(—Vide 2 *Sam.* vii. 2. 5 —*Deut.* xx. 5.—2 *Sam.* xx. 3.—)

This *Psalm* plainly shews to all Men the Duty of *Gratitude*, that we should always return *Thanks* for all *Mercies* we receive from the Hands of GOD; and also shew the like *Mercy* unto all others. That we should never too much trust to our own State, but, when we *stand*, take *Care*, lest we *fall*: which is very often suddenly, when we are careless, and off our *Guard*: for, when GOD leaves us to ourselves, we soon slide, and sink under the *Temptations* of the Devil. Therefore, we should never trust intirely on our *own* foolish *Security*, but commit ourselves wholly under the *Care* of GOD's *Protection*; knowing that He can both *[...]*, and *raise up*, whomsoever he pleaseth; and that we can do nothing

26   *The* Psalm-Singer's Jewel: *Or*,

thing of ourselves without His *Help:* For which Reason we should alway make a *grateful* Acknowledgment for what we receive, with the most hearty *Praises* and *Thanksgiving*; forasmuch as we know that our Labours will not be in vain in the LORD.

(—Vide *Psal.* xxiii.—*Psal.* xxx. 7, 5, 11.—*Psal.* cxlv. 8.—*Isai.* liv. 7, 8.—2 *Cor.* iv. 17.—2 *Chron.* xxxii. 24, 25.—*Jer.* xxxi. 18.—2 *Cor.* xv. 58.—)

The PRECEPT.

{ GOD *is my* Guardian, *Succour, and Relief,*
My Aid *from Foes, from Malice, Pain, and Grief:*
The LORD *my greatest* Thanks *and* Praise *shall have,*
For why?—There's no Repentance *in the Grave.* }

N. B. This was wrote on *Saul's* Persecutions after many Deliverances, when DAVID's Friends could yield him no Succour; but was forced to get Sanctuary for them in *Moab*, and go again to *Judea.* 2 Sam. xxii. 3. 6.

※※※※※※※※※※※※※※※※※※※※※※※※※

On PSALM XXXI.

DAVID, in this *Psalm*, being delivered from many great Dangers, ¹ returneth most hearty *Thanks* to GOD; shewing ³ what Trust he had in Him, even when *Death* was almost before his Eyes; and his Enemies ready to take him. He ⁵ then commits his *Spirit* to GOD, shews ¹³ how he was *despised* and *railed* on; and begs of GOD ¹⁷ to confound his Enemies; and ²³ that the *Faithful* would, by his *Example*, place both their Love, and Trust in GOD alone, who hath done so great Things for him, by preserving him out of their wicked Hands.

* (—Vide 2 *Sam.* xvii. 27. 29.—xix. 32.

This *Psalm*, (from the Time it was written,) shews to us the Uncertainty of *Court* Places; and the infallible *Success* of such as trust in GOD. For, DAVID being a little before in great *Power* and *Dignity*, and the second Man in the Kingdom to King *Saul*, was all on a sudden brought into extreme Misery by the Hatred of the *King*; whose Envy was stirred up against him by a great Number of *deceitful* Men. Notwithstanding all this, DAVID well considered the *moveable* Temper of this *World*, although he was in great *Prosperity*; and was not intirely cast down when the Storm fell upon him; for he trusted in the *Promises* of GOD, which he had learned from *Samuel*, and from his own upright *Conscience*; whereby he found *Deliverance.* From this we may learn, not to *trust* in *Man*, but in GOD; for though Man fail us, GOD will stand by us; Whose *Treasures* and *Mercies* are always laid up for his *Children* to guard them from all the Assaults of deceitful *Friends*, and open Enemies.

The

A New Exposition *of the* Book *of* Psalms, &c.

The PRECEPT.

{ LORD, *Thou'rt my* Hope, *no Trouble e'er shall move*
My Heart from Thee; *How boundless is Thy Love!*
LORD *take my* Spirit, *Thou canst it ever guard,*
And give me Heav'n, *at* last, *for my* Reward. }

N. B. This probably was wrote after DAVID's Reception at *Mahanaim*; which being compared with that *History*, will confirm the Conjecture of it. *

On PSALM XXXII.

HOLY DAVID, being, for his *Sins*, grievously afflicted with *Sickness*, here ¹ counteth them *blessed*, to whom GOD doth not impute their *Transgressions*. After he ⁵ had confessed his Sins, and obtained *Pardon* of GOD, he ⁸ exhorteth wicked Men to live a *godly* Life; and ¹¹ righteous Men to *rejoice* in the LORD with *Hope*.

* (—Vide 2 *Sam*. xiii.—*Psal.* xxxv. 13. 16. 25.—xxxviii.—)

In this *penitential Psalm* of INSTRUCTION, is contained the chief *Points* of our *Christian Faith, viz.* That to be *justified* by our *Faith*, is to have a free *Remission* of all our Sins; and the *Spirit* of *Regeneration* is always annexed with the Gift of *Righteousness*; which is received by *Faith*; and doth kindle in the Hearts, of them that are *justified,* an utter Loathing of Sin; and an earnest *Hope* and true *Obedience* to GOD. The *Conscience* being thus pacified, doth enjoy a true and *perpetual Love*, in all Storms that shall arise against us, &c. The *Prophet* also shews that it is a dismal Thing to be between *Hope* and *Despair*; for unless a Sinner is fully *reconciled* to GOD, he is in perpetual *Torment*. The Means to find *Mercy* is by *Repentance*, with *Faith*; and a good *Conscience*, in the *Holy Ghost,* is the *Fruit* of *Faith*; whereby we enjoy *Peace*, in Hopes of everlasting Life.

(—Vide *Rom*. iv. 6.—*Isai*. lv. 6.—)

The PRECEPT.

{ *How* Bless'd *is he, whose Sins are quite forgiv'n?*
All blotted out, and Pardon *sign'd in* Heav'n!
LORD, *touch my Heart to weep for ev'ry Sin,*
And, Then, by CHRIST, *I* Heav'n *shall surely win.* }

N. B. Probably this *Psalm* was wrote at the same Time as the vith; on Occasion of Delivery from Sickness; or, perhaps for the Grief of, *Amnon,* and *Absalom's* Miscarriages, and the *Reproaches* raised thereon. See the *Scriptures* before quoted. *

On

On PSALM XXXIII.

PRincely DAVID, in this *Pfalm*, ' exhorteth all the *Righteous* to *Praife* GOD, for ⁴ the Faithfulnefs of His *Word*, and the *Works* of His *Creation*; and that all Nations dread, and ſtand in Awe of Him for the Performance of His mighty *Counfels*, both for the *Juſt*, and Unjuſt. Shewing alſo, ¹² that they are *bleſſed* that truſt in GOD; His *all-ſeeing* Eye is over the whole World, ¹⁸ and His *Power* is over all: And that He will *preſerve* all ſuch as *love*, and place their *Hope* in Him, &c.

* Vide *Ver.* viii. and 1 *Sam.* viii. 10.—)

As all the *World* was made for the *Uſe* of *Man*, what can be more reaſonable than for *us* to conſecrate our whole Lives to the *Praiſe* and *Glory* of the great AUTHOR of it! and to SING forth His *Praiſes* for all His boundleſs *Mercies*; joining with the *ſolemn Sound* of *Inſtruments*, in a *ſerious* and *devout* Manner, which is acceptable to GOD, at all *Times*, and in all *Places*. Our *Author*, DAVID, alſo ſhews the wonderful Care and *Providence* of the *Almighty*, over His *People*, and *Church*; and how vain it is to truſt in any Thing but GOD, who provideth all Things for us; and hath placed us *over* all the other lower Part of his *Creation*; whoſe *Mercy* and Loving-kindneſs is ever towards us, and to all that *love* Him with a *pure* and upright *Heart*. So let us always *rejoice* in Him, and *praiſe* Him; for it becometh the Juſt to be thankful.

* (—Vide *Pſal.* xxxiii.—)

The PRECEPT.

{ GOD's *Eye is over all, that do Him fear,*
He loves *the* Juſt, *His* Counſel's *always near:*
Rejoice in GOD, *He doth all* Things *impart,*
And ſerve *Him, daily, with a* thankful *Heart.* }

N. B. Very probably this was compoſed for a triumphant Song after Victories; to ſubdue, and admoniſh the People to the Fear of GOD. See the above *Scriptures.* *

On PSALM XXXIV.

IN this *Pfalm*, holy DAVID, ' magnifies GOD for his great *Deliverance* from *Gath*; and ⁷ ſhews how GOD's Angels will defend the *Righteous*. He alſo ¹¹ exhorts others to the

Fear

Fear of GOD; [13] to speak no Evil: but [14] to do Good: for [15] His *Providence* is over all the *Righteous*, and [22] will deliver them out of all their Troubles.

(—Vide *Mark* ii. 25, 26.—1 *Pet.* iii. 10.—)

This glorious *Psalm* never ought to be out of our Hands or *Memories*, for its illustrious *Language*, grave, and *wise Sentences*. We are here taught, *first*, that, whensoever we *receive* any Favour at GOD's Hand, it is our *Duty* to return *Thanks*; and confirm our *Faith* in GOD, against all other *Temptations*. Secondly, to exhort *others* to do the like; that they may *believe* with us, and *trust* in GOD, and that such *Privileges* appertain to all such as love GOD, and his *Church*. Thirdly, That we should always *attribute* the *Deliverance* of the *Righteous*, and the *Destruction* of the Wicked to the *Power* and *Will* of GOD, and not to Man; for the Wicked only trust in Man, and are *Scoffers* of GOD, and can see on but one Side: But the *Righteous* discern on *both Sides*, i. e. the *Weakness* of one, and the invincible *Power* of the Other; so that they never forget His *Judgments* to come, as well as His *present Mercies*. So *Praise the* LORD *with me, and let us magnify His great and mighty Name together.*

(—Vide 1 *Sam.* xxi. 10. 15.—)

The PRECEPT.

{
Though many Troubles *to the* Just *befall,*
GOD, *at the last, will rid them out of all:*
O fear the LORD, *CHRIST is your* Guard *and* King,
Boast of His Mercy, *and His* Glory *sing.*
}

N. B. This *Psalm* was wrote by DAVID after he had escaped from *Achish*, by disguising himself with *Madness*; being forced thither by *Saul*. As *Psal.* lvith was his *Prayer*, this xxxivth was his *Song* of *Thanksgiving*; for himself, and his Companions.

✿✿✿✿✿✿✿✿✿✿✿✿✿✿✿✿✿✿✿✿✿✿✿✿✿✿✿✿✿✿✿✿✿✿✿

On PSALM XXXV.

HERE holy DAVID [1] prays to GOD to plead his Cause, and [3] *defend* him, and [8] to overthrow all his ungrateful and deceitful Enemies. He also shews [14] how good he had been to them, though they bore *false Witness* against him, and [15] rejoiced when he was in *Trouble*. He [24] then prays of GOD to be his *Judge*, and [26] confound his Enemies; that [27] he, and his *true Favourites*, might joyfully *magnify* His Name, for His *Mercy* and *Loving-kindness* vouchsafed to him and his People.

* (—Vide 2 *Thess.* 1. 6.

It is better to deal with an *open* Enemy, than with a fawning *Flatterer*; by Reason, we can be guarded against the Assault of the former, when there is no Defence,

Defence, only GOD, against a *flattering*, designing Knave; for, while he speaks fair to your Face, he is undermining to destroy you. We may see, by this *Psalm*, that, so long as *Saul* was an Enemy to DAVID, all that he had in Authority under him were *Flatterers*, whereby they so stirred up *Saul's* Rage against DAVID, as to destroy him, had not GOD stood his Friend. This is a worthy *Example* to be observed, and is dressed in the highest *Mode* of the World, both of the old and new Fashion; for when some Men are in Prosperity, too many will *counterfeit* Friendship: but, should a sudden Change of their State happen, they immediately, by Slanders and false Accusations, so unjustly kindle the *King's* Rage, as to cause him to be their Executioner. Therefore, when such Difficulties happen, it is best to *trust* in GOD*, Who is able to destroy all *flattering Courtiers*, or other Enemies of GOD's *Church* and *People*: For which Reason let us always maintain a *true* and *just* Cause, that GOD may stand our *Friend* in all Events; whereby we may *Praise* His Name, and sing of His Glory, as DAVID did. See the above *Scriptures* *.

The PRECEPT.

{ *Though cruel Foes on me false* Witness *bear,*
GOD *knows my Cause, He to the* Just *is near :*
His mighty Shield *will turn the Wicked's* Dart,
And safely guard *the Man of* upright *Heart.* }

On PSALM XXXVI.

WE have here, by holy DAVID, a Discovery of a wicked Man by his Words, *Deceitfulness*, and his evil Thoughts. DAVID also admireth GOD's *Mercy* above all Things; of which GOD's Children shall never want; but that all Workers of *Iniquity* shall be utterly cast down.

* (—Vide 1 Sam. xxii. 6. 23.

There is nothing more odious to Men of *Learning, Understanding,* and *Piety* than to hear the *Name* of GOD *prophaned*, His Power distained, and Men of *Merit despised*. We see by daily *Observations*, and by *Experience*, that more than one Half of the World take Delight in plaguing and vexing the other; and that (in Opposition to GOD, and good Men,) the Wicked torment the *Good*, by placing all good *Precepts* under *prophane Constructions*; being so blinded with their Sins, they make no Difference between *Good* and Bad.

And though such as live a *reprobate Life* may seem to have the upper Hand of those that delight in GOD's *Word*, and remark the *Actions* of *good* and holy Men, yet the LORD will defeat all their pretended Power in the End; and will so cast them down, as they shall not be able to stand in Competition with the Righteous: For GOD will most assuredly defend both His *Church* and *People*, and supply them with all necessary Comforts of this Life, and with the Hopes of His everlasting *Joy* and *Felicity*. Therefore, whilst we are in this wicked World, let us make it our *Rule* of Life, to shun the Company of all *Reprobates*

and

and *Scorners*, as much as possible; and give no Encouragement to such Fools as make a *Mock at Sin*. Let us, whensoever we fall into such *Company*, endeavour to *reform* their *Lives*, and not hear neither GOD nor His Divine *Ordinances* prophaned; but let our SONGS be of Him, and our *Talking* be of all His wonderous *Works*.

(—Vide *Psal.* cv. *Ver.* 2.—)

The PRECEPT.

{ *Though wicked Men muse* Mischief, *and intend*
To harm the Just, GOD *strikes them in the End:*
CHRIST *is the* Life *of all, His* Cross *shall be*
The Just *Man's* Shield, *to all Eternity.* }

N. B. This *Psalm*, to *Ver.* 5, very livelily describes *Saul's* Self-Flattery, Falseness, and Cruelty. See the above *Scriptures*. *

On PSALM XXXVII.

OUR princely *Author*, holy DAVID, in this *Psalm*, of *Instruction*, considering the Lives of *good* and *bad* Men, in this World, ¹ greatly exhorts us not to fret, or be grieved at the *Prosperity* of the Wicked, and *Afflictions* of the *Godly*, but ³ to *trust* in GOD: ¹⁰ Shewing that their Prosperity is but vain and transitory, and holds but a little While, because they are not in GOD's Favour. He shews also ¹¹ that, though the *Godly* undergo many *Hardships* and *Afflictions* in this Life, they shall ²⁷ find *Peace* at the *last*, when ³⁸ the Wicked shall be cut off, and destroyed.

* (—Vide *Psal.* xi.—xlix. lxxiii.—)

It is better to undergo the *Afflictions* of *this Life*, than the Torments of *Hell* in the *next*; by Reason, one is not to be compared to the Other: Those of *this Life* are but for a *Time*, but those of the *next*, they are *eternal*. Such as live in *Prosperity*, and enjoy all the Things of this Life, think but very seldom of true Godliness; they gnash their Teeth against the *Righteous*, and make good Men's Lives their Game and Ridicule. They despise both GOD, His *Church*, and His *People*, and would, if it were in their Power, lay all waste. They live in continual Security of their *present* Prosperity, and think it will last for ever; and, because they see others under *Poverty* and *Afflictions*, they think themselves on the right Side, and despise both the *Power* of GOD, and the *Religion* of His People. But, alas! GOD can, at any Time, bring down His *Judgments* on them in a Moment, and divest them of all their *Pride* and *Grandeur*, whilst the *honest* and *sincere* Man, (that has undergone their *Insults* and *Scorns*,) rests on His Divine *Providence*, whereby he stands unshaken; and at last lies down in *Peace* in his *Grave*, in *Hopes* of a joyful *Resurrection*. So let us commit ourselves unto GOD, and

The Psalm-Singer's Jewel: *Or*,

and not depend on Man, since He has promised us *Peace*, and will assuredly *save* all such as *love*, *fear*, and place their Trust in Him.

(—Vide *Job* xxi. 7.—*Mat.* v. 5.—)

The PRECEPT.

{ *Fret not to see the Wicked's prosp'rous* State,
For, well-got Wealth *will 'dure the 'longest* Date:
Transgressors from GOD's *Presence sure shall flee*,
But, godly Men *shall* rest *eternally*. }

N. B. From *Ver.* 25. it appears that holy DAVID wrote this excellent *Psalm* in his *Old-Age*, (as were *Psalm* xlix. and lxxiii:) he then taking a Survey of his Life, the Dealings of GOD with good and bad Men, and how Men dealt one with another, &c. &c. *

❊❊❊❊❊❊❊❊❊❊❊❊❊❊❊ ❊❊❊❊❊❊❊❊❊❊❊❊❊

On PSALM XXXVIII.

IN this *Psalm*, holy DAVID lying very *sick* of a grievous *Disease*, ¹ prayeth to GOD to turn away His Wrath from him, ⁴ although he most justly deserved it, for his Sins. He then ⁵ shews the Agonies of his *Grief*, as *wounded* with the *Arrows* of GOD's *Wrath*; being ¹¹ forsaken by his *Friends*, and ¹² cruelly treated by his Enemies: And, with a firm Confidence in GOD, ²² commendeth his Cause to Him, with Hopes of Recovery.

* Vide *Psal.* xl. xli.

It is a dreadful Thing to lie on a *Bed* of *Sickness* destitute of *Friends*, void of *Repentance*, and in *Despair* of GOD's *Mercy*. Though this is often the Case of the Wicked, by not living in the *Grace* of GOD, yet it was not the *Case* of DAVID, for he well knew that GOD had justly punished him for his Sins, and had also gave him *Patience*, a Heart of *Repentance*, and *Faith*; which appertained to his eternal *Salvation*. This worthy *Example* teacheth us, that all *Afflictions* are the worthy *Judgments* of GOD, laid on us for our Sins; and that *Prayer*, with *Faith* and *Patience*, is the only Means to find Comfort at His Hand. This warneth us also never to *despair* of GOD's *Mercy*, be our Torments ever so great, either in *Mind*, *Body*, or *Estate*, or our Enemies ever so inveterate against us: For GOD will never fail the *Righteous*, if they sincerely seek to Him for *Mercy*; for He loveth all whom he chastiseth in this World, and will at last receive all such as *love* and *trust* in Him, into His eternal *Glory*.

The PRECEPT.

{ GOD *knows the* Sore, *and* Ease *of ev'ry Part*,
Each faithful Friend, *and each* deceitful *Heart*:
He ne'er forsakes the Penitent *and* Just,
As love His Law, *and in His* Mercy *trust*. }

N. B. This

A New Exposition *on the* Book *of* Psalms, &c.

N. B. This *Psalm* seems to have been wrote at the same Time as the vith, the xiiith, the xivth, the xxxvth, and the xxxixth; when he was sorely oppressed, sometimes with Enemies, and at other Times with Sickness. See the *Scriptures* above quoted. *

On PSALM XXXIX.

*J*Eduthun being one of holy DAVID's chief *Singers*, he directs this mournful *Psalm* to him. And DAVID, being full of *Agonies*, sheweth ¹ that he was resolved to keep *silent*, lest he should offend G O D, in not bearing the *Afflictions*, He had laid upon him, *patiently*. But, being at last *wearied*, and tired of *this Life*, he vehemently breaks forth, and ⁴ desires that G O D would make an *End* of him; ⁸ pardon all his Transgressions, ¹⁰ *relieve*, ¹² *hear*, and *spare* him; *i. e.* that He would give him a true *Sense* of G O D, and not destroy his Soul; or, that he might not *despair* of His *Mercy*, but trust in Him, before he left this World, to be, here, no more seen.

* (—Vide *Rom.* xii. 19.—1 *Pet.* iii. 13.—)

This *penitential Psalm* is a glorious *Lesson* in the very *Agonies* of *Death*, for it contains a Mixture of *Prayers* suitable to every Case, in that *last State*. We are, *first*, taught not to trust to a *Death-Bed Repentance*, lest our *Pains* should deprive us of our *Senses*, and render us incapable of calling upon G O D: Also to bear our *Afflictions* patiently, and not think as G O D has unjustly punished us for our Sins; but that all Men must endure some *Hardship* or other in going out of this World. *Secondly*, as it is not then in the Power of Man either to augment, or lessen our bodily *Pains*, but by the *Power* and *Will* of G O D, we should fully rely on Him for *Help*, and earnestly pray to Him to deliver us out of our Pain and Misery, which Way he seemeth good. And, *lastly*, that in the Midst of our *Agonies*, we may not forget G O D, nor *despair* of His *Mercy*; but take all Things coolly that He lays upon us; beseeching Him to keep us in our perfect *Senses*, that our *Agonies* cause us not to offend; and that He would give us a Heart of true *Repentance*, to *forgive* all that have offended us; and so recover our *Strength* of *Faith*, that we may lie down in *Peace*; trusting in Him for a glorious *Resurrection*. Amen. Amen.

The PRECEPT.

{ *Think*, O *my Soul*, *how swift thy* Minutes *beat*,
Whilst circling Blood runs in its youthful Heat:
For, Measures *of a well-spent Life must rate*
All future Hopes *of an eternal* State. }

N. B. This *Psalm* has some *Connection* with *Psalm* the xxxvith, and xxxviith, only more deep and final. *

On PSALM XL.

AS the foregoing *Pfalm* fetteth forth holy DAVID's *Behaviour* under grievous *Afflictions*, this *Pfalm* ¹ fhews how he *magnified* GOD for His gracious *Deliverance*; and ³ commendeth the fame Divine *Providence* to all Mankind, by his own *Example.* He then ⁵ declaring the manifold *Mercies* of GOD, promifes ⁹ to give himfelf wholly to His *Service*; hoping ¹¹ for *future Deliverances*, and ¹⁴ *Confufion* to his *Enemies*, that GOD's Name might be more glorious.

* (—Vide Heb. x. 23, 24. 26, 27. 35, 36.—)

In this *grateful Leffon* are *three* Things appertaining to our *Salvation*, 1. GOD's infinite *Mercy* to us, whereby He fhews his *Pity* on us. 2. His *Righteoufnefs*, which fhews His continual Protection, and *Providence* over us. And 3. His *Truth*, whereby appeareth His conftant *Love* and *Favour* towards us. From hence we may *infer*, that though the Wicked generally *mock* GOD's Children, in their *Afflictions* yet the *Faithful* always *Praife* GOD for all *Mercies* and *Benefits* they receive; and that GOD will give them *Patience*, and a good *Heart*, to bear up manfully under all the *Afflictions* of this World, if they feek to Him with *Prayer*, and put their whole *Confidence* in His *Mercy.* DAVID, at the 6th, 7th, and 8th *Verfes* of this *Pfalm*, fets forth Himfelf in the Figure of *CHRIST*, which was to come; Who fhould be obedient even to the *Death* of the *Crofs*, to take away all the *Sins* of the World: For DAVID himfelf acknowledges his *Sins* to be more than he could number, though *CHRIST* finned not. Let us therefore not fin ever the more becaufe GOD is *merciful*, and gave his SON for us; but let us more endeavour to lead *godly Lives*, as becomes our *Profeffion* in *CHRIST JESUS*; that our *Prayers* may be heard of GOD at all Times, and at the *Hour* of *Death*; and that, at the Day of *Judgment*, *CHRIST* may take us into His bleffed Kingdom. Amen, Amen, LORD *JESUS*, come quickly.

The PRECEPT.

{ LORD, *place my* Hope *in* Thee *and Thy great* Pow'r,
Thou art my Rock, *my only* Fort *and* Tow'r :
CHRIST *is my* Song, *(moft* New) *I'll Him confefs,*
And daily triumph in His Holinefs. }

N. B. This *Pfalm* has fome Connection with the xxxviiith and xxxixth.

On PSALM XLI.

HOLY DAVID, being grievoufly *afflicted*, in this *Pfalm*, fheweth, ¹ that merciful Men are *bleffed* of the LORD in their *Sorrows*, for having *Pity* on him. He alfo complains

A New Exposition *on the* Book *of* Psalms, &c.

of the *Treason* and treacherous *Dealings* [4] of his Enemies, and of his own *Friends* [9] in the Manner of *Judas*, which was to come. He then [11] feeling the *Mercies* of GOD gently coming to him, that his Enemies might not triumph over him, [12] acknowledges and implores His gracious *Mercy*, and [13] *blesseth* Him for dealing so favourably with him.

(—Vide *John* xiii. 18.—)

We have here a just *Pattern* of false Friendship painted to the Life, in Imitation of the Book of *Job*: For when *good Men* are *afflicted*, the Wicked generally endeavour all they can to perfuade them that they have utterly lost the *Favour* of GOD. But, my Author, holy DAVID, by many Experiences, soon found out the Fallacy; and wicked *Achitophel* had drawn his Son *Absalom* from him, as well as many others; * who came to wicked and miserable Ends; yet GOD had so armed him with *Faith*, that he well knew his *Punishments* were inflicted on him for his *Sins*; and that though his Body suffered in this World, he well knew that he was not forsaken of GOD as they were; but that GOD would in Mercy save his Soul. Herein he also figures out *CHRIST*, shewing how he should be *betrayed*, even as he was, by treacherous *Dealings*: For as DAVID was betrayed and chaced away from his Kingdom by his Son, and recovered to it again; even so *CHRIST* should be betrayed by his *Disciple*, and nailed to the *Cross* by the Malice of the People. Hence let us all have *Pity* one for another, in our *Afflictions*, that GOD may have *Pity* on us; by Reason, our *Saviour* assures us, that *Blessed are the Merciful, for they shall obtain Mercy.*

* (—Vide *Mat.* v. 3, 4, 5, 6, 7, 8, 9, 10, 11, 12.—2 *Sam.* xv. 12.—)

The PRECEPT.

{ *He that relieves the* Poor *Man in Distress,*
And feeds the Orphan, *sure does nothing less*
Than lend to CHRIST; for surely he lays down
A simple Counter *for a heav'nly* CROWN. }

End *of the* FIRST BOOK.

※*※*※*※*※*※*※*※*※*※*※*※*※*※*※

On PSALM XLII.

1023. IN this *Maschil*, or *Psalm* of *Instruction*, holy DAVID, being drove away by his cruel *Persecutors*, [1] greatly *mourneth*, and longeth to be again in the *Congregation* of GOD's People; protesting that though his Body was separated from them, yet [2] his Soul and Heart was always there; of which his *Hope* never failed him in the Midst of all his Grief; because [9] he placed his whole *Confidence* in GOD. Then [11] raising up his disconsolate Soul, he returns Thanks to GOD for His present Help.

(—Vide *Psal.* lxxi.—lxxxiv.

In this *Pfalm* Hopes and *Fears, Joys* and *Sorrows* are ſtruggling; and it is an *Example* of true *Faith*, which holy DAVID left to the Sons of *Korah*, as a *Treaſure* to be kept by them for *Inſtruction*; they being *Singers*, and of the Number of the Levites: Wherein is ſhewed, that although he was in *Exile*, and ſpoiled of all his *Goods* and *Honour*, and that his Enemies alſo ſought for his *Life*, yet his *Deſire* was ſtill for the *Houſe* of GOD, amongſt the *Company* of *Singers*; counting all other Loſſes but as nothing in Compariſon to the Loſs of his *godly Companions*. And though he could not be with them, to *join* in *holy Worſhip*, yet GOD was always with him wherever he went; and becauſe he truſted in Him, He always afforded him Comfort; which *teacheth* us, that if GOD be for us, who can be againſt us. Hence let us always have a fervent *Deſire* to the *Church* of *CHRIST*, of which we are called *Members*; and take Delight in hearing GOD's *Word*, partaking of His holy *Sacraments*, and joining in His *Praiſes*. Let us ſtrongly oppoſe all the Enemies of our *Church* and People, that, by our *Faith*, we may overcome all the Powers of Darkneſs; that we may always *joyfully* appear in the *Congregation* of the *Faithful*; both in this World, and in that which is to come.

† The Word *Maſchil* ſignifies *Pſalms of Inſtruction*.

The PRECEPT.

Since GOD's *my* Aid, *why ſhould I be caſt down,*
Or torn with Grief? Hope *is my only* Crown:
LORD, *chear my Soul, I'll of Thy* Glory *ſing,*
For Thee I thirſt, O CHRIST! *my heav'nly* King.

N. B. This *Pſalm* was uttered after the *publick* ſolemn *Worſhip* mentioned in 2 *Kings* xxii. 2.—And alſo when DAVID was driven from it by *Saul*'s Inſurrection. (—Vide 2 *Sam.* xvii. 22.—*Joſh.* xiii. 5. 8.—*Pſal.* lxxi. and lxxxiv. were compoſed about the ſame Time.

On PSALM XLIII.

1023. THIS *Pſalm* has ſome Connection with the *former*, and on the ſame *Occaſion*; wherein holy DAVID prayeth to be delivered from all them that wrongfully had conſpired againſt him; that ⁴ he might *joyfully Praiſe* GOD in the *Congregation* as he uſed to do, before he was driven away; and alſo for his Deliverance.

Part of this *Pſalm* is only a *Repetition* of the *former*, which ſee, and the *Note* thereon.

The PRECEPT.

Since GOD *is* Judge, *why ſhould I dread, or fear*
Deceitful Foes, ſince JESUS *is ſo near?*
In Him I'll truſt, and His Deliv'rance *ſing;*
Whoſe Cup, *by Faith, will ſure* SALVATION *bring.*

N. B. Thi

N. B. This *Pfalm* was probably compofed on DAVID's returning over the River *Jordan*; and on Occafion of the renewed Interruption of Peace, by the *Revolt* of the ten *Tribes* after *Sheba*.

(—Vide 2 *Sam.* xix. 40.—2 *Sam.* i. 2.—)

On PSALM XLIV.

THIS *Mafchil*, or *Pfalm* of *Inftruction*, to the Sons of [1] *Korah*, remindeth to the *Faithful* the fundry *Mercies* of GOD towards His People; and [3] encourageth them to have their prefent *Hopes* and Confidence in Him. The *Faithful* then [4] alledging the *Covenant* made with *Abraham*, then what *Griefs* they underwent in keeping it; although [17] they were *true* and *faithful*: And [23] pray to GOD to ftir up to their *Redemption*.

(—Vide *Deut.* iv. 37.—*Rom.* viii. 26.—*Mat.* v. 10.—1 *Pet.* iv. 14.—)

This *Pfalm* of *Rememberance*, and *Prayer*, feems to be written by fome excellent *Prophet*, (perhaps DAVID) for the *Ufe* of the *People*, when the *Church* was in extreme Mifery; either at their Return from *Babylon*, or under *Antiochus*, or fuch-like Afflictions; from which we may *learn*, that GOD's free *Mercy* and *Love* is the only *Fountain* and Beginning of the *Church*; and that GOD delivered all His People for their *Faith* and *Good Works*.—And though we fuffer here wrongfully, and for *Righteoufnefs* Sake, it is a fure *Teftimony* of our Conformity with *CHRIST*, for which He bids us *Rejoice*, with the Affurance of being *Bleffed*: For *Salvation* is a fufficient *Ranfom* for all the *Tauntings*, *Miferies*, and *Slaveries* we undergo in this World. Therefore, let us always remember the *Words* of our bleffed *Saviour*, whenever we undergo any *Afflictions*, either for our *Sins*, or our *Religion* Sake, Who hath *promifed* us, that *Bleffed are ye when Men fhall revile you, and perfecute you, and fay all Manner of Evil againft you falfly for my Sake. 'Rejoice, and be exceeding glad, for great is your Reward in Heaven; for fo perfecuted they the Prophets which were before you.*

(—Vide *Mat.* v. 11, 12.—*Rom.* viii. 35.—)

The PRECEPT.

{ *Our Fathers old unto us do record* }
{ *The mighty Works, and Wonders of the* LORD: }
{ LORD, *let thy Precepts be our Rule and Guide,* }
{ *That we from Thee, and* CHRIST, *may never flide.* }

N. B. This *Pfalm* feems to be written at the fame Time as *Pfalm* the lxth and cviiith; when DAVID had that difficult *War* with the *Ammonites* and *Syrians*; who had probably over-run the *Tribes* beyond *Jordan*: And alfo with *Edom*, their Confederates, affaulting them at the fame Time; who, after the others, were fubdued by *Joab*, when he flew twelve thoufand of the *Edomites* in the *Salt Valley*. It is not probable that DAVID was always *fecure secure*, and exalted above Measure, by Reason, in the Midst of those *Conflicts*, GOD sometimes suffered his *Armies* to be *defeated*; which occasioned such Complaints in those *Psalms*; or as *Preventives* of his falling scandalously; which Difficulties being overcome, he straight lapsed into, *&c. &c.*

(—Vide 2 *Sam.* x. 1.—1 *Chron.* xix. 1.—2 *Sam.* viii. 13.—1 *Chron.* xviii. 12, 13.—2 *Sam.* xi. 1, 2.—)

On PSALM XLV.

THIS *Maschil*, or *Psalm* of *Instruction*, to the Sons of *Korah*, is wrote in the same *Style* as the *Book* of *Canticles*, being an *Epithalamium* or *Song* of *Loves*; and inscribed to him that excelleth, or could perform best on a six-stringed Instrument called *Shoshannim*, or a *Tune* so called; to which it was to be sung. Herein is described ¹ the *Majesty*, and personal *Accomplishments* of King *Solomon*; his ³ *Victories*; ⁶ *Governments*, ⁸ *Ornaments*, ¹⁰ *Attendants*, and ¹¹ *Marriage* with an *Egyptian* Heathen *Woman*; and ¹⁵ how she should be *blessed*, could she but renounce her *People*, the *Love* of her *Country*; and give herself wholly to her *Husband*, &c. All this is written by the *Author* under the *Similitude* of a *Bride* and *Bridegroom*; which shews what mutual *Love* ought to be between *Man* and *Wife*: But the real Meaning thereof, is CHRIST and His *Church*, and the Increase of CHRIST's Kingdom: CHRIST being here as the *Bridegroom*, and his *Bride* the *Church*, or the *faithful People* thereof: Shewing ¹⁵ how she is in her *Duty* to Him, with her *Attendants*, and ¹⁷ the joyful Gladness of her *Marriage*, &c.

(—See the BOOK of *Canticles* —)

This teacheth us how *pure* and *undefiled* CHRIST is; Who hath the *Government* of all upon his Shoulders: And with what *Love* and Respect we ought to submit to His GOSPEL and Divine *Ordinances*, since he is our King and Saviour. It also shews how joyful we ought to be when we approach His *Marriage-Feast*, and join our Hearts and *Souls* to His precious *Body*, by His holy *Communion*; having on our Wedding Garments, new, and without Spot, and a pure Heart within us; whereby we may so obtain His Favour, as to be admitted into His glorious Kingdom.

(—Vide *Heb.* i. 8.—2 *Cor.* i. 30.—*Mat.* xi. 22.—)

The PRECEPT.

{ *As* Solomon *the* Church *his* Bride *did call,*
And CHRIST *laid down His Life to save us all:*
So let me, JESUS, *love Thy Blessed* Name,
As to enjoy Salvation *by the same.* }

A New Exposition *on the* Book *of* Psalms, *&c.* 39

N. B. As there are many Hints in this *Psalm* that allude to the *Splendor* and *Plenty* of *Solomon*'s first Days, it is very probable that he was the *Author*; and that after he was reclaimed. But, as it is written *allegorically*, and speaks of *spiritual Things*, (otherwise means so) it must now be referred or compared to C H R I S T and His *Church*, and not to *Solomon*'s Person, nor His *Spouse, &c.*

On P S A L M XLVI.

HERE we have a *triumphant Song* committed to the Sons of *Korah*, and inscribed to him that excelled all in playing on the *Alamoth*, or *Virginals*, or a *solemn Tune* so called: wherein holy DAVID ¹ sets forth the *Church*'s Confidence in G O D, and *Thanksgiving* for the Deliverance of *Jerusalem*, after *Senacherib* and his Army were driven away; or some other sudden and marvellous Deliverance by the mighty Hand of G O D. He also ² exhorteth all the *Faithful* to behold the *Works* of G O D, and acknowledge His mighty *Power*; and to trust wholly to His gracious *Aid* and *Protection*.

* (—Vide 2 *Sam.* viii.—*Isai.* xxxvii.—2 *Kings* xv. 56.—*Prov.* xxviii. 1.—)

This *Psalm* is to comfort us, when Miseries seem to threaten us; and shews the mighty *Power* of G O D, in stopping the Rage of the Wicked, and defending the *Godly*; who give themselves wholly into His Hands; whereby His Name is *glorified*. And though the Affliction of the *Righteous* rage ever so much, yet the *Rivers* of GOD's *Mercies* are sufficient to give them *Comfort* in the greatest Dangers, if they put their *Trust* in Him. Therefore, the Wicked *war* in vain, when they fight against G O D and His *Church:* for G O D's *People* are undaunted in the greatest of Dangers, when the Wicked are driven down, and are shaken with every Wind. *The Wicked flee when no Man pursues them*, having a wicked Mind, and a guilty Conscience; *but the Righteous are as bold as a Lion*, because they place all their Trust and Confidence in G O D.

(—Vide *Prov.* xxix. 25.—1 *Chron.* ii. 6.—)

The P R E C E P T.

{ *Though* Surges *swell, and mighty* Tempests *fall,*
And dire Convulsions *shake Earth's reeling Ball:*
Why should we fear, if we are true *and* just,
And do in J E S U S *wholly put our Trust?* }

N. B. This *Psalm*, and the xlviith, were probably written on some eminent *Deliverance*, from a Combination of *foreign* and *intestine* Enemies; as in *Isaiah*, and *Kings*, above quoted. *

On PSALM XLVII.

THIS *Pfalm* holy DAVID committed to the Sons of *Korah*, ¹ exhorting all the People to the *Worſhip* of GOD, Who is everlaſting; and ⁴ greatly commends His infinite *Mercy* towards the *Poſterity* of *Jacob*. He then ⁶ exhorteth all People (⁷ with a double Command,) to *ſing Praiſes* unto GOD with *Underſtanding*, ſhewing ⁸ that He is both GOD, and *King*, over all the Earth: and hath ⁹ joined the mighty *Princes* of the World unto the Fellowſhip of His *Church*.

(—Vide 1 *Cor*. vi. 14.—*Pſal*. ciii. 17.—)

In this *Song* of *Praiſe* we are taught *four* principal Things, 1. With what fervent *Zeal* we are bound to ſeek the *Glory* of GOD; for that, in *ſinging* His *Praiſes*, we ſhould moſt endeavour to underſtand the *Matter* and *Words* we do ſing, leſt His Name ſhould be *prophaned*. 2. How careful *Princes* ought to be in eſtabliſhing the publick and holy *Miniſtry* of GOD, and to have it done in ſuch *decent Order* as to *amplify* it. 3. What great Difference there is between the *choſen People* of GOD, and many other Heathen Nations, proceeding from the infinite *Mercy* of GOD. And 4. That, in the End, all other Nations ſhall be Partakers of GOD's boundleſs *Mercy*, if they ſeek it with a *pure* Heart, &c. In this Pſalm is alſo figured *CHRIST*, that was then to come; that all ſhould be *obedient* to Him; and that He would ſhew Himſelf terrible to the Wicked. It alſo figures the glorious *Triumph* of His *Aſcending* into *Heaven*; and the *Enlargement* of the *Kingdom* even from *Euphrates* to *Egypt*, &c. as was promiſed. But, ſince *CHRIST* is now come, and died for our *Salvation*, let us have a true Regard for His holy *Goſpel*, and not prophane His divine *Ordinances*; but follow the *Pattern* that He, and His holy *Apoſtles*, have left for us, whereby we may be *Partakers* of His glorious Kingdom, which is to come.

(—Vide *Luke* xii. 32.—)

The PRECEPT.

{ Since GOD *is* King, *and* Ruler *of the Earth,*
All Praiſes *ſing, with* Judgment, *Joy and Mirth:*
For why? All Nations to His Power muſt yield,
He All ſupports, *as with a mighty* Shield. }

N. B. That the viiith, xviiith, and lxviiith *Pſalms*, are *Songs* of Victory, occaſional as this.

On PSALM XLVIII.

WE have here another *triumphant Song*, committed to the Sons of *Korah*, on the great Deliverance of *Jeruſalem* from the Hands of many Kings; for which ¹ mighty *Thanks* are

A New Exposition *on the* Book *of* Psalms, *&c.* 41

are given unto GOD; ² the *State* of the *City* praised; and GOD is to be *praised* for defending His *People*, ¹⁰ both for this Generation, ¹⁴ and for ever.

(—Vide *Psal.* lxxxix. *Ver.* 1, 2.—)

That GOD may be *praised* in His *Church*, He generally sheweth His Wonders, at certain Times, all over the World; because, as *Salvation* cometh from Him to all, He *willeth* that all should *believe*, and trust in Him. Herein we see, that when the Enemies of GOD behold the *City* wherein GOD was known, and the *Cilician* or Sea called *Mediteranean*, they were sore afraid, and returned back; but the People of *Jerusalem*, and of the Cities of *Judea*, where GOD was known, had great Reason to *rejoice*, that GOD was on their Side, and against their Enemies; whereby His *Blessing* appeared unto His People, by so marvellously *defending* them. The City of *Jerusalem* is here a Figure of *CHRIST's Church*, by the beautiful Situation, Strength of the Walls and Forts; which stands in *Safety*, only by the *Power* of GOD: From which we may understand, that whensoever his *Church*, or *People*, are oppressed by their Enemies, He is both able and willing to help us, whensoever He pleaseth, when Men and Arms fail us.

(—Vide *Psal.* xxxiii.—xlvi.—)

The PRECEPT.

⎧ *When spiteful Foes, with Malice, would oppress* ⎫
⎪ *The* Church *of CHRIST*; GOD *shields it in Distress*: ⎪
⎨ *He by His People is a* Refuge *known,* ⎬
⎩ *To Him they flee, and His great* Mercy *own.* ⎭

N. B. Although this *Psalm* seems to have some Connection with the xlvith, yet it seems to have been written a long Time after, either by *Isaiah*, or by *Hezekiah*, in the Days of *Ahaz* and *Jehoshaphat*; on GOD's destroying the *Assyrians*, that besieged *Jerusalem*. *Psalm* lxxvi. was probably composed at the same Time, they being Songs of Triumph.

(—Vide 2 *Kings* xviii. 19. 35, 36.—*Isai.* xxxvi. 37.—)

On PSALM XLIX.

HOLY David, being moved by the Holy Spirit, in this *Psalm*, ¹ exhorteth all Sorts of People in the World to give *Attention* to the Doctrine thereof; in a *grave* and *serious* Manner, by Way of *Preface*. He then wisely considers ⁵ the uncertain *State of such* Men as very *unhappy*; because ¹⁰ too many of them die without *Redemption*; trusting ¹¹ only to their own *Goods*, and not to the *Providence* of GOD. He also ¹⁵ exhorts all *just Men* not to envy such miserable worldly Men's

present

The Psalm-Singer's Jewel: *Or,*
present Prosperity, nor to be afraid of them, by Reason their
Reward is everlasting *Torment*; and that G O D will assuredly
preserve the *Righteous* at the Day of *Resurrection*.

(—Vide 2 *Thess.* i. 6, &c.—*Psal.* xxxvii.—*Job* xxvii. 19.—1 *Tim* vi. 7.—)

  Herein is the very *Portrait*, or Picture, of the Life, Death, and miserable *End* of *Worldly-wise Men*, or such *Misers* as set more Value on the Goods of this Life, than they do on the Kingdom of Heaven. These mercilefs Creatures are more like *Beasts* than Men, for what they gained by griping the *Poor*, and other knavish Dealings, they have not a Heart to make Use of; betraying their own *Trust*, in all Things they are concerned, to the Damnation of their own Souls. They abuse all that G O D sends them, as much as they do the *Grace* of G O D; starve themselves in the Midst of Plenty, and dare not use what G O D has bestowed on them. They are unjust Stewards to all, they heap up to themselves the Mammon of Darkness, to their own Damnation at the *Day* of *Judgment*; and follow their Fathers that lived so before them: (because they hated G O D, they have no Share in the *Kingdom* of Heaven.—On the contrary, they that have received the *Gifts* of G O D, and *trust* in Him, need never be afraid of such wicked abandoned Wretches; for though they have Power to hurt their Bodies, their *Souls* are out of their Reach; and *C H R I S T* will heal all their Grievances at the Day of Resurrection.

(—Vide *Psal.* xv. xxiv.—)

The PRECEPT.

{ *Fix not thy Mind too much on* worldly *Pleasure,*
 Nor grind the Poor *for to increase thy Treasure:*
 But, rather set thy Heart on Things *above,*
 Where C H R I S T resides, in holy Joy *and* Love. }

N. B. That *Psalms* the xxxviith and lxxiiid have some Connection with this.

※※※※※※※※※※※※※※※※※※※※※※※※

On PSALM L.

Cir. 1034. **T**HIS is a *Psalm* of *Asaph*, of *Advice* and *Instruction*, and was committed to the Sons of *Korah*, wherein is prophesied, ¹ that G O D will call all *Nations* by the *Gospel*, and ⁷ not require any other *Sacrifices* but ¹⁵ of the Heart. He also shews that GOD hateth all *Hypocrites*, *Slanderers*, and *wicked Worshippers*; and ²² exhorteth them to reform their Lives, from *outward* deceitful *Ceremonies*: And that ²³ the true *Worship* of G O D must be *spiritual*, and not hypocritical.

(—Vide *Job* viii. 13.—*Jam.* iii. 17.—)

  Invocation, and *Thanksgiving*, are the two principal *Points* of *Divine Worship*; i. e. to *call* earnestly on G O D by *Prayer*, with a pure Heart, for all Things we stand in Need of; and then return hearty *Thanks* for what we receive. And by
                 adding

A New Exposition *of the* Book *of* Psalms, *&c.* 43

adding to these *Faith*, and true *Repentance*, will, by the *Mercies* of GOD, and the *Merits* of His Son *JESUS CHRIST*, work out our *Salvation*. When GOD gave His *Law* in *Mount Sinai*, He appeared very terrible, with *Thunder*, and *Tempests*, as a Testimony that He will appear terrible at the *Day* of *Judgment*; to take an Account of the keeping of it. How will the Wicked then tremble that have *reviled* His *Name*, *despised* His *Son*, *oppressed* His *Church*, and *slain* His *People!* How will the *Hypocrite* and *Dissembler* then appear before GOD, when their Masks of Falshood shall be stripped off, and own the *Justice* of their Punishment!—How *glorious* then will the *Righteous* appear, who have *knit* themselves to *CHRIST*, obeyed His *Gospel*, and kept the *Faith!* This will be then called *true Wisdom*, and the worldly wise Man's, and the *Flatterer*'s Foolishness. Then will the *Conclusion* of this *Psalm* be fulfilled, viz. *Whoso offereth to me Praise and Thanksgiving, honoureth me; and to him that ordereth his Conversation aright, I will shew the Salvation of* GOD.—Which that we may all do, GOD grant, through the Merits of *JESUS CHRIST*. Amen.

(—Vide *Job* xxxvi. 13.—*Mat.* v. 3. 4. 8.—)

The PRECEPT.

$\left\{\begin{array}{l}\text{LORD, }\textit{in my}\text{ Sins, }\textit{take not my Life away,}\\\textit{But, me prepare for thy}\text{ Tribunal-Day:}\\\textit{Due}\text{ Thanks }\textit{and}\text{ Praise }\textit{to}\text{ GOD }\textit{will surely gain}\\\textit{His heav'nly Favour, ever to remain.}\end{array}\right\}$

On PSALM LI.

OUR princely, and most *penitent Author*, holy DAVID, being rebuked, by the Prophet *Nathan*, for his great Offence concerning *Bathsheba* and *Uriah*, [1] acknowledges his Sins to GOD, and [4] makes a very deep and mournful *Confession*. He then [7] begs for *Pardon*, and [9] *Remission*, and for a *new Heart*; and [12] to be restored again into GOD's *Favour*, that [13] his *Example* might be a Means to *convert* all others to forsake Sin, and *repent* as he did. He then, promising to be mindful of GOD's *Graces* for the future, and [14] to give Him Glory with a most contrite Heart; sheweth [16] that GOD delighteth not in outward *Sacrifices* for Sin, but in *Sincerity* of *Heart*. And, lest GOD should punish the whole *Church* for his Sake, he [18] prayeth for them; desiring He would rather increase His *Grace*, and Favour to them.

(—Vide 2 *Sam.* ii. 17.—2 *Sam.* xii 1. 15. 16.—)

This is one of the most principal *penitential Psalms* of holy DAVID, relating to *Repentance*, which never ought to be out of our Memories; by Reason we
can,

can, too many of us, sin as he did, but none *repent* with him. My penitent *Author* here differs, in *Duty*, quite from the Great Men of our Age, who glory in their Sins, and think, that, as mean Men dare not mention them, it is out of GOD's Power to *revenge* them. No, he well knew, that though he was a KING of great *Power*, he had the same GOD, as poor Men; and as willingly submitted to Him, with a sorrowful and contrite Heart, whereby he might receive both *Mercy* and *Forgiveness*. And finding the *Holy Spirit* colder in him, than it was wont to be at other Times, he desired GOD would *renew* it, by *Faith* and *Repentance*, whereby he might have Forgiveness of his Sins, and become a new Man. Let us all endeavour to follow this good *Example* of *Repentance*, and prostrate ourselves to the Throne of *Grace*, for all our past Sins; and resolve, with DAVID, to lead a *new* Life; whereby we may have Forgiveness; and obtain *Admission* into CHRIST's glorious *Kingdom*, where all our *Tears* will be wiped away.—*Rev.* vii. 17.

(—Vide *Psal.* vi.—which seems to have some Connection.)

The PRECEPT.

Touch me, O LORD, *that I in* Tears *relent*
As DAVID *did, and of my Sins* repent :
Guide Thou my Heart, *according to Thy* Will,
And let Thy Spirit *my Soul with Comfort fill*.

On PSALM LII.

HOLY DAVID, in this *Maschil*, or *Psalm* of *Instruction;* describeth ¹ the arrogant *Tyranny* of his Adversary *Doeg*, *Saul's* chief Shepherd; whose Flattery so raised the Fury of his wicked *Master*, that he caused *Abimelech*, and eighty-five innocent *Priests* to be slain. He then ⁵ foretels his Destruction; and encourages the *Faithful* to trust in GOD; who ⁶ should *rejoice* at his Downfall, and terrible End. He likewise ⁷ exhorteth all to take Notice of his *foolish Confidence*; and what his *Riches*, *Pride*, *Flattery*, and *Malice*, had brought him to: And as GOD would ⁸ *preserve* the *Faithful* for ever, he trusteth wholly in Him, and ⁹ *sings Praises* to His Name.

(—Vide *Psal.* xlix.—58.—)

This *Psalm* sets forth the very Nature of *Antichristians*, who would overturn all the *Laws* of *Christianity*, seduce the People to all Manner of Wickedness, and place themselves to be adored as Gods, if it were in their Power. It also shews how careful *Princes*, and others, ought to be in giving Credit to flattering, deceitful Villains; that they do not wrongfully destroy the People of GOD; especially the *Pastors* of the Church; by hearkening to their malicious Stories, &c. Let these wicked Wretches *Lives*, and terrible *Ends*, be a Warning to all that are

in

A New Expofition *on the* Book *of* Pfalms, *&c.* 45

in Power; not to truft in their *Riches*, but in GOD; left the like heavy *Judgments* fall on them: For fuch abandoned Wretches have been the Caufe of fo many *Maffacres* amongft the Chriftians. *From Popery and Slavery, Bloodfhed and Knavery, Libera nos Domine.*

The PRECEPT.

{ *They that refufe the* LORD *for their Defence,*
And, in vain Riches, *place their Confidence:*
How vain's their Truft, *whofe* Riches *fade away,*
Whilft juft Men's *Hope in* CHRIST *will ne'er decay?* }

N. B. This Pfalm was written on *Doeg*'s going to *Saul*, to tell him that DAVID was come to the Houfe of *Abimelech*, and probably *Pfal.* lviii.

(—Vide 1 *Sam.* xxi. 1. 10.—xxii.—1 *Kings* xxi,—)

On PSALM LIII.

THIS *Mafchil*, or *Pfalm of Inftruction*, holy DAVID infcribed to him that excelleth on the *Mahalath*, a Wind *Inftrument*, the fame as *Nebiloth*; or a *Tune* fo called; wherein he sheweth (from his Thoughts on *Atheifm*) the crooked *Nature*, *Cruelty*, and *Punifhment* of wicked Men; although they dreaded nothing, nor was the *Fear* of GOD before their Eyes. He then prayeth to GOD for the Deliverance of the Righteous, that they may rejoice, and *Praife* GOD for the fame.

(—Vide *Pfal.* xiv.—*Rom.* iii. 10.—)

The PRECEPT.

{ *Keep me,* O LORD, *from fuch as do blafpheme*
Thy mighty Power, *and do defpife Thy Name:*
Thy promis'd Aid, O LORD, *will me rejoice,*
And, to Thy Praife, *exalt my finging* Voice. }

N. B. This *Pfalm* being the very fame as *Pfalm* the xivth, excepting one *Verfe*, I refer you to the *Note* thereon.

On PSALM LIV.

WE have here another *Pfalm of Inftruction*, from holy DAVID, infcribed to him that performed beft on the *Neginoth*. The *Author* being brought into great Danger by
the

the *Ziphims*, who discovered to *Saul* where he was, ¹ begs of GOD to *save* him, and ⁵ to destroy his Enemies; promising ⁶ Sacrifice and free Offerings for so great a Deliverance; ⁷ which then he obtained by the *Mercy* of GOD.

(—Vide 1 *Sam.* xxiii. 19.—)

This is another *Example* of Mens *Treachery*, and GOD's *Mercy*; shewing how the *Righteous* fall often into *Perils* and *Dangers*, although they are in GOD's *Favour*, only to try their *Integrity*; and again, how wonderfully they are *preserved*, by the *Mercy* of GOD, on Account of their *Faith* and *Constancy*; while the Wicked fall into *Destruction*, and are cut off. Hence let all *Hypocrites* fear and tremble, and reform their *Lives* and *Actions*: Whilst *godly Men* rejoice in the *Favour* and *Love* of GOD.

(—Vide *Psal.* xxxiii. 1.—)

The PRECEPT.

{ *Though cruel* Tyrants *hourly on me rise,*
Me to destroy; and do the LORD *despise:*
GOD, *as He promis'd, by the* Just *will stand,*
And safely guard the Cause *they have in Hand.* }

N. B. This *Psalm* was made when the *Ziphites* came to deliver DAVID to *Saul*.

(—Vide 1 *Sam.* xxiii. 19. 24.—or else 1 *Sam.* xxvi. 1.—)

On PSALM LV.

1023. THIS is a *Maschil*, or *Psalm* of *Instruction*; and inscribed to the best *Player* on the *Neginoth*; wherein holy DAVID being in great Heaviness, ¹ prays to GOD for *Audience*, in ² his sad *Dejection*; complaining ³ not only of the Cruelty of *Saul*, but ¹² of the Falshood of his familiar *Acquaintance*. He then ¹⁵ begging of GOD to destroy them; most ardently promiseth himself ¹⁷ to *serve* GOD; being ¹⁸ well assured that He will *then* have *Pity* on him, as well as He hath had in Times *past*; ²² setting forth the *Mercy* and *Grace* of GOD, by his *Faith*, as if he had obtained his *Request*: And ²³ shews how the Days of wicked and deceitful Men are shortened.

(—Vide 1 *Sam.* xxiii.—2 *Sam.* xv.—xvi.—xvii.—xviii.—* 2 *Kings* vi. 16.—*Psal.* xxxiv. 7.—)

My *Author's Complaint* in this *Psalm* is worthy to be observed, by Reason it is an unparalleled Piece of *Deceit* and *Villainy*; for what could be more cutting to any one, than to have one's *own Son*, and chief *Counsellor*, with many other familiar *Acquaintance*, to contrive to take away one's *Life* wrongfully!—This was holy

A New Exposition *on the* Book *of* Psalms, &c. 47

holy DAVID's real *Case*; for *Ahitophel*, that had been his chief *Counsellor*, his Bosom *Friend*, and knew the very *Secrets* of his Mind, on all Occasions, had so drawn away his Son *Absalom*, (as well as many others of his *Friends*,) that they hourly sought his Life: Therefore he had great Reason to pour out his *Prayers* unto GOD as he did, when his very *Life* lay at Stake, had he fell into the Hands of such desperate and cruel Men; whose miserable *Ends* proved his *Prophecy*, and shewed the *Success* of his *Confidence*; and the *Mercy* of GOD to him testified His *Promise* in saving the *Righteous*, that His *Glory* might appear to all the World: Meaning * that the very *Angels* then fought, and were with him.

The PRECEPT.

{ *Though wicked Men do strive to harm the* Just,
Vain is their Hope, in GOD *they have no Trust:*
But righteous Men, that on the LORD *depend,*
Are safe from Foes, whilst GOD*'s their mighty* Friend. }

N. B. This *Psalm* was probably made on the *Intelligence* he had received of his Enemies; with the Plot that *Hushai* had laid against *Ahitophel*'s Counsel: the Wickedness perpetrated in *Jerusalem*, alluding to *Absalom*'s Conspiracy; foretelling the Event of himself, and them that followed him over *Jordan* in the Rebellion. (* See the *Scriptures* above quoted.)

※※※※※※※※※※※※※※※※※※※※※※※

On PSALM LVI.

OUR holy *Author*, DAVID, inscribes this *Psalm* to the chief Musician upon *Jonathelem-rechokim*, or to him that could play best on the *Michtam*; and, (being brought before *Achish*, King of *Gath*,) [1] greatly complains of his Enemies; and [2] earnestly makes his *Supplications* to GOD against their *Treachery* and *Violence*. He then [3] *rejoicing*, and trusting in GOD, promiseth [12] to perform the *Vows* he had taken upon him: *i. e.* never to forget his GOD.

* (—Vide 1 *Sam.* xxi. 10. 14.—1 *Sam.* xxxi. 10.—2 *Sam.* xxi. 12.—)

We see from this *Psalm*, that DAVID is still resolved to *Praise* GOD in His *Church*, though he was just then chaced away from it, into a strange Country; where he was as one dumb, amongst his Enemies; who could content themselves with nothing but his Life. But, as GOD has always *Mercy* in Store for the *Righteous*, He never fails to deliver them out of the Hands of the Wicked, when they trust in Him. If we but consider the *Dignity* of the *Person* of DAVID, and how he, (without any Fault,) was cast into such a miserable Condition; it will shew us a singular Example of true *Piety*, *Patience*, *Meekness*, *Constancy*, *Truth*, and *Righteousness*. Therefore, let us, (with him,) *rejoice* in GOD because of His *Word*; who hath, (by the *Merits* of His *Son* JESUS CHRIST,) delivered our *Souls* from *Death*, and our Feet from falling; let us pay our *Vows* in the *Presence* of GOD, and sing PRAISES to His Name for ever.

(—Vide *Psal.* xxxiv. 3—)

The PRECEPT.

{ *I'll* glory *in Thy mighty* Word, O GOD!
And will, with Joy, *declare Thy* Name *abroad:*
To Thee, O LORD *with thankful* Voice *I'll sing,*
And daily Praise *Thee,* O *my* GOD *and* King! }

N. B. Probably this *Psalm* was written at the same Time as *Psalm* the xxxivth; when DAVID feigned himself *mad,* before *Achish* the *King,* to make his *Escape* out of his Hands. See the *Scriptures* above quoted *.

On PSALM LVII.

THIS *Psalm* was inscribed to the chief Musician upon *Al-taschith,* or the best *Player* on the *Michtam,* or a *Tune* so called. Holy DAVID being in the *Desart* of *Ziph,* where the Inhabitants did betray him; and at length in the Cave with *Saul,* ¹ calleth upon GOD with a full Confidence, to have *Mercy* on him, and ³ take his Cause in Hand, according to His Promise: And ⁷ shews His *Glory* both in *Heaven,* and on *Earth* against his cruel Enemies. Then he sheweth ⁹ that his *Heart* was always in Frame to *Praise* GOD; promiseth ¹¹ to perform it in the Heathen Lands; shewing, ¹² that as GOD's *Mercy* aboundeth above the Heavens, so would he, ¹³ that His *Truth* should be known over all the Earth.

* (—Vide 1 *Sam.* xxiv. 4. 20.—)

From this *Psalm* we may infer, that all Things are under the *Power* and *Will* of GOD, that His *Promise* is sure, and that He will assuredly deliver His People, that His *Name* may be *glorified;* and not suffer the Wicked to overcome the *Righteous,* lest His *Power* be held in Contempt. We also see how ready *holy* DAVID was to *Praise* GOD; and how he called his *Heart,* (meaning his *Joy* or *Glory,)* and his *Lute,* (meaning his *Tongue,)* and *Harp* to *Praise* GOD; shewing that he would not only *Praise* GOD with his *Voice,* but with his *Heart* also: Importing thereby that GOD's *Mercies* did not only appertain to the *Jews,* but to the *Gentiles* also. So let us *Praise* His Name, *daily,* among the People; and sing of His *Glory* among all Nations.

(—Vide *Psal.* cviii. 4.—)

The PRECEPT.

{ *Under the Shadow of Thy mighty Wings*
I fix my Hope, O LORD, *Thou* KING *of* Kings!
Thy Mercy, LORD, *above the.* Stars *ascend,*
To Praise *Thy* Name, *my* Songs *shall never end.* }

N. B. This

N. B. This *Pſalm* is much to the Purpoſe of the former, only this ſeems to be that *Deliverance*, in the Care, and Aſſurance of the *Kingdom* to him at the very laſt. Alſo the xciiid *Pſalm* is on this his Acquittance from Imputation of *Treaſon*, and Aſſurance of the *Kingdom* from *Saul*'s own Mouth, &c. *

On PSALM LVIII.

OUR holy *Author*, DAVID, inſcribes this *Pſalm* to the chief Muſician upon *Al-taſchith*, or to the beſt Performer on the *Michtam*, or a *Tune* ſo called ; wherein he ¹ deſcribeth the Malice of his own Enemies, as well as *Saul*'s Flatterers ; ³ who both openly, as well as ſecretly, ſought after his Life, and many others. He then ⁷ appeals to GOD for Judgment on the Wicked, ſhewing ¹⁰ that the Righteous ſhall *rejoice* at their Puniſhment ; and that their Deſtruction ſhall be to the *Glory of* GOD, whereby His Judgment is made manifeſt.

(—Vide *Deut.* i. 17.—*Prov.* xxi. 15.—*Ecclef.* xii. 14.—)

Here holy DAVID painteth all wicked and corrupt *Judges*, in their own proper Colours. For *Saul* having called all his *Council* of State together, (to put a better Face on his Hatred againſt DAVID, who was abſent,) he ſo procured his own wicked Ends, as to have him *condemned* as a public Enemy, though he was innocent of all they laid againſt him. From this it appears, that there are ſeldom any greater *Injuries* committed, than thoſe that oppreſs under a falſe Cloak of *Law*, or pretended *Religion* ; by Villains who *pretend* to be over-much righteous, when they have not the Fear of GOD before their Eyes. My *Author* well knew the Nature of ſuch wicked People; and that what they had conſpired *ſecretly*, they would not be aſhamed to execute *publickly* ; for which Reaſon, he very juſtly in the *Name* of GOD, and as a *Prophet*, pronounceth *Sentence* againſt them ; as allowed by GOD himſelf. He alſo herein uſeth ſuch *Similitudes* as are agreeable to ſuch ambitious, covetous, and deceitful Men ; whoſe chief Purpoſe is to ſet themſelves *aloft*, and alſo their Children after them, by ſuch-like wicked Practices ; for which Reaſon GOD cuts them off in their wicked Courſes, and their Poſterity, either by conſuming them by a little at a Time, or by a ſudden Rage, to the *Joy* of His *People*, and His own Glory.

(—Vide *Pſal.* xxxvii. 38, 39.—xlix. 13. 19.—)

The PRECEPT.

{ Let Judges *juſtly hear the* poor *Man's Cauſe,*
No Bribes *receive, nor deaf to righteous* Laws :
On partial Judges GOD *will Vengeance take,*
But righteous *Men he never will forſake.* }

N. B. This *Pſalm* was written on that unjuſt and cruel *Sentence* and *Execution* done by *Saul*, and his Attendants, in deſtroying the City of *Nob* and the *Prieſts*.

(—Vide 1 *Sam.* xxii.—)

On PSALM LIX.

THIS *Psalm* holy DAVID inscribed to him that excelleth upon *Al-taschith*, or the best Player on the *Michtam*; wherein, ¹ being in great Danger of being slain, he prayeth earnestly to GOD to *save* him from his Enemies Fury; because ³ he was intirely *innocent*; desiring ⁵ GOD to destroy all such evil and malicious Men. He then ¹⁶ *sings* of *Mercy* and *Power*, in preserving him; and for delivering him safe out of the Hands of his Enemies.

(—Vide *Psal*. xvi.—)

This *Psalm* has some Coherence with the foregoing one, relating to his cruel Enemies; he being now in *Bed*, and his *House* beset, (by the Command of *Saul*,) was that very Night to be murdered, had not his *Wife*, *Michal*, let him out at the Window, down the Wall, to make his Escape out of their cruel Hands: From which we may infer, that a very weak Policy will disappoint and defeat the Designs of the Wicked, when GOD is on our Side. And though He often suffers the Wicked to oppress the Righteous for a Time, yet He never fails to *preserve* them in the End; and to bring Destruction on the Enemies of GOD's *Church* and *People*; to manifest His *Truth* and *Glory:* For which Reason, we must wait with *Patience*, under all Manner of Wrongs, till GOD, in His good Time, shall think fit to deliver us.

* (—Vide 1 *Sam*. xix.—*Psal*. v.—)

The PRECEPT.

{ LORD, *without Cause*, my Foes *would me devour*,
Save me, my GOD, *Thou art my* Fort *and* Tower:
Confound my Foes, O LORD, *I'll* sing *to Thee*,
For why? Thou art a loving GOD *to me.* }

N. B. The above *Note*, and *Scriptures*, shew on what Occasion this *Psalm* was written; if you have Recourse to the said *Sacred History*, as above quoted *.

On PSALM LX.

HOLY DAVID being now made *King* over *Judah*, after many Victories; ¹ sheweth by evident Signs, that ⁴ GOD *elected* him; assuring the People that ¹¹ He would *prosper* them, if they approve the same: And earnestly *prays* unto GOD to *finish* what he himself hath *begun*; on which holy DAVID wholly trusted, and ¹² greatly triumpheth, *&c.*

* (—Vide 2 *Sam*. viii.—1 *Chron*. xxiii.—)

This

A New Exposition on the Book of Psalms, &c.

This *Psalm* was inscribed to the best *Players* on the *Chustian-cluth*, &c. We may here learn, by this *Psalm of Prayer*, which is wrote in the Name of the *People*, that though the *Church* and G O D's *People* may seem, at some Times, to be utterly lost, (as it came to pass in the Time of the *Judges*, and when *Saul* was slain;) yet G O D is always mindful of His *Covenant* and *Promise*; by raising up the *Banner* of His holy *Word* more high at last than before; thereby stirring up Men to more heroic Spirits. The *Battle* our AUTHOR had with the *Assyrians*, and the *King* of *Zobab*, whom he overcame, and all the People that were then about him, (as he had before prophesied,) is shewn by the Spirit of this *Psalm*, wherein he says, he should divide *Shechem*, and measure out *Succoth*; that *Manasseh* should be his, and *Ephraim*, because it was a Place strongly peopled; *Judah* should be his Law-giver, because it was the *Tribe* where his Kingdom should be established; *Moab* and *Edom* should be in Subjection to him; and that *Palestine* should seem to be *glad* of him, though he knew they flattered and dissembled with him. Let us now take Notice, that all these *Actions* are rather to be applied to the *spiritual Enemies* of our *Church*, than to *Armies* that fight with outward Weapons; and that it is G O D alone, that defends us, and our *Church*, from all Enemies.

(—Vide *Psal.* xliv.—)

The PRECEPT.

{ Leave us not, L O R D, our righteous Cause maintain;
The Help of Man is only weak and vain:
In Thee I trust, O G O D, Thou canst tread down
Our mighty Foes, and us with Glory crown. }

N. B. This *Psalm* seems to be wrote when DAVID fought against *Aram Naharaim*; and against *Aram-Zobah*; when *Joab* returned and slew 12,000 in the Valley of *Salt*. *Psal.* xlivth was wrote at the same Time *.

✿✿✿✿✿✿✿✿✿✿✿✿✿✿✿✿✿✿✿✿✿✿✿✿✿✿

On PSALM LXI.

THIS *Psalm* holy DAVID inscribes to him that performeth best on the *Neginoth*; wherein he [1] earnestly begs to GOD for *Audience*; and [3] that He would *protect* him now, as at other Times. He then, confirming himself in his *Kingdom*, promiseth perpetual *Praises* to Almighty G O D.

* (-Vide 2 *Sam.* viii. 3. 5.—*Gen.* xv. 18.—*Exod.* xxiii. 31.—1 *Kings* iv. 20. 23.-)

DAVID being now in *Exile*, and driven from his *Church* and Friends, or in Danger of the *Ammonites*, and his Son *Absalom* pursuing him; was probably the Occasion of this *Address* to G O D; from which we may infer, that as there is always a continual *Battle* betwixt the *World* and the *Saints* of G O D, even so is the *Saints Hope* nourished by the continual Remembrance of the *Mercy* and *Providence* of GOD over them; Whose *Promise* is never changeable in preserving them. Holy DAVID here promiseth himself the *Kingdom*, and everlasting *Life*; which is promised to the *Righteous*, in like Manner; it being referred here, by the Prophet, to the

E 4   *Kingdom*

Kingdom of *CHRIST*, Whose *Kingdom* is not of this World; as is applied by the *Angel Gabriel*, &c. This affordeth great *Comfort* to the People of *CHRIST's Church*, in their greatest Miseries; knowing, that, if the World be ever so much against them, *CHRIST* will be for them, and take them into His *Kingdom*, Whose *Kingdom* standeth by *Mercy* and *Truth*.

(—Vide *James* iv. 4.—*Psal.* lxxxix. 11.—cxxx. 11.—2 *Sam.* vii.—*Luke* i.—)

The PRECEPT.

{ *Save me, my* GOD, *when unto Thee I cry*;
If Thou support'st, my Aid *is always nigh*:
Thy Truth, *and* Mercy, LORD, *to me extend*,
That I may Praise Thy Name, *World without End*. }

N. B. Probably this *Psalm* was wrote on his being far from *Judah*; when on the Expedition against *Hadadezer*, for the extending his *Empire* to the utmost Confine on *Euphrates*; as was *promised*, and compleated to *Solomon*. * See the *Scriptures* above.

※※※※※※※※※※※※§※※※※※※※※※※※

On PSALM LXII.

1048. **H**OLY DAVID inscribes this *Psalm* to his chief Musician *Jeduthun*; wherein he ¹ greatly professeth his *Confidence* in GOD, and ³ foretells the *Destruction* of his Enemies. He then shews ⁶ that GOD is his only *Salvation*; and ⁸ encourageth the GODLY to trust in Him; and ¹⁰ not in *Riches, Robbery*, nor *Oppression*; and ¹² that GOD is both *merciful* and *powerful*, and will *reward* all Men according to their Works.

* (—Vide 1 *Chron.* xvi. 41.—*Eccles.* vii. 8.—)

They that keep this *Psalm* in *Memory*, and consider well the holy AUTHOR's *Meditation* therein, have a strong *Defence* against all Temptations. DAVID being cast from his *Throne* by the Conspiracy of his Son *Absalom*, and compelled to fly, with a very few Men, beyond *Jordan*; was, from his sudden Change, tempted either to prove *unlawful* Things, or to fall into utter *Despair*. Under all this, he *trusted* in GOD with *Patience*, and constantly waited His good Time to help him; bearing all out with a lively and good Courage. From this *Example* we may infer, that, whensoever we undergo any grievous *Temptation*, we should never *murmur* against GOD, but rest on His *Promise*, and bear it patiently; for though DAVID was himself a KING, and *chosen* of GOD, yet he always called GOD his *Strength*, and trusted in Him: Whose godly *Petitions* should add Strength to our *Faith*, wherein we may be preserved from all cruel Enemies; knowing that *CHRIST* is both our *Judge* and *Saviour*, and will preserve the *Righteous*, and destroy the Wicked.

(—Vide 1 *Thess.* v. 14.—*Psal.* xxxvii. 7.—2 *Pet.* i. 6.—)

The

A New Exposition *on the* Book *of* Psalms, *&c.* 53

The PRECEPT.

{ Let me, O LORD, on Thy great Pow'r rely,
Thou art my SAVIOUR, Glory, and my Joy:
In Truth, and Mercy, GOD doth all exceed,
And gives to all according to their Deeds. }

N. B. This *Psalm* has some Coherence with the foregoing *Psalm of Prayer.* See the *Scriptures* before quoted *.

On PSALM LXIII.

DAVID, being in great Danger by *Saul*, in the *Wilderness* of *Judah, Ziph,* or *En-gedi,* ¹ declareth his earnest Desires to *serve* GOD again in the *Tabernacle*; shewing ³ that His *Mercy* and Loving-kindness was more dear to him than even *Life* itself. He then ⁴ promises to *magnify* GOD for His *Mercy* to him, Who ⁵ had filled his Soul with the *Marrow* of His GRACE; and ⁷ had kept him safe under the Shadow of His Wings. Then ⁹ foretelling the *Destruction* of his, and GOD's Enemies, sheweth ¹¹ that he himself, and all that were true to him, should rejoice at the untimely Ends of their Enemies; that GOD's *Name* might be glorified.

* (—Vide 1 *Sam.* xxiii. xxv.—2 *Sam.* xxiv.—)

This *Psalm* sheweth that, when our *Afflictions* are most dangerous, our *Constancy* and *Faith* ought to be strongest; and to call on GOD with more Fervency of *Prayer*, &c. DAVID being here suddenly cast down from his *Power* and *Dignity,* oppressed with *Hunger, Thirst,* and in Fear of his Life; yet, his Thoughts of GOD afforded him *Comfort*, in the Midst of these Miseries. And though nothing grieved him so much as his not having the Liberty to *Praise* GOD in the *Tabernacle*; as he was wont; and to hear his glorious *Worship* of GOD despised by his Enemies, who sought his Life without any Offence; yet we see how *fervent* his Desire was to be with his *Church*: He always having the *Worship* of GOD in his Mind; and contemplating thereon both Day and Night. The Rememberance of GOD, and His *Mercies*, afforded him more Pleasure than all the *Dainties* of the World; by Reason, he well knew GOD would deliver him, and his People; and that *Saul*, and all his wicked *Adherents* should come to untimely Ends; and that all that owned him as *King*, and were *true* to him, should rejoice with him, in the *Favour* of GOD.

The PRECEPT.

{ With fervent Zeal, O LORD, my Soul inspire,
That I for Thee may have a true Desire:
And let Thy CHURCH be all my Soul's Delight,
And Precepts guide me ev'ry Day and Night. }

N. B. Pro-

N. B. Probably this *Pfalm* was wrote by DAVID, when he abode in *Paran*, after he had fpared *Saul*, filenced, and convicted him; and was himfelf *juftified* and comforted by the Words of *Saul*'s own Mouth.—See the *Scriptures* above *.

On PSALM LXIV.

IN this *Pfalm* holy DAVID ¹ earneftly poureth forth his *Prayers* ² againft the *Confpiracy*, ³ falfe Reports, and ⁴ *Slanders* of his cruel Enemies. Then ⁷ foretelling the *Punifhment*, and Deftruction of his Enemies, he fhews, ⁸ that the *Juft* fhall rejoice at it; and that the fame fhall tend to the *Glory* of GOD.

* (—Vide 1 *Sam.* xxii. 8. 20. 22, 23, 24.—)

This *Pfalm* evidently fhews, that the Truft and *Conftancy* of the *Righteous* is not in vain; and that DAVID did not complain of his cruel Enemies without a Caufe; by Reafon, what State *Jealoufies, Accufations*, and *Plots* that were raifed and harboured againft him by cruel *Saul* and his *Affiftants*, were intirely groundlefs; neverthelefs DAVID remained conftant, and trufted in GOD, to the very End; Who never failed to *defend* him in his greateft Extremities, whilft his wicked *Cofpirators* were brought *down* by the *Power* of GOD, in all their vain Attempts and Undertakings; which fhews that GOD will never forfake the *Righteous*, though the Wicked be ever fo inveterate againft them; for they generally are caught in the Snares they lay for others; as the *Hiftory* of holy DAVID's *Life* makes manifeft.

(—Vide *Pfal.* xii. 3.—*Prov.* xxii. 22.—*Hof.* vii. 3.—*Rom.* i. 17.—)

The PRECEPT.

Defend me, LORD, *from Men of* Pride *and* Spite,
Who hourly ftrive againft my Soul to fight:
GOD *wounds the Wicked with His mighty Dart,*
And faves the Juft, *of pure and upright Heart.*

N. B. The *Scriptures* above quoted being compared with the Words of this *Pfalm*, fhew the *Occafion* on which it was written *.

On PSALM LXV.

WE have here, by holy DAVID, ¹ a *Pfalm* of *Praife* and *Thankfgiving* unto GOD by the *Faithful*, fignified by the *Names* of *Sion* and *Jerufalem*; ⁴ for His *chufing*, ⁵ *preferving*, ⁶ *and governing* them; and ⁹ for His manifold *Bleffings* and Increafe

A New Exposition *on the* Book *of* Psalms, &c. 55
crease poured forth over the whole Earth: And especially to
His *Church* and People.

    * (—Vide 2 *Sam.* xxiv.—1 *Chron.* xxi.—2 *Sam.* xxi. 1. 15.—)

    We are here *first* taught, from this SONG of PRAISE, that the *Benefits* of GOD are never so well known, and acknowledged, as they are in His holy *Congregations*; where we, in public, *Praise* G O D for them, in the Midst of all the People: G O D having gathered His *Church* unto Himself, in which He will be *Praised*; and where He will also *hear* the *Prayers* of all the People, and forgive their Sins; and bless the whole *Congregation*, with His *Benefits*, and *defend* them. *Secondly*, That He doth maintain all the *Societies* of good Men, and *preserve* them in the Midst of all Dangers. And, *Thirdly*, He doth send from Heaven *Rain*, to water the Earth, which affordeth all Things in great Abundance for our Necessities in this Life, by His gracious *Liberality*; shewing thereby, that there is no *Part*, nor *Creature* in the whole World, but what is governed by His *Divine Power* and Providence: So that all are in *Duty*, and Gratitude, bound to *sing Praises* for all His gracious *Benefits*.

The PRECEPT.

> *The* Field *sets forth the* Glory *of the* LORD,
> *But, grows more fragrant in his holy* Word:
> LORD! *as thy* Drops *do on the Earth distill,*
> *So let thy* Grace *my Soul with Comfort fill.*

N. B. The *first* Part of this *Psalm* seems to hint the *Author's* Sin in *numbering* the People; the *Scourge* of it in the *Plague*; and the *Grace* of G O D in removing it, by *Sacrifice*, in the Place where he appointed the *Temple* should be. The last *Part* magnifies the Earth's *Plenty* after the *Famine* continued the three first Years of his Reign in *Hebron*. See the above *Scriptures* *.

On PSALM LXVI.

HOLY DAVID, in this *Psalm*, ¹ exhorteth all Men to *Praise* GOD for all former *Deliverances*, and to behold and *meditate* on His wonderous *Works*; also to *Praise* G O D for His *Benefits* to the *Church*, and ⁷ setteth forth His Power against its Enemies. He ¹⁰ also sheweth how G O D hath delivered *Israel* out of Bondage, and sore Afflictions; and ¹⁵ promiseth Sacrifice. He then ¹⁶ sheweth what great Things G O D had done for him, and all *Israel*; and ²⁰ *Praiseth* G O D for the same, &c.

    * (—Vide 1 *Sam.* xxiv.—1 *Chron.* xxi.—)

    This *Psalm*, as well as many others, seems to be written for the continual Use of the *Church*, and for other private Occasions, in Order to remind the People of the wonderful Mercies of GOD, in preserving His People, in past Ages; as well as to give Thanks for every hourly Benefit we now receive, as Occasion shall offer, whether in private, or in public. The Condition of the *Church* is also here described, shewing that it is intirely under GOD's Providence, (as well as the other Part of the World,) and is subject to many Dangers; yet, as GOD always preserves the Faithful, it is their Duty to render Thanks and *Praises* to Him for all His Benefits; forasmuch as we know, that, if we delight in Wickedness, He will not hear us; but if we confess His Name in Righteousness, and *Praise* Him with a thankful Heart, He will receive us into His Glory. *Amen.*

(—Vide *Psal.* xxxiii. 1, 2, 3, 4.—)

The PRECEPT.

{ *Bear well in Mind what* GOD *for Thee hath done,*
To save thy Soul He gave His only SON!
O laud His Name, and never cease to sing
Due Thanks *and* Praise *to* CHRIST, *our Heav'nly King.* }

N. B. As the lxvth *Psalm* was probably wrote on the Sacrifice in the Floor of *Ornan*; this lxvith was probably wrote for the Use of the People, at the same Time. See the *Scriptures* above quoted *.

※※※※※※※※※※※※※※※※※※※※※※※

On PSALM LXVII.

THIS *Psalm* of *Prayer* holy DAVID inscribed to him that performed best on the *Neginoth.* Wherein he ¹ prayeth GOD to have *Mercy* on the whole *Church,* give them His *Favour,* and to enlighten them with His *Countenance;* to the Enlargement of His *Kingdom*; whereby ² His *Grace* might be known over all the World. He then ² doubly ⁵ exhorts all *People* to *Praise* GOD, that ⁴ they may rejoice in the *Justice* of His *Judgment* and *Government*; and ⁶ that His *Increase* may be on the Earth, as well as His *Grace* and ⁷ *Blessing*; whereby all the *Ends* of the World should *Praise* Him.

* (—Vide 1 *Sam.* xxi. 24.—)

Our holy *Author* here attributeth all Things to the infinite *Mercy* of GOD, both His *spiritual Blessings* belonging to His *Church*; and the *corporal Blessings* also; which he desireth GOD to *continue* unto us, as well as the former. He also herein foretelleth the Spreading of the *Church,* under CHRIST; and exhorteth all the *Godly* to give *Thanks,* and *celebrate* the *Praises* of GOD. This *Psalm* of *Prayer* should be generally used in the *Church.*

The

A New Exposition *on the* Book *of* Psalms, *&c.* 57

The PRECEPT.

{ *Bless us*, O LORD, *with* Mercy, Peace, *and* Love,
That we Thy Laws *may* know, *and well approve :*
May Earth increase, *and Thy great Name* adore,
With Thanks, *and joyful* Praises, *evermore*. }

N. B, This *Psalm* was probably set forth before the *Ark* in *Sion.* See the *Scripture* above quoted *.

On PSALM LXVIII.

IN this *Song*, or *Psalm* of DAVID, is [1] shewed what *Power* GOD has over His Enemies, and [3] that the Righteous shall rejoice at their Destruction, because they are not only the Enemies of the *Church*, but of their *Salvation*. He then [4] exhorteth all People to *Praise* GOD, for his wonderful *Mercies:* And shews [7] that GOD's *Favour* peculiarly belongeth to the *Church*, by His delivering them out of *Egypt*. He sheweth also [15] that the *Church* of GOD excelleth all other Things in the World, not only for its *external* Shew and Grandeur, but [16] for its *inward* Grace of GOD; because GOD Himself dwelleth there: And [17] that His *Promises*, *Graces*, and *Victories* do excel all the World. He then describeth the *Order* of the *Singers*, and *Instruments*, in the *Temple*, who daily sung *Thanks* and *Praises* to GOD, for all *Mercies* and *Victories*; desiring [30] GOD to destroy the Pride of the Mighty, who ornamented their Shoes with *Gold*, and *Silver*, only to shine above other Men. He also [31] foretelleth the *Gentiles* coming from foreign Lands to the true Knowledge and *Worship of* GOD; shewing [32] that by His Thunders he will make Himself known over all the World, against the Enemies of His *Church*, for our Salvation.

(—Vide 2 *Sam.* viii.—1 *Chron.* xv.—*Eph.* iv. 8.—)

Our holy *Author*, being about to carry the *Ark* of the *Covenant* into the Tower of *Sion*, in great Solemnity, composed several *Psalms*, (by the *Inspiration* of GOD,) to inflame the People to *Praise* GOD. This *Psalm*, amongst others, was one, which is wrote very *majestic* and *eloquent*; wherein he does not only point to the Matter in Hand, but mystically means CHRIST, and the Kingdom of Heaven. An *Ark* was a *Chest*, ornamented with *Gold*, *Cherubims*, &c. which was the visible Testimony and Representation of the *Shechinah*, or *Divine Presence* of GOD, and His internal Mercy, Blessings, *&c.* and the mystical *Godhead* of His Son *JESUS CHRIST*, that should come to put on our Flesh, and die for us. *Sion* meaneth the *Kingdom* of Heaven; and the *Ark* brought into it meaneth

meaneth *CHRIST's Ascension* into Heaven. The manifold temporal *Blessings* that GOD continually poureth upon us, and the *spiritual* and everlasting *Gifts* of *CHRIST* daily bestowed upon His Church, by the most holy *Ministry* and *Work* of the *Gospel*, are here likewise figured, and described; as appears more fully in the ivth of *Ephesians*, and the Book of *Hebrews*, by St. *Paul*, &c. &c.

The PRECEPT.

If GOD *arise, to take the* Cause *in Hand,*
His Foes shall fall; none can His Might withstand:
But, righteous *Men shall* sing, *with chearful Voice,*
Of His great Mercy, *and in Heart rejoice.*

N. B. It is very probable this *Psalm* was penned amidst those *Atchievements* in the foreign *Wars*; when the *Spoils* of the Nations were dedicated to the *Service* of the *Temple.* 2 *Sam.* viii.

On PSALM LXIX.

HOLY DAVID inscribes this *Psalm* to the best Performer on the *Shoshannim*; wherein he *(personating CHRIST and all His Members)* ¹ prayeth fervently to be delivered from his *malicious* and cruel Enemies; and ²² their cruel *Punishments*; shewing ²⁶ whereby such *Traitors* are accursed. He then taketh Courage, in his great *Afflictions*, and ³⁰ *Praiseth* GOD; which ³¹ was more esteemed than any other *Sacrifice* whatsoever; which afforded him great outward *Comfort*, under all Afflictions. He then ³⁴ exhorteth all Creatures to *Praise* GOD; and foretells the *Kingdom* of *CHRIST*, the Building of *Judah*; and where all the *Faithful*, and their *Seed*, shall remain, for ever and ever.

(—Vide *John* ii. 17.—*Rom.* xv. 3.—*John* xix. 28, 29.—*Acts* i. 16.—*Rom.* xi. 9.— *Mat.* xxvii. 48.—*Luke* i. 20.—*Rom.* xv. 3 —)

Herein DAVID's *Zeal* caused him to lament; either when he was offered to be driven out of the *Court* of *Saul*; or for his Son *Absalom*'s Treachery against him. However the Occasion was, it is evident that holy DAVID wrote this *Psalm* more (by the *Spirit* of *Prophecy*) of *CHRIST* to come, than the Matter just then in Hand; pointing out *Judas*, and *CHRIST*'s cruel Enemies, by *Example* of His own; which mystical *Interpretation* appears more clear in the above quoted *Scriptures*, in the New *Testament*. And as we know that all *Members* of the Body must be conformed unto the *Head*; so must we also conform to *CHRIST* and His Gospel, as long as our Church shall sojourn in this World, if we expect Happiness with *CHRIST* in the next.

The

The PRECEPT.

Save me, O LORD, *from Foes that would oppress*
My guiltless Heart, and plunge me in Distress:
For, well I know, all such as do rely
On Thee, and CHRIST, *their Souls shall never die.*

N. B. The xxiid and xlvth *Psalms* seem to have some Coherence with this lxixth, they all alluding to CHRIST, and His *Church*, &c.

On PSALM LXX.

THIS *Psalm* holy DAVID composed to bring GOD's former Deliverances to Rememberance; wherein he [1] earnestly prays to GOD to deliver him from his cruel Enemies; and [2] that they may be confounded and brought to Shame for *despising* him, &c. He then [4] sheweth that the Righteous shall greatly rejoice; and all those that seek the LORD shall surely be *comforted*.

* Vide *Psal.* iv. 13, 14.—Mat. xxvi. 36.—)

We are taught from this *Psalm* always to continue in *Prayer*, when under any Afflictions; and to bear all Things *patiently* till GOD, in His good Time, shall help us: And that the more our Enemies rage against us, the nearer they are to Destruction; and we to *Deliverance*. Hence we should never *mock* others when they are in *Misery*, lest the like fall on our own Heads; but, on the contrary, we should be *sorry* for their Afflictions, whether in Mind, Body or *Estate*; and do all we can to help them; forasmuch as our *Saviour* has promised, *Blessed are the Merciful, for they shall obtain Mercy*, which GOD grant to us all.

(—Vide Matt. v. 4. 7, 8.—)

The PRECEPT.

O LORD *of Hosts! help me, in Time of Need;*
Confound my Foes, that they turn back with Speed:
In Thee I trust, let me Thy Glory sing,
And Praise Thy Mercy, O my GOD *and King.*

N. B. Part of this *Psalm* is contained in *Psalm* the xlth. See the *Scriptures* above quoted * and the Note on the xlth Psalm.

On PSALM LXXI.

1023. WE have, in this *Psalm* of DAVID, an *Example* of his *Faith*, by which, and by GOD's *Promises*, he [1] prayeth to be delivered from his cruel Enemies: Shewing [5] that as He had

had trusted in GOD always, even from his *Youth*, and had been preserved; he ⁹ humbly begs that GOD would not forsake him in his *Old-Age*; left ¹¹ his Enemies should *taunt* him, and overcome him, when he had none to help him. He then ¹⁴ promiseth to *continue* his *Praises* more and more unto GOD, and ¹⁷ to *sing* of His Righteousness in his *Old-Age*, as he was wont in his *Youth*. Then ¹⁹ shewing what great Things GOD had done for him (and that He would still continue more of His Favours,) he ²² greatly *praiseth* the *Faithfulness* of GOD, and, (with his *Harp*,) ²⁴ *sings* of His *Truth*, in confounding his Enemies.

(—Vide *Psal.* xxv.—xxxi.—xlii.—)

We may infer, from this *Psalm*, that GOD is always stedfast in His *Promise*, in *preserving* the *Righteous*. For though wicked *Ahitophel* had drawn away DAVID's Son *Absalom* from him, and had conspired to take away his Life; yet GOD always delivered DAVID out of their Hands, and brought all his wicked Adversaries to miserable Ends. Hence, if we trust in GOD, as DAVID did, we need never fear what Man can do to us; and though they hurt our Bodies, GOD will preserve our *Souls*, if we trust in Him, and *Praise* Him from the *Ground* of our Hearts, for all the *Benefits* we receive from Him.

The PRECEPT.

{ *Defend me*, LORD, *Thou art my Strength and Stay*,
Nor me forsake, when I with Age *decay:*
Comfort my Soul; *my* Songs *shall Thee confess*,
And daily Praise *Thee in Thy Righteousness.* }

N. B. This *Psalm* refers to the *Sacred History* in the Second *Book* of *Samuel*, Chap. xv, &c. &c.

On PSALM LXXII.

1015. OUR holy *Author*, in this *Psalm*, ¹ beggeth for GOD's *Judgment* and *Righteousness* to his Successor and Son, *Solomon*; whereby he might *judge* ² the People with *Equity*, and *defend* the Poor and Innocent; that by his *Justice* ³ all Places might be inriched. He then shews ⁵ that, if he *ruled* according to GOD, all would embrace his *Religion*; and that it shall endure ⁷ to all *Ages*, in *Righteousness*, *Peace*, and *Felicity*; and that ¹⁰ all Nations shall pay him *Homage*, and bring *Riches*: ¹⁷ That his *Name* and *Power* shall endure for ever; and that in GOD ¹⁹ shall all *Nations* of the World be *blessed*.

* (—Vide

* (—Vide 2 *Sam.* vii. 12, 13, 14.—1 *Kings* i. 32. 49.—1 *Kings* iv. 21.— *Luke* i. 31, 32, 33.—*Zech.* ix. 9, 10.—*Matt.* xxviii. 18, 19, 20.—1 *Tim.* ii. 2.—)

This was holy DAVID's *last Prayer* in the *Close* of his Life; which he left for his SON *Solomon*, as a precious *Jewel*, after he was crowned *King*; wherein were all Rules necessary for him to observe in his *Office*. And, seeing that this Life is but for a little while, he in this *Psalm* setteth forth (by his *own* Kingdom and his *Son's*) the *Person* of *CHRIST*, and His *Kingdom*; which was *promised* by the Angel Gabriel: A *Kingdom* not made with Hands, eternal in the Heavens; prepared for the *Church*, and *People* of *CHRIST*.—So *Blessed be the glorious Name of His Majesty for ever, and let all the Earth be filled with His Majesty.* Amen. Amen Here ends holy DAVID's *Prayer*.

The PRECEPT.

{ LORD *save the* King, *and him preserve in* Peace, \
To rule with Justice; *and our* Land *increase*: \
And give us Grace, *that we may freely own* \
The wond'rous Works *that Thou for us hast done.* }

N. B. * Vide the *Scriptures* above, which have Respect both to *Solomon*, an *CHRIST*'s Kingdom.

End of the SECOND BOOK.

✳✳✳✳✳✳✳✳✳✳✳✳✳✳✳✳✳✳✳✳✳

On PSALM LXXIII.

THIS is a *Psalm* of ASAPH, who was one of the chief *Singers* * of holy DAVID; which Prophet herein teacheth (by [1] his getting Victory of a great *Temptation*,) that [3] neither the *Prosperity* of the Wicked, nor [14] the *Afflictions* of the *Godly*, ever ought to discourage the People from the *Worship* of GOD; but that it ought rather to *move* them more to *consider* GOD's *Providence*; and to *reverence* His *Judgments*, because [19] the Wicked vanish away; and [24] the GODLY enter into *everlasting Life*: And, in Hopes thereof, he [23] resigneth himself into GOD Almighty's Hands.

(—Vide *Psal.* xxxvii. 37, 38, 39, 40.—)

The *Author*, being here almost between *Hopes* and *Despair*, pauseth a while,— and at last considers, that GOD, for his *Promise* sake, would assuredly continue His *Favours* to the true *Godly*, and not to the Hypocrite; neither should the Wicked enjoy it, nor such as *glory* in their *Riches*, *Pride*, and *gay Apparel*; who *blaspheme* the Name of GOD, rail on His People, and esteem themselves above all other Men. This our *Author* learned from the Holy Spirit, by *Inspiration*, Who will always attend such as trust in GOD; and have a lively *Faith* in His *Mercies*. And, should the greatest Part of the World shrink from GOD, He promiseth always to defend them that wholly trust in His holy *Word*: And that, though their Flesh and Heart sink under the *Afflictions* of this *Life*, yet, before they

they leave this World, G O D has promised, to be *the Strength of* their Hearts, by Faith; *and their Portion for ever.* Ver. 26. See 2 *Chron.* xxix. 30 *.

The PRECEPT.

{ *Though* G O D *is great,* He's bountiful *and kind,*
To such as have a godly, honest *Mind:*
When all Things fail, C H R I S T *hath for them, in Store,*
A heav'nly Crown; *to last for evermore.* }

N. B. This seems to be the *first* Psalm wrote on this Subject, while DAVID began first to be exercised with his *Afflictions*; and *Saul* prospered; and his overcoming the Temptation by going into the *Sanctuary*; his dwelling with *Samuel* better enabling him to endure all Sorts of *Afflictions.* See 2 *Sam.* xviii, xix, &c.

On PSALM LXXIV.

IN this *Maschil*, or *Psalm* of ASAPH, is ¹ a grievous Complaint unto G O D of the Destruction and Desolation of the *Church* and true *Religion*; under the Names of ² *Sion, Temple, Sanctuary,* and *Altars.* He then trusting in the free *Mercy* and *Power* of G O D, by His *Covenant,* ¹⁰ beggeth for Succour at His Hands, ¹⁸ for the *Glory* of His *Name,* and for the eternal *Salvation* of His poor distressed Servants: Desiring ²² the utter Confusion of his proud, haughty, and cruel Enemies, that His People might *rejoice,* and *Praise* His Name.

* (—Vide *Dan.* ix. 4.—*Zach.* i. 12, &c.—)

As the *Punishment* and Destruction of an Enemy is generally the *Deliverance* of the People that are afflicted and distressed, they should always join their *Deliverance* with G O D's *Mercy, Power,* and *Glory,* Who was the AUTHOR of it. And as *Vengeance* only belongs to G O D, and not to Man, therefore, He destroys the Wicked, to maintain the *Truth* of His *Word,* for His *Glory* and *Honour*; that His wicked Enemies may neither hurt His *Church* nor *People*; nor *blaspheme* His Name, despise His *Mercy* and *Power,* nor hinder His People in in their *Worship* and true *Religion,* due to His holy *Name.* Our *Author* also herein hints the great Oppressions of the Church, either by the Tyranny of the *Babylonians,* or of *Antiochus*; and prayeth to G O D to deliver them; though the Yoke was laid on them for their Sins, &c. And, though the Church of G O D is often exposed as a Prey to the Wicked, we may be so well assured, that He will never lose His own Right, nor forsake His People; but will deliver them in His own due Time, if they remain *constant* to Him; for He will always preserve the *Godly,* and bring down the Wicked to the Ground.

(—Vide *Psal.* cxlvii. 5, 6.—)

The

A New Exposition *on the* Book *of* Psalms, &c. 63

The PRECEPT.

{ *Arise,* O LORD, *and all Thy Foes deface,*
That do despise Thy Church, *and Holy Place:*
Thou, LORD, *art* King! *Thou by the Just dost stand,*
Thy Mercy's known to ev'ry Age and Land. }

N. B. Some are of Opinion that this Psalm must be composed by *Daniel,* towards the End of the *Captivity* of *Babylon.* And, very possibly, the *Intercession* of *CHRIST* for His *Church* is herein figured; (that *Angel* of the Covenant;) and that this was, at that Time, *wrote* for their Use; whether the *Author* was *David, Daniel,* or *Asaph* *.

On PSALM LXXV.

IN this *Psalm* of DAVID, directed to *Asaph,* or to the chief Musician *Al-taschith,* [1] the *Author* greatly exhorteth the *Faithful* to *Praise* the Name of the LORD with him, for his wonderful *Promotion* to the Kingdom; shewing [2] that he would *judge righteously,* and [4] be a Terror to the Wicked. He sheweth also, [6] that all *Promotion* cometh alone from GOD; that [9] he will sing *Praises* to His Name for ever; and [10] that wicked Men shall be utterly thrown down; and the *Righteous* be exalted to *Honour.*

* (—Vide 2 Sam. ii, iii, v.—)

Herein is a *Figure* of the mighty and invincible *Power* of GOD; Who is the *Author* and *Governor* of all just *Policy* and *Kingdoms.* Here are also *two* principal *Duties* relating to *Magistrates, viz.* to be a Terror to those that do Evil, and encourage those that do Good; that the *Glory* may be given to GOD, Whose *Providence* ruleth over all the World. The *Wrath* of GOD is here compared to a Vessel of *Wine,* whereby the Wicked become so drunk, that they at last come to the very Dregs; which utterly destroys them; whilst the *Righteous* are *preserved,* and raised to Promotion and Honour.

(—Vide *Psal.* lvii. 1, 2, 3.—)

The PRECEPT.

{ *The* LORD *is* Judge, *and just are all his Ways;*
He puts down one, and doth another raise:
I'll bless His Name, *and His great* Pow'r *adore,*
And celebrate His Praise, *for evermore.* }

N. B. That whether this *Psalm* was composed by DAVID, and delivered to *Asaph,* or by *Asaph* himself, it is uncertain. But it appears most probably

bly to be written by DAVID himself, when he reigned in the City of *Hebron*, and was ready to receive the Kingdom of the whole Nation, by the Consent of all the *Tribes*: Or when *Abner* came peaceably to consult about removing the Remains of the Kingdom of *Saul* unto DAVID; else when it was performed by the ten *Tribes* themselves, after the Murder of *Ish-bosheth*. * See the *Scriptures* above quoted.

On PSALM LXXVI.

YOU have here another *Psalm*, or *Song* of ASAPH, directed to the chief Performer on the *Neginoth*; wherein is ¹ set forth the *Power* of GOD, and ⁴ His mighty *Defence* ⁸ and *Care* for His People in *Jerusalem*, by the Destruction of *Sennacherib*'s Army. He then ¹¹ exhorteth all the *Faithful* to thank and *Praise* GOD for the same; seeing He hath dealt so lovingly with His People.

*(—Vide *Psal.* xlvi. 1, 2, 3, 4. 11.—)*

We may infer from this *Psalm*, that GOD is able at all Times to *revenge* all Wrongs done to His *Church* and *People*; by Reason, all the Enemies thereof are not able to bring their Designs to pass, when GOD takes it in Hand to *defend* His People; for then are all the *Counsels* and Enterprises of Tyrants but foolish and vain. Herein are the *Gentiles* convinced, *taught*, and *converted*, and that from the *Wisdom* which CHRIST himself said, viz. *Divine Wisdom cannot be perceived of Flesh and Blood, without the Knowledge of the true* GOD, &c. So that the *true Church* may easily be known from all others, seeing that the *false one* is only feigned by *Hypocrites*, and tendeth only to *Folly* and *Ignorance*.

(—Vide Matt. xvi. 17.—1 Cor. xv. 50.—)

The PRECEPT.

{ Through all the World the Name of GOD *is known*;
CHRIST loves the Just; that His Salvation *own*:
Both Life, and Death, are in GOD's mighty Pow'r;
To save the Righteous, and His Foes devour. }

N. B. The xlvith *Psalm* was probably wrote on the same *Occasion* as this; it having some *Coherence* with it; which see *.

On PSALM LXXVII.

OUR *Author*, DAVID, directeth this *Psalm* to his chief Musician *Jeduthun*; wherein, in the Name of the *Church*, ¹ he rehearseth the Greatness of his *Afflictions*, and his grievous *Temptations*.

A New Exposition *of the* Book *of* Psalms, &c. 65

Temptations. Then [6] calling to Mind his former *Conversation,* and [11] the continual Course of GOD's *Works* in mercifully preserving His Servants; he fully [15] confirmeth his *Faith* against the like Afflictions and Temptations.

* (—Vide 2 *Sam.* xviii. 33.—xix. 1.—*Psal.* xxxix. lxii,—)

This precious *Psalm* teacheth, whensoever we undergo any grievous *Affliction,* or *Temptation,* to apply ourselves to *Prayer* and *Meditation*; till GOD, in his good Time, shall relieve us; and to call to Mind what great and marvellous *Works* He has done for His *Church,* and chosen People; which will afford us Comfort, in the Midst of our Afflictions. It also shews, that *Faith* and good *Works* are our only Anchor to trust to, in the Midst of all Storms and Dangers; and that as GOD brought His Children through the *Red Sea,* and turned the Waters again on their Enemies, so will He, in like Manner, destroy all the Enemies of His *Church*; and take His *chosen* People into the Kingdom of Heaven.

(—Vide *Exod.* xiv. 28, 29, &c.—)

The PRECEPT.

{ *To think on Thee,* O LORD, *my Heart incline*;
Teach me Thy Precepts, *and Thy* Laws *divine*:
For, Thou the Righteous *guard'st on ev'ry Side,*
And, as a Shepherd, *dost them* rule *and guide.* }

N. B. Probably this *Psalm* was composed after many *Mercies* received; and in some extreme *Distresses* following; from the *Mercies* declared, *Prayers,* and GOD's hearing him: *Viz.* as when he was in *Exile,* and had the fresh Tidings of his Son *Absalom's* Death, &c. *See the above *Scriptures* quoted. Some say this *Psalm* was wrote by *Asaph,* and not by DAVID; but which was the right *Author,* it is not well known; neither is it very material, if it was known, since the Matter thereof is *instructive.*

On PSALM LXXVIII.

THIS *Maschil,* or *Psalm* of *Instruction,* was, by our holy DAVID directed to *Asaph,* wherein GOD's People are exhorted to *learn, teach,* and *keep* His *Law*; to trust in GOD, and [4] remember His mighty *Works,* [12] in bringing their Fathers through the *Wilderness,* and [13] the *Red Sea.* [24] How He rained *Manna* for them to eat, and [25] fed them with the Bread of *Angels*: [36] And how they were false, and flattered GOD, yet He considered they were but Flesh, and forgave them. [42] They then rebelled against GOD, and forgot His *Mercy*; so that [44] He sent His Judgments on *Egypt,* and in *Canaan,* where

F 3 [56] they

⁵⁶ they *rebelled* afresh, and ⁶⁵ were punished; until ⁶⁷ GOD again vindicated them, and ⁶⁹ built His *Sanctuary* among them; and ⁷¹ set DAVID, and His *Posterity*, to *guide* and rule over hem, being the Tribe of *Judah*, whom GOD loved.

—Vide *Deut*. vi. 7.—*Exod*. xiv. 21. 24.—xvii. 6.—*Numb*. xx. 11.—*Pfal*. cv. 6.—*Numb*. xi. 1.—*John* vi. 13.—*Wifd*. xi. 4.—1 *Cor*. x. 4.—*Gen*. xlix. 3.—*Josh*. xi. 6.—xiii. 6.—1 *Sam*. iv. 10.—)

From this excellent historical *Pfalm* we see, in a few Words, the Effect of the *History* of the *Bible*, comprehending the Sum of GOD's *Mercies* and *Benefits* to His People, conveyed to the *Author* by the Infpiration of the *Holy Ghost*; in order that GOD's *Mercies*, on His chofen People, might never be forgotten, throughout all Ages to come.

(—Vide *Pfal*. xxxii.—*Rom*. ii. 12, 13.—xvi. 25.—)

The PRECEPT.

{ *In Times of Old*, GOD's *mighty* Works *were shewn*,
To Ifr'el's Race, who did His Mercy *own*:
So let me, LORD, *in* Gratitude *confefs*
Thy SON *my* Saviour, *and my Righteoufnefs*. }

N. B. This *Pfalm* was probably compofed by *Solomon*, as a *Memorial* to the People, when he had eftablifhed the *Worfhip* of the Temple: Commemorating the feveral *Paffages* of *Divine Providence* refpecting *Ifrael's* Afflictions in *Egypt*, until the Building of the *Temple*, for above 480 Years, *&c*. See 1 *Kings* vi. 1—2 *Chron*. iii. 1. and the *Scriptures* before quoted *.

※·※※※※※※※※※※※※※※※※※※※※※※※

On PSALM LXXIX.

THE Pfalmift ASAPH, in this *Pfalm*, fetteth forth, as it were, ¹ the grievous Complaints of the *Ifraelites* unto GOD, for what Oppreffion they had fuffered, by the Enemies of GOD, in His *Temple*, *City*, and *People*. ² How they had deftroyed them, and given their Flefh to the Beafts and Fowls of the Air; and ⁴ reproached them. ⁶ He then prayeth to GOD to pour out His *Wrath* on their Enemies, ⁸ to blot out their former Iniquities, and ⁹ to have *Mercy* on them; that ¹² their cruel Enemies might no longer terrify them; whereby they ¹³ might *Praife* His mighty Name, and *fing* of His *Glory*, for ever and ever.

* (—Vide *Jer*. x. 25.—2 *Kings* xxv.—2 *Chron*. xxxvi.—*Jer*. lii.—*Ifai*. lxiv.—*Dan*. ix.—)

A New Exposition on the Book of Psalms, &c. 67

The *Author* herein sheweth what Extremities G O D often suffereth His *Church* and People to fall under, only to prove their *Faith* and Constancy; before He puts forth His Hand to deliver them; for herein their very Friends durst not bury the Dead, for Fear of their Enemies. And, although they were of the *Seed* of *Abraham*, many of them were quite degenerate, and their greatest Enemies; and laughed at their *Religion*. And, though, in Respect to G O D, they were justly punished for their Sins; yet, in Consideration of their *Cause*, they were unjustly murdered. But, what could they look for else but *Ruin*, and even *Death* itself, when they were *Captives* among such cruel Enemies? Seeing then we have now nothing to trust to, but the *Power* and *Mercy* of G O D, and the Merits of His Son, *JESUS CHRIST*; how ought we to remain in *Faith* and good Works; and to daily *Praise* His great and holy Name for all the *Mercies* and *Benefits* we receive at His Hands, in whom we *hope* for eternal Salvation.

(—Vide *Isai*. xliii. 11. 21.—)

The PRECEPT.

{
L O R D, *give to me Thy saving Health and* Grace,
Pardon my Faults, *and all my Sins deface* :
Then shall I Praise *Thy great and mighty* Name,
And teach *all Nations to perform the same.*
}

N. B. Though on the Head of this *Psalm Asaph* is called the *Author*, yet it was more probably wrote by either *Daniel*, *Jeremiah*, or *Zachariah*; after *Jerusalem*'s Devastations and the Captivity of *Babylon* nearly expired; as *Isaiah* prophetically prayed and complained of, above 150 Years before those Things came to pass. * *Psal*. lxxiv. was on the same Occasion.—See *Dan*. ix.

❧:❀❧❀❧❀❧❀❧❀❧❀❧❀❧❀❧❀❧❀❧❀❧❀❧:❧

On PSALM LXXX.

*S*Hemaiah, the *Author* of this *Psalm* of *Prayer*, directs it to the chief Performer on *Shoshannim-eduth*, or to *Asaph*; wherein he ¹ imploreth G O D's Attention, and then ⁴ *prays* for Him to help the ⁵ *Miseries, Sufferings,* ⁶ and *Reproaches* of His *Church* and People; desiring Him ⁸ to consider their *first State*, when ⁹ His Favour shined towards them; and ¹² expostulates with His *Severity* towards them. He then ¹⁴ begs of G O D to return, and visit His *Church*, and ¹⁹ to re-establish it, and *finish* what He first begun; whereby His *People* might for ever call on His *Name*, and be *saved*.

(—Vide 1 *Kings* xiv.—2 *Chron*. xii.—)

This *Psalm* was made as a *Prayer* for the ten *Tribes*, to call upon G O D for Mercy; and to move their Hearts to *worship* G O D rightly in the Place appointed; whereby all the *Tribes* and People might be joined together again. It
also

also shews that *Repentance* only cometh of GOD; and that none can call on GOD, unless they are *regenerate* by the *Holy Spirit*, and raised from Death to *Life* by the Merits of *JESUS CHRIST*: Whereby we obtain *Forgiveness* of our Sins, and everlasting Life.

The PRECEPT.

{ O LORD, *Whose* Seat *is in the Heav'ns above*,
Send down *Thy* Beams of MERCY, *and Thy* Love:
Direct our Hearts, we on Thy Aid *rely*;
Shew us Thy Face, *and we shall never die.* }

N. B. This *Psalm* was probably composed after holy DAVID's mighty Conquests, and the Temple built; and yet abiding for some great *Calamity* sustained; which was the *Invasion* and Pillaging by *Shishak;* It being a *Prayer* for the *Church* by *Shemaiah;* who prophesied its *Punishment* and *Mitigation.* * See the *Scriptures* above quoted.

On PSALM LXXXI.

THIS is said to be a *Psalm* of MOSES, directed to the best Performer on the *Gittith*, (an Instrument brought from *Gath*;) which *Psalm* containeth, [1] An *Exhortation* to *Praise* GOD solemnly, with *Heart*, [2] *Voice*, and [3] *Instrument*, for all His gracious *Benefits*, and Divine *Providences.* GOD Himself is here [8] said to *call* unto the People, to *serve* Him only as the *true* GOD; [10] naming His Wonders wrought in *Egypt*; and that their Lusts [13] and Perverseness, which they gave themselves wholly up to, and their Enemies, had deprived them of the *Blessings* of *Canaan*.

(—* Vide *Exod.* xiv. 17.—xix. 20.—xxxii.—*Numb.* xiv.—)

This *Psalm* seems to be appointed for solemn *Feasts* and *Assemblies* of the People, to *Praise* GOD, and *remember* His *Works*. GOD is herein said to speak in Person to the People, because He is their only *Guide*; and that they are never able to give Him sufficient *Thanks* for their Deliverance from their corporal Bondage; and much less WE, for His *spiritual Deliverance* from *Satan*'s Tyranny, and our Sins; by the Merits of His SON *JESUS CHRIST.* He also herein condemneth all *false Assemblies* that are not attentive to hear His WORD, and keep it; and obey not His Call in the Holy *Scriptures*; nor yet return *Thanks* for the *Benefits* He so freely bestows on them. Hence let *us* be always mindful of H's *Word*, and obey His *Commands* in the Holy *Scriptures*; that our Names be not blotted out of the BOOK of Life; whereby we may, after this Life, enjoy the *full Fruition* of His holy *Kingdom*.

The

A New Exposition *on the* Book *of* Psalms, *&c.*

The PRECEPT.

{ *On solemn* Days Praise GOD *with one Consent,*
And, to your Voices, *join the* Instrument :
By Jacob's *Law, all should in Concert* sing,
To Praise *the* LORD, *and* CHRIST, *Our heav'nly* King. }

N. B. This *Psalm* so plainly agrees with the *History* of *Israel*, in the Wilderness, and with the *Words* and *Phrases* in the *Scriptures* above-mentioned *, that they plainly shew *Moses* to be the *Author*, (and not *Asaph*, as some pretend) when they refused to go up against the *Canaanites*; and were all sentenced to abide in the Wilderness, *&c.* See the *Scriptures* above quoted.

On PSALM LXXXII.

HOLY DAVID directed this *Psalm* to *Asaph*, wherein he sheweth ¹ That GOD is always present amongst *Judges, Magistrates,* and *Ministers* of the *Law* ; and ² threateneth their *Partiality :* And exhorteth them all to *judge* righteously, and not *unjustly* ; but to deliver the *Poor* and *Fatherless* from the Hands of the Wicked ; desiring GOD to undertake the Matter and execute *Justice* Himself, when the *Law* is perverted.

* (—Vide 1 *Sam.* xxiv.—*Psal.* lviii.—)

We may infer from this *Psalm*, that every Man can *judge*, though he not *judgeth*, i. e. every one can judge of a Matter, but not judge rightly to do *Justice* ; by Reason it too often happens, that *Thieves* and *Murderers* meet with *Favour* in Judgment. when the *Fatherless* and *poor* just Man's *Cause* is not heard; especially where *Bribery* perverteth *Judgment*. This is too often the Case, when *false Witnesses* are concerned; who will not only sell Men's Blood for *Gain*, but their own Souls into the Bargain: And that the Poor, for Want of Money, are little regarded, be their Cause ever so right.—But, alas! no *Titles* nor *Honours* can screen such Wickedness from the *all-seeing* Eye of GOD, nor save them from the Almighty's just Judgment at the last Day ; for they must render an *Account* of their *Works* as well as meaner Men. Then happy will they be that have *judged righteously*, and *suffered wrongfully :* For Vengeance is the LORD's, and He will surely repay it ; and reward all Men according to their Works.

(—Vide *Psal.* xciv. 1. 15. 21. 23.—)

The PRECEPT.

{ *Let earthly* Judges *make not righteous* Laws
A Trick for Gain, *let* Justice *rule the* Cause :
Protect the Poor, *for* GOD's *impartial Eye*
Surveys all Hearts, *and will all* Actions *try.* }

N. B. This

N. B. This *Psalm* seems to be DAVID's peaceful Appeal, or Conclusion, on the Occasion of *Saul's* unrighteous Judgment, and cruel Execution of the Priests *; as was also *Psal.* lviii. See the *Scriptures* above quoted

On PSALM LXXXIII.

*J*Ebaziel directed this *Psalm* to *Asaph*, wherein (in the Name of the People of *Israel*) he ¹ earnestly prayeth unto GOD to deliver them from ² the haughty, ³ crafty, cruel, and general Combination of their Enemies, both ⁵ at Home, and ⁸ afar off; who imagined nothing but their Destruction. They ¹³ then desire that such wicked People might be stricken with the Storms and ¹⁴ *Tempests* of GOD's accustomed Wrath; whereby they ¹³ may know the Power and Glory of GOD.

* (—Vide 2 *Chron.* xx. 1. 14.—*Judg.* vii. 21.—iv. 15.—vii. 25.—viii. 21.—)

This *Psalm* was composed as a Form of Prayer against the Dangers of the Church in the Days of *Jehoshaphat*; shewing that the Wicked are GOD's Enemies, who shall surely be cut off; and that the Righteous are His chosen People, whom He hideth in secret, in His holy Tabernacle, to preserve them from all Dangers. The Wickedness of the *Ammonites*, and the *Moabites*, is also here described; who provoked other Nations to fight against the *Israelites*, although they were their Brethren. Hence we may see, that all who are confirmed to GOD, and trust in HIM, are never utterly destroyed; and, where His true Church is, there He abideth also, Whose Glory is made manifest by destroying the Wicked, and His Mercy never fails to deliver the Just.

(—Vide *Dan.* ix. 9.—)

The PRECEPT.

When GOD *does strike the Wicked with His Rod,*
Feeling His Stripes, *they own that He is* GOD:
So purge me, LORD, *from ev'ry secret Sin,*
That I, through CHRIST, *may sure* Salvation *win.*

N. B. The Matter of this *Psalm* is so agreeable to *Jehoshaphat's* Prayer in the *Scripture* above quoted *, that there can be no Dispute of *Jehaziel* being the Author.

On PSALM LXXXIV.

1023. HOLY DAVID directed this *Psalm* to the best Performer on the *Gittith*, for the Sons of *Korah*; wherein he ¹ greatly shews what ardent *Desire* he has to come again

again into the *Public Worship* of GOD in the *Tabernacle*, to join in His *Praises*, with the holy *Assembly* of the *Saints*. He then ⁴ shews the *Blessedness* of those that are in the *Worship* of GOD, and the Happiness they enjoy in *Praising* Him; and ⁶ greatly praiseth the Courage of the People, that pass through the Wilderness, to assemble themselves in *Sion* : Shewing thereby, ¹⁰ that the *Worship* and *Praises* of GOD, in the Church, are more valuable than all else the World affords; and ¹¹ that GOD's *Grace* is a sure Shield and *Defence* to the Godly; and that ¹² He will surely *bless* all such as trust in Him.

* (—Vide 2 *Sam*. xix.—*Psal*. xlii.—*Psal*. cxxv.—)

Our holy *Author* herein shews that the *Church* is the only Place for the *Worship* and *Praises* of GOD; and although he was chaced from it by cruel *Saul*, and his own Son *Absalom*, yet his *Heart* was always with them. He then, having no settled Place, thought the very *Birds* were better than he, in such Cases; yet he trusted in nothing but GOD, by whose *Mercy* and *Power* he learned to rule his Life. He sheweth also that though GOD's People pass through the *Valley of Baca*, or a Wilderness only of *Mulberry-Trees*, and are forced to make themselves *Wells* for Water, or dig *Pits*, yet GOD will never fail them : Which *Similitude* plainly shews, that nothing will hinder GOD's People from His *Church*, if they take Delight in His Worship; and that they will undergo any Hardship for *CHRIST*'s Sake ; in Hopes that He will *increase* His *Blessings* more and more towards them; which is preferable to all the Enjoyments of worldly Men.

The PRECEPT.

{ He's surely bless'd *that doth in* GOD *delight,*
Resorts to Church, *and serves Him Day and Night:*
For why? the LORD *will sure His* Flock *defend,*
And give them Joys *that never shall have End.* }

N. B. This *Psalm* was probably wrote when the xliid was, when DAVID was about returning to *Jerusalem*, after his quelling *Absalom*'s Insurrection. See the *Scriptures* above quoted *.

On PSALM LXXXV.

THE *Author*, holy DAVID, composed this *Psalm* for the Sons of *Korah*; wherein he ¹ calls to Rememberance the mighty *Deliverance* of the *Israelites*; and acknowledges GOD's singular *Mercy*, in restoring them after the Captivity; whereby the Work of His *Grace* was completed. They then ⁵ complain of their long Affliction; and ⁷ beg of GOD to shew them

them *Mercy*; and [9] rejoice in the *Hope* of His *Promise*; with [12] Assurance thereof.

* (—Vide *Ezra* iv.—*Nehem.* iv. 6.—)

Herein is shewed that GOD's free *Mercy* was the Cause of their *Deliverance*; not only in withdrawing His Scourge, but in *forgiving* their Sins also; and that He so touched their Hearts as to make them *confess* them, and own His *Goodness*. From this we may infer, that our *Salvation* cometh only of GOD's *Mercy*; and that He will send *Prosperity* to His *Church*, when He has sufficiently corrected them: And that His Punishments are inflicted on the *Faithful*, only to *deter* them from the like Offences for the future. This *Deliverance* is also a Figure of CHRIST's *Kingdom*, wherein shall be perfect *Felicity*. And that although the *Faithful* are punished here for a Time, to try their Constancy in CHRIST, yet if they remain unshaken in their Faith, and in good Works, they sha'l surely enjoy His *Peace* in the *End*: For the *Justice* of GOD shall flourish in every Place, and His Mercy shall shine on all that *trust* in Him.

(—Vide 2 *Cor.* i. 3.—)

The PRECEPT.

GOD *to His People hath been wond'rous kind,*
Redeemed Souls should bear His Love *in Mind :*
Think, O *my Soul, on* CHRIST, *and Him adore,*
In Hallelujahs, *now, and evermore.*

N. B. This *Psalm* seems to be written after the *Captivity*, under some fresh Oppositions made against their *Worship*, and Safety in their own Land; which might, probably, be the Endeavours against rebuilding the *Temple*; which lasted above thirty Years. See the *Scriptures* above quoted *.

✦✦✦✦✦✦✦✦✦✦✦✦✦✦

On PSALM LXXXVI.

DAVID, in this *Psalm* of *Prayer* being sorely afflicted and forsaken, [1] prayeth to GOD for *Audience*, and [3] for *Mercy*; and [5] rehearsing the *Miseries*, and *Mercies* he had received, he [11] *prays* to GOD for *Direction*, whereby he might both *fear*, and *glorify* His Name. He then [14] sorely complains of his *proud* Adversaries; and [16] *prays* to GOD to have *Mercy* on Him, and [17] deliver Him out of their cruel Hands; whereby they might be ashamed of their Cruelty, and he himself be comforted.

* (—Vide 1 *Sam.* xvii, xviii, xix, xxi, xxii, &c—)

Our holy *Author*, being cruelly persecuted by *Saul*, leaveth this *Psalm* of *Prayer* to the *Church*, as an *Example* how to seek Redress against their cruel Enemies; shewing that he was not at any Enmity with his Adversaries, but that he rather
pitied

pitied them; though they were not only cruel againſt him, but againſt GOD alſo. This was a ſure Token that he believed that GOD would ſurely deliver him; becauſe he well knew His *Mercy* and former Goodneſs to His own People; even to all ſuch as *prayed* in the Name of *CHRIST*, and believed He ſhould come to be their *Judge*, *King*, and *Saviour.* From hence we are taught always to join ourſelves unto *CHRIST,* and to believe in Him; and, though cruel Tyrants torment and vex us, let us truſt that He will deliver us out of their deſperate Hands; foraſmuch as we know, by Him, that there *there is a certain Reward for the Righteous,* when *CHRIST* ſhall come to *judge* the Earth.

(—Vide *Pſal.* lviii. 11.—*Mat.* v. 12.—)

The PRECEPT.

{ Hear me, O LORD, in Thee I put my Truſt;
O join my Heart to Thee, O GOD moſt Juſt!
Thou, LORD, art kind, and all Thy Gifts are free,
And art a loving SAVIOUR unto me. }

N. B. We may gather from hence, that many Perſons now-a days are as cruel to the *Righteous* as *Saul* and his Adherents, who ſought the Life of holy DAVID; elſe our *Church* would not be in ſuch a State of *Jeopardy* as it now is. See the *Scriptures* before quoted *.

✽✽✽✽✽✽✽✽✽✽✽✽✽✽✽✽✽✽✽✽✽✽✽✽✽✽✽✽✽✽✽✽✽

On PSALM LXXXVII.

IN this *Pſalm,* our holy Author, DAVID, (in the Name of the *Holy Ghoſt,*) promiſeth¹ that the *Church* ſhall be eſtabliſhed for GOD's Public Worſhip on ³ *Mount-Moriah,* in *Jeruſalem,* after the Captivity of *Babylon*; although ⁴ it ſeemed to be as then in Miſery; and that there ſhould be nothing more comfortable to them, than ⁶ to be counted the *Members* thereof; wherein ⁷ they ſhould *Praiſe* GOD with both Voices and Inſtruments.

* (—Vide 2 *Sam.* xxiv. 18 — 2 *Chron.* xxi.—xxii. to xxix.—)

¹Herein are ſhewed the great Fruits of *Patience*; for, although the glorious *State* of the *Temple* of GOD did not juſt then appear, yet, on their waiting on GOD with Patience, He ſoon accompliſhed His *Promiſe*: For He fixed it on the Hills, very convenient for *Egypt,* and other Countries; in order that they might come to the Knowledge of GOD. From this we may infer, that all that are *regenerate,* and born again unto *CHRIST,* ſhall, by *Faith,* and *Good Works,* ſurely be ſaved: And although they come from all Quarters of the World, into *CHRIST's* CHURCH, they ſhall ſurely be called as *Citizens*; not only as *Members* of His earthly *Church,* but be *Partakers* of the *Kingdom* of Heaven, where the *Praiſes* of GOD have no End.

The Precept.

{ GOD *loves the* Church, *and doth therein abide*,
Adores *it more than any* Place *beside* :
The Joys *of* Heav'n *do here in* Plenty *spring*,
From Instruments, *and such as* Praises *sing*. }

N. B. The former Part of this *Psalm* very possibly alludeth to the *Place* where GOD had appointed His *Temple* to be built: And had revealed unto DAVID its *Splendor* and perpetual *Continuance.* See the *Scriptures* before cited *.

On PSALM LXXXVIII.

THIS is a *Maschil* or instructive *Psalm* of *Prayer* composed by HEMAN, and directed to the best Performer on the *Mahalath-Leannoth*, (the Name of an ancient Wind *Instrument* or *Tune* ;) for the Sons of *Korah*. Herein he [1] earnestly prayeth to GOD to hear him, being [4] grievously afflicted with *Sickness*, [6] *Persecution*, and [8] *Adversity*. He then [10] expostulates with GOD concerning the *Dead* ; [13] calleth on GOD by his Faith ; and striveth against Despair : Shewing [18] how his Lovers, Friends, and Acquaintance forsook him in the Midst of his Troubles.

* (—Vide 1 *Chron.* ii. 4.—1 *Kings* iv. 31.—*Psal.* v. 3.—)

This *Psalm* is a worthy *Example* for us to follow, when under any *Afflictions* ; directing us, always to *pray* to GOD earnestly, if we expect *Remedy* and *Salvation*. And although we are thrown down by *Afflictions*, and are counted as *Dead*, by Reason we are not able to be any ways profitable to the *Living*, in this World ; yet, if we put our whole *Trust* and Confidence in GOD, He is able to restore us, when all our *Friends*, in this World, have given us over and forsaken us. This also shews, that it is our only Time to call on GOD to *save* us, while we are in this World ; by Reason there is nothing to be done after Death, by us, towards our Salvation. neither in the Grave, nor yet at the Day of Judgment : *There being neither Knowledge, nor Wisdom, nor Device in the Grave, whither thou goest:* No! nothing but GOD's *Mercy* will then do us any Good towards the Kingdom of Heaven.

(—Vide *Eccles.* ix. 10.—*Psal.* vi. 5.—)

The Precept.

{ Give Ear, O LORD, *to my Complaint and Cry* ;
Thou art my Hope, *in Thee I trust* : *For why?*
The Dead *Thy Wonders can no Ways display* ;
LORD, *teach me Thee to* love—*and to* obey. }

N. B. That

N. B. That *Psalm* was composed by *Heman*, the *Ezrahite*; he being the Head of the *Family* of *Zarat*; and, with *Ethan*, were very famous for Wisdom, in the Days of DAVID and *Solomon*. See the *Scriptures* above quoted *. *Leannoth* signifies the VOCAL *Part*, to answer the Instrument.

On PSALM LXXXIX.

IN this *Maschil*, or *Psalm* of *Instruction*, *Ethan*, the Prophet, ¹ greatly *Praiseth* GOD for the certain Truth of His Covenant with DAVID; for His great ² *Mercy*, ⁵ *Truth*, ⁸ *Holiness*, ¹¹ *Power*, ¹⁴ *Justice*, and general *Providence* over him, and the *Faithful*. He then ¹⁵ shews the *Blessedness* of all those that rejoice and *Praise* GOD, and trust wholly in Him; especially ²⁰ unto DAVID, His Chosen and *Anointed*; and ²⁷ to his *Seed* and Kingdom, so long as they kept His *Statutes*. He then ³⁸ complains of the great *Ruin* and *Desolation* of the Kingdom of DAVID; so that ⁴² in all outward Appearance GOD had failed in His *Promise*; but ⁴⁶ by his earnestly *praying* to GOD for Deliverance from his Afflictions, and ⁴⁸ by mentioning the Shortness of his Life, confirmed himself otherwise; ⁵² whereby he *Praiseth* GOD.

* (—Vide 2 *Chron*. xii.—2 *Sam*. vii. 12. 17.—)

Our *Author* seems in this *Psalm* to personate holy DAVID, not only in the public *State* of His *Kingdom*, but also the State of the *Church*: Shewing that on GOD's *Promise* he grounded all his *Faith*; and that the very Angels *Praised* GOD for delivering the *Church*, as well as all *Nations*; He being both a merciful *Father*, and a powerful *Protector* unto all His People. He also shews, that what Power our *King* hath to defend us, is by the *Gift* of GOD, unto His Chosen and Anointed; and, though he meet with ever so many Enemies, He will surely *defend* him, according to His *Promise*, so long as he and his People remain *constant*, and trust in Him. Herein is also a Figure of *CHRIST* to come; and that, though His Kingdom seemed to be decayed by the People's Sins, yet a Root should remain to fulfil GOD's Promise, to continue as long as the Moon endureth. So let us always hold up a good Heart against all the Opposers of our *Church* and and *Religion*; and trust wholly on GOD's *Promise*; waiting with Patience under all Afflictions, till the Coming of the LORD *JESUS*, who will wipe all the Tears from our Eyes.

The PRECEPT.

{ *How* bless'd *are they that can in* GOD *rejoice*,
And sing *His* Praise, *with* Heart, *and chearful* Voice!
Their Hope *and* Glory *in the* LORD *doth lie*,
And they in Heav'n *shall be exalted high*. }

N. B. This

N. B. This *Pfalm* was probably wrote by *Ethan*, when the ten *Tribes* revolted, *Rehoboam* degenerated, and *Shishak* wasted *Judea*, and plundered the *Temple*: He then striving to comfort them by the *Faith* of GOD's *Promise**.

End of the THIRD BOOK.

On PSALM XC.

THIS *Pfalm* is the *Prayer* of MOSES, (the Man of GOD,) wherein he ¹ setteth forth the eternal *Favour* of GOD to His People; and greatly bewails ³ the Shortness, ⁵ *Vanity*, ⁸ *Sins*, and ¹⁰ *Miseries* of Man's Life. He then ¹² *prayeth* for GOD to turn our Hearts to *Wisdom*, ¹⁴ fill us with His *Mercy*, ¹⁵ *comfort* us in Affliction, and ¹⁷ *prosper* our Endeavours for ever and ever.

* (—Vide *Deut.* i. 3.—*Josh.* iii.—)

We are herein taught that GOD had chosen us to be His People before the Foundation of the World. He also shews us that Man's *Life* is but as a *Watch* of three Hours, in Comparison to a thousand Years with GOD; and that we are taken away as in a Moment when we think not. That for our Sins GOD shorteneth our Days, and that, if we arrive but to *fourscore* Years, our Days will be only a Trouble to us. Therefore we should always *meditate* on the Length of our Days, that we may apply our Hearts to true *Wisdom*; whereby we may attain the Kingdom of Heaven: Forasmuch as GOD hath promised, by His *Mercy*, to save all such as *trust* in Him.

(—Vide *Eccles.* xii.—)

The PRECEPT.

{ *As* Time *slides on, and all Things change their State,*
So passes Life *unto its final* Date:
LORD, *fix my Heart always to think on* This,
And, surely, I shall never do amiss. }

N. B. The *Title* of this *Pfalm* shews MOSES to be the Author; and wrote on *Israel*'s Sentence; or when the Rebel Generation that came from *Egypt* were quite wasted away: And their *Posterity*; (newly numbered and prepared on the Banks of *Jordan*,) were *new reformed* to the *Law*, by *Moses*: Who after his Death were to go into *Canaan*. See the *Scriptures* before cited *.

On PSALM XCI.

THIS *Pfalm* ¹ shews the *happy State* of the *Godly*, from their *Confidence* in GOD: And ³ that He will *defend* them from the Snares of all Enemies. That ¹² He will give His
Angels

Angels Charge over them, ¹³ in all *Dangers* and *Temptations*; and that ¹⁵ He will *hear* and *deliver* them out of all Troubles, that they may *glorify* His Name for their eternal *Salvation*.

(—Vide *Rom.* xvi. 20.—)

Hence we may obferve, that if we *truft* in GOD, and fervently *pray* to Him, He will keep us from all the *Temptations* of *Satan*; and will have a faithful *Care* over us in all Kinds of Danger: He having appointed certain *Angels* to be as *Minifters* of His Divine *Providence*, to keep His People; and to defend them in their feveral *Vocations*, for the very fame End. Hence let us all fhelter ourfelves under the Wings of GOD's *Mercy* and *Protection*; and be contented in our feveral *Stations*, wherein He has placed us, in this Life: Forafmuch as we know, that the Shortnefs and Troubles of this Life will be furely recompenfed with Immortality, by the Merits of His Son *JESUS CHRIST*.

(—Vide *Rom.* ii. 6, 7.—*Matt.* iv. 6. laft Part.—)

The PRECEPT.

{ *Come*, LORD, *and give to us Thy bounteous Grace*,
That we, with Thee, *may have a heav'nly* Place :
From Thee *and* CHRIST *Salvation only fprings*,
O fhade us under Thy Almighty Wings. }

N. B. The *Author*, and *Occafion* of this *Pfalm*, are unknown to me at prefent.

※※※※※※※※※※※※※※※※※※※※※※※※※※

On PSALM XCII.

THIS *Pfalm* was compofed for the *Sabbath-Day*, in Order ¹ to ftir up the Congregation to acknowledge ² GOD's *Loving-kindnefs*; and ⁴ to be *glad* in His *Works*. It fhews alfo ⁶ how ignorant the Wicked are of GOD's manifold *Works*, *Mercies*, and *Praifes*; and ⁹ how they fhall furely be deftroyed in their Iniquities; and ¹⁰ that the *Godly* fhall be exalted, and ¹⁴ *profper* throughout all Generations.

* (—Vide 1 *Sam.* xxiv. 16. 22.—)

This *Pfalm* teacheth us that the chief *Work* of the *Sabbath* is to *Praife* GOD for the *Mercies* we have received; and that His *Promifes*, *Mercies*, and Fidelity binds us all fo to do; both *Day* and *Night*: Alfo to *meditate* on His wonderous *Works*, and to *inftruct* one another, fo far as we are able; by Reafon we well know how *conftant* His *Judgments* are on the Wicked, that neglect fo great a *Duty*. We know alfo, how He will ftrengthen the *Faith* of fuch as feek after Him; and though the Righteous feem to wither for a little Time, yet GOD will raife them up at laft; and caufe them to flourifh, as the *Cedars* of *Lebanon*; and that their Children fhall have *Power* over the Wicked; and enjoy the Kingdom

78   *The* Pſalm-Singer*'s* Jewel: *Or,*

dom of Heaven, prepared for all ſuch as *worſhip* and *Praiſe* Him, with a free *Heart,* and with a willing *Mind.*

(—Vide *Rom.* xv. 5, 6. 33.—)

The P R E C E P T.

{ O Praiſe *the* L O R D *for his aſſiſting* Grace,
For *He's our* Guard, *in ev'ry* Time *and* Place :
When ye lie *down, for His Aſſiſtance pray,*
And Praiſe *Him,* riſing, *at the dawning* Day. }

•N. B. This *Pſalm* ſeems to be wrote by DAVID ; it hinting at *Saul*'s Declining, and his own Advancement to the *Kingdom* ; in which he was confirmed from *Saul*'s own Words ; and was acquitted from the Scandal of *Treachery* which he wrongfully had laid againſt him; on which he here *rejoiceth,* and giveth G O D *Praiſe.* See the *Scriptures* above cited *.

On P S A L M XCIII.

THIS *Pſalm* ſetteth forth the mighty Power of GOD by the Creation ¹ of the Heavens, ² the Earth, and ³ Waters ; Who ruleth over all, and by all His Name is magnified : and ⁵ for His merciful and loving Kindneſs to us, in giving us His holy *Word* and *Covenant,* which endureth for ever.

* (—Vide 2 *Sam.* viii.—*Pſal.* cxxxvi.—)

This *Pſalm* ſheweth unto us, that the invincible Power and Wiſdom of GOD formeth and governeth all Things, both in the Heavens, on the Earth, and in the Waters ; and is our only Defence in the Midſt of all Dangers, if we truſt in Him. He alſo, by His infinite Mercy, has beſtowed on us His moſt gracious Promiſe of Salvation, if we obey His Word, live in His Fear, and glorify His Name with holy Worſhip : Whoſe Promiſe is unchangeable, and endures for ever, and, for Whoſe gracious Gifts and Mercies, He cannot, by us, worthily be *Praiſed.*

(—Vide 1 *John* ii. 20.—)

The P R E C E P T.

{ *Thy* Seat, O L O R D, *within the Heav'ns was made,*
Before Thy Power *the* Earth's *Foundation laid :*
L O R D, *as Thy* Throne *abounds in* Righteouſneſs,
So guide *our* CHURCH, *and all Thy People* bleſs. }

N. B. Although no particular *Author* of this *Pſalm* is mentioned, yet it ſeems to me, from its *Style,* to be compoſed by holy DAVID, after he had ſubdued all the Nations by the *Power* and Command of GOD ; which tended to the *Glory* of G O D, and His own *Glory* likewiſe. See the *Scriptures* before cited *.

On PSALM XCIV.

Herein the *Author* ¹ earneftly *prayeth* unto GOD to take *Vengeance* on all the Wrongs he had received of his boafting, cruel, and blafphemous Enemies; and ³ reproves their futilous or foolifh *Notions* of GOD. He then fheweth that ¹¹ GOD certainly knows all the vain Thoughts of Man; and ¹² owns GOD's *Corrections* on the Righteous to be *Bleffings*; by Reafon ¹⁴ He *faveth* them at laft; and deftroyeth all the Wicked. He alfo fhews ¹⁶ that none can withftand the *Power* of GOD; and that ¹⁸ He was his only Help and *Comfort*, ²² under the *Afflictions* of all his cruel Enemies; and that He would ²³ affuredly deftroy them for their own *Malice*, and wicked Imaginations..

* (—Vide 2 Sam. xxi. to xxx.—Rom. xv. 4.—)

This *Pfalm* fhews that *Vengeance* only belongs to GOD, and not to Man; therefore we fhould not take His facred *Power* and *Office* out of His Hands; for He is a *juft Judge*, and will furely repay it. This alfo foretells the Danger of *proud*, haughty, and malicious Men, who, not only think themfelves above other Men, but alfo above GOD; and daily ftrive to deftroy both His *Church* and *People*. And though they vainly think GOD never fees their wicked Deeds, they are greatly miftaken, for His *all feeing Eye* knows every *Word* and *Deed*, and will accordingly reward them: And will have a fpecial Care over the *Righteous*. And fhould even wicked *Judges* themfelves pretend it *Juftice* to deftroy the *Church* of GOD, their Defigns would come all to nought; by Reafon GOD is above their earthly Power: And when all their Counfels fail, then GOD's *Judgments* are fure to be againft them; Who will *furely* reward all the Wrongs of the *Righteous*, and *punifh* the Wicked, that His *Name* may be glorious.

The PRECEPT.

{ *Seek not* Revenge *for ev'ry trifling Wrong,*
For Vengeance *only doth to* GOD *belong:*
Each Thought, *and* Deed, *the* LORD *doth truly know,*
To fave the Juft,—*and Wicked overthrow.* }

N. B. This *Pfalm* muft certainly be DAVID's Style, and wrote by him, when he was perfecuted by cruel *Saul*, and was forfaken by all his *Servants*. See the *Scriptures* before cited *.

On PSALM XCV.

THIS *Pfalm* contains ¹ an earneft *Exhortation* to *Praife* GOD, and ² to *fing Pfalms* in His Prefence in the *Congregation*; ³ for His *Power*, Goodnefs, and *Government* of the World; and ⁷ for

His *Election* of His *Church*. It also * admonisheth us, not to follow the Hard-heartedness and Rebellion of our Forefathers, (in the Wilderness,) lest we " enter not into the Land of Promise, *&c.*

* (—Vide *Deut.* i. 10.—*Num.* xiv.—2 *Sam.* viii.—)

Our holy *Author* herein shews, that G O D's *Worship* is not to be performed by dead *Ceremonies* only, but with *hearty Praises* and *Thanksgiving*; by Reason, as all Things are governed by G O D's *Providence*, so must all Men, from the Bottom of their Hearts, wholly give themselves up to His *Service*. And as He hath chosen us to be His *Flock*, we must obey His Voice in the Gospel; and not despise His *Divine Ordinances*, without Sense or Reason; nor rebel (as our Forefathers did,) against His sacred *Commands*; whereby we may enter into the *Rest* He has prepared for us, both in His *Church*, and in the Kingdom of Heaven.

(—Vide *Exod.* xvii. 1. 7.—*Num.* xiv. 22.—)

The PRECEPT.

{
To celebrate the Praises *of the* LORD,
In Psalms *and* Hymns, *sing ye with one Accord :*
For why? GOD *loves His* Saints, *and sure will* bless
All such as love the Paths *of Righteousness.*
}

N. B. This *Psalm* seems to be wrote by holy DAVID, to animate and call his *Subjects* chearfully to address themselves to G O D, during his perilous *Wars*, &c. See the *Scriptures* above cited *.

On PSALM XCVI.

THIS *Psalm* contains ' a precious *Exhortation* both to the *Israelites*, and 7 the *Gentiles* to *Praise* G O D; and 9 to *worship* His Name, *in the Beauty of Holiness*, for all His *Mercies* and *Benefits :* It also sheweth " that the very Heavens shall rejoice in His Name, and that the *Waters* 12 and *Fruits* of the Earth shall be joyful in His *Justice*, whereby He judgeth the whole World in Righteousness and in Truth.

* (—Vide 1 *Chron.* xv.—xxix.—*John* v. 39 —)

The *Doctrine* of this *Psalm* must now be referred to the Spreading of the *Kingdom of* CHRIST; by Reason, all Nations have just Cause to *Praise* GOD, for His sending His *Son* to reveal His *Gospel* to us. And as He will now *receive* all the *Faithful*, from all Nations, contrary to the Expectations in Times of old, how much the more ought *we*, His *chosen*, to *worship* Him contrary to their former Imaginations; and in that Manner as CHRIST Himself hath appointed, in His glorious Gospel! Who is sent to us, from GOD, for the very same Purpose, as was before told by His holy *Prophets*, by various Figures. And since the *Power* of

A New Exposition *on the* Book *of* Psalms, &c. 81

of GOD is manifestly shewn by His *Strength* and *Glory*, we cannot now plead any Ignorance on the *Worship* due to Him; He having, by *Regeneration*, and by the Merits of His SON *JESUS*, given us the Spirit of *Faith*, to work out our own Salvation. If then insensible *Creatures* shall have Cause to *rejoice* when GOD appeareth, how much more ought *we* to *rejoice* for the *Redemption* of our *Souls!* Hence, let us all well consider this, *and may the Lord give us Grace and Understanding.*

The PRECEPT.

{ *Let* Christians *all, with Heart and Voice, record*
The sacred Honours *of the heav'nly* LORD:
And let each tuneful Soul His Praise *express,*
And daily triumph *in His* Holiness. }

N. B. This *Psalm* seems to be wrote by DAVID, in *Praise* to GOD for *Victories* obtained; exhorting the subdued Heathens to submit to the *Government* of GOD in his *Kingdom*. See the *Scriptures* before cited *.

On PSALM XCVII.

Herein is ¹ a lively Description of *CHRIST's Kingdom*; ⁶ His *Glory*, and *Power*: And how dreadful it is to the *Worshippers* of *Idols*. It also ⁸ sheweth how *joyful* it is to the *Just*; and ¹⁰ exhorteth them to hate all Evil, and to do *Good*; whereby they may be *preserved* from the Hands of the Wicked: And *rejoice*, and ¹² *give Thanks* unto GOD, in Rememberance of His *Mercies* and *Benefits*.

(—Vide 1 *Chron.* xv.—xxix.—)

Herein is shewed that *CHRIST's Residence* is all *Felicity* and *spiritual Joy*; and that His *Gospel* should not only be preached in *Judea*, but throughout all Nations; in Order to keep all His Enemies in Fear of His mighty *Power*; and to bring the Wicked to a true *Obedience*, by His heavy *Judgments*, on all Idolaters. This is a precious Psalm for the *Meditation* of the *Godly*; here being figured *CHRIST's Divinity, Power, Humanity*, and even the Spreading of His *spiritual Kingdom* itself; as was foretold by the holy *Prophets*, and confirmed by *Himself*, and his holy *Apostles*. Here is also figured the *Exaltation* of the very *Person* of *CHRIST*; and GOD's *Word* made manifest to His *elect* and *chosen* People. Also the unspeakable *Joy* of *Conscience*, which was to follow; and the eternal *Salvation* of all such as are *justified* and *sanctified*, by attending and relying on the holy *Gospel*: By which all the *Righteous* may enjoy His holy Kingdom, to which it must be referred more than to any other *worldly* Transactions.

(—Vide *Heb.* i. 6.—*Mat.* xxviii. 18.—*Luke* xii. 49.—*John* xii. 32.—*John* xiv. 12.—*Eph.* iv. 10.—*Philip.* ii. 9.—iv. 4.—)

The Psalm-Singer's Jewel: *Or,*

The PRECEPT.

{ GOD's Grace *and* Light *springs daily to the* Just,
As love His Laws, *and on His* Mercies *trust :*
With Heart *and* Voice *His Holiness proclaim,*
And, as ye sing, *be mindful of the same.* }

N. B: This seems also to be wrote by holy DAVID, in *Praise* to GOD, for many *Victories* obtained; exhorting the subdued Heathens to submit to the *Government* of GOD, and his Kingdom. See the *Scriptures* before quoted *.

On PSALM XCVIII.

THE *Psalmist* here [1] exhorteth all *Israel*, with all Kinds of *Instruments* to *sing* and *Praise* GOD, for His *Power*, *Mercy*, and *Salvation* to them in His *Promise* by *JESUS CHRIST*. Also [7] that all *insensible* Creatures rejoice before the LORD for His *Righteousness*; because [9] *CHRIST* shall *judge* the whole World with *Equity* and *Truth*.

* (—Vide *Deut.* i. 10.—*Numb.* xiv.—2 *Sam.* viii.—*Isai.* lix. 16.—)

This *Psalm* varies but very little from the xcvth, being almost the same Words; *viz.* a Repetition of the *Prophecy* of the *Spreading* of the *Kingdom* of *CHRIST*; agreeing to those excellent *Hymns* of *Simeon, Zacharias,* and *Mary* the Mother of *CHRIST.* It also shews that *CHRIST* is our only *Mediator*, in the Work of our *Redemption;* and that this *Redemption* consisteth in the Justice of *CHRIST* Himself; and that all those *Mercies* and *Benefits* intirely flow from the free *Promise* and *Truth* of GOD Himself: For which *Performance,* we should give all the hearty *Praises* and *Thanksgivings* we are able; and that with all Kinds of Instruments; thereby meaning, that all the Tones of insensible *Creatures,* and Things joining with our *Voices,* are not able to *Praise* Him, as He worthily deserves, for the great and manifold *Blessings* He has so freely bestowed on us.

(—Vide *Luke* i. 46.—i. 68.—ii. 29.—)

The PRECEPT.

{ *Let ev'ry* Sound *now* Praise *the* LORD *of Might,*
Who all will judge *with Equity and Right :*
As CHRIST is now our new *and lasting* Song,
Think, O *my* Soul *!—what* He *for thee hath done.* }

N. B. Although this *Psalm* seems to be wrote by holy DAVID, in *Praise* for many *Victories* obtained, Heathens subdued to GOD's *Law,* and his Kingdom, *&c.* yet it must be referred to the Kingdom of *CHRIST;* which he then figured by his own *Life* and Transactions. See the *Scriptures* before cited *.

On

On PSALM XCIX.

WE have here set forth by the *Prophet*, ¹ a wonderful *Commendation* of the *Power*, *Equity*, and *Excellency* of the Kingdom of GOD, by *CHRIST*, over both the *Jews* and the *Gentiles*; exhorting ³ all to *Praise* and fear Him. He sheweth also ⁵ that all Nations shall *worship* GOD, and fall down before Him for all His *Mercies* and *Benefits*; and ⁸ for destroying all the wicked Inventions of the Enemies against His Church and People.

* (—Vide *Numb.* xiv.—2 *Sam.* viii.—)

This *Psalm* sheweth, that, whensoever GOD delivers His *Church* and People, all the Enemies thereof shall tremble; and that though the Wicked rage against GOD, yet the *Godly* shall *Praise* His mighty Name, and declare His Power. It also sheweth, that as *Moses*, *Aaron*, and *Samuel* were put in Office to *pray* to GOD for the People, so long as they remained in the *Priesthood*, as appointed by GOD Himself; even so should the People now *believe*, that GOD will *hear* them in like Manner as He had done those holy Men, in Times of old: And that all such as now desire to be heard, must follow the same *Faith* in *CHRIST JESUS*; which they foretold by the *Power* of GOD, and the *Spirit* of Prophecy. Seeing now that we have but one *Mediator*, *CHRIST JESUS*, let us wholly rely on Him, and His *Gospel*, for our *Salvation*; and daily consider what great Things the LORD hath done for us, and our Posterity: Unto Whom be all *Glory* and *Praise* for ever and ever.

(—Vide *Timothy* ii. 1.—*Mat.* xxvii. 39.—)

The PRECEPT.

{ On Cherubims GOD *reigneth over all*,
At His great POWER *all earthly* Princes *fall:*
He Justice *loves, and doth the* Just *defend*;
To His great NAME *be* Praises *without End.* }

N. B. * Though this *Psalm* seems to be wrote by DAVID, on his *Victories* obtained, &c. yet it must be referred to the *Kingdom* of *CHRIST*, of which he then foretold, as well as his own Success.

On PSALM C.

THIS *Psalm* contains ¹ a godly Exhortation for all People to *Praise* GOD chearfully, ³ for His *Greatness*, ⁵ for His *Mercy*, and for His *Truth*, which will endure to all Generations.

* (—Vide

84 *The* Pſalm-Singer's Jewel: *Or,*

* (—Vide 1 Sam. xvii, xviii, xix, xx, xxi, &c.—)

Though this *Pſalm* is very *ſhort*, yet it is very excellent; and was written to be uſed as a *Song* of *Praiſe* and *Thankſgiving* in general, in the Congregation: Whereby we may *Praiſe* G O D for all His *Mercies*. Herein is alſo figured the ſpiritual *Regeneration*, whereby we are called His *Sheep* and *People*; and that GOD is to be *worſhipped* only by that Means which He hath appointed in His *Goſpel*, by His Son *JESUS CHRIST*. Therefore, we muſt never be *weary* in well-doing, nor in *Praiſing* His holy Name for all the *Benefits* we receive of Him; ſeeing His *Mercies* towards us, and our *Poſterity*, have no End.

(—Vide *Pſal.* lxviii. 26. 32.—*Eph.* iv. 24.—)

The PRECEPT.

{ *To* Praiſe *the* LORD *let all the liſt'ning Earth*
Their Voices *raiſe, and* ſing *with awful Mirth:*
He all hath made, and over all doth reign,
His Truth *and* Mercy *ever ſhall remain.* }

N. B. This ſeems to be wrote by holy DAVID, and uſed as a *triumphant Song*, after any *Victory*, &c. Read the Chapters of *Samuel*, before cited *.

On PSALM CI.

PRincely DAVID, in this *Pſalm*, ¹ *Praiſeth* GOD for Ad*vancement*; and ² promiſeth to walk in perſonal *Integrity*, in his own Houſe; and that ³ no evil Perſon ſhall ever abide with him; neither the *Slanderer*, ⁵ nor the *Proud*. He ſheweth alſo ⁶ that he will encourage all ſuch as are *Good*; and that they only ſhould *ſerve* him: And that ⁷ both the *Lyar*, and the *Flatterer*, &c. ſhould not only be put out of his Houſe, but ſhould be puniſhed as the Wicked of the Land, and be cut off.

* (—Vide 2 *Sam.* ii. 1. 5.—*Exod* xxiii. 25.—*Joſh.* vii. 8.—1 *Chron.* xxviii. 9.— *Joſh.* xxiv. 15.—*Acts* xvi.—2 *Sam.* xiv. 18.—)

This *Pſalm* is a worthy *Pattern* to be obſerved in all *Families*, even from the *Throne* to the *Cottage*. Holy DAVID being juſt entered on his *Kingdom* in Hebron, and conſidering on the Faults of his Predeceſſor King *Saul*, reſolves to *live* in the *Fear of* GOD; and bind himſelf, and his Poſterity, as it were, in a ſolemn Vow to GOD to live *virtuouſly*; that his princely *Life* might not only be a worthy *Example* for all his *Subjects*, but for all *Princes*, *Governors*, and *Maſters* of *Families*. He firſt ſheweth, that the *Office* of a KING, is to *rule* with *Mercy* and *Judgment*, whereby he might be more *loved* than feared; and quell all the Deſigns of the Wicked by the *Laws* of GOD. And, as *Princes* are compelled, of Neceſſity, to have many others to aſſiſt in their *Counſels*, &c. he here reſolves not to receive any Man of an *evil Conſcience*; but that he will puniſh all *falſe Accuſers* even with *Death* itſelf; which are the general Poiſon of all Mankind: Nor will he ſuffer any *proud*, ambitious Man in his Preſence. He alſo vows to uſe no Manner of *Counſel* but what proceeds from honeſt, upright Men: That he
will

A New Exposition *on the* Book *of* Psalms, &c. 85

will be a *severe Judge* to the Wicked; and *a merciful Defender* of the *Godly:* whereby both his Kingdom might not only flourish, but that the *Church* of *CHRIST* might be defended, and *enlarged.* So let us all follow his noble *Example*, and say, with *Joshua, I and my House will serve the* LORD.

The PRECEPT.

{ *Let me of* Mercy, LORD, *and* Judgment *sing*,
And daily Praise *Thee, O my* GOD *and* King!
And let my House *for ever be inclin'd*
To Praise *and serve Thee with a willing Mind.* }

N. B. See the *Scriptures* above quoted *.

On PSALM CII.

THIS *penitential Psalm* of *Prayer* was probably appointed for the *Faithful*, during the seventy Years *Captivity* of *Babylon*; describing [1] a lamentable Mourning of the *Church*, representing more a dead Carcase, than a living Body. Then seeming [12] to have some little Hope of *Mercy* from GOD, by His *Promises*, and from [14] the *Prayers* of the People; they [18] appear more chearful: Shewing that GOD's *Praise* shall [22] be published in all Generations to come: And that His *Truth* shall continue for ever, and His *Praise* be glorious in all Nations, to all Posterity.

* (—Vide *Ezek.* xxxvii.—*Isai.* liv. lx.—*Jer.* xxiv. 12. 15.—xxix. 10. 12.— *Dan.* ix. 1 4. to 20.—*Mat.* xiii.—*Isai.* xxxiv. 11.—*Eph.* ii. 10.—*Heb.* ii. 10.—*John* i. 2.—)

This *Psalm* is a worthy *Prayer* for such as are afflicted, to pour forth their *Meditation* unto the LORD; and also shews how much the Afflictions of the *Church*, wounds the Hearts of the GODLY. It also shews, that, whatsoever we fail of our *Duty*, GOD is sure to keep His *Promise*, for which Reason we should wholly rely on Him for Help, under all Afflictions It shews likewise, that GOD is never more *Praised* than when *Religion* flourisheth, and the *Church* increaseth; which are chiefly accomplished under the Kingdom of *CHRIST*; and that their *Church* sorely lamented that they saw not the Time of *CHRIST*, as was promised. We see now, that, if all Things pass away, GOD's *Word* abideth, seeing He hath chosen His *Church*, and joined it to *CHRIST*, to continue for ever; by Whose *Mercies*, and *CHRIST's Merits*, we have sure Hopes of *Salvation*; if we live according to His Gospel, and abide in *Faith* and *good Works.* And since, by the *Promise*, and Power of GOD, our *Church* has the Conquest, and settled under *CHRIST*, let us never fall from the *Faith*, unto which we are called; but daily offer up our *Prayers, Praises*, and Thanksgivings to Him that sits on the Throne for ever.

The

The PRECEPT.

> LORD, *hear my* Pray'r, *and* guide *me in Thy* Truth,
> *And not, in* Sin, *destroy me in my* Youth:
> *And, as Thy* Mercy *doth for ever dure,*
> *Let* me, *and* mine, *abide for ever sure.*

N. B. The *Author of* this *Psalm* is not justly known, but it hints of *Sion* in her *Rubbish*, and *Restoration* approaching, when the Captivity were unloosing. Some imagine it to be wrote by *Daniel*, by Reason it agrees to the Time of his *Prayer*. See the *Scriptures* before cited *.

On PSALM CIII.

IN this *Psalm*, holy DAVID [1] greatly *Praiseth* GOD [2] for the *Pardon* of his Sins, [4] *Deliverances*, and [5] great *Bounty* to him; and [7] to his *Forefathers*. He also [13] shews what *Pity* GOD hath on His *Children*, by Reason of their Frailty; and [17] that His Loving-kindness will endure for ever, on the *Posterity* of the Righteous. He then [20] calleth on the very *Angels* to *Praise* GOD, as well as all others, that are the *Works* of the LORD; [22] and to all *Places* and *Dominions* to join with him, in that glorious *Part* of *Divine Worship*.

(—Vide *Psal.* cxlviii. 2. 14.—*Eph.* iv. 24.—)

This glorious *Psalm* of *Praise* was written by holy DAVID, as a *Thanksgiving* to GOD for *Recovery* and *Redemption*; the *Covenant of Grace*, and for all other *Mercies* and *Benefits*; and in *Commemoration* of the *Gospel* of *CHRIST*; concluding with a most magnificent *Description* of His Divine *Majesty*. It also shews that he counted himself but as dead, before he had *Remission* of his Sins; and that he was miraculously restored by the *Mercy* and *Grace* of GOD. And since Man, in *Affliction*, hath nothing in him to move GOD to *Mercy*, only *Prayer* and *Confession*, how much ought we to humble ourselves unto GOD, and beg *Pardon* for our Sins? Since we know *He is faithful and just to forgive us our Sins, and,* by His Promise, He will *cleanse us from all Unrighteousness*. On the which we should so fill our Thoughts, as to give GOD all the *Glory*.

(—Vide *John* i. 8.—ii. 1.—xx. 13.—1 *Tim.* i. 15.—*Mat.* xxvi. 28.—)

The PRECEPT.

> *By* me, O LORD, *Thy Name shall be ador'd,*
> *For Thou, in* Mercy, *hast my* Life *restor'd:*
> *To* Praise *Thy Name,* LORD, *let me be inclin'd,*
> *Nor let Thy* Gifts *e'er slip out of my* Mind.

N. B. As to the very Time this *Psalm* was written, it is very uncertain.

On PSALM CIV.

THIS excellent *Psalm* is an Exhortation to *Praise* GOD for His glorious *Works* of the *Creation:* viz. ¹ of the *first Day*, for the Heavens, Light, and Darkness. ³ Of the *second Day*, for the Firmament. ⁵ Of the *third Day*, for the Waters, Earth, and Fruits. ²² Of the *fourth Day*, for the Sun, Moon, and Stars. ²⁵ Of the *fifth Day*, for Fishes, Beasts, and creeping Things innumerable. And, *sixthly*, ²⁷ for His general *Providence*, and Care over them all, and His continual Decrements ³⁰ and Renovations.

Our *Author* then ³⁰ *sings* Glory to GOD, and admires His *Works*, and calls GOD also to *glory* in them; and ³¹ promiseth perpetual *Praises*, and begs that his Words may be acceptable unto GOD; and that all Sinners may be consumed by the Wrath of GOD; and exhorteth all People to *Praise* the LORD.

(—Vide *Gen.* i. ii.—*Psal.* xxxiii. 6.—cxxxvi.—*Heb.* i. 7.—*Eph.* iv. 24.—)

This glorious *Psalm* is as a *Mirrour* or Looking-glass, whereby we may see, at one View, the manifold WORKS of GOD, by the whole *Creation*; of which He is *Governor* of all, and *feedeth* all; and that the very *Angels* in Heaven are obedient to all. We may see also, that there is no Place in this World, (be it ever so barren) but some Signs of His *Blessings* appear; either by the *Sun, Moon, Clouds, Stars, Winds, Fowls, Trees, Earth, Herbs, Fruits, Stones, Beasts, Fishes,* and creeping Things innumerable; GOD having placed MAN over them all, and made all for His Service, whilst he is in this World. GOD hath also divided the Day from Night, so as to number *Days, Nights, Months,* and *Years*; *Summer* and *Winter, Heat* and *Cold:* For all which *Blessings*, let us daily render *Thanksgivings* and *Praises*; and more particularly for His eternal *Salvation* conferred upon us by the Merits of His SON JESUS, whom He sent into the World to die for our Sins; and by Whom we have eternal Life. So let us always fill our Thoughts with these Things, and give GOD the *Glory*.

The PRECEPT.

{ Great GOD! *the* Alpha *of both Heav'n and Earth!*
 And the Omega! *of all that had Birth:*
 Thou feedest all!—let me Thy Works *adore;*
 And sing Thy Praise, *Here, and for Evermore.* }

N B. Though the *Time*, and *Author* of this *Psalm* is not justly known; yet it was most probably wrote by DAVID.

On PSALM CV.

HALLELUJAH.

THIS *Psalm* is ¹ an Exhortation to *Praise* and *worship* the LORD, and seek Him by *Thanksgiving*, *preaching*, ³ *singing* His *Praises*, *Conference*, *rejoicing*, ⁵ *believing*, *praying*, and by *Meditation:* Being ⁶ for His keeping His *Covenant*, and ¹¹ *Mercy* with our Forefathers in *Canaan*; and ¹⁶ their descending into *Egypt*; and their Abode there: And ²³ the Plagues inflicted on *Egypt* for their Deliverance. Also ³⁹ GOD's mighty *Protection*, and ⁴⁰ *Provision* for them in the Wilderness; and ⁴³ His bringing them into *Canaan* ⁴⁴ for that very same End, *i. e.* to observe His *Statutes*, ⁴⁵ keep His *Laws*, and *Praise* His *Name* for the mighty Things He had done for them.

(–Vide Gen. xii. 17.—xx. 3.—*Exod*. vii. 20.—viii. 6.—xii. 29.— 1 *Chron*. xvi.*–)

The ancient *sacred History*, contained in this *Psalm*, is a worthy *Lesson* always to be remembered; wherein we have various *Examples* both of GOD's *Mercy*, and the *Truth* of His *Promise* to the Faithful; whereby we may confirm our *Faith*, and rest upon the same Foundation: We being now, by CHRIST, more bound to *celebrate* GOD's *Mercies* and *Benefits* than they were. And although the *Israelites* were exempted from the common Condemnation of the World, and were *elected* to be GOD's peculiar People, our *Author* here willeth them to shew themselves mindful of GOD's *Mercies*, by *Thanksgivings*; Whose *Mercies* had wrought their mighty Deliverance; His Power being thereby declared as lively as if He had spoke it then by His own Mouth. The *Promise* which GOD made first to *Abraham* was, that He should be His GOD, and also the GOD of all His *Seed* after Him, throughout all Generations; and shewed that they should not enjoy the Land of *Canaan* by any other Means, but by His Promise He had made to their Forefathers, to whom He had shewed Himself more plainly; who were to set forth His *Word* and Promise. We see also, that the very *Princes* of the Land were obedient to *Joseph's* Commandment, and learned Wisdom of Him: And that the very *Animal Plagues* arm themselves against Man, when GOD is his Enemy; from which *Plagues* all GOD's *Children* were exempted, by His *Mercy* and Divine *Providence* over them. Thus were the *Egyptians* destroyed, and His *chosen* People preserved; that they, and their *Posterity*, might call upon GOD, and *worship* and *Praise* Him in this World: Whereby we may know, that GOD is always mindful to *preserve* His CHURCH, and will surely keep His *Promise* throughout all Generations; to *preserve* the *Righteous*, and destroy the Wicked.

The PRECEPT.

{ *As* GOD, *in* Egypt, *did great* Wonders *show*,
That they His Statutes *should observe and know:*
So raise us, LORD, *that we, with Heart and Voice,*
Extol Thy Name, *and evermore rejoice.* }

N. B. Although

N. B. Although it appears, by the before-mentioned Transactions from *Abraham* to their Inheriting of *Canaan*, (and no farther,) that this *Psalm* was wrote by *Joshua*, in the End of his Life; by Reason it agrees with the Care he shewed for the same Thing, in his xxiiid and xxivth Chapters; as his Predecessor *Moses* left a Memorial like them, in *Deut.* xxxii.—Yet it appears more evident, from 1 *Chron.* xvi. that DAVID was the *Author*, and indited it for *Asaph*, to be sung as a Memorial when the *Ark* was carried into the City, &c.

On PSALM CVI.

THE *Psalmist* here ¹ exhorteth all to *Praise* G O D; ⁴ implores His *Mercy:* ⁶ Commemorating it, ¹³ and the People's Provocations in *Egypt*; and in the Wilderness; ³⁴ and in the Land of *Canaan*, at their first Enterance; and ⁴¹ under the *Judges:* Praying ⁴⁸ that the like *Favours* and *Mercies* may be shewed to them now; by gathering them from among the Heathen, that they might *Praise* the Name of the L O R D for ever and ever.

* (—Vide *Exod.* xiv. 27.—*Numb.* xxv. 12.—xx. 13.—*Psal.* xcv. 8.—1 *Sam.* vii. 7, 8.—*Psal.* cxxvi.—*Nehem.* ix.

The People here mentioned, being dispersed under *Antiochus*, magnify the Goodness of G O D among the Just and Penitent; and desire to be brought again into the *Land*, by G O D's merciful *Promise* and Visitation. Yet, after the marvellous *Works* G O D had wrought in *Egypt* for their Deliverance, their Ingratitude again appears, as is herein mentioned; and the wonderful MERCY of G O D, in saving them. They then *praying* to G O D to be gathered together, to *Praise* and *worship* Him, He then granteth their Request, for the *Truth* of His *Promise*; that His Name might be glorious in all the World. This *Psalm* evidently shews the *Patience* and *Goodness* of a merciful G O D, unto His People; Whose holy *Example* we ought to follow, one towards another, both in public and in private; rather than, for every little Offence, to tear one another in Pieces. It shews also, that we must now *reform* our Lives by the Gospel of CHRIST, if ever we mean to be saved; He having gathered His *Church*, which was dispersed, for the very same End. So *Blessed be the Name of the* G O D *of* Israel, *for ever and ever; and let all the People Praise Him, and say* Amen. Amen.

The PRECEPT.

O *save us*, L O R D, *by Thy most mighty Pow'r,*
From cruel Foes, *that would our Souls devour:*
And, when Thou com'st to set Thy People free,
In Thy great Mercy, L O R D, *remember me.*

N. B. This *Psalm* seems to be wrote by *Samuel*, in some Time of the Dispersion and Dread: It extending beyond the Time of the *Judges*, as is hinted in the 43d and 47th Verses. See in *Samuel* as before cited *.

End of the FOURTH BOOK.

On PSALM CVII.

OUR prophetical *Author*, in this *Psalm*, [1] kindly exhorteth all such as are *redeemed*, and the *Faithful*, earnestly to *Praise* GOD; especially [3] such as the *Tribe* of *Israel*; also for His Providence [4] over *Travellers*, [10] *Prisoners* set at Liberty; [18] *sick* Persons recovered; and [23] *Mariners* saved in Tempests. He shews also [33] how the *Impenitent* are punished; and [38] the *Righteous blessed*, and [42] rejoice at it: And that [43] wise Men will always *meditate* on the *Mercy* and *Loving-kindness* of the LORD.

(—Vide *Amos* viii.—*Luke* iv. 16.—*Isai.* xii. 18.—*Luke* i. 7.—)

This glorious *Psalm* (from former Examples, as well as from those more present,) shews the wonderful *Mercy* and *Providence* of GOD over Mankind, both by *Land* and *Sea*: in Order to teach us never to despair of GOD's *Mercies*, in our greatest Dangers and Afflictions. Here is one glorious *Verse* four Times repeated by the *Author*, after several *Mercies* that GOD had shewn to His People; which he desires always to be remembered and performed; saying, *Oh! that Men would therefore Praise the* LORD *for His Goodness; and declare the Wonders that He doth for the Children of Men!*—The great Benefits of GOD's *Mercy*, in past Ages, ought never to be out of our Memories; and, for the *Love* he beareth to His *Church*, we ought daily to *magnify* His Name, in all *Places* and *Assemblies*; knowing that He is as able to *destroy*, as He is willing to *save*; and doth, by His *Providence*, exalt us, and doth make us know ourselves by humbling us with Afflictions. And since our *Faith* is enlightened by His *holy Spirit*, and by the *Gospel* of His SON JESUS, let us always rejoice in the *Justice* of His *Word*, against the Wicked; and His *Truth*, in defending the *Righteous*; and, that His *Mercy* endureth for ever.

The PRECEPT.

GOD feedeth all, by His most powr'ful Hand,
And shews His Mercy both to Sea and Land:
Let all confess with Thanks, and freely own
The wond'rous Works that GOD for us hath done.

N. B. From the *Style* of this *Psalm*, it seems to be wrote by holy DAVID; though no particular Person is mentioned.

On PSALM CVIII.

HOLY DAVID, in this *Psalm*, [1] greatly encourageth himself to *Praise* GOD with *Heart*, *Voice*, and [2] *Instrument*, for

for [4] many past Deliverances: And [7] promiseth himself the like *Victories* over all his remaining Enemies for the future.

* (—Vide 2 Sam. viii. and x.—*Psal.* xliv.—lvii.—lx.—)

This *Psalm* is taken out of the lviith, and the lxth, wherein DAVID firmly declares that, as his *Tongue* is his *Glory*, his *Heart* shall go along with it, without any Hypocrisy, to *Praise* the LORD; assuring himself of the *Promise* of GOD concerning his *Kingdom*: Shewing, that he should divide *Shechem*, and measure *Succoth*; that *Manasseth* and *Ephraim* should be his, because it was strongly peopled; *Judah* be his Lawgiver, because it was the *Tribe* where his Kingdom should be established; *Moab* and *Edom* should be in Subjection to him; and that *Palestine* should seem to be glad of him, though he well knew they flattered and dissembled him. Let us always now take *Notice*, that these *Actions* are rather to be applied to the *spiritual Enemies* of *CHRIST's Church*, than to Armies that fight with outward Weapons: And that it is GOD alone that defends *us*, and our *Church*, from all Enemies. See the *Expositions* on the *Psalms* before-mentioned.

The PRECEPT.

Defend me, LORD, *with Thy great Pow'r and Might*,
When cruel Foes *do seek with me t fight*:
Let all sing Praise *to* GOD, *with Joy and Mirth*,
Whose Pow'r *and* Mercy's *over all the Earth*.

N. B. This *Psalm* was probably wrote on the same Causes as the xlivth, the lviith and the cxlviith, all of which see; and the viiith and xth Chapters of *Samuel* as before cited *.

On PSALM CIX.

IN this *Psalm* holy DAVID (under the Name of *Judas*) [1] complaineth to GOD of [2] the Falshood, [4] Treachery, and [5] Ingratitude of his cruel Adversary; and [6] expresses his great Dislike and Hatred against him, [10] and his Posterity. And [21] begging to GOD for Liberation to himself, he promiseth [30] to *Praise* GOD in the *Church*, [31] for his mighty Deliverances.

-Vide 2 *Sam.* xv. 31.—*Acts* i. 20.—*Psal.* lii.—*Mat.* xxiii. 23.—*John* vii. 49.-)

This terrible *Psalm* of DAVID, pointeth to the wicked Actions and Counsels of *Ahitophel*, with his Son *Absalom*; who, for no Cause, sought to take away his Life; even as *Judas* betrayed *CHRIST*; of which this was a true *Figure*, set forth by DAVID, by the *Spirit of Prophecy*. This *Psalm* must be used with great Care and Judgment, lest we draw in the Spirit of *Vengeance*, and false Zeal: for DAVID had no Spite against him or *Saul*, in any Case whatsoever, else he might have *avenged* himself on them, by several Opportunities which GOD gave him. No, he prayed all these *Judgments* to fall on his Enemies, for no other End, but that

that GOD might have the *Glory*, and his *Church* be kept in Safety ; and to deftroy the *Antichriftians*, and Enemies of the *Gofpel* ; which *Imprecations* we find in other *Pfalms*, as well as in this ; agreeable to the Writings of St. *Paul*, and many others. But our Cafe is now quite different from that of DAVID, fince *Chriftianity* is more fpread amongft us ; for what he then did, and faid, was to *enlarge* the *Church* of G O D and C H R I S T, that the Scriptures might be fulfilled ; and G O D have the Glory. So let us not mifapply fuch *Pfalms* to our own malicious Ends, left we bring on our own Heads thofe Things we pray for to others: Thefe being only written to fhew G O D's *Judgments* on the Perfecutors of His *Church*, and the *Love* he bears to thofe that efpoufe it.

(—Vide *Gal.* v. 12.—2 *Tim.* iv. 14.—*Acts* viii. 20.—1 *John* v. 16.—)

The PRECEPT.

> *Confound,* O L O R D, *with great Rebuke and Blame,*
> *All fuch as hate me, and defpife Thy Name:*
> *Shield me,* O L O R D, *from Men of* Pride *and* Spite,
> *And let Thy* Praifes *be my Soul's Delight.*

N. B. Some think this *Pfalm* points to *Doeg* and *Saul*, as well as to *Ahitophel*.

On P S A L M CX.

IN this *Pfalm*, holy DAVID ' prophefieth of the *Power* and everlafting *Kingdom* of C H R I S T ; and + alfo of His *Priefthood :* And 7 thas He fhall put an End to the *Priefthood* of *Levi*, and be made *Victor* over all His Enemies.

(—Vide *Mat.* xxii. 42.—*Heb.* i. 12.—1 *Cor.* xv. 24.—*Heb.* x. 13.—vii. 26.— *Ifai.* ii. 3,—*Luke* xxiii. 42.—*John* iii. 2.—*Acts* iii. 21.—1 *Cor.* xv. 28.— *Dan.* ii. 24.—)

This fhort, though precious *Pfalm*, feems to be an *Epitome* of the promifed *Gofpel* of C H R I S T : Shewing, *firft*, the Divinity of C H R I S T ; *fecondly*, His *Humanity*, and everlafting *Power* in the Kingdom of Heaven ; *thirdly*, his *Battles* and *Victories* againft His Enemies, vifible and invifible ; *fourthly*, what Time His *Kingdom* begun ; and by the Thief hanging on the Crofs, and whereunto *Pilate* did fubfcribe it in three feveral Languages ; and, *fifthly*, a plain Defcription of the *true Church*, &c. All which was, doubtlefs, C H R I S T Himfelf ; Who is now made to us *Wifdom*, *Juftice*, *Sanctification*, and *Redemption*. All thefe Things, both the *Church* itfelf, and the excellent *Gifts* wherewith it is adorned, is as the Dew falling down from the Womb of the Morning ; *fixthly*, He is a Prieft after the Order of *Melchizedeck*, which cannot be accomplifhed in any other King, only in C H R I S T ; nor no Power fhall be able to refift Him : Who fhall triumph much more glorious, when He fhall come to judge the whole World, in *Righteoufnefs* and Truth. The before-mentioned *Scriptures* will fet this in a clearer Light.

The

The PRECEPT.

{ *By* Melchi's *Order,* CHRIST's *our* Prieſt *for ever,*
Our great Salvation, Who will fail us never:
As Men, *and* Angels, *do His* Juſtice *own,*
So guide us, LORD, *to Thy eternal* Throne. }

N. B. When DAVID ſhewed the Continuance of his own Kingdom, he then *figured* thereby the above Kingdom of CHRIST: Of which this *Pſalm* is a *Song of Triumph.* The *four* following are on the ſame Score.

On PSALM CXI.
(HALLELUJAH.)

Herein holy DAVID poſitively declareth [1] that he will *Praiſe* GOD both with his *Voice* and *Heart,* [2] for the ſingular *Works* of His *Grace* towards His *Church:* And that [4] he will keep His *Works* always in Rememberance. He ſheweth alſo [7] that the *Works* of GOD are *Truth* and *Juſtice*; and that He hath performed His *Promiſe* [9] in *redeeming* His People: And [10] that to *fear* GOD is the Beginning of Wiſdom; and all that *love* Him, will be mindful of His *Covenant,* and PRAISE Him for His *Mercies,* for ever and ever.

(—Vide *Prov.* xxx. 8.—xxxi. 15.—*Pſal.* cxxxvi.—)

This *Pſalm* hath ſome Connection with the former, touching the wonderful *Mercies* of GOD in *redeeming* His People, by His Son *JESUS*; for which *Mercies* our *Author* herein voweth to *conſecrate* Himſelf wholly and only unto GOD; ſhewing that His very *Works* are ſufficient to make us *Praiſe* GOD; and that eſpecially for His *Benefits* towards His *Church*; and for His juſt and true *Government* of the ſame. He alſo ſhews that they are only *wiſe* that *fear* GOD, and keep His Commandments; and live according to the *Goſpel* of CHRIST; and *devote* themſelves wholly to the *Service* of GOD, by *Prayer, Praiſes,* and *Thankſgivings.*

(—Vide *Pſal.* cv. cvi.—*Rom.* ii. 29.—)

The PRECEPT.

{ *In Preſence of the* Juſt, *let all rejoice,*
And Praiſe *the* LORD, *with Heart, and Soul, and Voice*;
CHRIST *our Redeemer is, Who hath above*
A ſure Reward *for ſuch as do Him love.* }

N. B. That all ſuch *Pſalms* as have HALLELUJAH, or PRAISE THE LORD, ſet over them as a *Title,* were chiefly written by holy DAVID, or ordered by him, as Motives to a *godly* Life; and designed to be used when the People were gathered together in the *Temple*, as at solemn *Feasts*, &c. in order to exhort the People to *Praise* GOD for all *Mercies* in general; and that *Righteousness* should be sought out of his *Works*, by true *Faith*, in *CHRIST JESUS*: And even now to be used in all *Christian* Assemblies, and *Sacraments*, &c.

On PSALM CXII.
(Hallelujah.)

IN this *Psalm* is shewn ¹ the *Happiness* and *Felicity* that attends those that *fear* the LORD; ³ and practise *Righteousness*, ⁴ *Mercy*, ⁵ and *Charity*; and ¹⁰ that the Wicked shall consume away, for being *envious* against their Charity and Goodness.

* (Vide *Psal.* xli.—2 *Tim.* ii. 1.—iv. 8.—*Rom.* vii.—)

We may observe from this glorious *Psalm* what glorious Things are added unto us, by living in the *Fear* of GOD, *viz*. *Contentment* whilst we are in this Life, and the Enjoyment of *Heaven* hereafter; and that because all our Delight is always to do the *Will* of GOD, so far as we are able. Hence it appears, that, if we intend to be *happy* in the next World, we must *live* according to the *Gospel* of *CHRIST* in this; we must *love* Mercy, lend without Extortion, and *give* so far as we are able, without Ostentation; whereby we shall obtain the *Blessings* of GOD, both on ourselves, and our *Children*; whilst the Wicked die in Envy against us, by Reason their Eye is *evil*, because we are *good*. So let us all make this precious *Psalm* our godly *Pattern*, whilst we are in this Life, forasmuch as we are assured, by St. *Paul*, that *Godliness* hath *not only the Promise of Happiness in this Life, but also in that which is to come.*

(—Vide *Jam.* i. 9.—1 *Tim.* iv. 8.—*Isai.* lviii. 10.—*Eph.* iv. 29.—)

The PRECEPT.

> *A liberal Heart the* LORD *will surely bless,*
> *Who helps the Poor and Needy in Distress:*
> *His Righteousness, and Wealth, shall ne'er decay,*
> *Whilst wicked Men consume and melt away.*

N. B. See the *Scriptures* before-mentioned *.

On PSALM CXIII.
(Hallilujah.)

HOLY David, in this *Psalm*, ¹ exhorteth all the *Faithful* to *Praise* GOD ³ for His *Excellency*, ⁶ for His *Humility*, and for His general *Mercy*, Goodness, and *Providence* ⁷ over the *Poor*, ⁸ His *Church*, and all the World.

(—Vide *Psal.* viii.—cxxxv.—cxlvii.—*Matt.* xxi. 16.—)

This *Psalm* stirreth up the People to *Praise* GOD, and to consider that He created them for the same End. It sheweth also, that, as the *Glory* of GOD shineth over all the World, so should our *good Works*, by helping the *Poor* in their Need, and raising them to Honour; and to *instruct* those that are ignorant in the *Gospel* of *CHRIST*, that they may *glory* in His *Church*, which He so marvellously has ordained for them. We may also observe, in this *Psalm*, GOD's wonderful *Love* towards His People, and that chiefly towards such as were *Poor*, *viz.* *Joseph*, *David*, and *Daniel*, whom He, by His *Mercy*, so wonderfully raised; and also by the barren Women, *viz.* *Sarah*, *Rebecca*, *Anna*, &c. all of whom being the *Servants* of GOD, &c.—Now, seeing that the *Levitical* Priesthood is taken away, and we *Christians* only rely on *CHRIST*, let us always *consecrate*, and offer up our *Praises* and *Thanksgivings* to the *Throne* of GOD, with His Church, whom He hath appointed for the very same End. So *Praise* the LORD.

(—Vide *Psal.* cxvii.—*Isai.* liv. 1.—)

The PRECEPT.

{ GOD, *in* Compassion, *never fails the Just*,
But helps the Poor *that do Him love, and trust :*
Their Seed He raises up to mighty Fame;
Therefore, Praise ye the LORD's *most mighty Name.* }

※※※※※※※※※※※※※※※※※※※※※※※※※

On PSALM CXIV.

BY *Example* of dumb Creatures, holy DAVID herein exhorteth all the *Faithful* to [7] *fear* and *magnify* the LORD, for His past *Favours* and *Mercies* in delivering the *Israelites*, and preserving His *Church*.

* (—Vide *Exod.* xiii. 3.—xvii. 6.—*Psal.* lxviii. 8.—1 *Cor.* x.—*Acts* xvi.—)

This *Psalm* brings to *Rememberance* the wonderful *Mercies* of GOD; and celebrates the Deliverance of the Children of *Israel* out of the Land of *Egypt :* Being a true *Figure* of our everlasting Deliverance from *Satan*, *Sin*, and *Death*, by the *Coming* of *CHRIST*; for which we are more in Duty bound to *celebrate* the *Mercies* of GOD, than our *Forefathers*; by Reason we now have the *true Light* of the *Gospel*, and they had only *Types* and Shadows of it. We may here also observe, that when GOD had brought them from the *Egyptians*, (a People of a strange Language, unto them,) that they were then Witnesses of the *Power*, *Majesty*, and *Mercies* of GOD in delivering them, and relied wholly on GOD, as His chosen People. And, that as the dumb Creatures, *viz.* the Sea and *Mountains*,) in Similitude, then felt, and saw His mighty *Power*, how much more ought *we*, His People, now to *Praise* and *glorify* Him for our *Salvation* by *JESUS CHRIST!* So *Praise the* LORD *with me, and let us magnify His Name together.* Psal. xxxiv. 3.

The PRECEPT.

> *As* Mountains *shake, and mighty* Waters *stand,*
> *And all* Things *else obey the* LORD's *Command :*
> *So teach me,* LORD, *to dread Thy mighty Name,*
> *Thy* Mercy *own, and all Thy* Deeds *proclaim.*

N. B. This *Psalm* was (as is supposed) often used by DAVID, in the *Temple*, in Rememberance of GOD's *Mercies,* &c.

✶✶✶✶✶✶✶✶✶✶✶✶✶✶✶✶✶✶✶✶✶✶✶✶✶✶✶

On PSALM CXV.

THIS is a *Psalm* of *Prayer*, desiring [1] GOD would succour all such [4] as are oppressed with Worshippers of *Idols* ; exhorting [9] all the *Faithful* only to *trust* in GOD, and *fear* Him ; whereby [15] He will surely *bless* not only them, but their *Children* after them, according to His *Promise.*

* (—Vide 2 *Chron.* xx.—*Isai.* xlviii. 11.—xxxviii. 19.—*Rev.* xiv. 1, 2, 3.—)

This *Psalm* is of great Use to our *Commonwealth*, whereby we may *pray* to be defended from all prophane Nations, who worship *Idols* ; being a beautiful *Comparison* of *false gods*, unto the *Power* and *Goodness* of the *true One*. Herein we may see, that, as neither *Matter* nor *Form* can any Way commend *Idols*, there can be no Reason to esteem or *honour* them ; forasmuch as they can neither damn nor save, any farther than *deceiving* the Souls of those that trust in them. Hence let it be always our *Prayer* for GOD to save us from such *Idol-Worship* ; that we may rely on the *true* GOD of the House of *Aaron* and *Israel*, whom our GOD hath appointed as *Teachers* of the *true Faith* and *Religion* to all Generations that came after them. And since GOD's manifold *Gifts, Graces, Mercies, Wonders,* and *Works* are sufficient Testimonies of His *Truth* and *Goodness*, let us always rely on *Him* for Help, in all our Afflictions ; who never failed to *preserve* the Righteous, and destroy the Enemies of His *Church*, that His Name might be *glorious* in all the World. So let us never cease to *Praise* His *Name*, and *worship* Him according to the *Gospel* of His SON *JESUS*, by whom we have eternal Salvation. *Not unto us,* O LORD, *but to Thy Name be Glory.*

* (—Vide 1 *Sam.* ii. 30.—*Matt.* vi. 24.—†

The PRECEPT.

> *In* Idols *place no Confidence, nor Trust ;*
> *Their Help is vain, their* Makers *are but Dust :*
> *Trust in the* LORD, *for He's your only Guard,*
> *And, at the last, in Heav'n, your great Reward.*

N. B. It is supposed that holy DAVID composed this *Psalm*, and that it was referred to the *History* of *Jehoshaphat* ; or was indited for the Use of the Church. See the *Scriptures* before cited *.

On PSALM CXVI.

IN this *Pfalm*, holy DAVID, being in great Danger of *Saul* in the Defart of *Maon*, ¹ profeſſeth his great Love and Service to GOD for hearing and preferving him, when ³ he was near in Defpair of any Help; promifing for the future always ¹³ to be folemn, and drink the ufual Cup in his *Thankfgivings*; and ¹⁷ to offer his *Praiſes*, and ¹⁸ pay his Vows in the Houſe of the LORD, as an Atonement of GOD's *Mercies* towards him.

* (—Vide *Joſh.* xv. 55.—2 *Cor.* iv. 13.—*Iſai.* i. 14.—*Rom.* iii. 4.—*Matt.* xx. 20.—*Rev.* xix.—)

This *Pſalm* is a fingular Example of *Faith, Praiſe*, and Thankſgiving for any Mercies received from GOD. Our holy *Author*, herein, fetteth forth his *Love* in calling upon GOD, and avers Him to be *juſt* and *merciful* in helping him, when he was deſtitute of either Help or *Counſel*. He alſo ſhews how ſtrong his Faith was, that GOD would preferve him; knowing Man's Help to be only Flattery, without His *Divine* Protection. We may here alſo obſerve, how grateful DAVID was, in returning *Thanks* for his great Deliverance; by his promifing to make a ſolemn *Banquet*, according to *Law* and *Cuſtom* in thoſe Days, and drink a *Cup* in *Sign* of *Thankſgiving*: It being as a *Figure* of the Bleſſed *Cup* of our LORD *JESUS*, in His holy *Sacrament*. And, ſince GOD alone has the Power of both *Life* and DEATH, and can either *deſtroy* or *ſave*, let us always make it our conſtant *Rule* to return *Thanks* for all the *Mercies* and *Benefits* we receive at His Hands; and be as ready to acknowledge His *Favours*, and *Praiſe* His Name, as He is willing to *preferve* us: Let us always be mindful of the *Goſpel* of *CHRIST*, and not neglect that great and important *Duty* which *CHRIST* has commanded us, i. e. to *receive his bleſſed Cup of Salvation, and call upon the Name of the* LORD to ſtrengthen our *Faith* in *CHRIST JESUS*; whereby we may have free *Forgiveneſs* of our Sins, and die in *Charity* with all Men.

The PRECEPT.

> When unto GOD I pray'd, in Pain and Grief,
> He heard my Pray'r, and eas'd me with Relief:
> To GOD I'll offer humble Thanks and Praiſe,
> Receive the Cup, and call on Him always.

N. B. See the *Place*, and *Scriptures* before cited. *

On PSALM CXVII.
(HALLELUJAH.)

HOLY DAVID, in this *Psalm*, [1] chearfully exhorteth all *Nations* to Praise GOD, [2] for His loving *Kindness*, His *Mercy*, and His *Truth*, &c.

* (—Vide *Rom.* xv. 11.—*John* i. 17.—)

This short, though excellent *Psalm*, exhorteth all People in general to *Praise* GOD, because He hath *finished* His *Promise*, of giving everlasting Life to all by His SON *JESUS*; and in giving His *Grace* and *Truth*, by Whom He is to be *worshipped*; whereby we may know that the Kingdom of *CHRIST* is *spiritual*: This being the *Sum* of the *Gospel*, as expounded by St. *Paul*, and St. *John*. See the *Scriptures* before cited *.

(—Vide *Psal.* c.—)

The PRECEPT.

Let ev'ry Nation Praise GOD's *mighty Name,*
Declare His Power, *and exalt His* Fame;
Great is His Love!—*His* Mercies *ever sure,*
And Truth *to endless Ages shall endure.*

N. B: Altho' we have no particular *Author* mentioned in the ancient *Title* of this *Psalm*, yet, from its *Style*, it is conjectured to be wrote by holy DAVID, for *public Use*, in the *Congregations*; as a SONG of *Praise* and *Thanksgiving* in general unto GOD, for His fatherly *Grace*, Care, and *Protection*.

On PSALM CXVIII.
(HALLELUJAH.)

IN this *Psalm*, King DAVID [1] exhorteth all the *Faithful* to *Praise* and *confess* GOD, because His *Mercy* endureth for ever. He sheweth also [9] that it is better to trust in GOD than in *Princes*, [13] by his own Experience [17] and Faith: And [14] that his *Deliverance* should be His SONG, for His mighty *Salvation*. Then [19] foretelling of *CHRIST*'s *Kingdom*, [27] he sheweth His mighty *Power*; and [23] *Praiseth* GOD, that His *Mercy* endureth for ever.

* (—Vide 2 *Sam.* xxi. 16.—*Isai.* xxviii. 16.—*Matt.* xxi. 42.—*Acts* iv. 11.—*Rom.* ix. 33.—1 *Pet.* vi. 7.—*Numb.* vi. 23.—*Luke* i. 78.—1 *Thess.* v.—)

DAVID,

A New Exposition on the Book of Psalms, &c.

DAVID, being made KING, here impu*eth all to GOD's *Mercy* towards His afflicted *Church*; and does not only thank and *Praise* GOD for it himself, but exhorts all the *Faithful* to do the like. And though *Saul* was his greatest Enemy, from whom he was preserved, he doth not impute his *Deliverance* unto himself, but only unto the *Mercy* and *Power* of GOD; for which he promiseth *Praise*. and *Thanksgiving*; and willeth that the *Doors* of the *Tabernacle* might be opened unto all; whereby they may *join* with him in *Praises*, for delivering both him and the *Church*. And, though *Saul* and the chief Powers had refused DAVID to be King, yet GOD *preserved* him above them all, set him on the *Throne*, and delivered His *Church* from all its cruel Enemies. DAVID being here the very *Figure* of CHRIST, unto all the Faithful, they are all joyful in him, and pray for his Prosperity; because GOD, by him and his, hath *restored* Darkness unto *Light*, and hath brought *Salvation* to all Mankind. So let us all *Praise* the LORD for the *Truth* of His *Promise*, and say, *Blessed is He that cometh in the Name of the* LORD.

(—Vide 1 Pet. ii. 7.—Eph. ii. 20.—Heb. xiii. 16.—)

The PRECEPT.

{ CHRIST's my Defence, and Song; to Him I'll flee,
And is become a Saviour unto me:
My Song shall Praise Him, and His Name confess,
For He's the Gate of Joy and Righteousness. }

N. B. This seems to be penned for *a triumphant Song*, for *Victories* obtained, and his personal Deliverances, probably from *Ishbibenob*, &c. and of his *Advancement* to the Kingdom. All of which must be referred to CHRIST, of whom DAVID was a true *Figure*. See the *Scriptures* before cited *.

On PSALM CXIX.

THIS most glorious and *golden Psalm* of holy DAVID contains a general EXHORTATION to all the People of GOD, in order to frame their *Lives* and *Actions* according to His LAWS, and Divine PRECEPTS, and not to their own frail Opinions; in which he [1] setteth forth the *Blessedness* of those that live obedient to His *Ordinances*, and *love* and *fear* Him, &c. He then greatly magnifies GOD's mighty NAME, and prays to be instructed by Him, and [15] *meditates* on His divine *Promises*; and [71] greatly comforts himself in all his *Afflictions* and *Temptations*: Which he, through *Faith*, thought was for his own Good, and tended to his eternal *Salvation*. He also, herein, [105] shews the Light of GOD's holy WORD, and his own true *Zeal*; and [136] how he was grieved at the Wicked for their cruel Persecutions againſt him, and the Church, by their not living according to GOD's holy *Laws* and divine *Precepts*, &c. &c. &c.

*(—Vide *Pſal.* cxxiii.—cxxiv.—xcvi. 9.—*John* ii. 27.—)

This moſt precious *Pſalm* of INSTRUCTION, and divine MEDITATIONS, has 176 *Verſes*; and is divided into 22 *Octonaries*, each having eight *Verſes*, with proper *Titles* according to the *Alphabet* of the *Hebrew* Letters, &c. This *Pſalm* was anciently called *The Saint's Alphabet*, for the Scholars of *Sion:* Or, A choice and public *Repoſitory*, *Ark*, or *Cheſt* of 176 gold *Rings*, in 22 Diviſions; each *Ring* or *Verſe* being a golden PRECEPT to a godly Life, while we are in this World, and an *Hieroglyphic* of Eternity in the next.

(To comment ſtrictly on every *Verſe* of this long *Pſalm* would make a large *Volume* in *Folio*; which cannot be expected in this *Octavo*.)

As the whole BOOK of *Pſalms*, (apud *Luther*. and others) was formerly called, *The Leſſer Bible*, or, An *Epitome* of the holy *Scriptures* in general, ſo this cxixth *Pſalm* was, in like Manner, called, An *Epitome* of all other *Pſalms*; ſetting forth all the Excellencies and Perfections of the whole LAW of GOD contained in the holy *Scriptures*; in order to arm us with *Faith* to withſtand all the *Temptations* and *Afflictions* of this Life; and not to faint under GOD's *Chaſtiſements*; by reaſon they tend to our own Good, in the End, and to His Glory; if we faithfu'ly truſt in Him, with *Patience*.

St. *Ambroſe* ſays, that this cxixth *Pſalm* as far exceeds all other *Pſalms*, as the SUN exceeds the *Moon* in Luſtre; it being a choice *Pocket-Book* of GOD's LAW, according to *Moſes*; and the GOSPEL of CHRIST, in the New *Teſtament*.

It is alſo a worthy *Piece* of *Chriſtian Doctrine*, and adapted to every *Age*, *Sex*, and *Scene* of Life; whether in *Youth*, *Manhood*, or *Old-Age*; *Health*, *Sickneſs*, *Poverty*, *Proſperity*, *Temptation*, or *Deſpair*: And ought never to be out of our Hands, or Thoughts, at all Opportunities, if we would live in the *Fear* of GOD, according to the *Goſpel* of CHRIST, in Hope of eternal Life.

By a ſtrict Survey, I find there are but two *Verſes* in this long *Pſalm*, (viz. the 90th and 122d) but what mention the LAW of GOD, either under the Name of *Laws*, *Statutes*, *Precepts*, *Teſtimonies*, *Commandments*, *Ordinances*, *Word*, *Promiſes*, *Ways*, *Judgments*, *Name*, *Righteouſneſs*, or *Truth*, &c. &c. The Word LAW being diverſly taken in *Scripture*, though much to one and the ſame Meaning.

(—Vide *Jam.* xx. 10.—*Gal.* iii. 23.—*Luke* xxiv. 44.—*John* vii. 49.—*Mic.* iv. 2.—*Iſai.* ii. 3.—)

Holy DAVID complained of his diſtreſſed *Condition*, when he was wrongfully perſecuted by King *Saul*, ſaying, that he *was forced to fly, and hide himſelf in the Rocks and Caves of the Earth*; and alſo was obliged *to live amongſt the wicked Philiſtines*, &c.

Muſculus was of Opinion that DAVID had this *Pſalm*, of GOD's LAW or WORD, always along with him, as his only *Guard* and *Monitor* againſt the *Impieties*, *Temptations*, and *Allurements* of his Enemies: It being his daily *Meditation*; which appears very probable in the 92d *Verſe*, thus: *Unleſs Thy* LAW *had been my Delight, I then ſhould have periſhed in mine Afflictions*, &c. q. d. He ſhould have been drawn aſide by them, to join in their wicked *Actions* and *Impieties,* * if GOD's LAW had not been his only Safeguard.

It is alſo ſaid that the *Jews* always had a ſtrict Regard to this cxixth *Pſalm*, by Reaſon they always taught it to their *Youth*, of both *Sexes*; in order early to fix in in their Minds PRECEPTS to a godly Life: Which was probably penn'd by holy DAVID in the Days of his *Banishment*, under King *Saul*, (as before hinted,) at several *Times*, and in several *Places*, when he was chaced about by him, and his wicked *Adherents*: Which being now left to us a Monitor to all Ages, we ought to *read, mark*, and *learn*; and intirely rely on GOD's divine *Protection*, in every *Scene* of Life.

(—Vide *Ver.* 19, 23, 49, 54, 69, 75, 95, 107, 116, 150, 161.—)

The PRECEPT.

> LORD, guard *my Soul, and Thou my* Heart *incline*
> *To keep Thy* LAWS, *and* Statutes *most divine:*
> *Thy* Paths *are pure! Thy* Precepts *sure will lead*
> *To heav'nly* JOYS, *which never, never, fade.*

N. B. That *Herlackinden*, and *Greenham* wrote two large Volumes intirely on this *Psalm*, very tiresome to read; the last of which was printed in 1605, in a small *Folio*.

On PSALM CXX.

(ASCENSION 1.—*I called,*—)

Cir. 1058. **H**OLY DAVID, having prayed unto GOD to be delivered from his cruel Enemies, obtaineth his Desire; and herein complaineth of their flattering, lying, and deceitful Tongues, and declares his Judgment on them: And greatly lamenteth his long *Exile*, on Account of their Cruelty, &c.

* (—Vide 2 *Sam.* xxvii. 6, 7.—*Ezra* vii.—*Psal.* cxxvi.—*Gen.* x. 2.—2 *Chron.* xx. 19.—1 *Chron.* xvii. 17.—*Isai.* vi.—2 *Cor.* v. 1.—*Luke* xvi.—*Psal.* cxl.—*Prov.* xxv. 18.—*Ezek.* v. 16.—)

This *Psalm* chiefly pointeth to King *Saul*'s Flatterers against DAVID, such as *Doeg, Ahitophel*, &c. who drove DAVID out of *Judea*, and made him live long in *Exile* in *Ziklag*: From which we may see, that good Men are very often drove away from their own native Country, by the Cruelty of the Wicked; and that they have too often such wicked *Mesechites* and *Kedarites* amongst their own *Relations*, as holy DAVID herein speaks of, *i. e.* the greatest of Enemies: Some of the *Israelites*, as herein pointed at, having not only degenerated from their first *godly Fathers*, but turned envious against their own Brethren, and against all the *faithful* People of GOD, &c.

We may easily infer from this *Psalm*, that we never ought to be cast down when we suffer Afflictions for Righteousness sake; but rather ought to rejoice; though, at the same Time, it is very hard to be used ill for our Well-doing: For-*asmuch as we know that our Labours will not be in vain in the* LORD; and that all the *Slanders, Lyes*, and malicious Cruelties will, like sharp *Arrows, Fire*, &c.

turn

turn again on our Enemies, and not on us; if we faithfully rely on GOD for Succour, when the Help of Man faileth: Who hath always promised never to forsake the Righteous; but that He will assuredly destroy all the Enemies of CHRIST's People, Gospel, and Church.

The PRECEPT.

{ Thieves, Fire, and Sword, wound not with so much Wrong,
As a false Witness, and a lying Tongue:
LORD, give me Patience, when such Foes oppress,
And 'venge my Cause, in Truth and Righteousness. }

☞ The Reader is here to take Notice, that there are 15 Psalms, (from the cxixth to the cxxxvth) called Psalms of Ascension, Gradual Psalms, Songs of Degrees, or Songs of Rememberance, and GRATITUDE; which were sung by Ezra, and his Company, on the several Stages in their Journey out of Babylon: (And not on the 15 Steps or Stairs of the Temple, as some do imagine.) These 15 Psalms, I say, were particularly consecrated to commemorate the Return of the Israelites, as they came on their Way, in several Companies; which Psalms are said then to be put together, in a little Book by themselves, by Ezra, in order to declare and perpetuate the Benefits and wonderful Mercies of GOD to His chosen People: (Each Psalm having its Beginning as a Title, as above,) some coming from Babylon under Zorobabel, some under Ezra, and some coming under Nehemiah, &c.—See the Scriptures before cited *.

On PSALM CXXI.

(ASCENSION 2.—*I will lift up,*)

THIS *Psalm* [1] shews the wonderful Safety of all such as only trust in GOD; Who will always be watchful [6] both Day and Night to preserve them, and His Church; if they follow but this Example of holy DAVID.

(—Vide 1 *Sam.* xxvi. 19.—*Dan.* vi.—*Ezra* vii.—*Psal.* xci.—

Holy DAVID herein sheweth, that the highest Things in this World afford but little Help to Man; and that we must look over them all, into the very Heavens, if we would have GOD to be our Safeguard. And as his continual *Providence* is, at all Times, over the *Faithful*, He will not suffer either *Heat* or *Cold*, or whatever the Wicked shall contrive, to discommode or destroy His *Church* and People. Here, the *Israelites*, being on their Journey from *Egypt*, looked towards *Judea*, and saw the City overthrown, greatly comforting themselves, that GOD, by His *Mercy*, had defended them from the parching *Sun* in the Day-time with a *Cloud*; and with the Light of a *Pillar* of Fire in the *Night*; as they travelled on their Journey

Seeing now, that all these *Wonders* are only *Figures* of the spiritual Help, whereby the *Son* of GOD doth marvellously preserve and defend His Church, travelling through this World: Let us wholly rely on His *Gospel Ordinances* as

our

A New Exposition *on the* Book *of* Psalms, *&c.* 103

our *Rule* and Pattern, whilst we are in this Life; whereby we may raise our Thoughts above the Vanities of this World, even into the very Heavens, from whence all our Help cometh; and wherein we hope to be raised after this painful Life is ended; by the Merits of *JESUS CHRIST*, to Whom we seek for *Succour*, and eternal *Salvation*.

(—Vide *Exod.* xiii.—*Isai.* iv. 4.—*Gen.* xxxi. 40.—*Deut.* xxviii. 6. 2,—2 *Chron.* i. 10.—2 *Sam.* iii. 25.—*Acts* i. 21.—ix. 28.—)

The PRECEPT.

{ GOD *will the* just *Man safely* guard *and keep,*
By *Night, or Day*; awake, *or when* asleep:
In all his Business, *going in, or out,*
GOD, *as a* Fence, *will compass him about.* }

N. B. This *Psalm* is conjectured to be wrote by DAVID, though we have no particular Person mentioned.

On PSALM CXXII.

(ASCENSION 3.—*I was glad,*)

HOLY DAVID, in the Name of the *Faithful*, ¹ greatly rejoiceth that GOD hath accomplished His *Promise*, and hath ³ placed His *Ark* in *Sion*, for public *Worship*, and ⁵ civil *Justice*: Wherefore he giveth *Thanks*, and prayeth ⁶ for the *Church's Peace*, ⁸ and *Prosperity*; and for all the *Members* thereof.

* (—Vide 1 *Chron.* xxix. 9.—2 *Sam.* vi. 12. 20.—)

Our holy Author here greatly rejoiceth that GOD hath appointed a Place wherein His *Ark*, or *Divine Presence*, should abide, which was before removed from one Place to another. He also meaneth, by the artificial Workmanship and beautiful Joining of the Building, the *Concord* and *Love* that was amongst the Citizens, or *Tribes* that should come there to the *Worship* of GOD; Whose House was there placed as a *Throne* of *Justice*; and should have *Prosperity* both within and without, by the *Favour* and *Blessing* of GOD amongst the People. This being a true *Figure* of *CHRIST's* Kingdom, let us, (with holy DAVID) not only, for his own Sake, pray for it, but for all the *Faithful* of the *Church* of *CHRIST*, *Peace be within Thy Walls*, and *Plenteousness within Thy Palaces.*

(—Vide *Exod.* xxv. 21.—1 *Cor.* xi. 19.—*Rev.* xiv. 4. 9, 10, 11.—*Psa.* cxxxiii.—*Isai.* ix. 6.—)

The PRECEPT.

{ LORD, *let Thy* Church *be all my Soul's Delight,*
To Praise *by Day, and* meditate *by Night:*
And, that Thy Church *may more and more increase,*
LORD, *give to all* Prosperity *and* Peace. }

N. B. This *Psalm* was wrote by DAVID after the Ark was fixed in *Jerusalem*. See the *Scriptures* before cited. *.

On

On PSALM CXXIII.

(ASCENSION 4.—*I lift mine Eyes to the Heavens,*)

THIS *Pfalm* [1] shews holy DAVID's constant Dependence on GOD; and that [3] he *prays* for His *Mercy* to defend him and his from all proud, spiteful, disdainful, and [4] scorning Persons.

* (—Vide 1 *Sam.* xxiv.—*Nehem.* viii.—1 *Cor.* i. 24.—)

This *Pfalm* compareth the *State* of the *Godly* to that of *Servants*, and CHRIST the MASTER, on Whom all must *wait*, until it be His good Pleasure to bestow His *Mercies* and *Benefits* upon us. And as we have no other *Help* but what cometh from GOD, at every Need; how much the more ought we to *pray*, and rely on His divine *Providence* to assist us? Since He hath *promised*, that, when we have underwent all the *Oppressions* and *Scornings* of the Wicked, He will help us out of their cruel Hands; and that, if we be but *faithful* to Him, even *until Death*, he will surely give us a *Crown* of *Life*.

(—Vide *Pfal.* xxxi. 23.—*Prov.* xxviii. 20.—*Rev.* ii. 10.—)

The PRECEPT.

{ *Most mighty* LORD! *we all on Thee do wait,*
As Servants *waiting at their* Master's *Gate:*
We sue for Pardon, LORD, *till Thou forgive,*
For, at Thy Pleasure, *all must die, or live.* }

N. B. This *Pfalm* was probably wrote by DAVID, when *Saul* despised him, and his poor Train of *Attendants*. See the *Scriptures* before cited *.

On PSALM CXXIV.

(ASCENSION 5.—*If the* LORD *had not,*)

IN this *Pfalm* holy DAVID [1] shews that if GOD had not been on his Side, [2] when *Saul* pursued him, to take away his Life, both he and all his *Attendants* must have been *Victims* to their Cruelty; for which Deliverance [6] he greatly *Praiseth* GOD, and [8] owns Him to be their only Succour.

* (—Vide 1 *Sam.* xxiv.—*Pfal.* xci. 3.—*Rom.* viii. 31.—)

This *Pfalm* sheweth that GOD is always ready to help all such as trust in Him, in their greatest Dangers; and that the *Faithful* are always saved by that Means: And that though the Wicked rage ever so furiously against GOD's Church,

Church, and to destroy and swallow up His People, all their Enterprises are of none Effect, when GOD takes the Matter in Hand; forasmuch as His *Word* is *true*, and His *Mercy* aboundeth for ever to preserve them.

The PRECEPT.

{ *Why should we fear, when* Trouble *is at Hand?*
GOD loves the Just, *and faithful by them stands:*
Ungodly Foes in great Confusion flee,
Whilst godly Men *triumph in* Victory. }

N. B. This *Psalm* is supposed to be wrote by DAVID, when in the *Cave* with his *Attendants*, and *Saul* sought to destroy them. See the *Scriptures* before cited *.

On PSALM CXXV.

(ASCENSION 6.—*They that trust in* GOD,)

THIS *Psalm* shews ¹ the great *Safety* of the *Faithful*; and that such as trust only in GOD shall ² never be moved by the Schemes of the Wicked; and ³ that all such as are Workers of Iniquity shall inevitably perish.

(—Vide 1 *Sam.* xxiv.—*Matt.* vii. 22.—xxv.—)

This plainly setteth forth, that, if the World be ever so full of Mutations, the *Faithful* of GOD should never embrace any Wickedness; lest the Rod of the Wicked fall on them, and they be deemed as Hypocrites: But that they should always stand firm, and abide in the *Faith* of *CHRIST*; and withstand all the Efforts of the Wicked; whereby they attain everlasting *Salvation*: When the Righteous shall receive a *Come ye Blessed*, and the Wicked shall have a *Go ye Cursed*, &c. &c.

The PRECEPT.

{ *They that in* GOD *do place their Confidence,*
Trust in His Aid, *His Succour, and Defence,*
Shall never fail; for CHRIST, *inthron'd above,*
Will save all such, as do Him own, *and love.* }

N. B. Read the *Scriptures* before cited.

On PSALM CXXVI.

(ASCENSION 7.—*When the* LORD *had*,)

DAVID, in this *Psalm*, sheweth ¹ the ineffable Joy of the People after their Return from the Captivity of *Babylon*:
⁵ with

⁵ with the same *Promise* of Joy, to all such as endure the like *Afflictions*, with pious *Diligence* and *Prayer*.

* (—Vide *Jer.* xxv. 12.—xxix. 10.— *Ezra* i. 2.— vii. 9.— 2 *Chron.* xxxvi. ult.— *Isai.* xlviii. 20.—lv. 12.—)

As this Deliverance was wonderful, there was left no Excuse for *Ingratitude*; for which they had great Reason to *rejoice*, when GOD of His infinite Goodness had *gathered* and delivered His *Church*. From hence we may infer, that if Infidels confess the wonderful *Works* of GOD, how much more should the *Faithful* shew themselves thankful; and rejoice for such a *new Birth*? Therefore let us always be *joyful* in all such *Afflictions* as GOD shall lay on us to try us; forasmuch as we know, He is always as able to *defend* His *Church*, as He is to turn a barren and dry Ground into a running *Stream*; and that he will, at last, *reward* the *Sorrows* of the *Faithful*, who die from Sin, and *live* in CHRIST, with a *Crown* of Glory in His Kingdom: Where their Sheaves of *good Works* will be received with Joy.

(—Vide *Rom.* vii.—*Eph.* iv. 8.—*Col.* iii.—*Phil.* iii. 10.—1 *Cor.* ii. 9.—*Eph.* v. 19.—*John* vi. 38.—*Jam.* iii. 18.—)

The PRECEPT.

When GOD sav'd Isr'el *in their great Distress,*
In grateful Songs *they did His Name confess:*
Now teach *us,* LORD, *in* Gratitude, *to own*
CHRIST, *our* Redeemer, *seated on Thy Throne.*

N. B. This *Psalm* respects their *Deliverance*, and Liberty to restore the *Temple*, and its *Worship*, by the *Edict* and Bounty of *Cyrus*. See the *Scriptures* before cited *.

On PSALM CXXVII.

(ASCENSION 8.—*Except the* LORD *build,*)

THIS is a *Song* composed by SOLOMON; wherein he sheweth, ¹ that nothing in this World can stand and prosper whether *mechanical, domestical,* or *political,* without the *Blessing* and *Providence* of GOD: And ³ that though to bring up *Children* well is precious Care; yet *Grace* is the alone *Gift* of GOD, and their only *Safeguard.*

(—Vide 1 *Cor.* ix.—*Heb.* xiii. 17.—1 *Cor.* iii.—*Eph.* iv. 28.—)

This glorious *Family Psalm* shews how unable *Labourers, Watchmen, Parents,* (and even *Princes* and *Rulers*) themselves) are to bring their *Designs* to pass, unless GOD gives His *Blessing* to their Endeavours. If we contrive, GOD can disappoint, and defeat all our *Schemes,* in a Moment when we think not. Hence let it be our constant *Rule,* to crave GOD's *Blessing* on all our Endeavours; that our *Designs* may *prosper*. Let us always *pray* to GOD to give our Children His *Grace*, as we give them *Learning* and good *Examples*; whereby they need never be ashamed to appear before their Enemies, in the Doors of *Justice*; be they ever so wrongfully accused.

(–Vide *Isai.* lvi. 5.—*Luke* x. 20.—*Rev.* ii. 17.—*Gal.* iv. 19.—1 *Cor.* iv. 15.–)

The PRECEPT.

{ *Men* build, contrive, *and* watch, *and* ward *in vain*,
Unless the LORD *support, and them sustain*:
Bless us, O LORD, *give* Plenty *to our Land*,
And prosper *us*, *in all we take in Hand*. }

N. B. Though this *Psalm* is referred to *Solomon*, yet it is suggested to be composed by DAVID, his Father, for him; as an Acknowledgment, that all his Enterprises succeeded only in GOD, &c. &c.

On PSALM CXXVIII.

(ASCENSION 9.—*Blessed is every one*,)

HOLY DAVID, in this *Psalm*, setteth forth, ' that all are truly *Blessed* that live in the *Fear* and *Love* of GOD: And ⁵ that their *Children* after them shall enjoy the like *Benefits* and *Privileges*, if they continue in the *Fear* of GOD.

(—Vide *Deut.* xxviii. 30.—*Isai.* lvi. 5.—i. 7.—*Eccles.* ii. 24.—)

This *Marriage-Psalm* has Connection with the foregoing *Psalm*; which sheweth that GOD approveth not our *Life*, except we live according to His holy *Word*. And though the gay Part of this World esteem themselves, because they enjoy *Wealth*, *Honour*, and *Idleness*, yet the *Holy Ghost* approveth them best, that live by *Labour* and *Industry*, and in the *Fear* of GOD. In like Manner, GOD's *Favour* never appeareth more, than it does in the *Increase of Children*; by Reason He hath promised to inrich the *Faithful* with that Gift; and that, because of the *spiritual Blessing* He hath made to His *Church*, such temporal Things shall by Him be granted: For that, except GOD doth *publickly* bless His *Church*, He well knew that His *private Blessings* would be but little minded. So let us receive all that comes to us, by the *Power* of GOD, as His *Blessings*, with Chearfulness; that He may continue the same on our Posterity.

(—Vide *Matt.* xix. 12.—*John* xv.—*Matt.* vi.—)

The PRECEPT.

{ *Hail, wedded* Love!—*How* bless'd *both Man and Wife*,
When Virtue *guides them through the Scenes of Life!*
But, O how curs'd!—*when both in* Strife *contend!*
Unhappy here, *and Ruin in the* End. }

N. B This was wrote intirely to encourage all to live in the *Fear* of GOD; and *pray* for His *Blessings*, &c.

On PSALM CXXIX.

(ASCENSION 10.—*Many a Time have they afflicted,*)

THE *Church* and People of GOD having undergone many *Calamities* and *Afflictions*, the Psalmist herein ¹ shews that GOD was their only *Defender* and *Keeper*; and ⁵ that all the Schemes and Contrivances of the Wicked were of no other Effect, only ⁶ to work their own Destruction.

* (—Vide *Ezra* iv. 4, &c.—)

This shews that the *Church*, in all Times, hath had many cruel Enemies; and that *we* should always bear the same in *Remembrance*, in order to arm us against them; forasmuch as we well know that GOD never failed, in His own due Time, to break all the Snares that the Wicked laid for the *Righteous*; and to take the Yoke of Misery from off their Shoulders, so long as they endured their Punishments with *Patience*, and trusted in GOD. And though their wicked Enemies puffed up themselves with Pride, and seemed to domineer over both GOD and His *People*; yet GOD so took them off in their Bud, and their Posterity, that none would pity them; by Reason they grounded not their *Faith* in GOD, neither were they friendly to His People. So let *us* always *trust* in GOD, with full Assurance that He will deliver us from their *Bands* and Snares of Cruelty.

The PRECEPT.

> When GOD *supports, the Wicked strive in vain,*
> *For why? He will the just Man's Cause maintain':*
> *Aid us,* O LORD, *and be our great Defence,*
> *That we in* CHRIST *may place our Confidence.*

N. B. This seems to be wrote on the *People*'s going out of *Babylon*; and the cruel Conflicts they there underwent by their Enemies, who afterwards hindered them in their Work. The *Author* of this is uncertain. * Vide as above.

On PSALM CXXX.

(ASCENSION 11.—*Out of the Deep have I called,*)

IN this *penitential Psalm* holy DAVID ¹ mournfully prayeth to GOD to *hear* him, and ³ to *forgive* his Sins: In which, shewing his true *Hope*, he exhorteth all the *Faithful* to do the like.

* (—Vide 2 *Sam.* xxiv. 10.—*Psal.* lxix. 3.—xlii.—xxxviii. 4.—*Jam.* v. 16.—)

Holy DAVID, (in the Name of the *Faithful*) being grievously afflicted in Mind, calls on GOD from the very Bottom of his Heart, and in Remembrance of his

A New Exposition *on the* Book *of* Psalms, &c. 109

his Sins, to forgive him; well knowing, that, if GOD should mark all his Misdeeds, he should not be able to bear His *Judgment*, unless he vouchsafed His *Mercy* to him. This shews to us, as in a Glass, that we cannot ever appear *just* before the Face of GOD, unless He, in *Mercy*, forgive us our Sins: And that He hath promised if we confess our *Sins* and abide constant unto Him, He will *forgive* us our Sins; and, by the *Truth* of His *Word*, will cleanse us from all Unrighteousness.

(–Vide *Rom.* viii. 26.–*Psal.* ii. 7.–1 *Pet.* i. 18.–*Jer.* xxxi. 34.–1 *John* i. 8, 9.–)

The PRECEPT.

{ *When, from the Depth and Bottom of my Heart,*
To GOD *I cry'd, He did His Aid impart:*
In Mercy, LORD, *do Thou our Sins survey,*
That we may stand *at Thy* Tribunal-Day. }

N. B. This *Psalm* seems to be wrote by DAVID, on his *numbering* the People, and the *Famine* that followed. See the *Scriptures* before cited *.

On PSALM CXXXI.

(ASCENSION 12.—LORD, *my Heart is not haughty,*)

HOLY DAVID, being charged with *Ambition*, on his Desire to reign; in this *Psalm* he [1] protesteth his great *Humility* and *Modesty*, both to GOD and *Man*: And [3] exhorts all the *Faithful* only to trust in GOD.

(—Vide *Matt.* ii. 28.—v. 5—*Tit.* iii. 2.—*Psal.* cxlvii. 6.—)

This *Psalm* is a worthy *Example* of *Humility, Modesty*, and *Contentment*; in order to teach us not to be puffed up, nor aim at Things above our Reach, or Understandings; nor even to *despise* none that are under us; seeing it is in GOD's Power either to *raise* up, or cast *down*. It also teacheth us to behave ourselves *humble* and *meek* to both GOD and *Man*; to be contented in our several *Stations* wherein GOD hath placed us; and to rest ourselves wholly under His divine Care and Protection. Let this be a *Pattern* for all *Rulers* in general, in order to deter them from *Tyranny*: Whereby they may not oppress such as are under them, nor soar too high, lest they offend GOD, as much as they *despise* Man; be brought down to utter *Destruction*; and the *Cries* of the *Poor* be heard against them to their own Damnation. *Let all the Faithful wait on Thee, O LORD; and let our Trust be in Thee, for our Salvation.*

The PRECEPT.

{ *Be not puff'd up with* Wealth *or* Fame,
With Pride, *nor with a lofty* Name:
For CHRIST *appear'd in* humble Dress,
That we Salvation *may possess*. }

N. B. St. *Jerome* alludeth this *Psalm* to the Person of CHRIST; from DAVID's Spirit of Prophecy, &c.

I

On PSALM CXXXII.

(Ascension 13.—LORD, *remember* DAVID,)

1004. **H**OLY DAVID, in this *Pſalm*, ſetteth forth [1] what great *Troubles* and *Afflictions* he underwent, and what pious Zeal he had for *building* the *Temple*, and [8] reſting the *Ark* therein. He [9] then deſires GOD to eſtabliſh his *Church*, [11] according to His *Promiſe*; which being *obtained* [12] on *Condition*, he [14] reſteth fully thereon; and [15] *exhorteth* all the *Faithful* to do the like, for their eternal *Salvation*: And [18] that all the Enemies of *CHRIST*'s *Church* ſhall come to Shame; but His *Crown* and *Kingdom* ſhall for ever flouriſh.

* (—Vide 1 *Chron.* xv.—2 *Chron.* vi. 16. 41, 42.—vii.—1 *Kings* ix. 1. 10.—*Deut.* xii. 5.—1 *Sam.* iv. 11.—*Numb.* x. 35.—*Pſal.* lxxviii. 68.—*Nehem.* xii.—)

This precious *Pſalm* ought always to be *uſed* in our *Church*, that our *Faith* may be confirmed in the LORD JESUS; of whoſe *Perſon* DAVID was a true *Figure*. We may alſo obſerve, that this is the *true Church*; and is *eſtabliſhed* by GOD's own Appointment, for the *Faithful*; from Generation to Generation. And as *Salvation* cannot be attained by any other Means, but by our *Faith* in the *Goſpel* of *CHRIST*, how careful ought we to be in *obeying* His *Word*, and receiving His *Sacraments*, and to reſt ourſelves wholly on His *Merits* to ſave us: Whoſe *Throne* is everlaſting, and Whoſe *Power* is infinite, from GOD the *Father*.

The PRECEPT.

{ LORD, *let Thy* Prieſts *be cloath'd with* Righteouſneſs, *And all Thy* People *Thee with* Praiſes *bleſs*: *To keep Thy* Laws, LORD, *all our Hearts incline*, *CHRIST is our* Reſt, *and laſting* Joy, *divine*. }

N. B. The 8th, 9th, and 10th *Verſes* of this *Pſalm* were uſed by *Solomon*, at the Cloſe of his *Prayer*, at the *Dedication* of the *Temple*; and agree well with the *Acceptance* of it, as teſtified from Heaven; with the LORD's *Anſwer*, in a Viſion to *Solomon*: For which Occaſion it was compoſed by DAVID. Though ſome think it was made by *Solomon* himſelf. See the *Scriptures* before cited *.

On PSALM CXXXIII.

(Ascension 14.—*Behold how good!*)

AFTER the Civil *Wars* of eight Years were all ended, and the *Tribes* all were come together to anoint DAVID their King,

King, he then set forth this *Psalm*, ¹ to *exhort* all to *Friendship* and *Unity*, and to be as Brethren : Shewing, not only ² the Precioufnefs of Unity in this World, but ³ alfo the everlasting Bleffednefs of it in the World to come.

* (—Vide 2 *Sam*. v.—1 *Chron*. xi.—*Exod*. xxx 23.—xxviii.—*Pfal*. xlii. 6 — 1 *Cor*. xiii.—*John* xiv. 21.—*Matt*. xvii.—)

In this *Pfalm* are figured the feveral *Graces* that proceed from C H R I S T, the Head of the *Church*: 1. By *Ointment*, that He was *chofen* and *anointed* of GOD to fave the World: And 2. by *Hermon* and *Sion*, it meaneth the Plentifulnefs that was in the Country about *Jerufalem*, where Concord abideth. From which we may *infer*, that if we live in *Peace*, one with another, in this World, we shall be sure of *Peace* in the next: But, there is no *Peace* with the Wicked, neither in this World, nor in that which is to come. So let *Peace* abide always within our Walls, and *Plenteoufnefs* in our Palaces.

(—Vide *Pfal*. cxxii. 7.—*Ifai*. ix. 6.—*Matt*. v. 9.—*Eph*. iv. 3.—)

The PRECEPT.

How good and pleafant, L O R D, *it is to fee Brethren to live in* Peace *and* Unity !
Affift us, L O R D, *to us Thy* Bleffings *give*,
That we in Concord *may for ever live*.

N. B. See the *Scriptures* before cited *.

On PSALM CXXXIV.

(ASCENSION 15, and laft.—*Behold! Blefs ye the* LORD,)

THIS being the *laft Pfalm* of *Afcenfion*, holy DAVID herein ¹ exhorteth all the Godly to behold the *Temple* which GOD hath now placed for His divine *Worfhip*. Also to *watch* and keep all Things therein in *good Order*; and ² that they conftantly render *Prayers*, *Praifes*, and *Thankfgivings* unto GOD for His wonderful *Mercies* and Benefits; and ³ for *bleffing* and eftablifhing His *Church* amongft us.

* (—Vide 1 *Chron*. xvi. 4.—2 *Chron*. viii. 14.—*Eph*. vi. 18.—*Pfal*. xxv. 1.—)

This *Pfalm* fheweth the *Charge* that was firft given to the *Levites* and *Priefts*, not only to *guard* and keep the *Temple*, but alfo to beftow their Time, Day and Night, in *Praifes*, *Prayers*, and *Thankfgivings* unto G O D, for the *Salvation* of the People; fince He had fo beftowed His fatherly *Love* on them to eftablifh His *Church*, whereby they might be faved. Seeing now, that all thefe Things were only Shadows of C H R I S T, and His *Kingdom*, and that the *Promife* of GOD is now fulfilled by the Coming of the *Meffiah*, which He hath fent for our *Redemption*:

demption: Let us now, in His *Church*, render all the *Praises* and *Thanksgivings* we are able, for such wonderful *Mercies* and *Blessings*; and lift up our *Hearts* with our *Voices* in His holy *Sanctuary*; hoping for a *blessed Resurrection*, and Life in the World to come, by the *Merits* of His Son *J E S U S*.

(—Vide *Psal*. cxlv. 1.—1 *Pet*. iv. 7.—*Matt*. xvi. 15.—*Psal*. lviii. 11.—)

The PRECEPT.

{ *Let ev'ry* Servant *of the heav'nly* LORD,
Both Night and Day, Praise *Him with one Accord:*
At Home, *and* Church, *His* Mercy *daily own,*
Who sends all Blessings *from His holy Throne*. }

N. B. This *Psalm* hinteth on the *Levites* ministring in their *Courses*, either before the *Ark*, or in the *Temple*. See the *Scriptures* before cited *.

On PSALM CXXXV.

(HALLELUJAH.)

THIS is another *Psalm* of Exhortation: Wherein holy DAVID [1] inviteth all the Faithful to sing *Praises* unto GOD [4] for His *Election*, [5] *Power*, [6] *Decrees*, [7] *Providences* and Deliverances of the *Israelites*. And, whereas [15] vain *Idols* can do nothing to assist Man, he again [19] exhorteth all Kinds of People to *Praise* GOD.

* (—Vide 1 *Chron*. xvi. 4.—*Psal*. cxv.—cxxxiv.—)

This *Psalm* has Connection with the foregoing *Psalm*: Shewing, that GOD loveth the Posterity of *Abraham*, so long as they are constant to Him, and willeth that they should depend only on His Power; and that He will, at all Times, destroy the Enemies of His *Church*, to save His People. It also shews that GOD will surely *punish all Idolaters*, and *save* those that only *worship* Him, in Sincerity and in Truth. So *Praised be the* GOD *of* Israel *for ever and ever, Who hath visited and redeemed His People*.

(—Vide *Jer*. x. 13.—*Exod*. xii. 29.—*Numb*. xxi. 24. 34.—)

The PRECEPT.

{ O Praise *the* LORD, *His Name for ever bless,*
And daily triumph in His Holiness:
'Tis good and comely for His Saints *to sing*
Eternal Praises *to the heav'nly* King. }

N. B. The Word *Sion* being mentioned in the last *Verse* of the cxxxiiid, the cxxxivth, and the cxxxvth *Psalms*, sheweth that DAVID composed these *Psalms* before the *Temple* was built on that *Place*. See the *Scriptures* before cited *.

On PSALM CXXXVI.
(Hallelujah.)

WE have, in this *Pfalm*, ¹ a general Exhortation to *Praife* GOD for all *Mercies*; ⁵ for the vifible *Creation*, and all its *Works*; for *Redemption, Prefervation*, and ¹¹ for His bountiful *Mercies*, and ²¹ Loving-kindnefs towards His *Church*, &c.

* (—Vide *Gen.* i.—*Matt.* vi. 26.—2 *Chron.* vii. 3.—xx. 2.—)

This magnificent *Pfalm* has fome Coherence with the former, and was compofed for the fame Ufe, *viz.* for the *Congregation* in general to acknowledge the wonderful *Providence* and *Mercies* of GOD towards them, and their *Pofterity*. The grand *Chorus* that follows every *Verfe*, is a fingular Acknowledgment of GOD's *Mercies*, and fhews, that *they will endure for ever*, to all fuch as *love* and *fear* Him, and abide in the *Faith* of *CHRIST*. This *Chorus* was ufually a common Kind of *Thankfgiving* in general, for *Feafts* and Days fet apart for divine Worfhip, after any *Mercies* they had received from GOD; even to repeat, and remind them of *former* Favours: Shewing thereby, that GOD ha h promifed the like *Mercies* to them, and their *Pofterity*, as he had fhewn to their *Forefathers*; and on the fame Conditions. GOD's *Mercies* here are very wonderful, and even unto all *Creatures*, as well as to His *Church*, which He fhewed for the Space of forty Years; in order to teach us to be *patient* in our greateft *Afflictions*, and truft intirely on GOD's divine *Providence*; He having promifed always to *preferve* the *Faithful*, and deftroy the *Wicked*.

(—Vide *Pfal.* civ.—lxxviii.—cv.—cvi.—cvii.—)

The PRECEPT.

{ *Give* Thanks *to* GOD, *Who made both Heav'n and Earth,*
And Praife *His Name, Who gave to all Things Birth:*
GOD feedeth *all, His* Promife *is full fure,*
And, to the Juft, *His* Mercies *ever dure.* }

N. B. From the *Scriptures* before cited, DAVID muft certainly have been the Author of this *Pfalm*, which fee.*.

On PSALM CXXXVII.

Before *Chrift*, IN this *Pfalm*, ¹ the People of GOD, being in 1577. Captivity, greatly lament the *Decay* of true *Religion*, ³ and their being *derided*: and ⁵ avouch their *Conftancy* and

The Pfalm-Singer's Jewel: *Or*, and Zeal towards *Jerufalem*, in the Midft of their Griefs; and ? foretel the *Deftruction* of *Babylon*, for their cruel Ufage.

* (—Vide *Ezek.* vii. 16.—xxxiii. 21.—xxv. 12.—xxxv.—*Jer.* xlix. 7.— *Ifai.* xiii. 16.—)

This plainly fhews, that, although the Country was very *pleafant* whereto the People of G O D were banifhed, yet they lived in great *Sorrow* and *Anguifh*, and could not refrain from Tears; efpecially when the *Babylonians derided* them for their finging G O D's Praifes; and as if their *Silence* fhewed they had no more *Hope* in G O D to deliver them. No, their *Church* was fo dear to them, that their Tears burft out whenfoever they thought of it; and the Decay of G O D's *Religion* was fo grievous, that no *Joy* could make them *glad*, except it was reftored: So that G O D ufed them as *Rods* to punifh His Enemies. From this excellent *Pfalm* we may learn very *excellent* Things, *viz.* That whenfoever we remain *filent* under great Afflictions of barbarous Enemies, (efpecially for the *Gofpel* of C H R I S T,) when the Powers of Darknefs have their Time, we muft not only remain *conftant* in our *Faith*, but alfo in our *Zeal*; left we betray the *Truth* with our Silence, or forfake our *Duty* for the *Fear* of powerful Men. No, God forbid we fhould faulter, though we are obliged to be *filent*; feeing that fuch *Tyrants* are more like *Brutes* than Men, and never will go unpunifhed; who not only perfecute the *Church*, but *defpife* the Truth of G O D's *Word*; and cruelly ufe the Innocent.

The P R E C E P T.

> *Do Thou*, O G O D, *our Enemies confound*,
> *Thy Might can dafh their* Malice *to the Ground:*
> *Let us*, O G O D, *Thy* Mercy *ever* fing,
> *And own* Salvation *by our heav'nly* King.

N. B. This *Pfalm* feems to be compofed by *Ezekiel*, or fome other *godly Man*, at the Beginning of the *Captivity*, in order to ftir up the People not to fall from their *Religion* during the feventy Years *Exile:* Though fome fay it was made by DAVID *.

On P S A L M CXXXVIII.

HEREIN holy DAVID [1] greatly *Praifeth* G O D for His *Mercies* towards Him, in his Afflictions: And [4] that foreign *Princes* and *Strangers* fhall do the like, even *all together* in the *Worfhip* of G O D: [7] Affuring himfelf of the like *Comfort* of G O D's *Mercies* for the Time to come.

* (—Vide 1 Sam. xxvi.—1 Cor. xi.—*John* iv. 23 —)

DAVID, having attained the *Kingdom*, and brought the *Ark* into the City, thought alfo on the *Building* of the *Temple*, and *prophefied* that the fame fhould come

A New Expofition *on the* Book *of* Pfalms, *&c.* 115

come to pafs; and that all the *Kings* of the World fhould acknowledge and *celebrate* fo great a Benefit; that fhould be fulfilled by *CHRIST*. And, becaufe the Inftruments of *Satan* generally are amongft great Men, when the *Church* is perfecuted; he exhorteth all fuch to be armed againft fuch Battles, and to *pray* at all Times; and reft their Foundation of *Hope* intirely on GOD: Who cherifheth the *Oppreffed*, hateth the Proud, and fpareth the *Godly* for the Kingdom of Heaven.

(—Vide *Pfal.* xli.—cxix.—)

The PRECEPT.

{ *In Thy* blefs'd Courts, O LORD, *my* Voice *I'll raife,*
To blefs *Thy Name, and* celebrate *Thy* Praife:
Thy tender Care *is over all the* Juft,
That love Thy Name, *and in Thy* Mercy *truft*. }

N. B. This *Pfalm* feems to be wrote by DAVID, when *Saul* (by his fecond Confeffion) vindicated him in his *Reputation*, and confirmed him in his *Expectation* of the *Kingdom*. See the *Scriptures* before cited *.

On PSALM CXXXIX.

IN this *Pfalm*, holy DAVID ¹ fetteth forth the wonderful Knowledge of GOD over all his ² *Actions* ⁴ and *Thoughts*. He alfo ⁶ acknowledgeth that the *Works* of GOD are far above the Reach of Man, at all *Times*, and ⁸ in all *Places*: And ¹³ magnifies His Name, on his *Formation* in the *Womb*; ¹⁵ and the curious Texture of all his *Members*. He then ¹⁷ fhews how dear the *Thoughts* of GOD, and His *Works*, were unto him; and ¹⁹ defires He would deftroy the Wicked, try his *Integrity*, and ²³ lead him in the Way of *Righteoufnefs* for ever.

* (—Vide 2 *Sam.* xvi. 7.—*Pfal.* lxxvii. 12.—civ. 34.—)

This is a moft glorious *Pfalm* of *Meditation* on GOD's *Attributes*: Shewing that the all-feeing Eye of GOD infpects all our *Thoughts* and *Actions*, be they ever fo *private*, by Day or by Night. The curious *Structure* of Man may well be compared unto a *little World*, not only in Refpect of his *Body*, but alfo of his great *Underftanding* above all other terreftrial *Creatures*: He having a *Head*, and *Thoughts* to *conceive* and *invent*; a *Tongue* to *fpeak* and *argue*; and *Hands* to *act* beyond them all. GOD hath not only placed him *over* all the other earthly *Creation*, but has alfo endued him with an immortal *living Soul*; and hath *formed* him in his own *Image*, to *worfhip* and *ferve* him; and will, after this Life, give him a *Kingdom*, not made with Hands, eternal in the Heavens.—Let us at every Opportunity *meditate* on this moft *glorious Pfalm*, and the more we *meditate* on it, the more we fhall *admire* the wonderful *Works* of GOD; and what great Things He doth hourly for us: Forafmuch as we know He will lead us in the Way

116 *The* Psalm-Singer's Jewel: *Or,*

Way of all *Righteousness,* and give *Salvation* to all such as shall seek it, in the LORD *JESUS.*

(—Vide *Prov.* viii. 17.—*Matt.* vi. 33.—)

The PRECEPT.

> Great GOD! *to Thee are all my* Secrets *known,*
> In ev'ry Place, *awake, or lying down:*
> As nothing's hid from Thy *all-seeing* Eye,
> LORD, *guard my* Soul, *that I may never die.*

N. B. This *Psalm* was probably wrote with *Psal.* vii. xvii. xxvi. when DAVID was first accused, and then persecuted by Saul. See the *Scriptures* before cited *.

On PSALM CXL.

DAVID, in this *Psalm,* ¹ earnestly beggeth of GOD to deliver him from his cruel Enemies; *i. e.* ² from *malicious,* ³ *flattering,* ⁵ *proud,* and cruel Men. Then ⁶ acknowledging GOD to be his only Strength and *Safeguard,* in the Day of *Battle:* He ⁸ prays that He would destroy all his *spiteful, slanderous,* and ¹¹ *backbiting* Enemies; that ¹³ the *Righteous* might *Praise* Him, and abide in His divine *Presence,* in Peace and Safety.

* (—Vide 1 *Sam.* xviii. 19.—*Psal.* lii.—lxix.—cxx.—*Rom.* xii. 20.—)

This *Psalm* (as in a *Glass*) sheweth what Contrivances wicked Men have to bring their wicked Ends to pass; and how they will stick at nothing, neither in *Thought, Word,* nor *Deed,* when they intend to spoil the *Righteous,* and destroy the *Church* of GOD. It shews also, how soon they are *defeated* and overthrown, when GOD once takes the Matter in Hand, to *defend* the Godly: And how wonderfully they are *preserved* when they put their whole Trust and Confidence in His *Power* and *Protection.* Let it be, therefore, our chief Endeavour to *live* in the *Fear* of GOD, and trust wholly in His divine *Providence,* in all Manner of *Afflictions:* And earnestly *pray* to GOD to be our only Safeguard; Who hath Power both to *destroy* and to *save:* And will destroy the Wicked from the Face of the Earth, that the *Righteous* may *rejoice,* and that His *sacred* Name may be *glorious* in all the World.

(—Vide *Psal.* cxlvii. 6.—)

The PRECEPT.

> Protect *me,* LORD, *with Thy Almighty Care,*
> From *flatt'ring* Tongues, *and such as* cruel *are:*
> Thy tender Love *is over all the* Just;
> O *guard my* Soul, *for in Thee do I trust.*

N. B. This *Psalm* was probably wrote on *Saul's* first Machinations against DAVID. See the *Scriptures* before cited *.

On

On PSALM CXLI.

IN this *Pfalm* holy DAVID [1] earneftly *prayeth* to GOD that his *Prayer* may be heard; and that [3] he might be kept from all Kinds of Sin either [4] in *Thought, Word,* or *Deed*. That he might [5] be both *tractable* and *charitable,* and [6] be *juftified,* and [8] be *faved* from the Violence and Treachery of his cruel Enemies.

* (-Vide 1 *Sam.* xxiii. 13 -*Exod.* xvii.-*Jam.* iii.-*Matt.* xv. 19.-1 *Cor.* i. 9, 10.-)

This *Pfalm* is a Form of *Prayer* in general againft all Manner of *Vices,* and cruel Enemies: From which we may infer, that, under all Manner of *Afflictions,* we muft flee to GOD for Succour and Comfort; and patiently bear fuch Corrections and Chaftifements as proceed from a true and *loving Heart*; and receive them with Joy and Comfort; by reafon fuch Reproofs are for our own Good. And whenfoever we are wrongfully accufed, and perfecuted by cruel and malicious Men, we muft patiently wait on GOD, till He, in His good Time, fhall deliver us; Who will affuredly trap them in their own Snares, and *preferve* the *Righteous* out of their cruel Hands, if they *pray* to Him with a *faithful* and true Heart.

(—Vide *Pfal.* cxlv. 18, 19, 20.—)

The PRECEPT.

{ *Set Thou a* Watch *before my* Lips, *O* LORD,
That I may not prophane *Thy holy* Word:
And let me, LORD, *fo in Thy* Paths *proceed,*
Ne'er to offend, in Thought, *in* Word, *nor* Deed. }

N. B. This feems to be wrote when DAVID and his 600 Men were in the Wildernefs of *Maon,* when *Saul* had near encompaffed him, by the Treachery of the *Ziphites,* who were reftrained by the News of the *Philiftines* Invafion; but good *Jonathan* had before confederated with him, and approved him. See the *Scriptures* before cited *.

On PSALM CXLII.

DAVID, being in great *Fear* and *Diftrefs,* [1] crieth fervently unto GOD [4] to help him out of his great Dangers: Whereby [7] he might *Praife* His Name, and the *Righteous* be with Him as ufual, &c.

* (—Vide 1 *Sam.* xxiii. 29.—xxiv.—)

This *Mafchil,* or *Pfalm* of *Prayer,* fhews the great Effect of *Patience* under any Sufferings and Confinement; and that we fhould never *murmur* againft GOD,

GOD, in our greatest Extremities, when all our Friends have forsaken us; but rely wholly on GOD for Help, when all other Means fail; and wait for a joyful *Deliverance* from His Hands; Who is able to destroy our Enemies, and give us a *Crown* of Glory.

(—Vide *Matt.* v. 5.—*Psal.* xxxvii. *ult.*—)

The PRECEPT.

{ LORD, *Thou'rt my* Portion, *and my sure* Defence,
In *Thee I place my* Trust *and Confidence :*
To Thee I cry, O *help me in Distress,*
And slay such Foes, *as would my Soul oppress.* }

N. B. This was probably holy DAVID's *Prayer* and *Meditation*, when he was inclosed on every Side by cruel *Saul*, in the *Cave* or Strong-holds of *En-gedi*. See the *Scriptures* before cited *.

On PSALM CXLIII.

IN this *penitential Psalm*, holy DAVID ¹ earnestly prayeth to GOD for the *Remission* of his Sins; and ² acknowledges the *Justice* of his Punishments. He then ⁷ beggeth of GOD speedily to help him; ⁹ deliver him from his Enemies; ¹⁰ *teach* him in the Way of *Righteousness*, and ¹² destroy such as were his cruel Adversaries.

* (—Vide 1 *Sam.* xxiv.—xxiii. 29.—)

This *Psalm* of *Meditation* has Connection with the former, and on the same *Occasion:* Shewing, that we should always remain *faithful* in GOD's *Promises*, in our greatest Discomforts; and that we should always receive His *Afflictions* as *Messengers* to warn us to *Repentance* of our Sins. That we should, at all Times, trust ourselves to GOD's divine *Providence*; and shelter ourselves intirely under the Wings of his *Mercy*; Whose *Spirit* will frame our Hearts, by His *Grace*, to obey His *Word.* For, as soon as ever we *decline* from Him, and He forsakes us, we immediately fall into Error; and unless His *Mercy* restores us again, by His *Grace*, and Goodness, we must inevitably fall into Destruction both Body and Soul. And, since His *Grace* and *Promise* are our only *Safeguard*, let us never shrink from our *Duty* towards Him, lest He take His *Holy Spirit* from us, and leave us *comfortless*; nor be too daring in slighting and prophaning His *divine Ordinances*, lest we bring His heavy *Judgments* down upon us : But let us *pray*, with DAVID, *that He will guard us by His Holy Spirit, and lead us to the Land of Righteousness.* Ver. 10.

The PRECEPT.

{ *Let me,* O LORD, *Thy loving* Kindness *hear,*
Keep me from Foes, *and in my Cause appear :*
Teach me, O LORD, *to do Thy heav'nly* Will,
And guide my Spirit *unto Thy holy* Hill. }

N. E. This was probably penned by DAVID when in the Cave of *En-gedi*, and pursued by *Saul.* See the *Scriptures* before cited *.

On

On PSALM CXLIV.

DAVID, in this *Pfalm*, with great *Affection*, [1] bleſſeth GOD for his *Victories*, and [3] his *Humility* to poor Men. He then [5] imploreth GOD's further Aſſiſtance, [7] to deliver him from the Tumults of ſtrange People that flattered him: [9] Promiſing chearfully to *Praiſe* GOD with Voice and Inſtruments, for his great Deliverances: Wiſhing [12] the like Succeſs, [13] and Increaſe on all the Faithful, and their Poſterity.

* (—Vide 2 *Sam.* viii. 10.—*Pſal.* xviii.—xxxiii.—xliv.—cviii.—*Iſai.* xlv. 1.—)

Holy DAVID herein ſheweth, that it was GOD alone that gained him all his *Victories*, and not his own *Policy*; and that it was GOD only that had raiſed him from a poor *Shepherd*, to a valiant *Warrior*, and a mighty *Conqueror*; for which he had great Reaſon to *Praiſe* GOD for all His Favours towards him. He alſo deſires GOD to continue His *Benefits* towards His People; (counting the Procreation of Children, and good Education, amongſt GOD's gracious Benefits;) and even that none of His Bleſſings be wanted, on any Occaſion whatſoever, to all Generations, *&c.* So *Bleſſed are the People that hope only in* GOD, *yea, Bleſſed are they Whoſe* GOD *is the* LORD.

(—Vide *Pſal.* lxxviii. 70, 71, 72.—)

The PRECEPT.

> Bleſs'd be the LORD, *who gives me* Strength *to fight,*
> Loud Songs of Triumph ſhall my Soul delight:
> With Peace *and* Plenty, LORD, *Thy People bleſs,*
> That we may glory in Thy Righteouſneſs.

N. B. This *Pſalm* was probably wrote with the cviiith, in the Midſt of his foreign *Expeditions* againſt his cruel Enemies. See the *Scriptures* before cited *.

On PSALM CXLV.

(DAVID's *Praiſes.* HALLELUJAH.)

IN this excellent *Pſalm* holy DAVID [1] *Praiſeth*, [2] and *bleſſeth* GOD, [3] for His incomprehenſible *Greatneſs*, [7] *Goodneſs,* [9] and *Mercy*; and for His wonderful *Works* of the *Creation* in general. He ſheweth alſo, [10] that GOD is *Praiſed* by all His *Works*; and [11] that they ſhew His *Honour* and mighty *Power:* [13] That

[13] That His *Kingdom* is everlasting, and that all *Creatures* are *fed* by His *Bounty*. That [17] GOD also rejoiceth in all His *Works*; [19] fulfilleth just Men's *Desires*, [20] preserves them from Evil, and destroys their Enemies.

(—Vide *Psal.* ciii. 8.—*Dan.* vii. 14.—*Luke* i. 33.—1 *John* v. 14.—*Exod.* xxxiv. 6.—)

This glorious *Psalm* is called DAVID's *Praises*, as also may all the rest that follow; by Reason they continue the same Collaudation or *Praising* of GOD; as the *first* and *last Verses* of every *Psalm* testify.—To *Praise* GOD without *fearing* Him, is like *a sounding Brass, or tinkling Cymbal:* Or, that *we Praise Him with our Mouths, but in our Hearts we irreverently deny Him*. To *Praise* GOD *justly*, let this *Psalm* be our constant *Rule* and *Pattern*; that is, *with Heart and Voice*; for all the *Mercies* and *Benefits* he has bestowed on us; and that He alone may have the *Glory*, to whom *Glory* is due.—*All Thy Works bless Thee, O* LORD! *in Wisdom Thou madest them all! Thou openest Thy Hand, and they are filled with Good. The* LORD *preserves all those that love Him, and destroys the Wicked.— My Mouth shall daily sing the Praise of the* LORD: *And all Flesh shall bless the Name of the* LORD, *for ever and ever.*

(—Vide *Tit.* i. 16.—*Psal.* civ. 17.—)

The PRECEPT.

{ O LORD, I'll Praise *Thy great and mighty Name,*
Talk of Thy Works, *and celebrate Thy* Fame :
Thou sav'st the Just, *that on Thy* Aid *depend* ;
Thy Love *and* Mercy *never hath an End.* }

N. B. Probably this *Psalm* was wrote on the compleating of his *Victories*, and extending his Empire over the *Gentiles*, as GOD had promised; and the *establishing* his *Kingdom* for ever.

On PSALM CXLVI.

(DAVID's *Praises*. HALLELUJAH.)

IN this *Psalm* DAVID [1] declareth his continual *Zeal* to *Praise*; dehorting [1] us not to trust in *Princes*, no more than other Men; because all are mortal. He shews also [5] the eternal *Happiness* of those that trust only in GOD; [7] Whose *Word* is *true*, and [7] Whose *Judgments* are *just*; [8] Who loveth the *Righteous*, helpeth the poor *Strangers*, [9] relieveth the *Fatherless* and the *Widow*, and overthroweth the Wicked: And [10] preserveth His *Church* for ever. *Praise ye the* LORD.

(—Vide *Psal.* cxlv.—cxlvii.—cxlviii.—cxlix.—cl.

This *Psalm* has Connection with the former; and stirreth up all People to *Praise* GOD, and confide wholly in Him; Who is able to *save* us in all Dangers,

A New Exposition on the Book of Psalms, &c.

gers, when the Help of Man faileth. And although He often visiteth them with the *Afflictions* of *Hunger, Imprisonment*, and such-like, yet His *Love* and fatherly *Pity* never faileth to assist all such as *love* and *fear* Him. *Happy is he that hath the* GOD *of* Jacob *for his Help: And whose Hope is only in the* LORD GOD.

The PRECEPT.

{ Praise GOD, *my Soul, His Name I will confess*,
Who helps the Stranger *and the* Fatherless :
The Help of Princes *can no Life sustain*,
But, GOD's great Mercy *ever doth remain*. }

N. B. St. *Jerome* imagineth this *Psalm* to be made after the People's Return from *Babylon*; by Reason it hinteth on Releasing of *Prisoners*, Preserving of *Strangers, Fatherless*, and *Widows*, &c. It also referreth to CHRIST's being delivered from the Oppressions of Sin and *Satan*; and His *Church* and *Kingdom* preserved, &c. &c.

※※※※※※※※※※※※※※※※※※※※※※※※※※

On PSALM CXLVII.
(DAVID's *Praises.* HALLELUJAH.)

HOLY DAVID, in this *Psalm*, [1] exhorteth all the People to *Praise* GOD [2] for His *Care* of the *Church*; [5] for His *Power*; [6] His *Mercy*; [8] His *Providence*, and [12] for His *Blessings* upon the Kingdom: Also [15] for His Power and *Blessings* of His *Meteors*; and [19] for His mighty *Ordinances* in His *Church*, &c.—*Praise ye the* LORD.

(—Vide *Psal.* cxlv.—cxlvi.—cxlviii.—cxlix.—cl.—civ. 13, 14.—)

This *Psalm* has Connection with the former: Shewing, that, as GOD was the sole *Founder* of His *Church* amongst us, it is our *Duty* daily to *Praise* Him therein; seeing it is gathered together for the like Purpose, by His *Power* and infinite *Love* towards His People. Moreover, he hath not only left to us that excellent Treasure of His *Church*, but hath also given us His only SON JESUS CHRIST, to be our *Mediator* and *Redeemer*; by Whose *Gospel* we have eternal *Salvation*: Who in His last Appearance will *judge* both the Quick and the Dead, and render to every Man according to His *Works* in this Life. So *Praise the* LORD, *for He is gracious; and His Mercy endureth for ever.*

(—Vide *Psal.* cxxxvi.—*Matt.* xvi.—*Gal.* iii. 23.—)

The PRECEPT.

{ O Praise *the* LORD, *it is a comely Thing*,
Who all Things *made, and did* Salvation *bring :*
He feedeth all, *with* Plenty, Love, *and* Peace,
For which our Thanks *and* Praise *should never cease*. }

N. B. This *Psalm* was probably wrote after the People's Return from *Babylon*, as was the former.

On PSALM CXLVIII.

(David's Praises. Hallelujah.)

DAVID, in this *Pfalm*, earneſtly calleth on all Things both *celeſtial* and *terreſtrial* to *Praiſe* GOD: *viz.* ² the *Angels*; ³ the *Sun, Moon,* and *Stars,* the *Heavens* and *Waters* above them. Alſo ⁷ *Dragons* and *Depths*; ⁸ *Fire, Hail, Snow, Vapours, Wind*; ⁹ *Mountains, Trees:* ¹⁰ *Beaſts, Cattle,* creeping *Things,* and *Fowls;* ¹¹ *Kings, Princes, Judges,* and all People; ¹² *Young* Men, *Maidens,* Old Men, and *Children.* ¹⁴ Alſo to *Praiſe* GOD for His *Church*; and for the *Power* he has given to His *choſen* People, that He hath joined unto Him.—*Praiſe ye the* LORD.

(—Vide *Pſal.* cxlv.—cxlvi.—cxlvii.—cxlix.—cl.—*Iſai.* vi. 6.—)

This *Pſalm* hath Connection with the former; and ſheweth, that, as all *Things* are but as *Members* of their reſpective *Bodies,* they ſhould all join in GOD's *Praiſe,* and ſhew His Glory; *i. e.* both in *Heaven* above, in the *Earth* below, and in the *Waters.* This Exhortation teacheth us the great *Duty* we owe to GOD; and that the greater His *Gifts* are, the more we are in Duty bound to *Praiſe* Him; and to *glory* in His *Church*; which He hath placed amongſt us, according to the *Promiſe* that He made unto *Abraham,* and His Seed for ever.— So *Praiſe* the LORD, *for He hath exalted the Horn of His People: Which is a Praiſe for all His Saints; even for the Children of* Iſrael, *a People that are near unto Him.* Praiſe ye the LORD.

The Precept.

> Let all Things Praise *the great and mighty* LORD,
> In Heav'n *and* Earth; *for at His mighty* Word
> *All* Things *were* made; *all muſt on Him rely,*
> *And, by His* Power, *muſt all Things* live *or* die.

N. B. This *Pſalm* probably was penned after the Captivity of *Babylon;* as was the former.

On PSALM CXLIX.

(David's Praises. Hallelujah.)

HOLY David, in this *Pſalm*, ¹ earneſtly exhorts the *Saints* of GOD to *Praiſe* Him with their utmoſt *Power,* by by Reason [2] they are preferred before any other Nation; and, [3] to join their *Voices* with *Instruments*; and [5] rest themselves intirely under His divine *Providence*. He [6] then setteth forth the *Ministers* of *CHRIST*, and the *Power* of His *Gospel*; and [7] that *Judgment* shall be executed against the Enemies of the *Church*. *Praise ye the* LORD.

(—Vide *Psal.* cxlv.—cxlvi.—cxlvii.—cxlviii.—cl.—*Heb.* iv. 11, 12. 14.—)

This *Psalm* has Connection with the former; and beginneth as the xcvth, *viz.* *Sing to the* LORD *a new Song:* The Word *new* meaning to act under the *Gospel* of *CHRIST*, as a *new* People, by *Regeneration*, as the People of *Israel*; *CHRIST* being our *King*, in Whom we ought to be *glad*, and rejoice, as *Ver.* 2. And, as GOD is the Creator of both Soul and Body, so must we serve Him with both; with a free Heart, and with a willing Mind. *Let* Israel *therefore rejoice in* GOD *that created all; and let the Children of* Sion *be glad in the King of their Salvation. Let them Praise Him with the Lute and the Harp: And this Honour shall be to all His Saints*, in the LORD JESUS.

(—Vide *Psal.* xcv. 7.—2 *Cor.* x. 5.—*Isai.* xlv. 14, 15.—*Heb.* iv. ult.—)

The PRECEPT.

{ *Songs of* Salvation *let the Righteous* sing,
And joy in CHRIST, *their* Saviour, *and their* King:
Eternal Praises *unto* CHRIST *be giv'n*,
Inthron'd in State, *at* GOD's *Right-hand, in* Heav'n. }

N. B. Probably this *Psalm* was penned after the *Captivity*; and to keep the *Mercies* of GOD in Rememberance to all Generations, concerning His *Promise* to the *Faithful*.

On PSALM CL.

DAVID's *Praises.* HALLELUJAH.

THIS, being the last *Hallelujah*, [1] exhorteth all to *Praise* GOD both in *Heaven* and on *Earth*, [2] for His noble *Acts*, and according to His excellent *Greatness*. Also [3] to *Praise* Him with *Trumpet*, the *Viol*, and the *Harp*; [4] with the *Timbrel*, *Flute*, *Virginals*, and the ORGAN; [5] with the sounding *Cymbals*, and even with the *loud Cymbal*: And, [6] in the *Conclusion* of the whole, *Let every Thing that hath Breath, or Spirit*, PRAISE THE LORD, *&c. &c. &c.*

(—Vide *Psal.* civ.—cv.—cxlv.—cxlvi.—cxlvii.—cxlviii.—cxlix.—)

This *Psalm* has not only Connection with the four foregoing *Psalms*, but also with all other *Psalms* of *Praise* and *Thanksgiving*: By reason the *Mercy, Goodness,*

ness, and *Power* of GOD shineth not only in the *Heavens*, but also over all the *World*; in all *Places* and *Dominions*. And, as by His *Power* all *Things* were made, all are not able to *Praise* Him enough, according to His excellent *Mercy* and *Goodness*; and more particularly for His *Redemption, Government*, and *Salvation* of His *Church*, and *Monarchy* of the *World*; ruling in, and under His only Son the LORD JESUS; to Whom we seek for *Succour* whilst we are in this World; and hope for *eternal Life* in the World to come; in Whose eternal *Mansions Hallelujahs* have no End.—*So Blessed be the Name of the* LORD *for ever and ever: And may all the Earth be filled with the Glory of His Majesty.* Amen. Amen.

The PRECEPT.

{ *O* Praise *the* LORD, Praise *Him with one* Consent, }
{ Praise *Him with* Voice, *and ev'ry* Instrument : }
{ *Let* Organs, Trumpets, Drums, *and* Strings *accord*, }
{ *And all* Things *breathing* Praise *the mighty* LORD. }

DOXOLOGY.

O Spir't *of* Love! *Great* Source *of* Joy *and* Peace,
Our Praise *of* Thee *shall never, never, cease :*
To Thee, *Almighty* FATHER, Three *in* One,
Eternal Thanks *and* Praise *be ever done*.

HALLELUJAH.

WILLIAM TANS'UR, *Senior*.

End of the FIVE BOOKS *of* PSALMS.

An

An Alphabetical

DESCRIPTION

OF

PERSONS, of PLACES, and of THINGS.

AND

Wherein they are mentioned in the foregoing EXPOSITION; and in other Places in the Holy Scriptures: And of JESUS CHRIST, Poetically.

By WILLIAM TANS'UR, Senior.

A.

AARON—GOD's Messenger to King Pharaoh, &c. Psal. lxxvii. Levit. viii.

Abimelech—The general Name for the Kings of the Philistines. Psal. xxxiv. 1 Sam. xxii.

Abiram—The Son of Eliab, who was swallowed up alive. Psal. lv. Numb. xvi.

Abishai—The Father of a Song, &c. 1 Chron. ii. 28. Psal. xliv.

Abraham—That godly Prophet whose Seed had GOD's Promise. Psal. xliv. Gen. xii.

Absalom—The Son of David, who was hanged in an Oak. Psal. lxxxiv. 2 Sam. xviii.

Achitophel, David's false Counsellor; who hanged himself. Psal. lv. 2 Sam. xvii.

Achish—The King of Gath; to whom David framed himself mad. Psal. xxxiv. 1 Sam. xxi.

Adullam—An ancient City, mentioned in Joshua. Psal. cxlii. Josh. xv.

Agarims—A People from Sarah's Handmaid, Hagar; who were drove out of the Land. Psal. lxxxviii. Gen. xvi.

Ahaz, one who sought for Aid to King Ashur. Psal. xlviii. 2 Kings xvi.

Ajieleth-Afshahar—The Name of a common or Morning Song. Psal. xxii.

Alamoth—An ancient musical Instrument; or a solemn Tune. Psal. xlvi.

Aloes—The Juice of a Tree of the same Name, &c. Psal. xlv.

Alpha—The Beginning of all Things. Psal. civ. Rev. i. 8.

Altars—Places built for Divine Worship. Psal. xliii. Gen. xii. xxxv, &c.

Ammon—An ancient King of Judah, being an Idolater, was slain by his own Servants. Psal. lxxxiii. 2 Kings xxi.

Ammonites—A People which GOD forbid the Israelites to war with. Psal lxxxiii.

Amnon—The Son of David, who defloured

K

floured his Sister Tamar. Pfal. xxxii. 2 Sam. xiii. Deut. ii. xxiii.

Amorites—A People from Emori, who denied the Israelites Passage. Numb. xxi. Pfal. cxxxvi.

A.C. Anno Christi, the Year of CHRIST.

A. D.—Anno Domini, the Year of our LORD.

A. M.—Anno Mundi, the Year of the World.

Ant. dil.—Ante-diluvian, before the Flood.

Apostles—The Missionaries, or Persons sent by our SAVIOUR to preach His Gospel; being called twelve in Number.

Apud—At, to, by, with, in, nigh, near, among, before, or in Presence.

Angels—The blessed Messengers of Heaven, &c. Pfal. xci. Matt. iv.

Antichrist—A Person who is against the Doctrine of CHRIST. Pfal. li.

Antiochus—A cruel Tyrant, who spoiled the Temple, and ended his Life in a miserable Manner. Pfal. cvi. 1 Mac. vi.

Arabia—A Country between Judea and Egypt. Pfal. cxx. Ezek. xxvii.

Aram Naharaim—A Place mentioned in the xxivth of Genesis. Pfal. lx.

Aram-Zobah—The same as Syrians, a People. Pfal. xliv. 2 Kings xiii. 2 Sam. viii.

Ark—A small Chest, honoured as tho' it contained the Presence of GOD, &c. Pfal. cxxii.

Asaph—A renowned Chanter to King David; Heman's Brother. Pfal. lxxiii. 1 Chron. vi.

Asia—Where St. Paul preached the Gospel, (now under the Turks.) Pfal. xlviii. Acts xix.

Ashur—The Son of Shem: Also the People called Assyrians. Pfal. lxxxiii. Gen. x. Isai. viii.

Assyrians—The People of a fertile Land. Pfal. xlviii. 2 Kings xviii.

B.

Baal-Peor—An Idol, whose Worshippers were all destroyed. Pfal. cvi. Deut. iv.

Babel, or Babylon—Where the Israelites were captive 70 Years. Pfal. cxxxvii.

Baca—A Valley of Humiliation, or Mourning. Pfal. lxxxiv. 6.

Banquets—Feasts, Entertainments, &c. Pfal. xxxv.

Bashan—The Kingdom of Og, and Land of Giants. Pfal. lxviii.

Bathsheba—Uriah's and David's Wife, and Solomon's Mother. Pfal. li. 2 Sam. xi.

Benjamin—The youngest Son of Jacob. Pfal. lxviii. Gen. xliv.

Bethlehem—A City of the Tribe of Judah, where CHRIST was born. Pfal. cxxxii. Luke ii.

C.

Canaan—The Son of Ham; also a Country. Pfal. lxix. Gen. x.

Centurions—Certain Captains, one of which commanded 100 Men.

Chaldeans—A People of a Country, mentioned in Gen. xi. Pfal. cxxxvii.

Cassia—A sweet Shrub, whose Bark is spicy, like Cinnamon, &c. Pfal. xlv.

Congregation—A religious Assembly met together. Pfal. lxviii. xxvi.

Contemplation—A strict Thinking on the Works and Mercies of GOD, &c.

Cherubims—As Masters, &c. Pfal. xviii. lxxix. Gen. iii. 24. The second Order of Angels, &c.

Christian—A Person who owns, follows, and believes in the Laws and Ordinances of CHRIST.

Cilicia—An ancient City. Pfal. xlviii. Acts xxi. Pfal. lxviii. lxix.

Circa, Circiter, Circum, or Cir.—About, towards, near the same Time.

Cush—The Son of Aram-Naharaim. Pfal. vii. Judg. iii.

Cyrus—One of the ancient Kings of Persia. Pfal. cxxvi. Dan. v.

D.

David—The holy King of Israel, after GOD's own Heart, &c. &c. &c. Ruth iv.

Daniel—A godly Prophet, &c. See the Book of Daniel.

Dathan—One who, for Rebellion, was swallowed up alive. Pfal. cvi. Numb. xvi.

Deborah—An ancient Prophetess, who judged Israel, &c. Pf. lxviii. Judg. iv.

Doeg—King Saul's Herdsman; who told

Persons, of Places, and of Things. 127

...1 where David went to, and slew ny Priests. Psal. lii. 1 Sam. xxii.

...stical—Belonging to the Houshold Home Affairs, &c. Psal. cxxvii.

...logy—A Song devoted to GOD, ÏRIST, the Holy Ghost, and ssed Trinity, &c.

...ons—Flying Serpents, or cruel People. Psal. xliv. 19.

E.

—A Bird who reneweth Strength sucking Blood with her Beak, &c. ...l. ciii.

...ites—A People who denied the Usage of the Israelites. Psal. cxxxvii. ...mb. xx.

t—A Country in Africa. Psal. v. Gen. x.

...lation—A short, sudden, and fervent Prayer.

...edi—A City near the Red Sea. al. cxlii. 1 Sam. xxiv.

r—An ancient City mentioned in sh. xv. Psal. lxxxiii.

ata—An ancient City of Bethlehem. al. cxxxii. Gen. xxxv.

ireans—A Sect who placed all their appiness in the Pleasures of this Life.

n—A very wise Man mentioned in e Book of Kings. Psal. lxxxix. Kings iv.

...pia—A Country near Egypt, and e River Nile. Psal. lxviii.

...rates—A River mentioned in Gen. Psal. cxxxvii.

...iel—A godly Prophet. See the ...ok Ezekiel.

, or Esdras, a famous Scribe. Vide e Book Ezra. Psal. i, &c.

hites—A People descending from ash, &c. Psal. lxxxviii. 1 Kings iv.

F.

...unatus—A Person in whom St. Paul eatly delighted, &c. 1 Cor. xvi. ...ii, &c.

lity—Faithfulness, Trustiness, Integrity, and Honesty.

G.

...—An ancient City taken by Ha...el. Psal. lvi. 2 Kings xii.

...al—A City of Syria. Psal. lxxxiii. tile—A Heathen, or a Pagan, &c.

Gilead—A City, a Country, and a Mount: Also a People called Gileadites. Psal. vi. Gen. xxxi. Numb. xxvi.

Gittith—A musical Instrument or Tune. Psal. viii.

Gomorrah—A City destroyed by Fire and Brimstone from Heaven. Psal. xi. Gen. xix.

Gospel—The good Tidings or Writings of the four Evangelists, &c. Psal. xlv. Luke ii.

Grace—The Gift which God bestows on Mankind, &c.—Also to adorn and ornament any thing.

Gracious—Tender, kind, merciful, and beneficent.

H.

Hadadezar—The King of Zobah, who was discomfited by David. Psal. lxvi.

Hallelujah—Praise the LORD. Rev. xix. And to many Psalms, &c.

Ham—The Son of Noah; who, being drunk, mocked his Father, and was cursed. Psal. lxxviii. Gen. ix.

Heman—One of King David's excellent Singers. Psal. lxxxviii. 1 Chron. i.

Hebron—A Cave in Canaan; which Abram bought to bury in. Psal. lxv. Gen. xiii.

Hermon—A Mountain dedicated unto GOD. Psal. cxxxiii. Deut. iii.

Hezekiah—A godly King of Judah, of noble Actions. Psal. xlviii. 2 Kings xvi.

Holy—Sacred, innocent, divine, and pure.

Holy Ghost—The Holy Spirit of GOD, &c. Acts v. Psal. li. 11.

Horeb—A Mountain called Sinai. 1 Kings xix. Psal. cvi.

Horn—The Strength, Power, and Defence of GOD, &c. Psal. xviii. cxxxii. Deut. xiii. 17.

Hyssop—Meaning the Water of Life. Vide Psal. li. 7. Numb. xiv. 6.

I.

Jabin—the King of Hazor; who oppressed the Israelites 20 Years. Psal. lxxxviii. Judg. iv.

Jacob—the godly Son of Isaac; in whose GOD is all our Trust. Psal. lxxxi. Rom. ix.

K 2 Japhet,

Japhet—The Son of Noah who was blessed by his Father, &c. Psal. xlviii. Gen. v.

Jeduthun—A Singer, a Musician, and a Praiser of GOD. Psal. xxxix. 1 Chron. xvi.

Jehosaphat—The Son of Asa, a virtuous King. Psal. xlviii. 2 Chron. xvii. Also the Son of Ahilud, David's Recorder. 2 Sam. viii. 17.

Jehovah, one of the Names of our GOD. Psal. lxxxiii. Exod. vi.

Jemini—A Land belonging to the Tribe of Benjamin. Psal. vii. 1 Sam. ix.

Jerusalem, the Head City of Judea. Psal. cxiv. 1 Kings viii.

Jews, a People well known by most of the World. Psal. ii. Acts ii.

Joab—King David's chief Captain. Psal. lx. 2 Sam. ii. and slew Abner. 2 Sam. iii.

Job—A patient and upright Man. Vide the Book of Job. Gen. xlvi. 13.

Jonathan—The Son of Saul whom David loved, &c. Psal. liv. 2 Sam. i. and many others.

Jordan—A River in Judea, ebbing and flowing with two Heads. Psal. cxiv. Numb. xiii. Matt. iii.

Joseph—The elected Son of Jacob, who was sold into Egypt. Psal. lxxix. Gen. xxx, &c.

Joshua—The Names of several godly Men, &c. Psal. cv. Josh. i. 1 Chron. vii. Hag. i.

Isaac—The Son of Abraham. Psal. cv. Matt. i.

Isaiah—A good and godly Prophet. Psal. xlviii. Ecclus. xlviii. 23.

Ishbibenob—A mighty Giant. Psal. cxviii. 2 Sam. xxi.

Ishmaelites-The People to whom Joseph was sold. Gen. xxxvii. Psal. lxxxiii.

Israel—A Name which GOD gave to Jacob. Gen. xxxii. Also, the elected People of GOD descending from Jacob. Psal. lxxx. Deut. iv.

Israelites—An elected People whom GOD called His Servants. Psal. cxiv.—Levit. xxv.

Jubal—The first Inventor of the Harp and Organ, &c. Psal. cl. Gen. iv.

Judah or Judea—The Land of the 12 Tribes. Psal. xlviii. 2 Kings xxi. Matt. iii.

Judith—A very chaste Widow. Vide Judith viii. Psal. lxviii.

Judgments—Heavenly Punishments—Reason, Prudence, Decision, &c. Psal. lxxii. cxix.

K.

Kedar or Kedarites—A Place and a People mentioned in Psal. cxx. Gen. xxv.

Kishon—A River in Galilee, near the Hill Tabor. Psal. lxxxiii. Judg. iv.

Korah—A People descending from him, &c. Psal. xliii. Gen. xxxvi.

L.

Leamoth—An humble Song or Tune. Psal. lxxxviii.

Lebanon—A Place in Syria yielding much Frankincense. Psalm lxxii. Deut. i.

Levi—The third Son of Jacob. Psal. cxxxv. Gen. xxix.

Leviathan—A very large Fish, called a Whale. Psal. lxxiv. Job iv.

Levites—The People of the House and Tribe of Levi. Psal. cxxxiv. Exod. iv.

Libertines—The Freemen of Rome, who, being Jews or Proselytes, had a Synagogue or Oratory to themselves.

M.

Mahalath—A musical Instrument, or a Tune. Psal. liii.

Malahath-leannoth—A petitional Song or Tune. Psal. lxxxviii.

Manna—Food sent from Heaven for the Israelites. Psal. lxxviii. Exod. xvi.

Manasseh—The Son of Jacob, &c. Psal. lx. Gen. viii.

Meditation—A strict and close Thinking on the Laws, Works, and Mercies of GOD.

Mediterraneum—A midland Sea between Europe, Asia, and Africa. Psal. xlviii.

Melchizedeck—The King of Salem. Gen. xiv. 18. Heb. v. 6. John xviii. 10. Psal. cx. See Shem, Gen. v. who is thought to be Melchizedeck, and Noah's Son.

Merab—King Saul's eldest Daughter. Psal. v. 1 Sam. xviii.

Meribah—A Place mentioned Exod. xvii. Pſal. lxxxi.

Meſopotamia—Part of Aſia and Syria. Pſal. lx. Acts ii.

Meſſias—The SAVIOUR of the World, JESUS CHRIST. Pſal. lxxxvi. John i. 14.

Michael—An Archangel. Dan. xii. Rev. xii.

Michal—Saul's Daughter, and David's Wife. 1 Sam. xviii.

Michtam—A Pſalm, or a certain Tune. Pſal. xvi.

Midianites—A People from Midian, Abraham's Son. Pſal. lxxxiii.

Miriam—The Daughter of Amram; who gave Thanks, &c. Pſal. lxviii. Exod. xv.

Mizar—An Hill or Mountain. Pſ. xlii. 6.

Moab—The Son of Lot, from whence deſcended the Moabites. Pſal. lx. Gen. xix.

Moabites—A wicked People deſcended from Moab the Son of Lot. Pſal. lxxxiii. Gen. xix.

Moſes—The Son of Amram, who foretold of CHRIST to come. Pſal. lxxvii. Deut. xviii.

Mount-Moriah—The Mountain where Abraham offered his Son Iſaac. Pſal. xv. Gen. xxii.

Mount Sion—The holy Mount of the LORD in Jeruſalem; whereon ſtood the holy City of David. Pſal. xlviii. 2 Sam. v. Vide the heavenly Jeruſalem, in Pſal. lxxxvii. &c.

Muth-Laben—A muſical Inſtrument, Pſal. ix.

Myrrh—A precious Gum, &c. Pſal. xlv. Exod. xxx. Matt. ii.

N.

Nob—A City which was deſtroyed by Saul. Pſal. xi. 1 Sam. xxii.

Naphtali—The Son of Jacob. Pſal. lxviii. Gen. xxx. Alſo a City. Tob. i.

Nathan—The Prophet who reproved David. Pſal. xv. 2 Sam. xii. Alſo David's Son. 2 Sam. v.

Najoth—The Name of a Dwelling-place. 1 Sam. xix. Pſal. xi.

Nazarenes—Certain Jews who profeſſed Chriſtianity.

Nazareth—The City where CHRIST was conceived and brought up. Matt. ii.

Nazarites—The People of Nazareth, whoſe Hair parted in the Middle, who would not own CHRIST, but would have had him thrown down from their Hill. Matt. xiii. Luk. iv.

Nazarites, a Sect, who, under a Vow, abſtained from Wine, &c.

Neginoth, a mournful Tune or Inſtrument. Vide Pſal. vi.

Nehiloth, a muſical Inſtrument or Tune. Pſal. v.

Nethinims—The inferior Servants to the Prieſts and Levites; whoſe Buſineſs was to draw Water, and cleave Wood.

New Song—The Song which is of CHRIST, now come, &c. Pſal. xcvi. The old Law being called the Schoolmaſter. Gal. iii. 24, 25.

Nile—The famous River in Egypt. Exod. vii.

O.

Obed-Edom—A City, whoſe People were called Edomites. Pſal. xxiv. 2 Sam. vi.

Oblations—Things given to GOD as a Sacrifice, &c.—or Alms given to the Poor, &c.

Og—The great gigantic King of Baſhan. Pſal. cxxxv. Numb. xi.

Olive-mount—An Hill two Miles from Jeruſalem, where grew many Olives. Matt. xxi.

Omega—The Ending of all Things. Pſal. civ. Rev. i. 8.

Oreb—The Prince of the Midianites. Pſal. lxxxiii. Judg. vii. Alſo a Rock.

Ornan—The glorious Light of the Sun, &c. Vide Pſal. lxvi. 1 Chron. xxi.

P.

Paleſtina—A Country, and People of Syria. Exod. xv.

Parable—An allegorical Speech, or a wiſe Sentence, &c. Pſal. xlix.

Patriarchs—Fathers of Families, ſuch as Abraham, Iſaac, Jacob, &c.

Peſtilence—A Plague, or contagious Diſtemper, in Man or Beaſt. Pſal. xci.

Pharaoh—The King of Egypt, who reſiſted Moſes and Aaron, to ſtay the Iſraelites. Pſal. lxxiv. Exod. v.

Phariſees—

Pharisees—A Sect, who, from their own Opinion of Godliness, despised all other People in the World; even as some Culemites now think and say, that all are damned only themselves; who put a literal Construction on all they read, and depend only on Faith without Works.

Philistines—The People of Palestina. Psal. lvi.

Philologus—A Lover of Learning and GOD's Word. Rom. xv.

Phineas—The Son of Eleazar; who stood before GOD's Ark. Psal. cvi. Judg. xx.

Political—Belonging to State Government, &c. Psal. cxxvii.

Precepts—A godly Rule to live by, whether in Prose or in Verse. Psal. xix. cxix.

Priests.—The Levites of the Sons of Aaron; being divided into 22 Ranks, each Rank serving weekly in the Temple.

High-Priests—Such as were admitted into the Holy of Holies.

Prophet—A Foreteller of Things to come, such as Abraham, David, Jeremiah, &c.

Psalmist—A Composer of Psalms, &c. Hence David is so called, &c.

Publicans—Tax-gatherers.

Q.

Q. D. or **q. d.** Quasi dicat. As if it were said; or, as if he should say.

R.

Rabbies—The Doctors or Teachers of Israel.

Rahab—Strong and Proud. Also, a large, wide Street, &c. Psal. lxxxix. Josh. ii.

Rehoboam—The Son of Solomon. Psal. xcviii. 1 Kings xi.

S.

Sacrament—That religious Ceremony which is a visible Sign of an invisible Grace, as instituted by Christ for the Sanctification of our Souls.

Sacrifice—An Offering offered unto GOD; to devote or give up, &c. Psal. iv. cxvi.

Sadducees—A Sect who denied the Resurrection of the Dead, and the Existence of Angels, or of Spirits.

Salvation—Our great Preservation from eternal Death, &c. Psal. lxxxiii. cxviii, &c.

Salem, or **Shalem**—An ancient City: Gen. xiv. Afterwards called Jerusalem. Psal. lxxvi.

Samaritans—The Offspring of the Assyrians who were of a mixed Profession, partly Jewish, partly Heathen, &c.

Samuel—A godly Prophet who anointed Saul, &c. 1 Sam. ii. Psal. xcix. See the two Books of Samuel.

Sanctuary—An holy Place of Worship, or a Place of Refuge. Psal. xlvi.

Saul—The Son of Kish, and first King of Israel, who sought the Life of David, his Son-in-Law, but at last killed himself. Psal. cxviii. 1 Sam. xix. xxxi. 2 Sam. xxi.

Saviour—The Son of GOD, JESUS CHRIST. Psal. cxviii.

Sceptre—A princely Staff, &c. Vide Psal. cx.

Scribes—The ancient Writers and Expounders of the Law, &c.

Selah—A Word signifying to consider, to lift up the Voice, &c. or for ever. Psal. iii. Also a City. Judg. i.

Sennacherib—The King of Ashur, who was slain by his own Children. Psal. xlvi. 2 Kings xix.

Seraphims—A certain first Order of Angels. Isa. vi. 3. Above the Cherubims.

Shalm.—A musical Instrument. Psal. xcviii.

Sheba—An ancient City. Psal. xxxiv. Isai. xliii.

Shechem—An ancient City. Psal. lx. Gen. xii. Judg ix.

Shem—The Son of Noah. Gen v. 32. Luke iii. 36. He is blessed. Gen. ix. 26. His Posterity. Gen. x. xi. 1 Chron. i. 17. Shem is thought to be Melchizedeck, which see.

Shemaiah—Many Mens Names. Vide Psal. lxxx. Ezra viii. 1 Kings xii. 1 Chron. iii.

Shigaion—A Psalm or Tune. Psal. vii.

Shilo—An ancient City. See Salem. Vide Psal. lxxviii. Josh. xviii.

Shiloah—

Persons, of Places, and of Things.

Shiloah—A River near Mount Sion. Isai. viii. Psal. lxv. John ix.

Sihon—The King of the Amorites. Psal. cxxxv. Deut. ii.

Shishak—A Place of Joy, &c. Psal. lxxx. 1 Kings xi. 4.

Shoshannim—A certain Tune or Instrument. Psal. xlv.

Sinai—A Mountain or Wilderness. Exod. xvi. Gal. iv. Psal. lxviii.

Sion—A City and a People. Ps. cxxxiii. cxlix. Josh. xix. 1 Kings iv.

Sisera—The King of Canaan's chief Captain. Psal. lxxxiii. Judg. iv.

Sodom—A City destroyed by Fire and Brimstone from Heaven. Psal. xi. Gen. xix.

Soliloquy—A short Dialogue or Discourse that a Man holds with himself.

Solomon—The Son of David by Bathsheba. Psal. xlv. 2 Sam. v.

Spiritual—A devout, holy, and divine Contemplation, and Life, Doctrine, &c.

Statutes—The divine Laws and Ordinances of GOD and CHRIST, &c. Psal. xix. cxix.

Syrians—The People of Syria. Psal. xliv. 2 Kings xiii. 2 Sam. viii.

T.

Tabernacle—A Place of Worship. Also the Kingdom of Heaven. Psal. xv.

Tabor—An high Mountain of Galilee, where CHRIST was transfigured. Psal. lxxxix. Acts xxi.

Temple—The ancient Place of Divine Worship. Psal. cxxxviii. &c.

Tetrarchs—Persons that had princely Power over four Provinces.

Tarshish—A City in Cilicia. Psal. xlviii. Gen. x. Acts xxi.

Theology—The Art and Study of Divine Matters, &c.

Tubal-Cain.—The first Brasier and Smith. Gen. iv.

Tyrus. A City near Libanus. Psal. lxxxiii. 2 Sam. v.

U.

Vide, Vid.—See thou, or Look on, &c.

Uriah—The Husband of Bathsheba, who was killed in Battle thro' Joab. Psal. li. 2 Sam. xi.

Uzzah—A Man's Name. Vide 2 Kings xxi. 1 Chron. vi, &c.

Z.

Zachariah—The Son of Jeroboam, and John Baptist's Father. Ps. lxxix. 2 Kings xiv. Luke v.

Zalmon or Zion—The same as Sion, which see, &c. &c.

Zalmunna—A certain King. Vide Psal. lxxxiii. Judg. viii. 5.

Zarat—The Root of a People called Zarites.

Zealots—A certain Sect of mere Murderers, who, under Pretence of Law, thought themselves authorised to commit any Outrages whatsoever.

Zeb—See Psal. lxxxiii. Judg. vii. 25.

Zebah—A King of Midian. Ps. lxxxiii. Judg. viii.

Zebulon—The tenth Son of Jacob. Ps. lxviii. Gen. xxx.

Ziklag—A City given unto David, and burnt by the Amalekites. Psal. cxxi. 1 Sam. xxx.

Ziph, or Ziphims—A City and Desart; also a People. Psal. lvii. Josh. xv. 2 Sam. xxiii.

A Poetical

A Poetical DESCRIPTION of JESUS CHRIST.
By WILLIAM TANS'UR, Senior. A. D. 1760.

A. M.
4036.
A. C.
32.

WHEN great *Tiberius Cæsar* reign'd as King,
And *CHRIST*'s great Name did in *Judea* ring;
Then *Publius Lentulus* writes to *Rome*,
To tell the *Senate* who was thither come.
" We have, says he, a Man, the *Gentiles* call
" *Prophet of Truth*; whose Virtues exceed all:
" His Works and Goodness greatly found abroad,
" And His *Disciples* call Him *Son of* G O D, &c."
The SAVIOUR great, on whom the *Christians* call,
Was well-proportion'd, straight, and somewhat tall.
His *Hair* was brown, like to a Chesnut bright,
Parting i'th' Middle, like a *Nazarite:*
Straight to His Ears it grew, quite from His Crown,
And, on His Shoulders, did, in *Curls*, hang down.
On His fair *Face* no Wrinkles did appear,
Grey were His *Eyes*, quick, sharp, and very clear.
His *Nose* and *Mouth* were beautiful and fair,
His *Beard* was thick, with short and forked Hair.
His *Countenance* was ruddy and mature,
His *Voice* was pleasant, and His *Words* were pure.
His sage *Behaviour* did the World surprise,
His *Speech* was graceful, modest, grave, and wise.
He, ev'ry Sin, with Strictness did reprove,
And, all admonish'd, courteously, with Love.
Before His *Lips* He always Guard did keep,
None saw Him *laugh*, though many saw Him *weep*.

A. M.
4037.
A. C.
33.
Ætat.
suæ.
xxxiii.

He cur'd *Diseases* by G O D's Pow'r and Might,
He *rais'd* the *Dead*, and gave the *Blind* their Sight.
As He in *Beauty* did the World exceed,
So were His *Actions* both in *Word* and *Deed.*
He, for a sinful *World*, His *Life* laid down,
To give His *Saints* a lasting Heav'nly *Crown*.

⎧ O Blessed SAVIOUR! mighty PRINCE of Peace! ⎫
⎨ To Praise Thy NAME, O let me never cease: ⎬
⎨ Since on Thy Aid must ev'ry Soul depend, ⎬
⎩ Me raise to Thee, where Joys do never end. ⎭

(—Vide Dr. *Cave*'s Historia Literaria, &c.

The Right and Present

USE of PSALMODY,

According to the SERVICE of the

CHURCH of ENGLAND, &c.

Being a New, General, and Correct

CALENDAR of PSALMS,

Adapted to every

SUNDAY, FESTIVAL, and HOLIDAY
throughout the whole YEAR;

Concordant to the

COLLECT, EPISTLE, and GOSPEL for the Day, &c.
And to all other VICISSITUDES of HUMAN LIFE, &c.

By WILLIAM TANS'UR, Senior, Psalmodist.

THE *Reader* is here to obferve, That all fuch *Pfalms* as contain cruel *Imprecations* againſt GOD's, DAVID's, and CHRIST's Enemies, are not (amongſt us) to be taken as *Wiſhes*; but are rather to be underſtood as *Predictions* and *Denunciations:* Or, that GOD's juſt *Judgments* will furely fall on fuch obſtinate obdurate Sinners, as are mentioned in *Pfalm* XXXV, *Ver.* 4, 5, 8, *&c.* and *Pfalm* CIX.

[Vide *Hooker*'s Eccleſiaſtical *Policy*, Fol. 213.]

The Right and Present

USE of PSALMODY, &c.

NOTHING has rendered PSALMODY more contemptible, of late Years, than the whimsical Caprice of some ignorant *Parish-Clerks*, &c. by their setting out malicious *Psalms*, in their *Congregations*, adapted to their own foolish Taste and Temper; intirely forgetting, at the same Time, that they are leading a *Christian Congregation* into Envy and Hatred.

First, the *Parish-Clerk* (or some other Person, supplying his Disabilities) invokes, or *calls* on the People, then present, *To sing to the Praise and Glory of God*, &c. and immediately imposes on them (too often) all the *Curses* he can gather from holy DAVID's *Psalms*, quite contrary to the *Laws* of *Christianity*; for, if Cursing might have been lawful amongst the primitive *Jews*, it is *now* absolutely abolished by *CHRIST* and His *Apostles*; Who instructed us to *bless*, and not to *curse*, &c.— *Ex. gr.*

Suppose the *Collect*, *Epistle*, *Gospel*, and *Sermon* for the *Day* should recommend unto us the *Mercy* of GOD, &c. as His darling *Attributes*, what would be more contradictory to the *Service* of the *Day*, than to set out *Psalms* of *Curses*, *Fire*, *Flame*, *Gibbets*, *Axes*, *Hammers*, &c. as may be found in the BOOK of PSALMS? Or such as *Psalm* XCV, Verses 5, 6, 7, 8.—*Psalm* LXXXIII, Verses 15, 16, 17, 18.—*Psalm* CXXXVII, Verses 7, 8, 9 10.—Or the latter Part of *Psalm* CIX, &c.—On the Contrary, when we go to the *House* of GOD, and approach the *Throne of Grace*, we should lay aside all *Malice* and Rancour, and bear no Ill-will to our Neighbours, on any Account whatsoever, &c. Hence let it be the Practice of *Parish-Clerks*, for the future, to conform to the *Laws* of *Christianity*, in setting out PSALMS according to the following *Directions* in this CALENDAR, which I have compiled for the very same End; that *Heathenish Passions* may not in the least be stirred up amongst us.

N. B.

N. B. That, though the following *Beginnings* are according to the *Old Version* of *Psalms*, the Words of the *New Version* of both PSALMS and *Verses* may be likewise applied in the same Manner, and answer the same *End*, with a very little Trouble, *&c.*

First Sunday in Advent.

Psalm.   Verses.   Beginnings.
50. 2d Met. 1, 2, 3, 4.—The God of Gods, the Lord, *&c.*
18. ——— 6, 7, 8, 9.—Upon the Harp unto Him sing. Gl. P.
51. 2d Met. 1, 2, 3, 8.—Have Mercy on me, Lord, after.
118.——————25, 26.—Thou art my God, I will confess. G. P.

Second Sunday in Advent.

89.——15, 16, 17, 18.—Blessed are they that know aright.
86.——— 11, 12, 13.—O teach me, Lord, Thy Way, and I. G.P.
96.——— 12, 13, 14.—The Heav'ns shall joyfully begin.
117.——— 1, 2, 3, 4.—O all ye Nations of the World. G. P.

Third Sunday in Advent.

143.——1, 2, 6, 10.—Ld. hear my Pray'r, and my Complaint.
80.— 8, 9, 10, 19.—O take us, Lord, unto Thy Grace. G. P.
119.—33, 34, 35, 36.—Instruct me, Lord, in Thy right Way.
22. —— 26, 27, 28.—The Poor shall eat, and be suffic'd. G. P.

Fourth Sunday in Advent.

100. ————— ————All People that on Earth do dwell.
37.————— 3, 4, 5.—Trust thou therefore in God alone. G. P.
80. —— 1, 2, 3, 4.—Thou Shepherd that dost Isr'el keep.
55. —— 24, 25, 26.—Cast all thy Care upon the Lord. G. P.

Christmas-Day.

81. —— 1, 2, 3, 4.—Be light and glad, in God rejoice.
118 —19, 21, 22, 15.—I will give Thanks to Thee, O Lord. G.P.
85.——8, 9, 10, 11.—I'll hear what God the Lord doth say,
110.—————2, 3, 4.—The Lord shall out of Sion send. G. P.

St.

St. Stephen's Day, the first Martyr.

Psalm.   Verses.   Beginnings.
31.———5, 7, 14, 24.—Into Thy Hands, Lord, I commit. G. P.

St. John the Evangelist's Day.

19. —— 7, 8, 9, 10.—How perfect is the Law of God!
32.————5, 6, 7.—I did therefore confess my Faults. G. P.

Innocents-Day.

10. —— 17, 18, 19.—Thou hearest, Ld. the Poor's Complaint.
8.————1, 2, 8.—O God, our Lord, how wonderful. G. P.

First Sunday after Christmas-Day.

104.————1, 2, 3.—My Soul praise the Lord, speak good, &c.
89.—26, 27, 28, 30.—His Kingdom I will set to be. G. P.
98.————1, 2, 3, 4.—O sing ye now unto the Lord.
97.———— 8, 9, 10.—For all the Idols of the World. G. P.

Circumcision, or New-Year's-Day.

36.———— 7, 8, 9, 10.—Thy Mercy is above all Things.
32.———— 1, 2, 11.—The Man is blest whose Wickedess. G. P.

Second Sunday after Christmas-Day.

68.—29, 21, 20, 34.—Thy God hath sent forth Strength for thee
2. ——— 11, 12, 13.—See that ye serve the Lord above. G. P.
125. —— 1, 2, 3, 4.—Those that do place their Confidence.
62.————7, 6, 8.—My Glory and Salvation doth. G. P.

Epiphany, or Twelfth Day; being Christ's Manifestation to the Gentiles.

68.—29, 21, 20, 34.—Thy God hath sent forth Strength for thee.
68.———— 19, 20.—Thou hast received Gifts for Men. G. P.

First Sunday after Epiphany.

143.— 9, 10, 11, 12.—Lord, unto Thee I lift my Soul.
72.———————19, 20.—Praise ye the Lord of Hosts and sing. G. P.
113.——— ————Ye Children which do serve the Lord.
67. ——— 1, 2, 3.—Have Mercy on us, Lord. *Gloria Patri.*

Second

Second Sunday after Epiphany.

Psalm.	Verses.	Beginnings.
19.	1, 2, 3, 4.	The Heav'ns and Firmament on high.
85.	7, 8, 13.	O Lord, on us do Thou declare. G. P.
102.	23, 24, 25, 26.	The whole Foundations of the Earth.
37.	23, 31, 3.	The just Man's Mouth, &c. Glo. Pat.

Third Sunday after Epiphany.

32.	6, 7, 10, 11.	The humble Man shall pray therefore.
107.	20, 21, 22.	For then he sent to them his Word. G. P.
87.	1, 2, 3.	That City shall full well endure.
103.	11, 18, 19.	And as the Space is wond'rous great. G. P.

Fourth Sunday after Epiphany.

100.		All People that on Earth do dwell.
125.		{ Those that do place their Confidence. { Gloria Patri.
143.	9, 10, 11, 12.	Lord, unto Thee I lift my Soul.
132.	11, 13, 15.	The Lord himself hath Sion chose. G. P.

Fifth Sunday after Epiphany.

103.	1, 2, 3, 4.	My Soul, give Laud unto the Lord.
71.	5, 6, 8.	Thou art the Stay whereon I rest. G. P.
147.	1, 2, 3, 4.	Praise ye the Lord, for it is good.
43.	3, 4, 6.	{ O Lord, send out Thy Light and Truth. { Gloria Patri.

Sixth Sunday after Epiphany.

67.	1, 2, 3, 4.	Have Mercy on us, Lord.
19.	8, 9, 10.	{ The Lord's Commands are righteous. { Gloria Patri.
71.	1, 2, 3, 15.	My God, my God, in all Distress.
65.	17, 18, 19, 20.	Full oft I call to Mind God's Grace. G. P.

Septuagesima Sunday; or, Third Sunday before Lent.

33.	5, 6, 7, 8.	For by the Word of God alone.
105.	4, 5, 7, 42.	Seek ye the Lord, and seek, &c. G. P.
102.	23, 24, 25, 26.	The whole Foundations of the Earth.
130.	3, 4, 5.	O Lord, our God, if Thou survey. G. P.

Sexagesima Sunday, or Second Sunday before Lent.

56.—10, 11, 12, 13.—I glory in the Word of God.
5.———7, 9, 11. { Lord, lead me in Thy Righteousness.
                 { Gloria Patri.
94.—11, 12, 13, 14.—The Lord doth know the Heart of Man.
31.———1, 2, 4.—O Lord, I put my Trust in Thee. G. P.

Quinquagesima Sunday; or, next Sunday before Lent.

112.———1, 2, 3.—The Man is blest that God doth fear.
146.———7, 8, 9.—The Lord doth send the Blind, &c. G.P.
37.—23, 24, 26, 31.—The Ld. the just Man's Steps doth guide.
133. — — — —O what a happy Thing it is. Glo. Pat.

Ash-Wednesday; or, First Day of Lent.

51.—11, 12, 13, 14.—Cast me not, Lord, out from thy Face.
130.———1, 2, 3, 4, 5.—Lord, unto Thee I make my Moan. G.P.

First Sunday in Lent.

119.———1, 2, 3, 4.—Blessed are they that perfect are.
91.—11, 12, 14, 15.—For why? unto His Angels all. Glo. Pat.
25.———1, 2, 3, 4.—I lift my Heart to Thee.
61.———3, 4, 5.—Upon the Rock of Thy great Pow'r. G.P.

Second Sunday in Lent.

32.———1, 2, 6, 11.—The Man is blest whose Wickedness.
130.———6, 7, 8.—My Soul to God hath great Regard. G.P.
89.—15, 16, 17, 18.—Blessed are they that know aright.
7.——— 10, 11, 17.—I take my Help to come from God. G.P.

Third Sunday in Lent.

5.—7, 9, 10, 11.—Lord, lead me in Thy Righteousness.
51. 2d Met. 7, 10, 11.—With Hyssop, Lord, besprinkle me G. P.
107.— 1, 2, 21, 22.—Give Thanks unto the Lord our God.
71.——— 3, 4, 5, 6. { Save me, my God, from wicked Men.
                { Gloria Patri.

Fourth Sunday in Lent.

125.——— 1, 2, 3, 4.—Those that do place their Confidence.
79.———8, 9, 15.—Bear not in Mind our former Sins. G. P.
105.—16, 17, 18, 23.—God call'd a Dearth upon the Land.
77.———13, 14, 15.—Thy Works, O Lord, are all upright. G.P.

Fifth

Fifth Sunday in Lent.

Psalms.	Verses.	Beginnings.
51. 2d. Met.	1, 2, 3, 4.	Have Mercy on me, Lord, after.
130.	3, 4, 5.	O Lord our God, if Thou survey. G. P.
17.	5, 6, 7, 8.	Within Thy Paths which are most pure.
25.	20, 21, 22.	Preserve and keep my Soul. Glo. Pat.

Sixth Sunday in Lent.

146.————1, 2, 3, 4.—My Soul, praise Thou the Lord always.
88.———11, 12, 13, 14.—Dost thou unto the Dead declare. G. P.
145.——13, 14, 15, 16.—The Lord is just in all his Ways.
114.————————7, 8. { O Earth, confess Thy sov'reign Lord.
                          Gloria Patri.

Good Friday.

69.—18, 19, 20, 22, 23, 36.—O Lord of Hosts, to me give Ear.
22.—11, 14, 18, 19, 22. { O Lord depart not now from me.
                            Gloria Patri.

Easter Sunday.

16.————8, 9, 10, 11.—I set the Lord still in my Sight.
57.—10, 11, 12, 13.—My Heart is set to laud the Lord. G. P.
89.————5, 6, 7, 14.—The Heav'ns do shew with Joy and Mirth.
118.—19, 20, 21, 22.—I will give Thanks to Thee, O God. G. P.

Easter Monday.

30.————1, 2, 3, 4.—All Laud and Praise with Heart, &c. G. P.

Easter Tuesday.

118.———12, 13, 15. { The Lord is my Defence, and Strength,
                         Gloria Patri.

First Sunday after Easter.

104.————1, 2, 3.—My Soul praise the Lord, speak good, &c.
2.———11, 12, 13.—See that ye serve the Lord above. G. P.
145.———1, 2, 3, 4.—Thee will I laud, my God and King.
89.————3, 4, 6.—With mine Elect, saith God, have I. G. P.

Second Sunday after Easter.

Psalm.   Verses.   Beginnings.
81.——1, 2, 3, 4.—Be light and glad, in God rejoice.
43.———3, 4, 5. { O Lord send out Thy Light and Truth.
                 Gloria Patri.
103.—10, 11, 12, 17.—According to our Sins, also.
118.——17, 18, 26.—Set open unto me the Gates. Glo. Pat.

Third Sunday after Easter.

119.—9, 10, 11, 12.—By what Means may a young Man best.
39.———12, 13, 14. { When Thou for Sin dost Man rebuke,
                     Gloria Patri.
115.—9, 10, 11, 12.—Such as be Fearers of the Lord.
118.——12, 13, 15. { The Lord is my Defence and Strength.
                     Gloria Patri.

Fourth Sunday after Easter.

89.———1, 2, 3, 4.—To sing the Mercies of the Lord.
25.———12, 13, 14.—Whoso doth fear the Lord. Glo. Pat.
42 ———1, 2, 11, 15.—Like as the Hart doth pant and bray.
96.————9, 10, 11.—Fall down and worship ye the Lord. G.P.

Fifth Sunday after Easter.

113.———————————Ye Children which do serve the Lord.
34.———12, 13, 14.—Who is the Man that would live long. G.P.
68.———18, 19, 20.—Thou didst, O Lord, ascend on high.
68.—————3, 4.—But righteous Men before the Lord. G.P.

Ascension-Day.

81.———1, 2, 3, 4.—Be light and glad, in God rejoice.
18.————9, 10.—The Lord descended from above. G.P.
47.——— 5, 6, 7, 8.—Our God ascended up on high.
24.———— 9, 10.—Ye Gates and everlasting Doors. G.P.

Sunday after Ascension-Day.

15.——1, 2, 3, 4.—Within thy Tabernacle, Lord.
125.——— 1, 2, 3, 4.—Those that do place their Confidence. G.P.
48.——-8, 9, 10, 13.—O Lord we wait, and do depend.
24.————3, 4, 5.—Who is the Man, O Lord, that may. G.P.

L   Whit-

Whit-Sunday.

Psalm.	Verses.	Beginnings.
119	5, 6, 7, 8.	O would to God it might Thee please.
Veni Creator	11, 12.	To us such Plenty of Thy Grace. *G. P.*
104.	1, 2, 3.	My Soul praise the Lord, speak good, &c.
105.	1, 2, 3, 4.	Give Praises unto God the Lord. *Gl. P.*

Whit-Monday.

145.	1, 2, 3, 4.	Thee will I laud, my God and King.
47.	7, 8.	{ God o'er the Heathen reigns, and sits. Gloria Patri.

Whit-Tuesday.

147.	1, 2, 3, 4.	Praise ye the Lord for it is good.
143.	8, 9, 10.	Let me Thy Loving-kindness in. *G. P.*

Trinity Sunday.

81.	1, 2, 3, 4.	Be light and glad, in God rejoice.
Veni Creator.	13, 14.	{ Grant us, O Lord, through Thee, to know. *G. P.*
33.	1, 2, 3, 4.	Ye Righteous, in the Lord rejoice.
2.	8, 9, 10.	I have anointed him my King. *Gl. P.*

First Sunday after Trinity.

18.	1, 2, 3, 4.	O God, my Strength, and Fortitude.
Veni Creat.	1, 2, 3, 4.	Come, Holy Ghost, eternal God. *G. P.*
119.	33, 34, 35, 36.	Instruct us, Lord, in the right Way.
34.	7, 8, 9.	The Angel of the Lord doth pitch. *G. P.*

Second Sunday after Trinity.

92.	5, 6, 7, 8.	O Lord, how glorious, and how great.
97.	10, 11, 12, 13.	For Thou, O Lord, art set on high. *G.P.*
99.	1, 2, 3, 4.	The Lord doth reign, although at it.
31.	23, 24.	Ye Saints, love ye the Lord alway. *G. P.*

Third Sunday after Trinity.

113.		Ye Children which do serve the Lord.
37.	4, 5, 6,	In God set all thy Heart's Delight. *G. P.*
55.	24, 25, 26.	Cast all thy Care upon the Lord.
86.	8, 9, 10.	Among the gods, O Lord is none. *G. P.*

Fourth Sunday after Trinity.

Psalm.	Verses.	Beginnings.
103.	8, 9, 10, 11.	The Lord is kind and merciful.
25.	8, 9, 10.	God's Mercy is full sweet. *Gloria Patri.*
101.	1, 2, 3, 4.	I Mercy will and Judgment sing.
86.	3, 6, 7.	Thy Mercy, Lord, on me express. G. P.

Fifth Sunday after Trinity.

119.	165, 6, 7, & 8.	Great Peace and Rest all such shall have.
34.	12, 13, 14.	Who is the Man that would live long. G.P.
37.	37, 38, 39, 40.	Mark and behold the upright Man.
4.	7, 8, 9.	{ The greater Sort crave worldly Goods. { Gloria Patri.

Sixth Sunday after Trinity.

32.	1, 2, 5, 11.	The Man is blest whose Wickedness.
145.	6, 7.	{ The Lord, our God, most gracious is. { Gloria Patri.
103.	1, 2, 3, 4.	My Soul give Laud unto the Lord.
86.	5, 6, 7.	Lord, Thou art good and bountiful. G.P.

Seventh Sunday after Trinity.

100.	—	All People that on Earth do dwell.
95.	6, 7.	{ Come let us bow, and praise the Lord. { Gloria Patri.
23.	—	The Lord is only my Support.
105.	1, 2, 3, 4.	Give Praises unto God the Lord. Gl. P.

Eighth Sunday after Trinity.

119.	Two last Staves.	Stretch out Thy Hand, I Thee beseech.
25.	20, 21, 22.	Preserve and keep my Soul. *Glo. Pat.*
125.	1, 2, 3, 4.	Those that do place their Confidence.
27.	15, 16.	I utterly should faint, but that. *Gl. P.*

Ninth Sunday after Trinity.

19.	7, 8, 9, 10.	How perfect is the Law of God.
78.	14, 15, 16.	He clave the Rocks i' th' Wilderness. G.P.
34.	1, 2, 3, 4.	I will give Laud and Honour both.
86.	11, 12.	O teach me, Lord, Thy Way, and I. G.P.

Tenth Sunday after Trinity.

Psalm.	Verses.	Beginnings.
65.	1, 2, 3, 4.	Thy Praise alone, O Lord, doth reign.
5.	1, 2, 3, 6.	Incline thine Ear, O Lord, and let. G. P.
135.	1, 2, 3, 4.	O praise the Lord, praise ye His Name.
115.	9, 10, 11, 12.	Such as be Fearers of the Lord. Gl. P.

Eleventh Sunday after Trinity.

96.	1, 2, 3, 4.	Sing ye, with Praise, unto the Lord.
36.	7, 8, 9, 10.	Thy Mercy is above all Things. Gl. P.
67.	1, 2, 3, 4.	Have Mercy on us, Lord.
84.	11, 12, 13, 14.	{ For why? within Thy Courts one Day. Gloria Patri.

Twelfth Sunday after Trinity.

103.	8, 9, 10, 11.	The Lord is kind and merciful.
62.	7, 8.	My Glory and Salvation doth. Glo. Pat.
106.	1, 2, 3, 4.	Praise ye the Lord, for it is good.
56.	10, 11, 12, 13.	I glory in the Word of God. Glo. Pat.

Thirteenth Sunday after Trinity.

100.		All People that on Earth do dwell.
2.	11, 12, 13.	See that ye serve the Lord above. G. P.
139.	1, 2, 3, 4.	O Lord, thou hast me try'd and known.
80.	1, 2, 3, 4.	Thou Shepherd that dost Isr'el keep. G.P.

Fourteenth Sunday after Trinity.

119.	113, 114, 115, 116.	All Thoughts that vain and wicked are.
146.	4, 5, 6, 7.	Blessed and happy are all they. Gl P.
16.	8, 9, 10, 11.	I set the Lord still in my Sight.
128.		Blessed art Thou that fearest God. G. P.

Fifteenth Sunday after Trinity.

1.	1, 2, 3, 4.	The Man is blest that hath not lent.
55.	24, 25, 26.	Cast all thy Care upon the Lord. G. P.
37.	23, 24, 25, 26.	The Lord the just Man's Steps doth guide.
147.	5, 6, 7, 8.	Sing unto God, the Lord, with Praise. G.P.

Sixteenth

Sixteenth Sunday after Trinity.

Psalm.	Verses.	Beginnings.
103.	1, 2, 3, 4.	My Soul give Laud unto the Lord.
27.	4, 5.	One Thing of God I do require. G. P.
28.	6, 7, 8, 9.	To render Thanks unto the Lord.
33.	5, 6, 7.	For by the Word of God alone. G. P.

Seventeenth Sunday after Trinity.

145.	13, 14, 15, 16.	The Lord is just in all his Ways.
107.	20, 21, 22.	For then God sent to them his Word. G. P.
77.	11, 12, 13, 14	I will regard and think upon.
149.	1, 2, 3, 4.	Sing ye unto the Lord our God. Gl. P.

Eighteenth Sunday after Trinity.

125.	1, 2, 3, 4.	Those that do place their Confidence
110.	1, 2, 3, 4.	The Lord did say unto my Lord. G. P.
141.	1, 2, 3, 4.	O Lord, upon Thee do I call.
34.	17, 18, 19.	The Lord is ever nigh to them. Gl. P.

Nineteenth Sunday after Trinity.

92.	1, 2, 3, 4.	It is a Thing both good and meet.
25.	5, 6, 7.	Thy Mercies manifold. Gloria Patri.
34.	1, 2, 3, 4.	I will give Laud and Honour both.
119.	5, 6, 7, 8.	O would to God it might Thee please. G. P.

Twentieth Sunday after Trinity.

89.	1, 2, 3, 4.	To sing the Mercies of the Lord.
107.	46, 47, 48.	Save us, O Lord, who art our God. G. P.
95.	1, 2, 3, 4.	O come let us lift up our Voice.
103.	8, 9, 10, 11.	The Lord is kind and merciful. G. P.

Twenty-first Sunday after Trinity.

103.	1, 2, 3, 4,	My Soul give Laud unto the Lord.
35.	8, 29, 3.	O let my Soul, my Heart, and Voice. G.P.
11.	4, 5, 6, 7, 8.	Our God, that in the Temple is,
30.	1, 2, 3, 4.	All Laud & Praise, with Heart, &c. G.P.

Twenty-second Sunday after Trinity.

Pfalms.　　Verſes.　　　　　Beginnings.
73.——23, 24, 25, 26.—Lord, what is there that I can wiſh.
37.———26, 27, 28.—He always gives moſt lib'rally. G. P.
100.————————— —All People that on Earth do dwell.
84.——5, 6, 7, 8.—O! they are bleſſed that may dwell. G.P.

Twenty-third Sunday after Trinity.

1.———1, 2, 3, 4.—The Man is bleſt that hath not lent.
80.————1, 2, 4.—Thou Shepherd that doſt Iſr'el keep. G.P.
105.———40, 41, 42.—God brought his People forth with Mirth.
92.——12, 13, 14, 15.—The Righteous flouriſh ſhall on high. G.P.

Twenty-fourth Sunday after Trinity.

57.——10, 11, 12, 13.—Awake, my Joy, awake, I ſay.
116.————3, 4, 5.—Upon the Name of God the Lord. G.P.
23. 2d Met. ———My Shepherd was the living Lord.
107.——23, 24, 25.—Thy Faithfulneſs, O God, to praiſe. G.P.

Twenty-fifth Sunday after Trinity.

92.——1, 2, 3, 4.—It is a Thing both good and meet.
34.————8, 9, 10.—Taſte and conſider well therefore. G.P.
29.——1, 2, 3, 4.—Give to the Lord, ye Potentates.
33.———11, 16, 18.—Bleſſed are they, to whom the Lord. G.P.

☞ Mark well, That if there ſhould be more than 25 *Sundays* after *Trinity-Sunday*, before *Advent-Sunday* comes in again; then you may uſe ſuch *Pſalms* as are adapted to ſuch *Collects, Epiſtles,* and *Goſpels* as ſhall be read, until the Service begins again at *Advent*: By reaſon the whole Order of this CALENDAR is carefully ſuited to the *Collect, Epiſtle,* and *Goſpel* for the Day, as near as the Matter will bear in Harmony one with another.

St. Andrew, *the Apoſtle.*

145.—13, 14, 15, 16.—The Lord is juſt in all his Ways.
94.—11, 12, 13, 14.—The Lord doth know the Heart of. G.P.

St. Thomas, *the Apoſtle.*

37.——3, 4, 6, 23.—Truſt thou therefore in God alone.
27.————15, 16.—I utterly ſhould faint, but that—G. P.
　　　　　　　　　　　　　　　　　　　　　　Converſion.

Conversion of St. Paul, the Apostle.

Psalm.   Verses.   Beginnings.
23. ——————— —My Shepherd is the living Lord.
51. 2d. Met. 10, 11, 12.—O God, create in me a Heart. *Gl. P.*

Purification of the Blessed Virgin Mary.

118.——1, 2, 3, 4.—O give ye Thanks unto the Lord. *G. P.*

St. Matthias, the Apostle.

18.——29, 30, 34.—Unspotted are the Ways of God. *G. P.*

Annunciation of the Blessed Virgin Mary.

2.——6, 7, 8.—I have anointed him my King. *Glo. Pat.*

St. Mark, the Evangelist.

106.——1, 2, 3, 4.—Praise ye the Lord, for it is good.
68.——18, 19, 20.—Thou didst, O Lord, ascend on high. *G.P.*

St. Philip and James, Apostles.

103.——14, 15, 16.—The Lord that made us, knows, *&c. G.P.*

St. Barnabas, the Apostle.

9.——1, 2, 3, 4.—With Heart and Mouth unto the—*G. P.*

St. John Baptist.

94.—11, 12, 13, 14.—The Lord doth know the Heart of Man.
132.——13, 14, 15.—With my Salvation I will cloath. *G. P.*

St. Peter, the Apostle.

145.——11, 12, 16.—The Eyes of all, Lord, wait on Thee.
62.——7, 6, 8.—My Glory and Salvation doth. *Glo. Pat.*

St. James, the Apostle.

121. ——————— —I lift mine Eyes to Sion Hill.
27.——9, 11, 16.—In Wrath turn not thy Face away. *G. P.*

St. Bartholomew, *the Apoſtle.*

Pſalm.   Verſes.   Beginnings.
77.——11, 12, 13, 14.—I will regard and think upon.
  4.——— 7, 8, 9.—The greater Sort crave worldly. G. P.

St. Matthew, *the Evangeliſt.*

125.——1, 2, 3, 4.—Thoſe that do place their Confidence.
 86.——11, 12, 13.—O teach me, Lord, Thy Way—Gl. P.

St. Michael, *and all Angels.*

31.——19, 20, 21, 24.—How plentiful Thy Mercies be!
96.———12, 13, 14.—The Heav'ns ſhall joyfully begin. G P.

St. Luke, *the Evangeliſt.*

111.———— 1, 2, 3.—With Heart I do accord.
107.———20, 21, 22.—For then God ſent to them His—G. P.

St. Simon *and* Jude.

 15.——1, 2, 3, 4.—Within Thy Tabernacle, Lord.
139.———3, 4, 5.—No Word is on my Tongue, O Lord. G.P.

All Saints Day.

145.——8, 9, 10, 16.—Thy Saints do bleſs Thee, Lord, and do.
 89.——14, 15, 16.—In Righteouſneſs and Equity. Glo. Pat.

Preparation-Pſalms for Sundays, &c. before the H. Sacrament.

 4.—————5, 6.—Sin not, but ſtand in Awe therefore. G.P.
18.————29, 30.—Unſpotted are Thy Ways, O God,
19.——7, 8, 9, 11.—How perfect is the Law of God.
19.——12, 13, 14.—O Lord, what earthly Man doth. G. P.
25.————5, 6, 7.—Thy Mercies manifold.
27.—————4, 5.—One Thing of God I do require.
37.————3, 4, 5.—Truſt thou, therefore, in God alone. G. P.
42.—————1, 2.—Like as the Hart doth pant and bray.
51.————7, 8, 9.—With Hyſſop, Lord, beſprinkle me. G.P.
51.——10, 11, 12.—O God, create in me a Heart.

103.

The Psalm-Singer's New CALENDAR, &c.

| Psalm. | Verses. | Beginnings. |

103.———8, 9, 10.—The Lord is kind and merciful. G. P.
119.———1, 2, 3, 4—Blessed are they that perfect are.
119.———5, 6, 7, 8.—O would to God, it might Thee please.
119.—33, 34, 35, 36.—Instruct me, Lord, in the right Way. G. P.

Psalms for Sacrament-Days.

2.———11, 12, 13.—See that ye serve the Lord above. G. P.
26.———6, 7, 8.—My Hands I wash, and do proceed. G. P.
36.———7, 8, 9, 10.—Thy Mercy is above all Things.
43.———3, 4.—O Lord send out Thy Light and—G. P.
96.———7, 8, 9.—Ascribe unto the Lord therefore. G. P.
116.———10, 11, 12.—The wholesome Cup of saving Health. G. P
116.———14, 15, 16.—Therefore I'll offer up to Thee. G. P.

Gunpowder Plot, Nov. 5, A. D. 1605.

18.———1, 2, 3, 4.—O God my Strength and Fortitude.
64.———5, 6, 7.—A wicked Work they have decreed. G. P.
125.———1, 2, 3, 4.—Those that do place their Confidence.
94.———21, 22, 23.—They did consult against the Life. G. P.

Martyrdom of King Charles the First, Jan. 30, 1648.

94.—19, 20, 21, 22, 23.—When with myself I mused much.
79.—9, 10, 11, 12, 15.—O God, that giv'st all Health and. G. P.

Restoration of King Charles the Second, May 29, A.D. 1660.

18.—46, 47, 48, 49.—For it is God that gave me Pow'r.
144.——— 8, 19.—A new Song I will sing to Thee. G. P.
85.—1, 7, 12, 13.—Thou hast been merciful indeed.
18.—15, 16, 17, 18.—And from above the Lord sent down. G. P.

On the King's Accession to the Throne.

21.———1, 2, 3, 4.—O Lord how joyful is the King.
72.———6, 7, 8.—Lord, make the King unto the Just. G. P.
61.———6, 7, 8.—God will the King in Health—Glo. Pat.

Psalms sung before Rulers, Corporations, &c.

58.——— 1, 11.—Ye Rulers that are put in Trust. G. P.
81.———1, 2, 3, 4.—Be light and glad, in God rejoice.
87.———6, 7, 8.—Of Sion they shall say abroad. G. P.

| Psalms. | Verses. | Beginnings. |

119.———137, 139.—In ev'ry Thing, Lord, thou art just. G.P.
133.——————————O what a happy Thing it is.

On a National Cessation of Arms, &c.

66.———7, 8, 9, 10.—The Lord of Hosts doth take our—G.P.

Psalms exhorting to Charity, Liberality, &c.

37.———26, 27, 28.—He always gives most lib'rally.
41.———1, 2, 3, 4.—The Man is blest that doth provide.
72.———12, 13, 14.—For God the needy Sort will save.
78.—————4, 5, 6.—To Jacob he Commandment gave. G.P.
145.———11, 12, 13.—The Eyes of all do wait on Thee. G. P.
146.—————8, 9.—God doth defend the Fatherless. G. P.

Thanksgiving for Victory.

9.———1, 2, 3, 4.—With Heart and Mouth unto the Lord.
18.————33, 37.—God did in order put my Hands.
21.———11, 12, 13.—Lord, they much Mischief did—Gl. P.
28.———6, 7, 8, 9.—To render Thanks unto the Lord.
98.———1, 2, 3, 4, 6.—O sing ye now unto the Lord.
20.———6, 7, 8, 9.—Our Hopes are fix'd. G. P. (New Ver.)

On a welcome Rain.

65.—8, 9, 10, 11, 14.—Lord, when the Earth is chopt—G.P.

On welcome fair Weather.

29.———3, 4, 10, 11.—God's Voice doth rule the Waters. G.P.

On Feast-Days or Wakes; being the next Sunday after some Saint's Day, to which their Parish-Church was dedicated, &c.

81.———1, 2, 3, 4.—Be light and glad, in God rejoice.
84.—9, 10, 11, 12.—O Lord of Hosts, to me give Heed. G.P.
26.—8, 9, 11, 12.—O God, thy House I love most dear.
150.———————————Yield unto God the mighty Lord. G.P.

On a public Fast, in Time of War, Conspiracy, Rebellion, &c.

118.——5, 6, 8, 9.—The Lord himself is on my Side.
5.—7, 9, 10, 11.—Lord, lead me in Thy Righteousness. G.P.

Psalms.   Verses.   Beginnings.
20.———1, 2, 7, 8.—In Trouble and Adversity.
33.—16, 18, 19, 20.—But lo, the Eyes of God attend, G. P.

Psalms after a Wedding.

128. ——————————— Blessed art thou that fearest God. G.P.
67.—1, 2, 3, 4, 6, 7.—Have Mercy on us, Lord. *Glo. Pat.*
133. ——————————— O what a happy Thing it is. *Glo. Pat.*

Psalms adapted to the several Vicissitudes of Human Life: As hinted in the Preface.

Confession of Sins.—Psal. 6. 32. 38. 51. 102. 130. 143.
Praying to God.—Psal. 25. 54. 67. 70. 72. 86. 143.
Tempted with Evil.—Psal. 22. 64. 69.
Life tedious.—Psal. 42. 63. 84.
Sorrow and Trouble.—Psal. 13. 31. 44. 54. 56.
Ease, &c. restored.—Psal. 30. 34. 103. 104.
God's Laws and Precepts, &c.—Psal. 119.
Praise and Thanksgiving to God.—30. 34. 103. 104. 105. 106. 107. 108. 111. 113. 119. 144. 145. 146. 147. 149. 15.
The Seven Penitential Psalms, 6. 32. 38. LI. 10. 130. 143.
Mercies received.—Psal. 8. 30. 103. 92. 138. 144.
God's Word excellent.—12. 19. 119.
Wicked Men miserable.—1. 11. 37. 119.
Righteous Men blessed.—1. 15. 24. 32. 92. 112. 119. 128.

Psalms sung in the Funeral-Service, which is the last good Office, and Period of all human Glory.

90.—13, 11, 9, 15.—Instruct us, Lord, to know and try.
90.———3, 4, 5, 6.—Thou grindest Man through Grief—
39.———5, 6, 7, 8.—Lord, number out my Life and Days.
39.————2, 13, 14.—When Thou for Sin dost Man—*Gl. P.*
88.—11, 12, 13, 14.—Lord, dost Thou to the Dead declare.
89.—49, 48, 45, 53.—Lord, who is he that liveth, and.
102.——9, 10, 19.—The Days wherein I pass my Life. G.P.
103.—14, 15, 16, 17.—The Lord who made us, knows our—
40.—1, 2, 14, 15, 21.—I waited long, and sought the Lord, &c.

End of the CALENDAR.

AN ABSTRACT

OF THE

LIFE of Holy DAVID,

Concordant to the Book of PSALMS:

SHEWING

On what Occasion several Psalms were composed, &c.

By WILLIAM TANS'UR, Senior, Philo. *Music* and *Theology*.

SECT. I.

Of DAVID's Birth. *He is anointed* King; *and for* playing *before King* Saul, *is made* Armour-Bearer, *&c.* Ruth iv. 12.

A. M. 2919.
Before *Christ*,
1058.

DAVID, whose *Name* signifies *Beloved*, the true *Prophet* of *CHRIST*, and *King* of *Israel*, was not only a Man after GOD's own Heart, but was also one of the greatest Men for *Virtue* and *Valour* in all Antiquity. He descended, in a direct *Line*, from *Judah*, the Son of *Jacob*; and was the youngest of the eight Sons of *Jesse*, and was born, and lived, in a small City called *Bethlehem*, of the *Tribe* of *Judah*, from the Generation of *Pharez*, as appears in *Ruth* iv. ver. 12 to 22, *&c.*

When DAVID was about Twenty-two Years of Age, [13] the

1 Sam. xvi.

LORD ordered *Samuel* to anoint him *King*; and [11] though he was only a *Shepherd* to his Father, he [12] was very *fair* and *beautiful*: This being about six Years before

before *Samuel*'s Death; who exhorted DAVID to study *Justice*, that his *Name* might be famous to all Generations.

Now [17] the *Spirit* of GOD going from King *Saul*, into DAVID *, *Saul* was [14] sorely afflicted with an *Hypochondriac* Disorder, which greatly impaired his Senses; who, hearing of DAVID's great Skill in *Musick*, [19] sends for him to play before him on his *Harp*. His Father *Jesse*, on this Request, [20] immediately sends DAVID to *Saul*, with a *Present* of *Bread*, *Wine*, and a *Kid*, which he kindly received: And made such Musick with his *Harp* and *Voice* before him, that he [23] recovered him to his right Senses as before.

This grand *Performance* gained DAVID such Applause, that the King took him [21] to be his *Armour-bearer*; where he remained, greatly in his royal Favour, two or three Years, tho' in many Troubles: But, having Leave, he [15] returned again to his Father, and followed his old *Employment* among the Flocks, &c. 1 *Sam*. xvii.

SECT. II.

DAVID *carries Presents to* Saul; *and kills* Goliath.
1 Sam. xvii.

JESSE now [13] having three Sons in *Saul*'s Camp, sendeth [17] DAVID to carry *Cakes* and *Cheeses* to his three Brothers: Where [18] hearing of the forty Days Challenge of the *Goliath* of *Gath*, he, [37] from Experience of GOD's Assistance in killing a *Lion* and a *Bear*, [32] undertakes to fight the *Giant* himself: Though *Saul* greatly feared his Success; and [25] had promised any one his Daughter to Wife that would do the Jobb, and overcome him.

---

* (Vide *Hedio* & *Rufinus*, *Jos*. *Antiq*. Lib. 6, and P. *Heylyn*'s Hist. of *Palestine*.)

N. B. *That* Flavius Josephus *was a learned* Writer, *of great Truth and Esteem amongst the* Jews; *who was chief* Governor *of both* Galilees, *the Upper and the Lower; and bravely defended the City* Jotapata *against* Vespasian. *He was born but five Years after the* Death *of CHRIST, and wrote the* History *of the Destruction of* Jerusalem *forty Years after it; to which he was an Eye-witness: Whose* Works *(as well as many others) I have as carefully consulted, to compleat this short* History, *as I have our* Sacred Bible; *to which I refer the* Reader, *should any* Controversies *happen herefrom,* &c. &c.

The Life of Holy DAVID:

Saul, on seeing DAVID's Courage, [38] puts off his Armour, and puts it on DAVID; which [39] DAVID puts off again, because he had not proved it: Chusing [40] no other Weapon than a *Staff*, a *Sling*, and five smooth *Stones*; which he had put in his Shepherd's Bag.

Now the *Giant* [33] was a Man of War, and great *Stature*, [7] whose Height was six Cubits and a Span; having [6] *Boots*, and [5] an *Helmet* of Brass; a *Coat of Mail* which weighed 5000 Shekels, and [6] a *Target* of Brass between his Shoulders; the [7] Head of his *Spear* weighed 600 Shekels of Iron, and its *Staff* was like a Weaver's Beam; and one, bearing a *Shield*, marched before him.

Both Armies being now [3] together in the Valley of *Shocho*, DAVID, (though but a Youth and a [56] Stripling,) marched boldly in Presence of all the People, [25] in the Defence of G O D, to meet *Goliath*. Then [40] taking a *Stone* out of his Bag, he, with his *Sling*, threw it into the Forehead of *Goliath*, and brought him to the Ground: Then [51] standing boldly on his Body, he cut off his Head with his own Sword; which he [54] afterwards carried to *Jerusalem*; but he put his Armour in his Tent.

When the *Philistines* [51] saw their *Champion* fall, they fled; and the Armies of *Israel* [52] and *Judah* shouted, and followed them to the Gates of *Gath*; where many fell wounded, and they took their Tents, &c.

N. B. It is here to be observed, that, [55] on *Saul*'s asking who DAVID was? That his Countenance was so changed, by lying in the Fields, that none at Court did remember they ever had seen him before; although he had beforetime been so great a Favourite.

DAVID now [5] shewing himself a Man of Courage and great Wisdom, *Jonathan*, the Son of *Saul*, greatly loved him, as well as his Father; by Reason he did all Things to the *Glory of* G O D, amongst the Heathens, as well as amongst the *Israelites:* So that *Jonathan* [3] made a *Covenant* with him, and [4] gave him his *Garment*, his *Sword*, his *Bow*, and his *Girdle*; and DAVID had great Power in the House of *Saul*, and [5] was greatly beloved by him and all his Servants.

1 Sam. xviii.

N. B. That there were two Sorts of Shekels, *one being* Half an Ounce, *and the other but the* Quarter of an Ounce.—*Quære Which?*

Concordant to the Book of PSALMS, &c.

SECT. III.

Saul, *being false to* DAVID, *contrives his Death by several Ways; which* DAVID *prudently avoided.* 1 Sam. xviii.

THIS *Section* shews the wavering State of *Court Favourites*: For, ⁶ as DAVID was returning from the Slaughter of *Goliath* and the *Philistines*, behold, the Women came out of the Cities *singing* and *dancing*, with *Timbrels*, and Instruments of Joy, by Course, saying, as they met *Saul*, " Saul *hath* " *slain his Thousands, and* DAVID *his Ten Thousands,* &c." which ⁸ so enraged *Saul*, that ever after that Day he bore DAVID Hatred, and ⁹ daily contriv'd to take away his Life several Ways: For, the very next Day, he ¹⁰ (falsely) relapsed into his old *Disorder*, and sends for DAVID again to play before him, as before; when he ¹¹ twice threw his *Javelin* at him, to stick him against the Wall; which Strokes DAVID avoided, by being on his Guard: Which ill Success ¹² made *Saul* ever after afraid of DAVID, because the LORD was on DAVID's Side, and ¹⁴ not with *Saul*.

Saul seeing this Scheme of none Effect against DAVID, he ¹⁵ next makes him Captain over 1000 Men, in order to dispatch him that Way; and ¹⁷ also promised him his Daughter *Merab*; in which he was not so good as his Word, for he gave her to *Adriel*: But his other Daughter *Michal* loving DAVID, he gave her to him in Marriage, only to be a Snare to him to take away his Life amongst the *Philistines* (A): But, for all this Deceit, DAVID ²⁷ slew 200 of them, and brought their *Foreskins* to *Saul* his Father-in-law; being ²⁵ all he desired of DAVID for his Daughter *Michal*: For which Victory *Saul* was more afraid of him, and *Michal* more lov'd him.

SECT. IV.

Jonathan *makes a* Covenant *to tell* DAVID *all his Father's Intentions.* DAVID *getteth* Goliath's *Sword; and acteth mad before King* Achish, &c. 1 Sam. xix.

JOnathan now ¹ finding his Father's Resolution for DAVID's Life, ² makes a *Covenant* with DAVID always to let him

---

(A) On this Deceit of Marriage, DAVID penn'd *Psal.* v.

know

know his Father's Intention: And ¹² *Michal* also let him down the Wall when the House was beset, ᵃ and laid an *Image* in Bed; and ¹⁴ said that DAVID was sick, in order to save his Life ᵇ,

1 Sam. xx.   &c. So DAVID fled to *Ramah* to *Samuel*, and ¹⁸ told him what was done; and they went and dwelt together in *Naioth*: Which being told unto Saul, he ²¹ sent Messengers thrice after him ᶜ; and ²² went also himself: But DAVID fled. DAVID now being fled from *Naioth*, ² greatly complaineth to *Jonathan*; and ⁵ great Feasting being at *Saul*'s House, *Jonathan* lets DAVID know how all Matters went, both for and against him, (though ³³ to the Hazard of his own Life) by ²⁰ shooting three *Arrows* near the Place where he lay in secret, and ³⁷ by hearing what passed between him and a Boy. Then sending the Boy back, *Jonathan* ⁴¹ spoke to DAVID, and kissed him; where they both wept together, confirming ⁴² their Sincerity to each other, in a very moving affectionate Manner; and ⁴² so parted: *Jonathan* returning to the City of his Father,

1 Sam. xxi.   and ¹ DAVID fleeth to the City of *Nob*, to *Ahimelech* the Priest; of whom he (² by framing many Sham-*Excuses*, of being sent, by the King, on private Business) obtained not only hallowed *Cakes*, &c. but also *Goliath*'s Sword, to guard him: But *Doeg*, *Saul*'s Herdsman, ⁷ being there at the same Time, DAVID immediately flees from *Ahimelech* to *Gath*, where

1 Sam. xxii.   being accused, and afraid of King *Achish*, he ¹³ framed himself *mad*; by which Hypocrisy he got clear off, and ¹ fled from thence to the Cave of *Adullam* *.

✥ ❀ ✤ ❀ ✤ ❀ ✤ ❀ ✤ ❀ ✤ ❀ ✤ ❀ ✤ ❀ ✤ ❀ ✤ ❀ ✤ ❀ ✤ ❀ ✤ ❀ : ✤

SECT. V.

Seven Thousand and Two Hundred Men join to DAVID *in Adullam.*

DAVID now ² being in a lonely *Cave*, all his Friends (as soon as they heard of it) as were in Debt, vexed, or troubled in Mind, gathered to him; being about 400 able

---

ᵃ On watching the House to kill him, *Psal.* lix.
ᵇ Here was composed *Psal.* xi. and cxl.
ᶜ When abroad with *Samuel*, *Psal.* lxxiii.
* In this disconsolate Place he prayed, as *Psal.* lvi, and praiseth GOD, as *Psal.* xxxiv.

Men:

Men: And David headed them as their *Prince* or *Captain* [d]. [It is also said that many of *Saul*'s Men deserted, and joined to David, to the Number of near 6800; all Men of great Valour, active, tall, and nimble; skilful in Bows and Arrows, austere in Look, and could throw Stones right or left-handed, &c. which David carefully received, and placed in *Order* under *Captains*, in *Bands* [†], &c. &c.]

Then [4] David, taking Care of his *Parents*, to shelter them from *Saul*'s Fury, with the King of *Moab*; he [5] leaves the Cave or Hold, by the Order of *Gad*, the Prophet, and fled to the Forest of *Hareth*.

Now *Saul*, [6] on hearing of David's Success, called his Men together under a Tree, in *Ramah*; and [8] greatly complained of their Infidelity towards him [e]; on which [9] *Doeg* told him how *Ahimelech* the Priest had relieved David, and gave him a Sword, &c. on which *Saul* sends for him; who, [14] then speaking favourably of David, [18] *Saul* caused eighty-five innocent *Priests* to be slain in cold Blood; even by wicked *Doeg*'s Instigation; putting all the City of *Nob*, where the Priests dwelt, to the Sword; sparing neither Man, Woman, nor sucking Child; Ox, Ass, nor Sheep; only [20] *Abiathar*, the Son of *Ahimelech*; who fled to David, and told him what Cruelty was done; for which News David [21] kept him with him in Safety. ‡ *Vide* 1 *Chron.* xviii. 16.

SECT. VI.

David *saves the City of* Keilah, *marches to the* Wilderness, *where* Jonathan *comforts him*, &c. 1 Sam. xxiii.

DAVID now [1] hearing that the *Philistines* were gone to fight against the City of *Keilah*, he [2] asked Counsel of the LORD twice what to do; Who [4] ordered him to go and

---

[d] Here he composed *Psal.* xxvii.—See 2 *Sam.* xxii. 1, 2, 3, 4, with *ver.* 6, 10.—2 *Sam. ver.* 45.

[†] See 1 *Chron.* xii. 1, 2, 22.

[e] *On this Complaint of* Saul, *or on his* Son, 1 *Sam.* xx. 30, 31. *it is thought* David *wrote* Psal. vii. 3, 4, 7, 12. *Also* Psalms xxvi. lxiv. cxxxix.

‡ *On hearing of this Flattery and Cruelty he composed* Psalms xii. lii. *and* xxxvi.

save the City; which he⁶ accordingly did, with great Slaughter; and brought away all their Cattle: Which ⁷ *Saul* hearing of, went with an Army, in great Haste, thinking to destroy DAVID and all the City ᵉᵉ.

DAVID ⁹ now being informed of *Saul's* mischievous Intention, asked Counsel again of the LORD, whether *Saul* would come or not; or, whether the *Lords* of the City would deliver him into *Saul's* Hand; Who ¹¹ told him they so intended: On which DAVID ¹³ marched off from the City, with about 600 Men, to the Wilderness of *Ziph*: Which *Saul* hearing of, proceeded no farther on that Enterprize; but sought after DAVID, in the Woods, to take his Life.

Jonathan, ¹⁶ on hearing where DAVID was gone, steals away, unknown to his Father, and goes to him in the Wood to comfort him; telling him that his Father should not find him; that ¹⁷ he should be soon KING, and that his Father well knew it. Then renewing their old *Covenant* with each other, *Jonathan* left him, but not without Tears on both Sides.

1 *Sam.* xxiii.

The *Ziphims* now ¹⁹ hearing of *Saul*, hasted to him in *Gibeah*, and ²⁰ told him they would do all that was in their Power to deliver DAVID into his Hands, which ²¹ greatly pleased *Saul*: But ²⁶ DAVID shunned their Company by retiring into another Quarter ᶠ; and *Saul* ¹⁶ being told that a Party of *Philistines* had invaded the Land, he ²⁸ returned from pursuing DAVID any more at that Time.

SECT. VII.

DAVID *cuts off* Saul's *Skirt; and* Saul *owns* DAVID's *Clemency, and his own Sin in pursuing him,* &c. 1 Sam. xxiv.

DAVID, being now ¹ in the Holds of *En-gedi*, (a City in *Judah*, of a natural Defence, *Josh.* xv. 62.) *Saul* ³ takes 3000 Men of *Israel*, and went again in Pursuit of him, on the *Rocks*, amongst the wild Goats; and ⁴ coming among the

---

ᵉᵉ *On the cruel Judgment of* Saul, *and his Courtiers, to slay the innocent* Priests *of the* LORD, *and to destroy the City, he composed* Psal. lviii.
ᶠ *On this Escape was wrote* Psal. xvii. *See ver.* 11, *and probably* Psal. xiv.

Sheep-

Sheep-folds, he left his Men, and went into an old *Cave* to do his Eafement, wherein (to his great Surprize) he finds DAVID and his Men fitting in both Sides the *Cave* g; who ⁵ would immediately have deftroyed *Saul*, had not DAVID hindered them: But, he ⁶ neverthelefs cut off the *Skirt* of *Saul*'s Coat; which he afterwards forely repented, becaufe he knew that *Saul* was the LORD's *Anointed*. But ⁸ letting *Saul* go off unhurt, he ⁹ called after him, and fhewed him his *Skirt*, and ¹⁰ greatly reproved him for hearkening to falfe Tales; feeing ¹¹ that GOD had put it in his Power to take his Life: Which when *Saul* faw and heard, he ¹⁷ forely wept, and owned DAVID's *Clemency* towards him, and confeffed his Sin in fo doing ʰ: Telling DAVID that he fhould be KING; and fwearing ²³ him not to deftroy him, nor his Seed: Which ²³ DAVID accordingly complied with. So *Saul* went home, and DAVID went up again, with his Men, into the *Hold*.

SECT. VIII.

Nabal's *Churlifhnefs, and* Abigail's *Generofity to* DAVID.
1 Sam. xxv.

SAmuel now dying, DAVID ¹ goes down to the Wildernefs of *Paran*, where, ⁴ hearing of churlifh *Nabal*, in *Maon*, he ⁵ fends ten young Men to his *Sheep-fhearing*, defiring him to fend fome Victuals, it being a good Time; who ¹⁰ being refufed any, they foon returned back: On which DAVID ¹³ in Anger took 400 Men, under Arms, to deftroy his Houfe, (leaving 200 more behind him) for that they had been a *Safeguard* to his Flocks: But, they were prevented by *Abigail*, Na-

---

g *Juft before* Saul *came into the Cave* DAVID *compofed* Pfalms cxlii *and* cxliii.
ʰ *On this, and fuch like Occafions,* DAVID *compofed* Pfal. xxviii. *See ver.* 21, 25. —*On the* Repentance *of an Enemy, he cheareth himfelf, as* Pfal. lvii. xcii. cxxiv. cxxv.—*On longing for Liberty and* GOD's Worfhip, *he compofed* Pfal. lxiii —*His Prayer in Adverfity was* Pfal. lxxxvi. *See ver.* 1, 14, 17 —*On Vengeance on his Enemies,* Pfal. xciv.—Pfal. cxix. *was here probably penned, or often repeated; wherein he breathes from the very Bottom of his Soul, his divine Thoughts and pious Meditations on* GOD's Law, Mercies, &c. *See* Pfal. cxix; *and my* Expofition *thereon.*

bal's Wife, by her meeting them on the Road, with her Ass-load of rich *Provisions*; which ³⁵ DAVID kindly receives, blesses her, and falls in Love with her; for she was a generous, fair Woman. *Abigail* then ³⁶ caused *Nabal* to make a Feast in his own House for DAVID; and *Nabal*, getting drunk, lay on the Floor till Morning: Then ³⁷ sickening, with fretting at *Abigail*'s Generosity, he ³⁸ lingered on for ten Days, when the LORD smote him for his Greediness and Ingratitude, that he died; and ⁴² DAVID took his *Abigail* to *Wife*: He also then ⁴⁴ took *Ahinoam* to Wife; *Saul* having given DAVID's Wife *Michal* unto *Phalti* the Son of *Laish*.

SECT. IX.

Saul, *and his Army, being asleep,* DAVID *took away his Spear,* &c. 1 Sam. xxvi.

THE *Ziphims* now ¹ telling *Saul* that DAVID was on the Hill of *Hachilah*, he chose out 3000 of his best Soldiers, and planted them very near him ²: Which ³ DAVID being aware of, he ⁴ sent out *Spies* to view their Armies; *Abner* being ⁵ then *Saul*'s chief Captain.

Then DAVID ⁶ took *Abimelech* and *Abishai*, his chief Captain, and marched privately down to *Saul*'s Army, by Night; and finding ⁷ *Saul* asleep, with his *Spear* sticking in the Ground, just by his Head, and a Pot of *Water*, and his Men lying asleep all round him, he ¹⁰ privately took away the *Spear* and Water *; but ⁸ *Abishai* would fain have killed *Saul* with his own *Spear*, as he lay sleeping, had not DAVID hindered him; because he ¹¹ knew that none should kill the LORD's Anointed: and that ¹² it was the LORD that had laid them all in such profound Sleeps, &c.

As soon as they were returned back from *Saul*'s Army to the Top of an *Hill*, afar off, DAVID ¹⁴ in the Morning, called out aloud, and awaked *Saul* and his *Soldiers*; and ¹⁵ greatly taunted *Abner*, for having no better Care of his Royal *Master:* Which ¹⁷

---

¹ On *this he composed* Psalms xvii. liv. and lxiv.
* Or Cruse of Oil. Vide *Jos.* Ant. and *P. Heylyn*'s Hist. of *Palestine*, &c. 4d. Edit. p. 559.

the.

the *King* hearing, he knew DAVID's Voice, and called to him; and [21] greatly owned his Folly, and Sin, in seeking after him; especially [19] when DAVID shewed him his *Spear*, as a Token of his Mercy towards him. Then *Saul* [21] owned DAVID to be his Son, and *blessed* him, and returned again to *Gibeah*; and DAVID went on towards *Gath*.

SECT. X.

DAVID *obtains* Ziklag *for his Residence, and kills the wicked* Canaanites, &c. 1 Sam. xxvii.

DAVID [1] still being in some Fear of *Saul*, (and, in some Measure, of GOD's Protection) thought it best to go and hide himself amongst a *Party* of the *Philistines*; thinking, that, in so doing, *Saul*, in all Probability, would then leave off from pursuing him any further, (as it so prov'd;) on which [2] he took 600 of his Men, with all their *Houshold*, and marched to *Achish* the King of *Gath*, having with him his two *Wives Abinoam* and *Abigail*; desiring [5] the King to give him and his some Place of *Residence*; on which [6] he gave him the City of *Ziklag*.

DAVID and his Men remained here about sixteen Months [k], in which Time [8] they went and invaded the *Geshurites*, the *Gezrites*, and the *Amalekites*, sparing [9] neither Man, Woman, nor Child to tell the Tale; bringing away all their Sheep, Oxen, Asses, Camels, and Wearing Apparel, and returned again to King *Achish*: These being the wicked *Canaanites* which GOD had appointed to be destroyed.

On this Return, the King [10] asked DAVID where he had been riding that Day; to which he answered, against the *South* of *Judah*, the *Jerahmeelites*, and the *Kenites*; which [11] the King then believed; and (thinking now that DAVID utterly hated the People of *Israel*, and they him,) said, for that, he should now be his Servant for ever, &c. &c.

---

[k] *In this disconsolate Place it is thought that* DAVID *composed* Psalms xiii. cxx. cxxi.

SECT. XI.

Saul *consults the* Witch *of* En-dor, *and hears his* Doom.
1 Sam. xxviii.

*S*Amuel now¹ being dead, and *Saul* (as GOD commanded in *Exod.* xx. 18. and *Deut.* xviii. 10.) had drove all the *Sorcerers* and *Soothsayers* out of the Land; and⁴ all the *Philistines* were assembled in Bands, and pitched their Tents in *Shunem*, to fight against *Saul*; and *Saul* also had assembled his Army, and pitched in *Gilboa*: King *Achish*¹ commanded DAVID to go with him to Battle against the *Israelites*, promising him, ² for which, that he should be the Keeper of his Head for ever; which DAVID durst then by no Means deny, though it was a great Grief to him to fight against the *People* of GOD.

As soon as *Saul* saw the powerful Armies of the *Philistines*, he⁵ was sore afraid, and ⁶ asked *Counsel* of the High-Priest, (as if of GOD) what to do; but, being no Ways answered, as he expected, he, ⁸ in *Disguise*, with two others, goes to consult with a *Witch*, at *En-dor*, about the Matter.

The *Witch*, now suspecting *Saul* might do her some Harm, was unwilling to begin her *Art*, till *Saul*⁹ had sworn not to betray her; which he accordingly did. Then, telling *Saul*, that she must, of Necessity, raise some *Spirit* to consult with, demanded of him, who he would she should raise; to which ¹¹ he answered, *Samuel* (little considering that *Satan* hath no Power over *Saints* after this Life;) on which ¹² (to her great Surprise) an *evil Spirit* directly appeared in *Samuel's* Shape, which put her into a double Fear; because she then knew that he had deceived her, in Disguise, *&c.*

Saul, on seeing her thus affrighted, ¹³ bid her not be afraid, but proceed; and ¹⁴ asked her what she saw, that so surprised her; to which she said, *one rising out of the Earth, with a venerable Look, and in a* sacerdotal *Mantle, or Vest.*

As soon as *Saul* saw the Spirit, (which he took to be *Samuel*) he bowed himself to the Earth, in great Fear; and being ¹⁵ asked, by the Spirit, why he so disquieted him; he told him, he was in a great Distress, and that GOD had intirely left him; and the *Philistines* were also gathered against him; therefore he desired he would tell him what to do; to which the

Spirit

Spirit anſwered, [16] *as he had not obeyed the* LORD, *nor done well to* DAVID, (Chap. xv. 28.) *nor* [18] *done his utmoſt Endeavour to ſlay the wicked* Amalekites, *the* LORD *would* [19] *now deliver him into the Hands of the* Philiſtines ; *and that, To-morrow, he, and his Sons, ſhould be with him among the Dead* ; *and that* DAVID (*whom he hated*) *ſhould be made* King, *and rule in his Stead.* So the Spirit vaniſhed.

Saul, on hearing this dreadful *Sentence*, [20] fell to the Ground, and was ſorely troubled ; which [21] when the *Witch* ſaw, ſhe (probably in Hopes of Reward) told him, that ſhe had done all ſhe could for him, and had doubly ventured her Life for his Sake, *&c.* deſiring him to eat ſome Bread with her, and ſo go hence, (for that he had not eaten any that Day) which [22] he much refuſed, until his Servants perſuaded him. *Saul*, now a little recovering himſelf, ſat upon the Bed, and eat ſome *Veal-Pye*, which [23] the *Witch* then made in Haſte (although ſhe was very poor ;) ſo [25] they went away that Night, ſorely troubled. *Thus have I cleared this dark* Paſſage, *concerning the Witch of* En-dor, *&c.* The Sequel of *this* is in *Sect.* XIII.

SECT XII.

DAVID, *on being diſmiſſed from King* Achiſh, *is guided by a young Man to the* Amalekites *Army* ; *recovering all they took from* Ziklag. 1 Sam. xxix.

AT this Time the *Philiſtines* [1] gathered their Armies to *Aphek*, and the *Iſraelites* at *Jezreel* ; and, DAVID [2] coming a little behind, with King *Achiſh*, (to join the other *Philiſtines*) [3] ſome of the Chiefs thought he might be a little treacherous, and not do his utmoſt againſt the *Iſraelites* ; on which they [7] ſent him and his Men back ; although [9] the King liked him as an Angel. But he [1] coming again to *Ziklag*, found his City pillaged and burnt by the wicked *Amalekites* ; and [2] his Wives, and their Children all taken *Priſoners* ; on which [4] they ſorely wept ; and, had DAVID himſelf then been there, they intended to ſtone him to Death, if they could have laid Hands on him ; but [6] DAVID comforted himſelf, and his Men, in the LORD his GOD.

DAVID, on this difmal *Scene*, [3] afked *Counfel* of the LORD, Who ordered him to follow them; which [10] he accordingly did, with about 400 Men; leaving 200 others behind, (who were weary, and not able to pafs the River *Bafor*) to ftay by the Baggage.

As DAVID was marching after them, behold, [11] he found a poor *Egyptian* in the Field, who was in Want, (whom the *Amalekites* had left, being fick) and [11] had neither eat nor drank for three Days and three Nights; when DAVID had [12] well refrefhed him with Food, he afked him [15] to guide him to the Company that had left him in that miferable State; which the young Man complied with, on DAVID's fwearing not to deliver him into their Hands, nor kill him.

DAVID now coming up to the *Amalekites*, (as the young Man directed) behold, [16] he found fome lying drunk on the Ground; others dancing, finging, and making merry with what they had taken from the Land of the *Philiftines*, and the Land of *Judah*; little thinking the *Vengeance* of GOD was juft at their Heels.

Then DAVID [17] forely fmote them, and mingled their Blood with their Wine; none efcaping, only 400 young Men, who rode away on Camels; recovering every Thing they had taken away, both Men, Women, Children, Oxen, Sheep, &c. as GOD had before told him. DAVID, [21] on returning back, met the 200 Men they had left behind, who defired Part of the *Plunder*: But [22] fome of the wicked Sort refufed to give them any, becaufe they were not in the Action: On which [24] DAVID ordered all to have Share alike, and [25] eftablifhed it as a *Law*, fo always to do for the future.

Then DAVID [26] coming again to *Ziklag* he gave the Elders thereof Part of what they had taken; telling them, that, that was the Spoils of the Enemies of the LORD; even [27] to *Beth-el*, *South-Ramoth*, *Jattir*, *Aroer*, [28] *Siphmoth*, *Efhtemoa*, [29] *Rachal*, the *Jerahmeelites*, and the *Kenites*; to them of *Hormah*, *Chor-afhan*, [30] *Hathach*, and [31] to *Hebron*; and all other Places where DAVID and his Men had ufed to haunt; as a grateful Acknowledgment of the *Favours* he had received of them.

SECT.

SECT. XIII.

Saul *and his three* Sons *slain, hanged, burnt, and buried,* &c.
1 Sam. xxxi.

NEXT Day ¹ the *Philistines* making a great Slaughter among the *Israelites*, in *Mount Gilboa,* ² wherein *Jonathan, Abinadab,* and *Malchishua,* the Sons of *Saul*, were slain; *Saul*, being wounded and weary, ⁴ desired his *Armour-bearer* to stab him, lest he should die by the uncircumcised; but, he refusing, *Saul* fell directly on his own Sword himself; and ⁵ his *Armour-bearer* on his likewise: But *Saul*, not dying directly, called to a young Man, an *Amalekite*, to dispatch him *; which he immediately did, taking his *Crown* and *Bracelet*, which he afterwards carried to DAVID. Thus ⁶ *Saul*, his three *Sons*, and *Armour-bearer*, fell, and came to miserable Ends in one Day, as the evil Spirit, in *En-dor*, had the Day before told them, for *Saul's* leading a wicked Life, &c.

Now another Party of the *Israelites*, over the *Valley*, seeing the others flee; they fled also; and left their Cities to the *Philistines* to dwell in; who ⁸ coming the next Day, to *plunder* the Dead, they found *Saul*, his three Sons, and his Armour-bearer. Then ⁹ cutting off *Saul's* Head, they carried it to the *Philistines*, as a Token of Victory; ¹⁰ and hanging up their Bodies, some Time, near the Walls of *Beth-shan*; which the People of *Jabesh-Gilead* took, by Night, and ¹² burnt their Bones; and ¹³ buried the Remains thereof under a Tree at *Jabesh*; and fasted and mourned seven Days, according to Custom.—*Vide Jer.* xxxiv. 5.—1 *Chron.* x. 12.

SECT. XIV.

DAVID *lamenteth* Saul *and* Jonathan's *Deaths; slays the Messenger; and is made* King *at* Hebron. 2 Sam. i.

DAVID not having been three Days in *Ziklag*, he received the sad Tidings of the Death of *Saul* and his three Sons, by the *Amalekite*; who ¹⁰ then brought him *Saul's*

---
* See *Josephus's* Antiquities.

Crown.

Crown and Bracelet, that were on his Arm, when he difpatched him; as a Teftimony of the Truth, in Hopes of a great Reward for his Trouble: On which DAVID [12] forely lamented, and the young Man [2] falfly wept, in Sympathy along with him: But, [9] although the young Man faid, that he difpatched *Saul* by his own Order, DAVID, [5] after feveral fevere Queftions, [15] ordered his Servants to flay him, for [16] being *Regicide* to the LORD's Anointed. A juft *Reward* for all fuch as forfake their own native Country, and feek Wealth for Bloodfhed, as he [3] had done.

Then DAVID paid his laft Duties to the Dead, and [17] greatly lamented *Saul*, and [16] *Jonathan* his whole Delight; ordering [14] all the chief Women to mourn in *Scarlet* trimmed with Gold; and to be decorated with the richeft *Jewels.—See Chap.* iii. 31, *and Chap.* xiii. 31.

After this DAVID [1] (by Counfel of GOD, [2] by the High-Prieft) took his two Wives, *Ahinoam* and *Abigail*, and [3] all his Men, with their Houfhold, and went to the City of *Hebron*; and he was made KING of *Judah*; where [4] a Party of the Men of *Judah* brought him Word, that a Party of *Jabefh-Gilead* had ftole *Saul* and his *Sons* away by Night, and buried them in the chief Place of that *Province*; on which DAVID [5] fent them great Thanks; telling them [6] that, as he was now made KING, nothing fhould be wanting in him to their Affiftance, &c. And DAVID [11] reigned in *Hebron* about feven Years, and fix Months [1].

2 Sam. ii.

SECT. XV.

Ifh-bofheth *made* King *by* Abner; Joab *killeth* 360 *of his Men; and* Abner *killeth* Afahel. 2 Sam. ii.

ABNER now, [8] (who had been *Saul*'s chief Captain) hearing that DAVID was made KING, taketh *Ifh-bofheth*, the Son of *Saul*, from *Mahanaim* to *Gibeon*, and [9] made him *King* over eleven *Tribes* of *Ifrael*, in the 40th Year of his Age; where he reigned about two Years. *Chap.* v. 5.

---

[1] *On this Glimpfe of* GOD'*s Mercy he compofed Pfalm* ci. *being a* Thankfgiving, *and Refolution to lead a more* godly *Life than his Predeceffor,* Saul.

Then

Then *Abner*, [12] *Ish-bosheth*'s Servant, and [13] *Joab*, DAVID's Servant, with eleven others on each Side, went to meet other Parties by the Pool of *Gibeon*; and each Party sat by the Pool on the opposite Sides: But, [14] after some Taunts given to *Joab* by *Abner*, they [15] all arose to battle, Man for Man, Sword in Hand; wherein *Abner* [23] being defeated, stabbed *Asahel* under the fifth Rib to the Heart, on which he fell; which [24] *Joab* and *Abishai* seeing, they pursued him and his Army, till the Sun went down, to the Top of an Hill before the City of *Giah*; where, [25] in the Night, *Abner* called out for Mercy, for taunting him; on which *Joab* [25] blew a Trumpet, for his Men to stop from pursuing him. So *Abner* [29] and his Men walked all Night through the *Wilderness*, and over the River *Jordan*, to their Tents in *Mahanaim*; and *Joab*, [30] and his Men, returned back to *Hebron*.

When *Joab* [30] had called his Men together, he wanted only *Asahel*, and 19 others; but *Abner* [31] wanted 360, who were slain in the Battle; which greatly confirmed DAVID's Kingdom. And they buried *Asahel* in his Father's Sepulchre in *Bethlehem*.

SECT. XVI.

Abner *revolteth to* DAVID; Joab *killeth him*; *and* DAVID *mourneth*, &c. 2 Sam. iii.

NOW continued a War between DAVID and *Ish-bosheth* for near two Years, in which DAVID [1] became more strong, and *Ish-bosheth* weaker, and discouraged. *Abner* [7] having now taken *Rizpah*, one of *Saul*'s Concubines, *Ish-bosheth* greatly reproved him for it; which *Abner* resenting, he directly [8] sent Messengers to DAVID to covenant a *Peace* with him; to revolt *Ish-bosheth*, and to deliver him the whole Kingdom, &c. This DAVID [14] complied with, on his bringing again *Michal* his Wife, whom *Saul* had before given to *Phalti*; 1. *Sam*. xviii. 25. On this DAVID [14] sends to *Ish-bosheth* for his Wife, on which he took her from *Phalti*, who [15] followed her, sorely weeping; but, *Abner* sent him back again, and her to DAVID; and also [17] persuaded the *Chiefs* of *Israel* to join with DAVID.

2 Sam. iii.

Then *Abner*, taking twenty of his best Men, went privately to see DAVID, where they were kindly feasted, and sent away peacefully:

peacefully ᵐ: But, *Joab*, and other Servants ²³ coming to DA-
VID juſt as they were gone, and hearing, by the Servants, how
Abner had been there privately, he ²⁴ was very angry, thinking
²⁵ he might get in more Favour than he, he in a Rage ²⁶ (unknown to DAVID) ſends for *Abner* back again; when ²⁷ taking
him aſide pretending to whiſper with him, in a friendly Manner, he ſtabbed him to the Heart, in Revenge of his Brother
Aſabel, on which he died on the Spot; as *Chap.* ii. 23.

This private *Murder* ſoon coming to DAVID's royal Ear, he
greatly lamented, by Reaſon, he well knew that he had no
Ways contrived *Abner*'s Death in ſuch a ſly cruel Manner; willing, ²⁹ that the Blood of *Abner* ſhould be on *Joab*; viz. *that
his Houſe might never be without Poverty, the Sword, running Sores,
or Lameneſs*: Commanding *Joab* ³¹ and all People elſe to mourn
for *Abner*; on which ³² they all wept at his *Funeral*, &c. and ³³
DAVID himſelf followed his *Corps* to the Grave, in *Hebron*;
weeping even till the Sun went down, and eat not; he being
a wiſe and valiant Man. DAVID alſo ³⁵ prayed that GOD
would reward the Doer of that Evil according to his Wicked-
neſs; and compoſed an *Epitaph* in Rememberance of *Abner*, &c.
(*Apud. Joſ. Antiq.*)

༺༺༺༺༺༺༺༺༺༺༺༺༺༺༺*༺༺༺༺༺༺༺༺༺༺༺༺༺༺༺

SECT. XVII.

Iſh-boſheth *killed*; Baanah *and* Rechab *gibbeted*; *and*
DAVID *proclaimed* KING *over all* Iſrael. 2 Sam. iv.

KING *Iſh-boſheth* ¹ on hearing that *Abner*, his chief Captain, and Kinſman was dead, he was greatly diſcouraged;
and ² having two *Captains* in the City of *Beroneth*, called *Baanah* and *Rechab*, they ⁵ came in Diſguiſe to *Iſh-boſheth*'s Houſe
in the Afternoon, as he lay on his Couch taking his Nap, pretending ⁶ to his Servants, that they were *Merchants*, and came
to buy Corn: And, he having no *Guard* then about him, they
entered his Apartment, and ſtabbed him to the Heart: Then,
cutting off his Head, they travelled all Night through the *Wilderneſs*, and carried it to DAVID, in the City of *Hebron*.

DAVID ¹⁰ on ſeeing the *Head*, greatly blamed them for their

ᵐ DAVID, *in Hopes of greater Mercies from* GOD, *here compoſed* Pſalm lxxv.

Cruelty,

Cruelty, knowing they had done it only for the Sake of Reward: On which he ᴸ ordered his Servants to cut off their *Hands* and *Feet*, and hang their Bodies on *Gibbets*, over the *Pools* in *Hebron*; in order to deter others from committing such like cruel Actions for the future: And also to bury the Head in the Sepulchre with *Abner*, in that City. (Chap. iii. 32.)

*** (The *Reader* is here to take Notice, that ᵗ *Jonathan* had a Son called *Mephibosheth*, who was lamed by being dropped out of his *Nurse's* Arms, as she carried him out of the Battle, when his *Father Saul* was slain; of whom I shall say more in *Sect*. xxii.)

These Executions being over, ᴵ all the *Elders* and chief *Officers* of War, and near 200,000 of the *Tribes* of *Israel*, bearing Arms, came to DAVID in *Hebron*, with Corn, Wine and Provisions of all Kinds: And holding there a *Feast* for three Days, they set DAVID at the Head, and all marched after him; and ᴶ with one Voice proclaimed him KING over all *Israel* ⁿᵘ; he being ⁴ then about 30 Years old. And he reigned in all about 40 Years; i. e. 7 in *Hebron*, and 33 in *Jerusalem* *.

2 Sam. v.

SECT. XVIII.

DAVID *twice beats the* Jebusites, *and takes Possession of* Jerusalem. 2 Sam. v.

SEVEN Years after DAVID was proclaimed KING he ⁶ advanced towards *Jerusalem:* And the *Jebusites*, having then Possession of the *City*, shut the Gates against him, and, by Way of Defiance, brought all the Blind and Lame out of the City, and set them as a *Guard* against DAVID, and his Troops; thinking, by the Strength of their City, that such *Invalids* were sufficient to make DAVID retreat.

. This foolish Mockery so enraged DAVID, that he (for Example sake) was resolved to attack their *Castle* first; promising ᵃ that he who first scaled the Walls should be made his chief

---

ⁿ *See* Psal. lxx. *and* lxxviii.   ⁿ *Here he composed* Psal. cxxxiii.

* Or *Jebusalem*; said first to be built by *Melchisedeck*, Prince and High Priest of *Salem*. Vid. P. Heylyn's Hist. of *Palestine*, p. 561.

Commander,

Commander, becaufe he knew the *Jobb* was a little hazardous: On which *Joab* directly wins the *Prize*, and called to DAVID from the Top of the *Battlements* of the *lower Gate*, to make good his Promife, which was accordingly done. (1 *Chron.* xi. 6.)

Then having cleared the *Caſtle* of all the *Jebuſites*, DAVID made it his *Reſidence* for his Family, and 9 called it THE CITY OF DAVID: And having all fine *Materials* and *Workmen* ſent him by *Hiram* King of *Tyre*, he beautifies the whole Town, and built a fine *Palace* therein; fortified the upper Town, laid the lower Town to it, and walled it round; and gave *Joab* the Command and Care of it, as he before had promiſed: And the LORD was with DAVID, &c.

Now there was in the Town, in the Time of ſacking, one very rich Man, and another very poor Man, which eſcaped the Fury of the *Soldiers*, by being DAVID's *Friends* and *Favourites*; and were then preſerved by his Royal Order.

Now 17 other *Philiſtines*, on hearing that DAVID was made KING, came into the Valley of *Rephaim*, againſt him; but he ſmote them ſorely, as GOD had commanded him. Theſe alſo 21 came again a ſecond Time, more ſtrong, and DAVID, 23 by Counſel of the LORD, (by *Abiathar*, Who directed him 24 by a walking Noiſe over the *Mulberry-Trees*, where they lay in the Wilderneſs,) killed many of them thereunder, and 21 putting the reſt to the Rout, he got conſiderable *Booties* from their Camps, and brake and burned many of their *Images*p. 1 *Chron.* xiv.

SECT. XIX.

The Ark *removed.* Uzzah *ſtruck dead; and* Michal *made barren, for deſpiſing* GOD's Praiſe, &c. 2 Sam. vi.

THE *Wars* now being a little over, DAVID 'gathers about 30,000 of his chief Men, in the City of *Baale*, to fetch the *Ark* of GOD from the Houſe of *Aminadab* in *Gibeah* *, (it being a Kind of *Cheſt* which was ſuppoſed to contain the *Spiri*

---

p *On theſe* Victories *was ſung* Pſal. xviii.
* Where it had been near 20 Years. Vide *Heylyn*, p. 557.

or *Residence* of GOD; and built on *Cherubims*, and called *The* LORD *of Hosts*, &c.) Then putting ³ the *Ark* into a *new Cart*, *Uzzah* and *Ahio* (the Sons of *Aminadab*) drove it; and DAVID ⁵ and the People of *Israel* sung *Psalms*, and played on all Kinds of *Instruments* made of *Fir*; and on *Harps, Psalteries, Cymbals*, and *Cornets*, &c. as they walked before the *Ark*.

When they came ⁶ to *Nachon*'s Threshing-floor, the *Ark* began to shake in the Cart; on which *Uzzah* put his Hand to hold it steady, and was, ⁷ by the LORD, immediately struck dead on the Spot; he not having an express *Order* to touch it ᵠ: On which *Breach* DAVID ⁸ was greatly displeased, and ⁹ feared to touch it himself; nor ¹⁰ would he then have it brought to his own House, but ordered it to be carried to the House of *Obed-Edom*, a *Levite*, which was accordingly done. (1 *Chron.* xv. 25.)

Some Time after ¹¹ DAVID being told how GOD had blessed *Obed-Edom*, with great *Riches*, (on Account of the *Ark* being at his House,) who was very poor before, he went, with great Gladness, and fetch'd it from thence, to his own House in *Jerusalem* ʳ; offering ¹² up to GOD several Beasts as he went, for a Burnt-offering: Having it carried by the *Priests* and *Levites*; with seven *Choirs* of Singing-Men, and *Instruments of Joy*; and ¹⁴ DAVID *danced* and *sung* before them, wearing a Linen *Ephod* or *Girdle*, ornamented, like a *Priest*'s, and bare-headed; which ¹⁶ his Wife *Michal* seeing through a Window, as he passed, she greatly despised him for so doing: Which plainly shews, that such as set their Minds on the Pleasures of this Life, and live in Luxury, generally despise *Religion*, and the *Praise* and *Glory* of GOD. And, ¹⁷ bringing the *Ark* to the House of DAVID, they set it in the Midst of the *Tabernacle* as DAVID had made for it; and ¹⁷ offered a Peace-offering unto the LORD; which being over, DAVID ¹⁹ ordered to every one of the People of *Israel*, both Men and Women, a *Cake* of Bread, a large Piece of *Flesh*, and a Flagon of *Wine*: Then giving them his *Blessing* in the Name of *The* LORD *of Hosts*, they all departed to their own Homes ˢ. (See 1 *Chron.* xvi. 4.)

DAVID now ²⁰ returning home to *bless* his own Houshold, was met by his Wife *Michal*, who, (jealous) said, *How glorious has the King been To-day among the* Maidens, Servants, *and*

ᵠ *On this* Psal. xv. *was composed.*   ʳ *Here was uttered* Psal. xviii. xxiii.
ˢ *Here was composed* Psal. xxiv.

vain

vain Fellows! *bare-headed like a* Fool: To which DAVID answered, "GOD *rather bless'd me than thy Father* Saul; *therefore, I will* serve, sing, *and* play *before the* LORD.—And *Michal* never after had any *Child* by DAVID to the Day of her Death, for making Mock of him, and GOD's *Praises*; though she ever so much desired it. (See 1 *Chron.* xvi. 8.)

SECT. XX.

DAVID *in full Tranquillity proposeth to build the* Temple, *but is forbidden by the* LORD, *by the Prophet* Nathan. 2 Sam. vii.

KING DAVID now living in a *Palace* of *Cedar*, as fine as Hands could make it, and at *Rest* from his Enemies, next resolved to build a *Temple*, and *dedicate* it to the *Service* and *Worship* of GOD, and (according to the *Prediction* of *Moses*, *Exod.* xxvi. 7.) communicated his Design to *Nathan* the Prophet, who first greatly encouraged him to proceed; but the *Word* of GOD coming to *Nathan*, by Night, ordered him to tell DAVID not to proceed, but "leave it to be done by his Son *Solomon*, that should succeed him; for that He had not dwelt in any House since He had brought the Children of *Israel* out of *Egypt*, but in *Tents* and *Tabernacles*; and that He had not only took him from the Sheep-folds, and destroy'd his Enemies, and now made him King over all *Israel*; whereby he might be great in the World; but that "he should now rest till *Solomon* should build *Him* an House; and that He would establish it to him and his Seed for ever, if he walked in the Fear of GOD, &c.

(See 1 *Sam.* xvi. 12.—*Psal.* lxxviii. 70.—1 *Kings* viii. 20.— v. 5.—vi. 12.—1 *Chron.* xxii. 10—*Heb.* i. 15.—*Psal.* lxxxix. 31, 32.—) Now *Solomon*'s Beginning figureth the Accomplishment in *CHRIST*.)

As soon as *Nathan* had delivered his Message from GOD, DAVID immediately goes to the *Ark*, and fell on his Face and *worshipped*; *blessing* and *praising* GOD for all his *Mercies*

Here was uttered Psal. cx.

Concordant to the Book *of* Psalms, &c. 173

and *Benefits* to him; and for his mighty *Promises* to his Posterity: Then concluding his *Benediction* with an *Hymn*ᵘ, and *Prayer*, he departed, believing all that *Nathan* had told him would surely come to pass ᵛ. (See 1 *Chron*. xvii.)

SECT. XXI.

David *subdueth the* Moabites, *and* Syrians, *and settleth his Houshold, Servants*, &c. 2 Sam. viii.

DAVID not loving to sit idle, in a little Time meditates a War against a Party of the *Philistines* called *Moabites*, in order that he might leave his Kingdom all in *Peace* to his Successor *Solomon*. To compleat this *Victory*, he summoned his Troops together to the Number of about 20,000 Foot and 170 Horse, and marched against them; and ³ sorely smote *Hadadezer* their King, and ⁴ took the City of *Metheg-ammah*, with 1000 Chariots, 700 Horsemen, and 20,000 Foot; houghing or cutting all the Leaders of the Horses Feet, reserving only 100 Horses and Chariots for himself; recovering all the Lands bordering on the River *Euphrates*, &c. in the Valley of Salt. The *Syrians* now ⁵ coming to succour *Hadadezer*, David slew 220,000 of them; and took all the rest Prisoners, and ⁶ put them in Garrisons; and they became Tributaries, bringing to David large Gifts of *Gold, Brass*, &c. of great Value; which ⁷ he took to *Jerusalem* for sacred Uses: For which ⁶ the LORD preserved David wheresoever he went ʷ.

Now *Toi*, King of *Hamath*, hearing how David had drubbed the *Philistines*, ¹⁰ sent his Son *Joram* to rejoice with David on these Victories, he bringing him many *Vessels* of *Gold* and *Silver*, of great Value, which *Toi* had formerly taken in War; in order to *mediate* for a *Peace*, and to make a League with David, lest he should fall on him in like Manner; by Reason he well knew that he was very powerful and *victorious*, and ¹⁴ that the LORD always preserved him, he converting ¹¹ all rich Gifts and Spoils to sacred Uses. David, now loving

---

ᵘ *Here was uttered* Psal. xviii. *and* xxiii.
ʷ *Here probably were uttered* Psalms ii.—iv. ver. 2.—ix.—xx.—xxi.—xxx.—xcv.—xcvi.—xcvii. *See my* Exposition *on each.*

N *Peace,*

Peace, kindly accepts the rich Present that *Toi* had sent him; and agreeing to the *Proposals* that his Son *Joram* had brought, dismissed him with great Honour and Satisfaction: And, being ¹⁵ a Lover of *Honour* and *Justice*, ¹⁴ built *Garrisons* in *Edom* for Soldiers; and, according to Promise, he ¹⁶ made *Joab* his General, *Jehoshaphat* his Recorder, ¹⁷ *Zadok* and *Ahimelech* (or *Abiathar*) his Priests, *Seraiah* his Secretary or Scribe, ¹⁸ *Benaiah* over the *Cherethites* and *Pelethites*, his Body-Guards, and DAVID's own *Sons* were his chief *Rulers*, &c.

SECT. XXII.

DAVID *findeth* Jonathan's *Son* Mephibosheth, *restores his Lands, and makes* Ziba's *Sons his Overseers*, &c. 2 Sam. ix.

DAVID having put all his *Family* into a regular Order, next ¹ enquires after the *Family* of his Father *Saul*, that, if his beloved Brother *Jonathan* had any of his Family left, he might make them some grateful Amends for their Father's *Love* towards him; as he formerly promised. (1 Sam. xx. 15.)

Now, after a strict Enquiry, *Ziba* ³ told DAVID that *Jonathan* had a Son alive in the House of *Machir*, in *Lo-debar*, called *Mephibosheth*, or *Eliam*, the Father of *Bathsheba*; and that ⁴ he was lame in his Feet, by a Misfortune at five Years old, by his *Nurse* dropping him, in a Fright, as she run with him in her Arms, out of that bloody Battle, wherein his Father and Grandfather were slain, &c. in order to save his Life. (2 Sam. iv. 4.) See *Sect.* xvii.

On these joyful *Tidings*, DAVID ⁵ directly sends for *Mephibosheth*, who ⁶ fell on his Face to reverence him; but DAVID, ⁷ bidding him arise, told him that he would restore him all the Lands he had took from his Grandfather *Saul*, and that he and his Sons should for ever be his darling *Guests*, and eat with him at his Table; on which *Mephibosheth* returned Thanks, and ⁸ owned himself too mean to enjoy such princely Favours, &c. DAVID also ¹⁰ made *Ziba* and his 15 Sons, and 20 Servants, *Overseers* and Tillers of *Mephibosheth*'s Land, which they kindly received; and promised carefully to perform. (See 1 Chr. xviii.)

And *Mephibosheth* ¹¹ eat at the King's Table, having one Son called *Micha*.

SECT.

SECT. XXIII.
Joab *subdues the* Ammonites *for using* DAVID's *Messengers ill*, &c. 2 Sam. x.

A Little after, *Nahash* the King of the *Ammonites* died, and ¹ *Hanun* reigned in his Stead, to whom DAVID shewed great Kindness for his Father's Sake: But, ² sending his Servants to *comfort* him on his Father's Death, some of the *Chiefs*, contrary to all Reason, persuaded King *Hanun* ³, that DAVID's Servants were only *Spies*, and not Friends: On which, ⁴ instead of using them honourably, they *shaved* off half their *Beards*, and cut off their *Garments* close to their *Buttocks*, and sent them shamefully away. DAVID ⁵ hearing of this cruel *Usage*, sent other Messengers to meet them, on their Return, to order them to stay at *Jericho*, till their *Beards* were grown; which was accordingly done.

The *Ammonites*, now conscious of the *Breach* they had made with DAVID, and fearing his Anger, immediately ⁶ sent 1000 Talents to the King of *Surus*, and hired the *Syrians* of the House of *Beth-rehob*, and of *Zoba* 20,000 Foot, of the King of *Maacab* 1000, and of *Ish-tob* 12,000 all under Arms; calling in all *Allies* they could make, to meet DAVID.

DAVID ⁷ hearing of these *Preparations* for War, immediately sent *Joab* to meet them near the City of *Rabbath*; and ⁹ as soon as he saw their *Army*, he chose all his best Men, and set them in Order for Battle against the *Syrians*; and ¹⁰ put his other Men, under the Command of *Abishai*, his Brother, against the *Ammonites*: Charging ¹² all to be valiant, and ¹¹ to help each other if Occasion required, resigning himself intirely to the *Power* and *Will* of GOD ¹³.

The Enemy first marched out of *Rabbath* with their *Auxiliary-Troops*, and drew up in the Field into two Bodies; and *Joab* drew up his in the same Order to meet them: Who giving them the first On-set, the ¹⁴ *Syrians* fled before him; which the *Ammonites* seeing, they fled also before *Abishai*, and went again all together into the City. *Joab* having thus drove them, he went again to *Jerusalem*.

Hadarezer now, not content with this run-away Battle, sends to *Chalama*, a King of *Syrus* beyond *Euphrates*, to hire an Army of 80,000 Foot, and 10,000 Horse; which ¹⁷ DAVID hearing of, immediately gathers a mighty Army, and paſſed with them himſelf over the River *Jordan*, and killed of them at *Halem* 40,000 Foot, and 70,000 Horſe; taking 700 Chariots, and *Hadarezer*'s chief General *Shobach*. (See 1 *Chron.* xix. 18.)

When this dreadful Drubbing was over ¹⁹ the People of *Meſopotamia* ſent Ambaſſadors with great Preſents and Addreſſes to DAVID for Peace, and delivering themſelves wholly to him, he returned to *Jeruſalem* in Peace and Safety ˣ.

SECT. XXIV.

DAVID *debaucheth* Bathſhebah, *and her Huſband* Uriah *treacherouſly ſlain.* 2 Sam. xi.

ABOUT a Year after this, DAVID ¹ (according to Cuſtom in the Spring-time) ſends *Joab* once more to War againſt the *Ammonites*, who then laid all the Country waſte; and driving the People into *Rabbath*, the Metropolis, laid Siege to it. Mean while DAVID tarried in *Jeruſalem*.

A. M 2069.
Before *Chriſt*
2035.

And though DAVID was undoubtedly a *juſt* and *pious* Man, and very ſtrict in *Obedience* to the *Law* of GOD, and his Country, yet, alas! GOD ſuffered him to fall into Sin, for Example to others; whoſe Sin not only teaches us the *Frailty* of Fleſh and Blood, but alſo teacheth us a *Leſſon* of unfeigned *Repentance*. For, one Day, as DAVID, was juſt riſen from his *Couch*, in the Cool of the Evening, on the *Terrace* of his Houſe, ² looking down he ſaw *Bathſheba* the Daughter of *Eliam*, and Wife of *Uriah*, waſhing herſelf: And ſhe being a beautiful Woman of an exquiſite *Shape*, ſo enamoured DAVID that he ⁴ ſends for her to his Bed, where ſhe lay all that Night, and returned to her Home the next Morning. Soon afterwards, finding herſelf with Child, ſhe ſent *Meſſengers* to let DAVID know of it, that he might ſome Way conſider how to conceal it; for that ſhe knew it would be Death to her, ſhould it be known, according to the *Laws* of her Country, did not DAVID prevent it: Her Huſband *Uriah* then being *Joab*'s Armour-bearer in the Camp.

ˣ *On this ſee* Pſalms xliv.—lx.—lxi.—lxii.—xciii.—xcvi.—xcvii.—xcviii.—xcix.—c.—cviii.—cxvii—cxviii.—cxlv.—cxlvi.—cxlvii.—cxlviii.—cl.—*and read their ſeveral* Expoſitions.

On this News from *Bathſheba*, DAVID [6] directly ſends for *Uriah* her Huſband, and, after aſking him [7] many *Queſtions* about the State of the Army, and how the Siege went on at *Rabbath*, he [8] (to ſmother the Matter, and lay the Child to *Uriah,*) ordered him to go home to his *Wife*; ſending a Meſs of Meat after him: But *Uriah*, [9] by drinking with the *Guards*, neglected the King's *Order*, and ſlept with them all Night at the Gate: Which [10] DAVID hearing of, he greatly reproved him for not paying the *Benevolence* due to his Wife, ſeeing he had been ſo long from her; *Uriah*, on this Reproof, [11] told the King, that *he did not think it honourable to indulge himſelf in his* Wife's *Arms, while his* General *and* Fellow-Soldiers *lay on the Ground, in an Enemy's Country.*

DAVID [12] then bids him, a ſecond Time, to go to his *Wife* that Night; and return to the Camp next Day: But, he ſtaying again with the *Guards* whilſt the King was at Supper, they ſo ply'd him with Liquor, by *Healths*, that he entirely forgot both his *Wife*, and the King's *Order*.

DAVID, now hearing of *Uriah*'s ſecond Neglect, was determined to puniſh him privately; and [13] accordingly ſends for him the third Day in the Morning, and made him ſo drunk that he lay on the Couch that Night: Mean while DAVID went and lay again with his Wife *Bathſheba*.

On the Morrow, [14] DAVID writes a *Letter* to *Joab* (which prov'd to be *Uriah's Dead-warrant*) and ſent it by *Uriah*, that *Joab* ſhould make the firſt Attack, and put him in the Front of the Battle, with many other Ragamuffins, to be ſlain.

Poor *Uriah*, knowing nothing of the *Scheme*, nor that his Life was in Danger, chearfully undertakes the Poſt that *Joab* had fixed him; by Reaſon *Joab* promiſed [16] to back him with his beſt Men: But, alas! *Uriah* was deceived, for *Joab* had given his Men *private Orders* to retreat, and leave *Uriah* in the Lurch, according to the King's Order.

Uriah then, vigorouſly and innocently leading the Front, was greatly preſſed againſt the Wall of the City by the *Rear*; and the *Ammonites*, throwing open the Gates directly on him, the Rear then retreated, and left poor *Uriah* [17] to be cut in Pieces, with ſome few others; although he fought manfully, after he received many Wounds, and fell on his Face towards the Enemy, and died like a *Man of Honour*; whilſt others retreated, as *Traitors*, cowardly.

This vile *Action* being over, and *Joab* [18] sending Word what was done, the Messenger did not forget letting DAVID know that *Uriah* was killed, according [*] to his former *private* Instructions. DAVID, [25] on hearing this *News,* without any seeming Dullness or Gloominess of Conscience, said, *The Fate of War falleth on one as well as another, therefore none should think it hard when their Friends fall,* &c. bidding him tell *Joab* to make his next *Attack* more sure, by a stronger Force against the City.

Now [26] *Bathsheba* hearing also that her Husband *Uriah* was slain, she sorely wept, and kept in close *Mourning* for several Days: But, that Sorrow being soon over, DAVID [27] sent for her to his House; and to make her the sooner forget her *Sorrow,* he made her his *Wife,* and she bare him a Son; but, it being unlawfully begotten, it greatly displeased the LORD.

✺✺✺✺✺✺✺✺✺✺✺✺✺✺✺✺✺✺✺✺✺✺✺

SECT. XXV.

Nathan *reproveth* DAVID *of* Adultery *and* Murder; *who sorely* repenteth: *And taking the City* Rabbath, *putting them to cruel Deaths,* &c.

GOD thus suffering DAVID to *sin,* as willingly raised him again by giving him an Heart of unfeigned *Repentance,* and took him again into his Divine Favour, by [1] sending *Nathan* the Prophet, to tell him his Error. Now, *Nathan,* being a *Prophet* of great *Wisdom* and *Chearfulness,* not willing to tell DAVID of his *Error* point-blank, at once, acquaints him of it by Way of *Parable* thus: *There were (said* Nathan) *two Men in one City, one* [2] *very rich, having many Sheep, Oxen,* &c. *and another* [3] *very poor, having only one* Ewe-lamb, *which he raised up with his* Children, *loved it as his* Daughter, *and* [3] *it slept in his Bosom: And behold the rich Man, refusing to use his own, hath* [4] *not only took away the* poor Man's *Ewe-lamb by Night, and dressed it for his Use, but has also slain the* Owner *to conceal the Crime.*

Then said DAVID, *Oh! Villain, to do such an unjust Thing! he* [6] *shall not only make a fourfold Satisfaction, but* [5] *shall also die into the Bargain.* Then [7] *said Nathan* unto DAVID, THOU ART THE MAN: *Hath not* [8] GOD *made thee* KING *over* Israel, *and delivered thee from the Hands of* Saul, *and gave thee Wives for thy*

thy *Bosom*? Why [9] hast thou thus despised GOD's *Command*, and slain innocent Uriah, only to have his *Wife*? For this *Sin* GOD shall raise up Evil in thy *Family*, and [11] take thy *Wives* from thee, and give them to others, who shall lie with them before thy Face, openly, because [12] thou hast done this *Sin* secretly.

Then said DAVID [13] to *Nathan*, 'I have sinned against the LORD:' And *Nathan* said, The LORD will forgive thee, thou shalt not die; but [14] the *Child* that is born, for that Sin shall surely die.

Nathan was no sooner departed, but [15] the Child sickened; and although DAVID [16] privately wept, fasted, and prayed to GOD to save it, yet [19] it died on the seventh Day [y]: After which DAVID [20] washed himself, changed his *Garments*, worshipped in the House of GOD; and eat again in his own House, seeing he could not restore the Life of the Child [y]. So DAVID [21] again comforted his Wife *Bathsheba*, and [24] she bare him a *Son*, whom he called *Solomon*, who was greatly loved of GOD. (1 *Chron.* xxii. 9.—*Matt.* i. 6.)

Then DAVID [29] went and took the City of *Rabbath*, and [30] took the King's *Crown*, which weighed 60 Pounds of *Gold*, and precious Sardonyx Stones, and wore some of them on his Head for *Ornaments*: And [31] putting many People of that City, and others unto cruel Deaths by Saws and Axes, in burning Kilns, and under Harrows; for being Enemies to GOD and His People; and he then returned to *Jerusalem*.

SECT. XXVI.

Amnon *debaucheth* Tamar. Amnon *killed by* Absalom; *he fleeth, is forgiven, and returneth.*

DAVID now being a good and holy Man, GOD accepted his *Repentance*, and took him again into his Favour; and also promised to secure his Life and Kingdom, as was before hinted by *Nathan* in *Verse* 13. But, alas! his *Glory* was greatly eclipsed by the Trouble he had from his own Children; viz. [14] by *Amnon defiling* his Sister *Tamar*, by the Contrivance of his Cousin *Jonathan*; [29] by *Absalom* causing *Am-*

2 *Sam.* xiii.

---

[y] *Here he composed* Psal. li. *Also* Psalms v.—x.—xxxii.—xxxviii.—cxxx.—cxliii. *on other Calamities.*

non to be flain in the City of *Baal-hazor*, at a *Sheep-shearing*, when he was intoxicated with Liquor; and ³⁰ by *Absalom*'s fleeing to *Geshur*, for near three Years, &c.

But DAVID ¹ longing to see *Absalom* again, ² by the Instigation of *Joab*, ⁶ in Conjunction with an old Woman of *Tekoah*, forgave him his Crime; so that ²⁴ he lived for two Years amongst his Servants; and ³⁰ at last set fire to *Joab*'s Field of Barley, to bring Matters to pass to bring himself again into his *Father*'s *Presence*; which ³³ he at last accomplished, by *Scheme* and Stratagem.

2 Sam. xiv.

SECT. XXVII.
Absalom *gaining the Hearts of the People, is made King at* Hebron, &c. 2 Sam. xiv.

*A*Bsalom ²⁵ now being the *Beauty* of the Age, and admired by the People, (whose Hair weighed 200 Shekels, or five Pounds, every Year it was polled) he then ¹ fitted up a great Number of *Chariots*, and *Horses*, and *fifty Men* to guard him; who doing many valiant Exploits, drew all the Hearts of the People to him. Then ⁴ longing for Honour, and promising to do more Justice to the Nation, (blaming his *Father*'s Conduct,) he thought himself able to undertake any Enterprize; ⁵ kissing all that came near him, &c. ᶻ About four Years after, having ⁷ about 200 Men, he, by *Scheme*, got Leave of his Father to go to *Hebron*, under Pretence of going there to *Divine Worship*, &c. When ¹² by *Signal* of a *Trumpet*, many resorted to him, where he made a great Feast; and ¹² also sent for *Achitophel*, his Father's chief Counsellor; where they proclaimed him KING against his Father DAVID.

2 Sam. xv.

SECT. XXVIII.
DAVID *leaveth* Jerusalem *for Fear of* Absalom; Hushai *is sent to give* DAVID *Intelligence: And* Shimei *curseth* DAVID, &c. 2 Sam. xv.

DAVID, ¹³ on hearing how *Absalom* his Son had degraded him for his Mercy and Good-will, and how he had re-

---

ᶻ *On this* DAVID *composed* Psalms xiv.—liii.—See 1 Kings ii. 11.

belled

belled against him, greatly feared some Evil was plotting against his Life; by Reason, he knew that *Achitophel* was a lucky and wise Counsellor: On this [10] DAVID flees from *Jerusalem*, over *Jordan*, to escape what might happen from his cruel Son, taking with him 600 Men, (besides [12] *Ittai*, and his 600 Men that followed him in his former Banishment by *Saul*) and left the Government of his House to his ten *Concubines*; charging [14] *Abiathar*, *Zadok*, and other *Levites*, to stay by the *Ark* in *Jerusalem*; assuring them [15] that GOD would soon deliver them; and that they should give him *private Intelligence* on whatsoever should happen, &c. But, on DAVID's Departure, [23] all the Country wept, because he went away very sorrowful.

DAVID [30] then going barefoot, and all weeping, up the *Mount of Olives*, and praying GOD to turn *Achitophel*'s *Counsel* to nought, he meets with his Friend *Hushai*, in a very ragged mournful Condition, who offered himself to go with him, [33] which DAVID refused; but, on the contrary, [34] persuades him to go and join with *Absalom*, in Order that he might, by *Ahimaaz* and *Jonathan*, privately know how all Things went against him, [35] by their sending [25] Word to their Fathers, *Zadok* and *Abiathar*, the Priest, &c. to overturn the Counsel of *Achitophel*[a]. So [37] *Hushai* went on to *Absalom*, who was then gone from *Hebron* to *Jerusalem*.

No sooner was *Hushai* [1] gone, but DAVID meets with *Ziba*, who said, he was a Servant to *Mephibosheth*; having two Asses laden with Cakes, Raisins, Figs, and Wine for DAVID; who, falsly, informed him [3] that his Master *Mephibosheth* was then in *Jerusalem*, and expected to be made King; on which DAVID gave him all the Lands that *Mephibosheth* had been Master of.

2 *Sam.* xvi.

DAVID now [5] arriving at *Bahurim*; behold *Shimei* came out, and cursed him, and threw Stones at him, calling him Murderer, [8] concerning *Ish-bosheth* and *Abner*; telling him that *Absalom* had very justly took the Kingdom from him; on which DAVID greatly lamented; and hindered *Abishai* from taking off his Head, seeing his Life [11] was in Danger even by his Son, &c.

---

[a] *Here were repeated* Psalms iii.—lxxvii.—cix.

SECT.

SECT. XXIX.

Hushai's Counsel rather chosen than Achitophel's; Messengers sent to DAVID, but pursued by Absalom's Soldiers, &c.

HUSHAI now [16] being with *Absalom* in *Jerusalem*, *Absalom* [20] asked *Counsel* of *Achitophel* what to do; and he accordingly counselled him [21] to go and dwell with his Father's ten *Concubines*, and lie with them; in order, that, when the People knew his Father DAVID hated him, they would then probably enlarge his

2 Sam. xvi.   Army; which [25] he accordingly did; (for *Achitophel's Counsel* was then counted as great as an *Oracle* of GOD, both to DAVID and *Absalom*;) he not chusing any *Peace* should be made between Father and Son. Moreover, [1] that *Ab-*

2 Sam. xvii.   *salom* would let him have 12,000 Men, that he might follow DAVID that Night; (for, he being weary with travelling, and very weak in Number, he might the better overcome them;) and that [2] he would only kill DAVID, and let his Men escape; and afterwards bring them to him: And [3] when DAVID is slain, then will all the People be at Peace, &c. Which Counsel [4] greatly pleased *Absalom*, and all his chief Adherents.

Then *Absalom* [5] called to *Hushai*, to have his Opinion of the Matter; who informed him [7] that *Achitophel's Counsel* was not good, by Reason [8] DAVID's Army were all good Men, (though weary with travelling) and that DAVID seldom lodged in the Field, in the Night, with his Men; but that [9] he generally lodged in some *Cave*; and, his Men [10] being all lion-hearted, will no Ways shrink from their *Master* till every one are cut off; so that in following *Achitophel's Counsel* he would be certainly overthrown. Therefore my *Counsel* is, [11] that you gather all *Israel* you can, even from *Dan* to *Beer-sheba*, and go with them yourself into Battle, till [12] you find him; then may you, by your large Number, not only slay him, but every Soul also.

Hushai's Counsel now being heard, it was [14] more approved than *Achitophel's*, and was immediately ordered to be obeyed with the greatest Strictness. No sooner was this agreed on, but *Zadok* and *Abiathar* [15] sends their Sons, *Ahimaaz* and *Jonathan*, to let DAVID know what was designed against him; but they were no sooner gone, but [18] a young Man (who saw them) went and told *Absalom* of their going; and he sent Soldiers after them, to bring them back.

SECT. XXX.

Achitophel's Counsel *set at nought by* Hushai; *on which he hanged himself.* 2 Sam. xvii.

NOW *Ahimaaz* and *Jonathan*, knowing they were pursued, went [17] to a House in *Bahurim*, and, there being a *Well* in the Court, they both got therein, and [19] the Woman of the House, to save them, shut down the Cover thereof, and spread *Chaff*, *Bran*, and threshed Corn, &c. over it, so that no *Well* appeared.

Absalom's Soldiers [20] now coming to the House to inquire after *Ahimaaz* and *Jonathan*, the Woman told them they were both just gone over the *Brook*; on which the Soldiers returned again to *Jerusalem*; and *Ahimaaz* and *Jonathan* [21] went to DAVID, and let him know what *Counsel Achitophel* had given against him, &c. and how they were then pursuing him.

Then DAVID [22] and all his Men arose in great Haste, and travelled all Night, and got safe over the River *Jordan* before Day-light, and went to *Manahanim* [b] ; and *Absalom*, [24] and his Army, went over the River also (*Amasa* being his chief *Captain*, in the Room of *Joab*;) and [25] pitched in the Land of *Gilead*.

Mean While [3] *Achitophel*, hearing that his *Counsel* was set aside, by the *Counsel* of *Hushai*, he rode home on his Ass, and settled all his Affairs; and, in a *Pet*, went and hanged himself.

SECT. XXXI.

Absalom's *Army overthrown;* himself hanged in an Oak; *and killed by* Joab.

NOW *Shobi* of *Rabbath*, *Machir* of *Lo-debar*, and *Barzillai* [27] of *Rogelim*, hearing that DAVID and his *Host* were

---

[b] *See* 2 Sam. xv. 23.—*Here* DAVID *composed* Psalm lv.

in *Mahanaim*, they [23] brought them *Beds*, *Basons*, earthen *Vessels*, *Wheat*, *Barley*, *Beans*, *Lentils*, and parched Corn; also [29] *Sheep*, *Kine*, *Cheese*, *Butter*, and *Honey*, knowing them to be very weary, hungry, and thirsty in the Wilderness [c].

Then DAVID [1] drew up all his *Host* together, which were 40,000 tall, beautiful, fighting Men, and set over them *Captains* of Thousands, and of Hundreds; and divided his Army into three Parts, *i. e.* [2] one third under *Joab*, another under *Abishai*, and the other under *Ittai*; and fain would have headed them himself, had his Men been willing; they [3] telling him that his Life was worth ten Thousand of theirs; and that a *good Governor* ought not to be in the Field of Battle: So he, [4] by their Desire, sat in the Gate as they all passed by him, giving them all his *Blessing*; and, leaving all to the Management of his three Officers, he sat alone in the Gate, waiting for *Tidings*, &c. [d]

2 Sam. xviii.

DAVID's Army now being all in regular *Order* for Battle, he called to his three *Commanders*, desiring [5] that they would use the *young Man Absalom* mildly, for his Sake, and not kill him, for that his Heart *yearned* for him, though he had wickedly took up Arms against him, &c. This *Charge* was also heard by all the Army, that all might shew *Mercy* to *Absalom* should he happen to fall into their Hands.

No sooner was this *Charge* given, but [6] both Armies met by the Wood of *Ephraim* (which belonged to the People called *Ephraimites*;) where DAVID's Army [7] slew 20,000 of those of *Absalom*; many [8] taking to the Wood for Shelter from the Sword. Now *Absalom* [9] riding in the Wood, on a Mule, under an *Oak*, behold the *Oak* caught hold on his tangled Hair, and took him off his Mule, and his Mule run away and left him; which DAVID's Soldiers seeing, [10] they ran and told *Joab*, their Commander; and he [11] commanded the Messenger to kill him, telling him he would give him 100 *Shekels*, and a *Girdle*, which [12] the Man refused: On which JOAB [14] stuck three Darts into *Absalom* as he hung in the Tree, although [15] *Abishai* and *Ittai* reminded him of DAVID's *Charge*, to save the young Man, his Son: Then [15] coming up ten of *Joab*'s Armour-bearers, they slew *Absalom*, and [17] cast his Body into a Pit in the *Wood*, and covered it with Stones. Hence did Justice overtake him, for

---

[c] Here DAVID composed Psalm xxxi.   [d] Here he prayed, as Psalm xxv.

rebelling

rebelling againſt his Father. Then *Joab* [16] blew a Trumpet, to call his People from purſuing the Remainder of *Abſalom*'s Army any farther; for that he pitied their Frailty, in being ſo deluded to War againſt DAVID; ſo what were left returned privately to their own Homes.

SECT. XXXII.

DAVID *mourneth for* ABSALOM; *comforteth his Soldiers; forgiveth* Shimei, Ziba, *and* Mephiboſheth; *and bleſſeth* Brazillai.

THE Battle being over, *Joab* [21] ſends *Cuſhi* to let DAVID know what was done; and, [23] *Ahimaaz* running after him, came up firſt to DAVID, as he [24] ſat waiting for *Tidings* in the Gate of *Mahanaim*. The Meſſengers then [32] telling DAVID of their great *Victory*, and, after ſome Heſitations, that *Abſalom* was ſlain amongſt the reſt, he [33] went up into his *Chamber*, and grievouſly wept, ſaying, *Oh! my Son* Abſalom, *my Son, my Son!—Oh! that I had but died for thee! O my Son!—*

When [1] DAVID's Grief was told unto *Joab*, then [2] was all their Joys of Victory turned into *Mourning*, on [4] DAVID hiding his Face from his Soldiers, and not appearing to rejoice with them as he uſed to do: On which *Joab* [5] went to him, and much reflected on him, telling him [6] that he was not his Soldiers' Friend, to weep at their Victory, *&c.* and [7] that, if he did not come out that Night into the City, and ſpeak *comfortably* to his Army, they ſhould all quit the Place, and leave him; and that he would draw all the Army to War againſt him; on which [8] the King appeared in public, and [12] knit his Soul to them, and [13] they to him.

2 Sam. xix.

Then making *Amaſa* Captain before *Joab*, *Abſalom*'s Army came and joined unto DAVID, to [15] conduct him ſafe over the River *Jordan*, towards *Bahurin*ᵉ. *Shimei*, with 1000 Men, came to meet him, where [23] he forgave him for curſing him, though *Abiſhai* would have perſuaded him to the contrary. *Ziba* alſo, and [17] his 15 Sons, and 20 Servants [18] rowed a Boat over the River for the King.

ᵉ *On this he wrote* Pſalm lxxvii.

David alfo ²⁴ forgave poor *Mephibosheth* for not going with him, he being lame; and alfo ²⁵ *Ziba* for deceiving and flandering *Mephibosheth*; and inftead of giving *Mephibosheth* all his Lands again, he ²⁹ gave him but half of the Lands of *Ziba*.—See 1 *Kings* ii. 8, 9.—2 *Sam.* xvi. 3.

David alfo ³¹ would have had virtuous *Barzillai* and his Family along with him to *Jerufalem*, who had greatly affifted him in Time of War, but he ³⁷ begged to be excufed on Account of his *Old Age*, being 80 Years old; on which he difmiffed him with his Kiffes, and his Bleffing: But *Barzillai* let him have his Son *Chimham* with him, becaufe he ³⁸ greatly loved him, and defired to keep him for his Father's Sake.

SECT. XXXIII.

Judah *and* Ifrael *contend about* David, *and proclaim War againft him by* Sheba's *Inftigation. He is again brought to* Jerufalem, *and cleanfeth his Houfe.* Gibeon *faved by throwing* Sheba's *Head over the Wall*; *and* Amafa *is killed by* Joab.

WHEN David ⁴⁰ arrived at *Gilgal* with *Chimham*, and all the People of *Judah*, and half the People of *Ifrael*, ⁴¹ the other Part of *Ifrael* was angry with them for conducting David thither without their whole Confent: But ⁴² the Men of *Judah* telling them David was near *a-kin* to them, they were angry, claiming ⁴³ a greater Right to David than they; and that they fhould have had the Honour of bringing him thither before them, &c. On which mighty Words arofe between them ¹. In the Heat of this *Difpute* ¹ ftarted up one *Sheba*, a wicked Man, and, founding a Trumpet, faid, We have no Right with David, nor any of the Sons of *Jeffe*. Then, proclaiming *War* againft David, all *Ifrael* left him, and followed *Sheba*: But ² the Men of *Judah* ftuck faft to David, and ³ took him to *Jerufalem*, where they eftablifhed him on the Throne; where were the ten *Concubines* he had left behind him to keep Houfe: But he put them out under *Confinement* till the Day of their Deaths, and lay no' more

2 *Sam.* xx.

---

¹ *On this he compofed* Pfalm xliii.

with them, becauſe his Son *Abſalom* had defiled them ᶠ. (See Chap. xvi. 22.)

David ⁴ then ſent *Amaſa*, his chief Captain, to call all the Men of *Judah* to join in Arms; but ⁵ he not returning the third Day as David expected, he ⁶ ſent *Joab* and *Abiſhai* with 600 Men to ſeek him, leſt *Sheba* ſhould do more Miſchief than *Abſalom*. When ⁸ they came to the City of *Gibeon* they met *Amaſa*, and many *Forces* following him, coming to David; on which *Joab* coming to meet him ⁹ in a ſeeming friendly Manner, whilſt he took him by the Beard, pretending to kiſs him, he ¹⁰ maliciouſly ſheath'd his Sword in his Belly (as he before had ſerved *Abner*,) ſo that his Bowels fell out on the Ground; for no other Cauſe, but only that David had put him in an higher *Office* than himſelf. Then ¹³ ordering his bloody Body to be taken out of the Road, and covered, he ¹⁴ and *Abiſhai*, and the Army marched after *Sheba* to the City of *Abel-maacha*, (where he was ſheltered) and ¹⁵ beſieged it; and would have deſtroyed all the Inhabitants had not ¹⁶ a virtuous wiſe *Woman*, of the old Faſhion, who had ſeen the World, called to *Joab* from off the Walls, to prevent it; whoſe Importunities ²¹ cauſed the Governors to cut off *Sheba*'s Head, and to throw it over the Walls into *Joab*'s Camp, on receiving of which ²² *Joab* ſounded a Retreat, and they all returned back to *Jeruſalem* to David, (and ſo ſaved the City.) Where ²³ he was once more declared *General* over the Armies of *Iſrael*. *Benaiah* was alſo Captain over the *Cherethites* and the *Pelethites*, being 600 Guards; ²⁴ *Adoram* was made Treaſurer; *Jehoſhaphat* was made Recorder; ²⁵ *Sheva* was made Scribe; *Zadok* and *Abiathar* were made Prieſts; and ²⁶ *Ira* was the King's chief Favourite.

SECT. XXXIV.

Saul's *Sons hanged*; Mephiboſheth *ſpared*; *and* David *praying, ſtoppeth a cruel* Famine. *&c.* 2 Sam. xxi.

NOT long after this, ¹ a ſore three Years Famine happened in David's Country, which the People imputed to be occaſioned by the Cruelty of King *Saul*, in ſlaying ſo many Peo-

---

ˢ *On this was compoſed* Pſalm xxx.

ple;

ple; and that they having not revenged themselves on his *Sons*, for their Father's Deceit and Cruelty, was the very Cause that GOD suffered such dreadful Calamities to fall on them: Which they greatly complained of to DAVID.

DAVID then, ² willing to appease the Wrath of GOD, by His Counsel, ⁸ ordered the seven Sons of *Saul* to be taken up, and delivered up to them, who ⁹ hanged them on a *Gibbet* before the LORD: And ¹⁰ *Rizpah* sorely wept for her Son *Armoni*, &c. But ⁷ DAVID spared her Son *Mephibosheth*, the Son of *Jonathan*, as he before had promised.

Then DAVID ¹² went to *Jabesh*, and took the Ashes of the Bones of *Saul* and *Jonathan*, and ¹³ the Bones of them that were hanged, and buried them all together in the Grave of *Kish*, the Father of *Saul*: And then praying to GOD in Behalf of the People, He ¹⁴ again sent *Rain* on the Earth, and it yielded them *Corn* and *Fruit* in great Abundance. (See 1 *Sam.* xxxi. 13.)

SECT. XXXV.

Three Philistine *Battles against* DAVID; *wherein four Giants are slain by* Abishai, Sebbichai, Elhana, *and* Jonathan: *And of* DAVID's *divine* Songs *and musical* Instruments.

SOON after this ¹⁵ the *Philistines* made War against *Israel*, when DAVID went himself with his Army ¹⁶. The chief Champion of the *Philistines* was *Ishbi-benob*, of the *gigantic* Race, the Point of whose Spear weighed 300 Shekels of Brass, (or near 10 Pounds) besides tushed Chains crossing his Shoulders. This mighty Man, as his Army was fleeing before *Israel*, turning quick on DAVID, as he ran after him, would have slain him on the Spot with his Sword, had not ¹⁷ *Abishai* stepped between and slew the Giant; for ¹⁵ DAVID was very weary and faint with running after him: On which DAVID's Officers sware that he should never any more go into Battle, lest they should lose the *Flower* and Glory of the whole World.

After this ¹⁸ there was another Battle with the *Philistines* at *Gob*; when *Sebbichai*, one of DAVID's pick'd Soldiers behaved very valiantly, by slaying *Saph*, and others of the Race of the Giants, &c. Also another Battle in *Cob*, where ¹⁹ *Elhanah*

hanah flew another Giant, whose Staff of his *Spear* was like a Weaver's Beam.

Not long after this²⁰ the *Philistines* once more hazarded their Lives and Fortunes against DAVID in *Gath*, where another mighty *Giant* appeared, having six Fingers on each Hand, and six Toes on each Foot, and six Cubits high. In this Battle²¹ *Jonathan*, (the Nephew of DAVID) behaved very valiant, for he not only²² flew the *Giant*, but gained such a Victory, as put an entire End to the War against *Israel*. These four Giants²² are said to be the Sons (or Brothers) of the great *Goliath* of *Gath* ; and that they arose against DAVID, to revenge their Father's Death. * (See 1 *Sam*. xvii. 4. 1 *Chron*. xx. 4, 5, 6, *&c*.)

These Battles being over, DAVID¹ returned Thanks to GOD for the several *Victories*, in Token for the several *Mercies* and *Benefits* he⁴⁹ had received at His Hands ʰ.   2 *Sam*. xxii. A worthy *Example* for all Men to follow.

He⁵⁰ also made many divine *Songs*, *Odes*, *Psalms*, or *Hymns* to the *Praise* of GOD; and also made many *Instruments*, and taught the *Levites* how to use them on Sabbath and Feast-Days, in Divine Service.

The *Instruments* were of three Kinds, i. e. The *Cinnare Kind*, consisted of ten Strings on each, and struck with a *Bow*, as a *Viol* or *Violin*. The *Nabal Kind*, contained twelve Chords or *Strings*, pulled or struck with the Thumbs and Fingers, or with a *Plectrum* made of a split *Quill*, or thin Piece of *Horn*, in a melodious, concording Manner. The *Cymbal Kind* were made of solid Pieces of *Brass* or *Bell-metal*, like Iron *Wedges*, and suspended on Rows of Iron *Pins* by Holes drilled half through each Piece; and struck with a small *Rod* of Brass or Iron in each Hand, as we do a *Drum* or *Dulcimer*, &c. &c. (Vide *Joseph. Ant.*)

※※※※※※※※※※※※※※※※※※※※

SECT. XXXVI.
Of DAVID's *Thirty-seven* Worthies, &c.   2 Sam. xxiii.

DAVID now, (finishing his *Psalms*)¹ set on high, (the Anointed of the GOD *of Jacob, and the sweet Singer of*

ʰ *Here was uttered* Psalm xviii.—See 2 *Sam*. xxii.

* Vide *Exod*. iii. 11. and *Psal*. cxxxvi. Being of the Race of *Og*, whose *Bed-stead* was near six Yards long, and two Yards and a Half wide.

all Israel;) and ⁴ shone as the Morning Sun in the Firmament; ⁵ a *Comfort* to all good *Magistrates*, and ⁶ a *Terror* to the wicked ones that should oppose him ⁷: He then ⁸ chose out 37 valiant Men, as *Worthies*, to be with him, as *Examples of Merit* and *Gratitude, viz.*

The first was *Adino*, his chief, who sat in the Seat of Wisdom: Who slew 800 or 900 Men in one Battle. Also *Eleazar*, ⁹ who obtained a great Victory against the *Philistines*: And ¹¹ *Shammah*, a mighty Victor. These three ¹⁵, on DAVID's longing for some *Water* from a *Well* in *Bethlehem*, ¹⁶ rushed through an Army of the *Philistines*, and brought it safe to him; which ¹⁷ receiving, he poured it on the Ground, as an *Offering* to GOD, for so great a *Mercy*: Seeing they had obtained it at the Hazard of their Lives. There were ¹⁸ also *Abishai*, who slew 300 Men in one Battle: And ²³ *Benaiah*, who slew a *Lyon* in a Pit of Snow, and an *Egyptian* with his own Spear. Also,

Asahel.
Elhanan.
Shammah, the Harodite.
Elika, the Harodite.
Helez, the Paltite.
Ira, the Tekoite.
Abiezer, the Anethothite.
Mebannai, the Hushathite.
Zalmon, the Ahohite.
Maharai, the Netophathite.
Heleb, the Netophathite.
Ittai, the Benjamite.
Benaiah, the Pirathonite.
Hiddai, the Gashite.
Abi-albon, the Arbathite.

Azmaveth, the Barhumite.
Eliahba, the Shaalbonite.
Shammah, the Hararite.
Abiam, the Hararite.
Eliphelet, the Maachathite.
Eliam, the Gilonite.
Hezrai, the Carmelite.
Paarai, the Arbite.
Igal, the Gadite.
Zelek, the Ammonite.
Naharai, the Beerothite.
Ira, the Ithrite.
Gareb, the Ithrite.
Uriah, the Hittite.

In all 37, as mentioned in 2 *Sam.* xxiii. and in 1 *Chron.* xi. xii. which see.

---

¹ *Here was composed* Psal. xxxvii. *and* xl.

SECT. XXXVII.

DAVID *numbereth the People, and repenteth of it; and by chusing three Days* Plague, *he appeaseth* GOD's *Wrath by* Prayer; *and erecteth an* Altar *for* Divine Worship: *Then, proposing to build a* Temple, *is ordered to leave that to his Son* Solomon, *which he accordingly did, leaving him the* Plan *and* Materials, *&c.* 2 Sam. xxiv.

DAVID now being very desirous to know how many Thousands of Men might be found able to bear *Arms,* amongst the People, (forgetting GOD's Command to *Moses,* that there should be paid for every *Head* two Shekels *) he commanded *Joab* to go and number them; who would fain have persuaded him to the contrary, but all to no Purpose. On which *Joab* took with him many principal *Tribes,* and *Scribes,* and went round all the Country of the *Hebrews;* and in about ten Months returned to DAVID at *Jerusalem,* with a *Roll* of all the People, (except of the Tribe of *Benjamin* and of *Levi.*) The Number of *Israelites* were 800,000 Men; and the *Tribe* of *Judah* 500,000; in all 1,300,000 Men able to bear Arms †.

These *Lists* were no sooner delivered, but DAVID began to be very sorrowful, and greatly repented what he had done, beseeching GOD to *appease* his Wrath, and pardon his Offence: On which "GOD, by His Angel, sent the Prophet *Gad* to DAVID, giving him the Choice of three *Evils,* to chuse which he would should fall on the *Land, viz.* a seven Years Famine, a three Years *War,* or a three Days *Plague,* or *Pestilence:* So DAVID chose the latter, chusing rather to fall under the Hands of GOD, than to lie under the Rage and Mercy of worldly Enemies. So GOD smote *Israel* the next Day with a *Pestilence* that there died, in the three Days, 70,000 Men; some dropping *suddenly;* others *scorched* up with Heat; some struck *blind;* and others languishing for many Hours in *Tortures,* and great Agonies; ending their Lives in a thousand different Ways too tedious here to mention. (Vide *Joseph. Ant.*)

DAVID during this Time, prostrated himself on the Ground,

---

* Or one Shilling. *Exod.* xxx. 12.—*Numb.* i. 2. † Vide *Heylyn* on the World, p. 549.

The Life of Holy DAVID:

with *Prayers* to GOD in Behalf of the People; and looking towards Heaven, he beheld the Angel of GOD hovering his *Wings* over the Threshing-floor of *Ornan*, in *Jerusalem*, with a naked Sword in his Hand; on which DAVID said, that, as he was the *Shepherd*, he deserved to be punished, and not the *Flock*, who had no Ways offended; praying that he would punish him, and his *Posterity*, and save the People [k]. Hereupon GOD's Angel [18] sent *Gad* again to DAVID, commanding him [21] directly to repair to the *Threshing-floor* of *Aranuah*, or *Ornan*, and build there an *Altar* to offer *Sacrifice* to GOD; that the *Plague* might cease from the People.

As soon as this was told, [19] DAVID hasted to the Floor of *Ornan*; who [20] seeing DAVID coming, hasted to meet him, and humbled himself before him. Now *Ornan* had been one of DAVID's chief Friends, for which Reason he did not spoil him, when the *Fortress* of the *Jebusites* was taken, as before hinted. When DAVID had told *Ornan* that he was come to buy the *Threshing-floor*, to build thereon an *Altar* for GOD's *Worship*, he [22] immediately would have given it him, But [24] DAVID refusing, purchased it for 50 Shekels of Silver, and erected an *Altar* thereon, and [25] offered *Sacrifices* unto GOD, and the Plague ceased: (it being the very Ground whereon *Abraham* had offered up the Ram instead of his Son.) So the Angel put up his Sword into the Sheath, of whom DAVID was sore afraid [l]. (Vide *Joseph. Jewish Antiq.*)

DAVID now seeing that GOD had heard his *Prayer*, and accepted his *Sacrifice*, decreed that in this very Place he would build a *Temple* to GOD: But GOD, sending the Prophet *Nathan* to tell him that it should be built by his Son *Solomon*, who should succeed him, he immediately commanded near 180,000 Men to prepare Materials of *Wood*, *Stone*, *Iron*, *Gold*, *Silver*, *Brass*, &c. to be ready for his Son to build it according to the *Plan* that he left him.

To make a more strict Enquiry concerning the *Temple* of *Solomon*, read in the First Book of *Chron.* Chap. xxii. of DAVID's *Preparations*, Ver. 5.—His *Charge* to his Son, Ver. 16: And to *Princes*, Ver. 19.—Chap. xxiii. Of the Number and Order of the *Levites*, Ver. 3.—Chap. xxiv. Of the Sons of *Aaron*, Ver. 19: The *Kohathites*, Ver. 26: And the *Meraites*, Ver. 26.—

---

[k] *Here was composed* Psal. cxxx. xiii.   [l] *See* Psal. lxv. lxvi. lxvii.

Chap.

Chap. xxv. Of the Singers, Ver. 11.—Chap. xxvi. Of the *Porters*, Ver. 19: And other Officers, Ver. 32.—Chap. xxvii. Of David's Martial Officers, and Houshold, Ver. 34.—Chap. xxviii. David recommends the Work to them, and his Son *Solomon*, Ver. 10: And gives them G O D's *Plan* to work by, Ver. 19.—Chap. xxix. Then David and his Princes making further *Freewill Offerings* towards it, Ver. 9: He blesseth GOD, Ver. 20: And offers Sacrifices, &c. Ver. 21 ᵐ.

✻✻✻✻✻✻✻✻✻✻✻✻✻✻✻✻✻✻✻✻✻✻✻✻✻✻✻✻✻✻✻

SECT. XXXVIII.

David, *destitute of Warmth, takes a Virgin to lie with him.* Adonijah *desires to be King, but* Solomon *is chosen, and crowned,* &c. 1 Kings i.

DAVID, now ¹ drawing near the *Verge* of his *Life*, began to be destitute of his wonted natural Warmth, on which ² he desired that a young *Virgin* might attend him and lie at his Bosom: Hereupon ³ they sought through all the Coasts of *Israel*, and, after great Inquiry, found one named *Abishag*, a *Shunamite*, of the *Tribe* of *Issachar:* (*Josh.* xix. 17.) and ⁴ she lay with him only to cherish him; for, probably through Impotence, he knew her not, though she was young, fair, and beautiful.

Now *Adonijah* (the Son of David by *Haggith*, and Brother-in-law to *Solomon*) ⁵ hearing that David's Dissolution was very near, he ⁷ by the *Counsel* and Assistance of *Joab* and *Abiathar*, set up many Chariots and Horses, and 50 Men to run before him, in Order to *usurp*, and take the Crown from *Solomon:* But ²⁸ the same being told unto David by *Bathsheba* ¹¹ by the Order of *Nathan*, the Prophet, *Zadok*, the Priest, and *Benaiah*, he ¹³ was soon set aside, and ³⁹ *Solomon* proclaimed KING, ⁴⁰ with *Musick*, and great Acclamations of Joy, ³⁵ according to the *Order* of his Father David; who ⁴⁸ gave him his *Blessing* accordingly ⁿ. *Adonijah* then ⁵³ humbling himself to his Brother *Solomon*, he ⁵³ forgave him the Fault at that Time.

ᵐ *Here was penn'd* Psal. lxxxvii. *Hedio* & *Rufinus*, and *Joseph. Ant.*   ⁿ *Here be uttered* Psalm lxxii. Vide

SECT. XXXIX.

David's *last* Charge *to his Son* Solomon. 1 Kings ii.

A. M. 2989.
Before *Christ*
1015.

DAVID, now breathing out his *last Moments*, in the Presence of his Son *Solomon*, gave him his *last Charge*, as follows: " *My Son* Solomon, " *I am now going the Way that all have gone before me, and* " *to where all Flesh must follow me*; *I* charge *thee be strong,* " *and shew thyself a Man*; *walk in the Ways of the* LORD *thy* " GOD, *and keep his* Statutes, Commandments, Judgments, " *and* Testimonies, *according to the Law of* Moses, *that* GOD " *may confirm his Promise to thee and thy* Posterity *on the* " Throne *of* Israel *for ever. Take thou also great Heed of* Joab, " *and remember how he took the Blood of* Abner *and* Amasa " *causless, and not in War: Let not his hoary Head go to the* " *Grave in Peace. But shew great Kindness to the three Sons of* " Barzillai, *and let them eat at thy Table, for they shewed me* " *Kindness when thy Brother* Absalom *took up Arms against me.* " *Though I once forgave* Shimei *for cursing me, yet he is not guilt-* " *less*; *let not his Head lie down in Peace, but in Blood. Do* " *Justice to all Men*, &c. "." According to this Charge, so even did *Solomon* in all Things; after his Father's Death, he orders *Adonijah, Joab,* and *Shimei* to be slain by *Benaiah,* as in Ver. 24. 34. 46. expelling all his Father's Enemies, and cherishing his Friends. Chap. iv.

DAVID having thus exhorted his *Son*, and communicated all his Affairs to him, he peaceably gave up the *Ghost*, being about 70 Years old; having reigned King over *Israel* 40 Years; i. e. seven Years in *Hebron*, and thirty-three in *Jerusalem*.

SECT. XL.

Of David's Character, Riches *left*, Funeral, *and* Monument.

THUS ended the Life of Holy DAVID, a Man after GOD's own Heart, only in the Matter of *Uriah* (whose Sin teacheth us *Repentance)* and in numbering the People. He was a *just* and *wise* Man, and adorned with all *Virtue* requisite for a KING.

a KING. He was valiant beyond Comparison, a brave PRINCE, and an undaunted *Soldier*; and exhorted his Soldiers to follow his *Example*, in all Events. He was *moderate, just,* and *courteous*; *favourable* to those afflicted; and *generous* to those of Merit. He took Part of all Hardships with his Soldiers; and underwent many Dangers for the Sake of *CHRIST*, to establish the GOSPEL, which was then to come. He was such a Prophet, *Prince,* Poet and Musician, as never will be forgotten; whose Writings, *Laws,* and *sacred Songs* none can behold without Sorrow or Transport; and will not only endure to the last Age, but, if strictly practised, will qualify us for the Kingdom of Heaven.

In fine, he was a Man after GOD in most Actions, and they that were against him were against GOD: He bare the true Figure of *CHRIST* in all Things (who sprang from his Loins) and foretold of his *Life, Death,* and *Resurrection,* above 1000 Years before it came to pass: By whom all may have eternal Life, &c. &c. &c.

It is said that DAVID left more *Riches* behind him, than all other Kings of any Nation whatsoever; and that his Son *Solomon* who succeeded him, buried him royally, with great *Riches* and Solemnity in *Jerusalem,* in a magnificent *Tomb*; out of which 3000 Talents, or 16,425,000 l. if Gold; if Silver, 1,026,500 l. was taken out by *Hircanus,* the High-Priest, 300 Years after, to give to *Antiochus,* to deliver the Siege of that City; and that DAVID's Monument might not be destroyed *.

I shall conclude this *sacred History* with the last *Benediction* of Holy DAVID from *Psalm* lxxii, typically speaking of GOD himself, in the Name of his Son *Solomon,* and of *CHRIST's* everlasting Kingdom: *And Blessed be the Name of His Majesty for ever; and may all the Earth be filled with His Glory.* Amen. Amen.

> *In fine let all from Sin and Malice fly,*
> *And learn of* DAVID *how to live and die.*

(* Vide *Hedio* & *Rufinus,* and *Joseph. Ant.* Lib. vii.)

A *New*, and *Select* NUMBER of
PSALMS, MEDITATIONAL HYMNS,
AND
SPIRITUAL SONGS, &c.

Set to MUSIC in

Two, *Three*, and *Four Musical* PARTS, in *Score*;

FOR THE

USE of PARISH-CHURCHES, &c. and other Occasions.

By WILLIAM TANS'UR, Senior, *Psalmodist*.
(*By Way of* Supplement *to his Royal Melody.*)

Praise *ye the* LORD *with* Psalms *and* Hymns,—*With Voice and chearful Heart*:
For *He's the Giver of all Things*,—*And doth all Things impart.*
And, *when opprest, His Aid implore*,—*That He may Succour send*:
Who *hath for all His Saints in Store*—*Such Joys as never end.*   W. T.
(Vide *James* i. 27.—v. 13.—*Rev.* iv. 11.)
Sing *to* GOD's *Praise, with lofty Hymns*,—*His wond'rous Works rehearse* :
Make *them the Theme of your Discourse*,—*And Subject of your Verse.* (*Psal.* cv. 2.)

SOLILOQUIES.

A Meditational SOLILOQUY, *when going to join in Psalmody.* W. T.

    LORD! give me DAVID's well-tun'd Heart,
        For *Voice* alone is vain :
    Then shall I *rightly* bear a *Part*,
    And not *Thy* WORD prophane.

A Meditational SOLILOQUY, *when leaving Psalmody.* W. T.

    GREAT GOD! Who gav'st to all Things Birth,
        To THEE all *Praise* be giv'n :
    Let me *adore* THY NAME on *Earth*,
    And *sing* THY Praise in HEAV'N.

☞ For your INSTRUCTIONS *to the Art of* MUSIC, *I refer you to my* New
Royal Melody ; *or to my* New Musical GRAMMAR *and* DICTIONARY :
Both *of which are correctly printed in Score in* Octavo, *with a new* Frontispiece, &c.

[197]

PSALM-TUNES, HYMNS, &c.

PRECEPTS *Tune*. PSALM I, &c. *For Two Voices*. W. T.

THE Man is *bleſt* that ne-ver goes a-ſtray, By falſe Ad-—-vice, nor ſtands in Sinners Way: Nor ſits in--fect-ed by ſuch ſcorn-ful *Pride*, Whom GOD condemns, and Pi—e—ty derīdes.

Their *Guilt* ſhall not the horrid DAY endure,
Nor yet approach th' *Aſſemblies* of the *Pure:*
For GOD approves the Ways the *Righteous* tread,
:ll: But ſinful Paths to ſure Deſtruction lead. :ll:

To

PSALMS *and* HYMNS.

To PSALM IV. *For Three Voices.* W. T.

6. OF-fer to God the *Sa-cri--fice* — Of Righteousness and *Praise*:

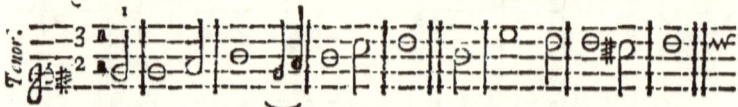

6. OF-fer to God the *Sa-cri--fice* — Of Righteousness and *Praise*:

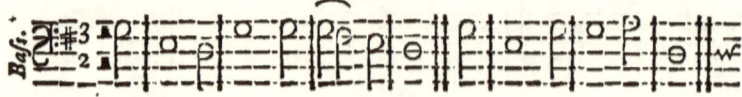

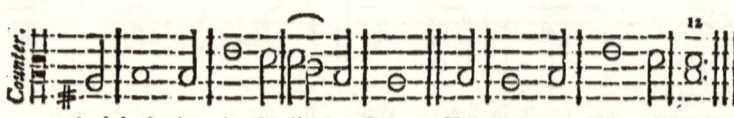

And look that in the liv-ing Lord — You put your Trust al-ways.

And look that in the liv-ing Lord — You put your Trust al-ways.

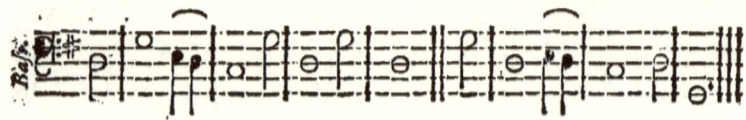

7.
The *greater Sort* crave worldly Goods, — And *Riches* do embrace:
But, Lord, grant us Thy Countenance, — Thy *Favour*, and Thy *Grace*.

8.
For Thou thereby shalt make my Heart — More joyful and more glad
Than they who of their *Corn* and *Wine* — Full great Increase have had.

9.
In *Peace*, therefore, lie down will I, — And take my Rest and Sleep:
For Thou, O Lord, dost only me — Preserve and safely keep.

An

PSALMS *and* HYMNS.

An HYMN *for* CHRISTMAS-DAY.
(Luke II. *from Verse* 8. *to Verse* 14.)

1.

AS watchful *Shepherds*, in the Night,
    They by their *Flocks* did stand:
An ANGEL came, in heav'nly Light,
    And GLORY deck'd the Land.

2.

Fear not, *said He*, glad *News* I bring
    To sinful Men forlorn:
Lo, CHRIST the LORD, the promis'd KING,
    This *Day* for you is born.

3.

To DAVID's City go with Speed,
    And there you'll surely find
The *Woman's* antient promis'd *Seed*,
    The SAVIOUR of Mankind.

4.

Let this be unto ye a *Sign*;
    Ye Him shall find array'd
In *swathing Clothes*, A BABE DIVINE!
    And in a *Manger* laid.

5.

Then next appear'd a shining *Throng*
    Of ANGELS in Array;
All joining in this heav'nly SONG,
    To usher in the *Day:*

6.

" GLORY to GOD, th' *eternal* KING,
" *And heav'nly* Peace *on Earth;*
" Good-Will *to Men, with* Joy, *we bring,*
" *At the great* SAVIOUR's Birth."

7.

Now, let all Men, with Pleasure, join
    The sweet celestial *Choir:*
And this bright *Scene* of LOVE *divine,*
    With thankful Hearts admire.

HALLELUJAH.

PSALMS and HYMNS.

To PSALM IX, *New Version. In Four Parts.* W. T.

1. TO celebrate Thy *Praise*, O Lord, I will my Heart prepare:
1. TO celebrate Thy *Praise*, O Lord, I will my Heart prepare:
1. TO celebrate Thy *Praise*, O Lord, I will my Heart prepare:

To all the lift'ning World Thy *Works*, And *Wonders* I'll de--clare.
To all the lift'ning World Thy *Works*, And *Wonders* I'll de--clare.
To all the lift'ning World Thy *Works*, And *Wonders* I'll de--clare.

2 The *Thoughts* of them shall to my Soul—Exalted *Pleasure* bring:
 Whilst to Thy Name, O Thou most High!—Triumphant *Praise* I sing.
3 Thou mad'st my haughty *Foes* to turn—Their Backs, in shameful Flight:
 Struck with Thy *Presence*, down they fell,—And perish'd at Thy Sight.
4 Against insulting *Foes* advanc'd,—Thou didst my *Cause* maintain:
 My *Right* asserting from Thy *Throne*,—Where *Truth* and *Justice* reign.

— To Father, Son, &c. —

PSALMS and HYMNS.

An HYMN *on the* Excellency *of* DIVINE WISDOM.
Prov. iii, iv, vi, vii, viii, &c.   *By* W. TANS'UR.

1 HOw *bl.ſt* is he that WISDOM finds,
   And KNOWLEDGE doth behold!
   Such *Merchandiſe* is more eſteem'd
   Than *Pearls* and precious *Gold*.

2 In her Right-Hand is *Length of Days*,
   Her Left doth *Honour* ſway:
   Her Paths abound in *Plenteouſneſs*,
   And *Peace* is all her Way.

3 She's like a *Tree of Life*, to all
   That do on her depend:
   And ev'ry one that her retains,
   Hath ſure a faithful *Friend*.

4 By WISDOM GOD hath made the *Earth*,
   As mortal Men may ſee:
   With UNDERSTANDING form'd the *Heav'ns*,
   His *Dwelling-place* to be.

5 By *Knowledge*, he hath made the Sea,
   O vaſt CREATOR's *Skill!*
   Likewiſe the *Clouds* to bring forth *Rain*,
   And on the *Earth* diſtil.

6 My SON, let WISDOM ne'er depart,
   On JUDGMENT lay faſt hold:
   They'll be as GRACE unto thy Neck,
   And LIFE unto thy *Soul*.

7 Then ſhalt thou walk in *Paths* moſt ſafe,
   And *fearleſs* take thy *Sleep:*
   Thy Feet from Stumbles ſhall be free,
   GOD will thee GUARD and keep.

8 Thou ſhalt not *fear*, when GOD ſhall bring
   On wicked Men great Woe:
   Thy *Confidence* in GOD ſhall keep
   Thee *ſafe* from ev'ry Foe.

9 WISDOM will ſurely thee *promote*
   To *Honour* and *Renown:*
   Embrace her, and ſhe'll be thy Aid,
   And thee with GLORY *crown*.

10 For, WISDOM *Rubies* doth ſurpaſs,
   And all that's Excellent:
   She dwells with PRUDENCE, alſo doth
   All *curious Things* invent.

11 If after KNOWLEDGE thou wilt try,
   As if for fineſt *Gold:*
   Likewiſe for UNDERSTANDING too,
   Thou both ſhalt then behold.

12 My *Son*, thy *Father's Counſel* take,
   Thy *Mother's Law* embrace:
   And bind moſt firmly to thy Heart,
   All *Ornaments* of *Grace*.

13 Keep firm thy Heart with *Diligence*,
   From all *bad Counſel* fly:
   Walk in the *Paths* of *Righteouſneſs*,
   And thou ſhalt never die.

202 PSALMS and HYMNS.

To PSALM XI, *New Version.* In *Four Parts.* W. T.

1. Since I have plac'd my *Trust* in God,—A *Refuge* always nigh:

1. Since I have plac'd my *Trust* in God,—A *Refuge* always nigh:

1. Since I have plac'd my *Trust* in God,—A *Refuge* always nigh:

Why should I, like a tim'rous *Bird,*—To distant *Mountains* fly?

Why should I, like a tim'rous *Bird,*—To dis-tant *Mountains* fly?

Why should I, like a tim'rous *Bird,*—To dis-tant *Mountains* fly?

2 Behold, the Wicked bend their *Bow,*—And ready fix their *Dart:*
Lurking in *Ambush* to destroy—The Man of *upright* Heart.
3 When once the firm *Assurance* fails,—Which public *Faith* imparts:
'Tis Time for *Innocence* to fly—From such deceitful Arts.
4 The Lord hath both a *Temple* here,—And righteous *Throne* above:
Where He *surveys* the Sons of Men,—And how their *Counsels* move.

A Fu=

PSALMS *and* HYMNS.

A FUNERAL HYMN. W. T.

1.

John xi. 25.   THE *Resurrection*, and the *Life*,
     I am, faith CHRIST, moſt high:
   And whoſoe'er believes aright
vi. 40. In *Me*, ſhall never die.

2.

   And, whoſoe'er doth truly live
    And doth depend on *Me:*
John viii. 5c. Shall never die. if he believe,
    Nor *ſecond Death* e'er ſee,

3.

   I know that my REDEEMER lives,
    And, at the *latter Day*,
Job ix. 25. On *Earth* ſhall ſtand, and *Judgment* give,
    To whom All muſt obey.

4.

   And though the *Worms* my *Skin* deſtroy,
    A *Seed* ſhall ſtill remain:
Job xix. 29. My *Fleſh* ſhall ſee the LORD with Joy,
    And never die again.

5.

   And I, myſelf,—(Oh joyful Sight!)
Job xix. 27. The very *ſame* ſhall be:
   And with theſe *Eyes*, with Luſtre bright,
    My dear REDEEMER ſee.

6.

1 Cor. xv. 55. *Death! where is now thy deadly Sting?*
    CHRIST ſhall the *Conqueſt* give!
Pſal. xvi. 11. His *Saints* in Heav'n ſhall ever *ſing*,
    And with *Him* ever live.

DOXOLOGY.

   To Father, *and* Holy Ghoſt,
    The undivided Three:
   The One, *ſole* Giver *of all* Life,
    GLORY *for ever be.*

PSALMS and HYMNS.

To PSALM XVI, New Version. In Four Parts. W. T.

1. PRotect me from my cru--el Foes,--And shield me, Lord, from Harm:

Be--cause my Trust I still re--pose — On Thy Al--migh--ty Arm.

2 My Soul, all Help but Thine doth slight,—All Gods but Thee disown:
  Yet can no Deeds of mine requite—The Goodness Thou hast shown.
3 But those that strictly virtuous are,—And love the Thing that's right.
  To favour always, and prefer,—Shall be my chief Delight.

DOXOLOGY.

To Father, Son, and Holy Ghost, the undivided Three:
The One, sole Giver of all Life, Glory for ever be.

A MEDITATIONAL HYMN on DEATH.

HARK! from the *Tomb*'s a doleful Sound,
    My Ears, attend the Cry:
" Ye living Men, come view the *Ground*,
" Where ye muſt ſhortly lie.

" *Princes*, this *Clay* muſt be your Beds,
" In Spight of all your *Pow'rs*:
" The *Tall*, the *Wiſe*, and *rev'rend* Heads
" Muſt lie as low as ours."

Great GOD! is this our certain *Doom!*
    And are we ſtill ſecure?
Still walking downwards to our *Tomb*,
    And yet *prepare* no more?

Grant us the Pow'rs of quick'ning *Grace*,
    To fit our Souls to fly
(Whene'er we drop our dying *Fleſh*)
    To THEE, above the Sky.—*Amen.*

A FUNERAL HYMN: *From the 39th* PSALM.

LORD, make me underſtand mine *End*,
    And Day's uncertain *Date:*
That I may fully apprehend
    The Frailty of my *State*.

Our Days, alas! are but a Span,
    LORD, when compar'd to Thee:
The beſt Eſtate of ev'ry Man
    Is only Vanity.

Prepare, O LORD, our Souls for *Death*,
    And to our *Cry* give Ear:
For we are *Pilgrims* here on Earth,
    As all our Fathers were.

O ſpare us, LORD, our *Torments* Eaſe,
    Our failing *Faith* reſtore:
Leſt *Death*, in Sin, ſhould on us ſeize,
    And *We* ſhall be *no more*.

    — *To Father, Son,* &c. —

PSALMS and HYMNS.

To PSALM XX, *New Version.* In *Four Parts.* W. T.
For VICTORY *in Time of* WAR.

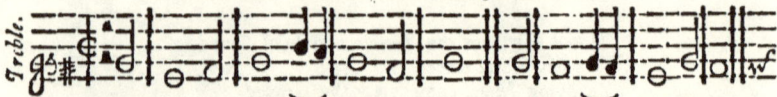

6. OUR *Hopes* are fix'd, that now the LORD—Our *Sov'reign* will defend:

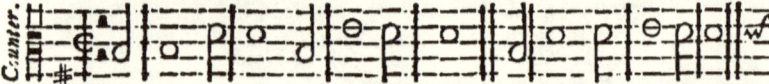

6. OUR *Hopes* are fix'd, that now the LORD—Our *Sov'reign* will defend:

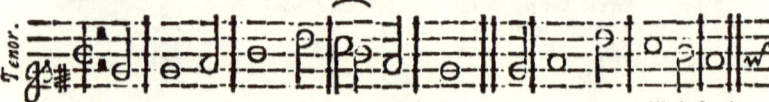

6. OUR *Hopes* are fix'd, that now the LORD—Our *Sov'reign* will defend:

From Heav'n re—fist-less *Aid* af—ford,—And to his *Pray'rs* at-tend.

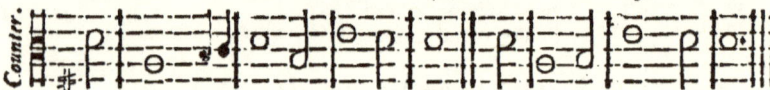

From Heav'n re—fist-less *Aid* af—ford,—And to his *Pray'rs* at-tend.

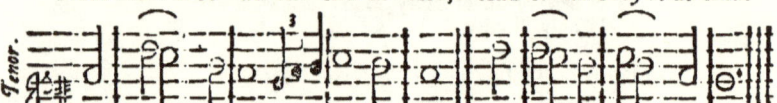

From Heav'n re-fist—less *Aid* af—ford,—And to his *Pray'rs* at-tend.

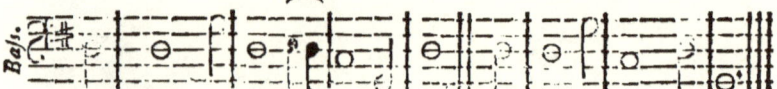

7 Some trust in *Steeds* for *War* design'd,—On *Chariots* some rely:
  Against them all we'll call to Mind—The Pow'r of GOD most high.
8 But from their *Steeds* and *Chariots* thrown,—Behold them thro' the Plain,
  Disorder'd, broke, and trampled down,—Whilst our firm *Troops* remain.
9 Still *save* us, LORD, and still proceed—Our rightful *Cause* to bless:
  Hear, KING of Heav'n, in Times of Need,—The *Pray'rs* that we address.

(DOXOLOGY, OR HALLELUJAH.)

An

An HYMN for EASTER-DAY.

1.

1 Cor. i. 7. SINCE CHRIST, our *Passover*, is slain
A *Sacrifice* for all:
Let all, with thankful Hearts, agree
To keep the *Festival*.

2.

Not with the *Leaven*, as of Old,
Of *Sin* and *Malice* fed:
But, with unfeign'd *Sincerity*,
And *Truth*'s unleaven'd Bread.

3.

om. vi. 9. CHRIST being rais'd by Pow'r *divine*,
And rescu'd from the *Grave*:
Shall die no more, *Death* shall on Him
No more *Dominion* have.

4.

Ver. 10. For that He dy'd, 'twas for our Sins
He once vouchsaf'd to die:
But that He *lives*, He lives to GOD,
For all *Eternity*.

5.

r. 11. So count yourselves as dead to *Sin*,
But *graciously* restor'd:
And made, henceforth, *alive* to GOD,
Through JESUS CHRIST our LORD.

DOXOLOGY.

O Holy, Holy, Holy LORD,
All Things *declare Thy Fame*:
Let all, in Trinity, accord;
To praise *Thy mighty Name*.

PSALMS *and* HYMNS.

To PSALM XXV. Compoſed in *Three Parts.* W. T.

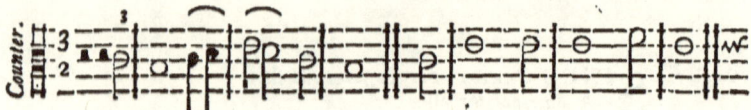

1. I Lift my Heart to Thee,—My God and *Guide* moſt juſt:

1. I Lift my Heart to Thee,—My God and *Guide* moſt juſt:

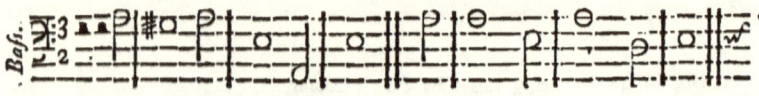

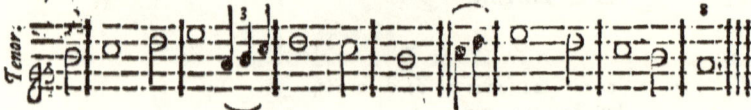

O ſuf--fer me to take no Shame,—For in Thee do I truſt.

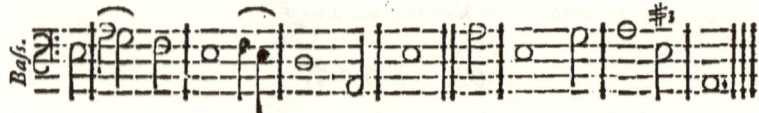

O ſuf--fer me to take no Shame,—For in Thee do I truſt.

2.
Let not my Foes rejoice,—Nor make a Scorn of me:
Nor let them e'er be overthrown—As put their Truſt in Thee.

3.
Let Shame all them befal—As harm Men wrongfully:
And Thy juſt *Paths,* and Thy right *Ways*—Unto me, Lord, deſcry.

4.
Direct me in Thy *Truth,*—And teach me, I Thee pray:
For Thou'rt my *Sav'our,* and my God,—On Thee I wait alway.

PSALM

PSALM XXV, *New Version*.
For a PUBLIC FAST *in Time of* WAR.

1.

TO GOD, in whom I trust,
   I lift my *Heart* and *Voice*:
O! let me not be put to Shame,
   Nor let my *Foes* rejoice.

2.

Those who on Thee rely,
   Let no *Disgrace* attend:
Be that the shameful Lot of such
   As wilfully offend.

3.

To me Thy *Truth* impart,
   And lead me in Thy Way:
For Thou art He that brings me *Help*,
   On Thee I wait alway.

4.

Thy *Mercies*, and Thy *Love*,
   O LORD, recal to Mind:
And them, O LORD, continue still,
   As Thou art ever kind.

5.

Consider, LORD, my *Foes*,
   How vast their *Numbers* grow:
What lawless *Force* and *Rage* they use,
   And boundless *Hatred* show.

6.

Protect, and set my Soul
   From all their *Malice* free:
Nor let them e'er be overcome,
   As put their Trust in Thee.

DOXOLOGY.
To GOD, *the* Father, Son,
   Be Praise *in Persons* Three:
As in Beginning, was, is now,
   And shall for ever be.

210 PSALMS and HYMNS.

To PSALM LVII, *New Version*. In *Four Parts*. W. T.

1. THY *Mercy*, LORD, to me extend,—On Thy *Protec-tion* I depend:

1. THY *Mercy*, LORD, to me extend,—On Thy *Protec-tion* I depend:

1. THY *Mercy*, LORD, to me extend,—On Thy *Protec-tion* I depend:

I to thy *Wings* for Shelter haste,—Till this out-rageous *Storm* is past.

I to thy *Wings* for Shelter haste,—Till this out rageous *Storm* is past.

I to thy *Wings* for Shelter haste,—Till this out-rageous *Storm* is past.

2 To Thy *Tribunal*, LORD, I fly,—Thou sov'reign *Judge*, and GOD most High:
Who *Wonders* hast for me begun,—And wilt not leave thy *Work* undone.
3 From Heav'n *protect* me with Thy *Arm*,—And shame all those as seek my *Harm*:
To my Relief Thy *Mercy* send—And *Truth*, on which my *Hopes* depend.
4 Be thou, O GOD, exalted High,—And, as Thy *Glory* fills the Sky:
So let it be on *Earth* display'd,—Till thou art here, as *there*, obey'd.

PSALMS and HYMNS.

An HYMN, from the 103d PSALM.
On RECOVERY from SICKNESS.

1.

Pſal. xxx. 1. MY GOD, ſince Thou haſt rais'd me up,
Thee I'll extol, with thankful Voice:
Who haſt ſecur'd me from thoſe Harms,
That would have made my Foes rejoice.

2.

Ver. 2. With Troubles worn, and Pains oppreſt,
To Thee I cry'd, and Thou didſt ſave:
Thou didſt ſupport my ſinking Hopes,
And Life didſt reſcue from the Grave.

3.

Ver. 4. Wherefore rejoice, ye Saints of His,
Proclaim the Praiſes of the LORD:
Let's call His Goodneſs all to Mind,
And His *Fidelity* record.

4.

Ver. 5. His Anger is but ſhort, His Love,
Which is our Life, doth longer ſtay
Grief may continue for a Night,
But Comfort riſes with the Day.

5.

Ver. 11, 12. My Glory ſhall proclaim GOD's Praiſe,
And what I vow'd, I now will give:
And ſtrive that in my grateful Verſe,
Thy Fame eternally may live.

DOXOLOGY.

To Father, Son, *and* Holy Ghoſt,
The bleſt, *and undivided* Three:
The One, *ſole* Giver *of all* Life,
GLORY, *and* Praiſe *for ever be.*

PSALMS and HYMNS.

To PSALM LXIII. For *Three Voices*. W. T.

4. LORD, as Thy *Mercies* far surmount—This Life, and wretched Days:

4. LORD, as Thy *Mercies* far surmount—This Life, and wretched Days:

My *Heart*, and *Voice*, shall give to Thee—Due *Honour*, *Thanks*, and *Praise*.

My *Heart*, and *Voice*, shall give to Thee—Due *Honour*, *Thanks*, and *Praise*.

5.
Ev'n whilst I live, I will not fail—To *worship* Thee alway:
And in Thy *Name* will I lift up—My Hands when I do pray.

6.
My Soul is, as with *Marrow*, fill'd,—Which is both fat and sweet:
Therefore, my *Voice* shall *sing* such *Songs*—As are for Thee most meet.

7.
When on my *Bed*, I think on Thee,—And in the silent *Night*:
And under *Covert* of Thy *Wings*—Rejoice with great Delight.

HYMN for CHRISTMAS-DAY.   W. TANS'UR.

Luke ii. 10.
WHAT joyful *News* did *Angels* bring
    On this most blessed Morn?
Glad *Tidings* of a *New-born* KING,
    That JESUS CHRIST was born!

John iv. 20.
Who did our Nature on *Him* take,
    And did *Himself* debase,
Col. i. 20.
Our *Peace* with GOD alone to make,
    And save all Human *Race*.

Psal. cxviii.
A mighty *Work* the LORD hath wrought,
    That we a SAV'OUR find,
Rom. xi. 11.
To *save* our Souls; who now hath brought
    SALVATION to *Mankind*.

1 Sam. ii. 1.
Now let us *sing*, *love*, and *admire*!
    With *Notes* above the Sky:
Luke ii. 14.
And join with *Heav'n's* celestial *Choir*,
    " GLORY to GOD on *high!* "

Sing *Hallelujah* to the LORD,
    To CHRIST be Glory still:
Ver. 14.
Peace to Earth may Heav'n afford,
    And unto Men *Good-Will*. — AMEN.

An HYMN for the HOLY COMMUNION.

Rev. xix. 5.
ALL ye who faithful Servants are
    Of our Almighty KING:
Both High and Low, both Small and Great,
    His *Praise* devoutly sing.

Ver. 7.
Let us *rejoice*, and render Thanks
    To *His* most holy Name:
Rejoice, rejoice, for now is come
    The *Marriage* of the LAMB!

Ver. 8.
His *Bride* Herself has ready made,
    How pure and white *Her* Dress!
Which is *Her Saints* Integrity,
    And spotless *Holiness*.

Ver. 9.
How, therefore, *blest* is ev'ry One
    Who to the *Marriage-Feast*
And *holy Supper* of the LAMB
    Is call'd a welcome *Guest*!

— *To Father, Son, &c.* —

214 PSALMS and HYMNS.

To PSALM LXXIII. For *Three Voices*. W. T.

23. WHat Thing is there that I can wish,—But in the *Heav'ns* above?

23. WHat Thing is there that I can wish,—But in the *Heav'ns* above?

For, on the *Earth* there nothing is—Like GOD that I can love.

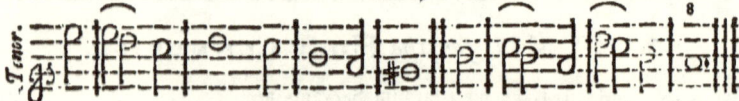

For, on the *Earth* there nothing is—Like GOD that I can love.

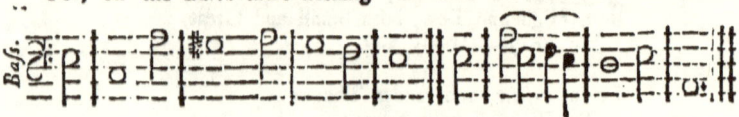

24.
Tho' *Flesh* and *Spirit* both should fail,—The LORD will me restore:
For of my *Heart* He is my *Strength*,—And *Portion* evermore.

25.
But, lo all such as Him forsake,—He will destroy each one:
And those that trust in any Thing,—Except in GOD alone.

26.
Therefore I will draw near to GOD,—And ever with Him dwell:
In GOD alone I'll put my Trust,—And will His *Wonders* tell.

A Me-

PSALMS and HYMNS.

A Meditational HYMN *on* GOD's Providence, &c.

1.
WHEN all Thy *Mercies* O my God!
My rising Soul surveys;
Transported with the View, I'm lost
In *Wonder*, LOVE, and *Praise*.

2.
But, how can *Words* with equal Warmth
The *Gratitude* declare;
That flows within my ravish'd Heart,
Yet Thou canst read it there.

3.
Thy PROVIDENCE my Life sustain'd,
And all my *Wants* redress'd,
When in the silent *Womb* I lay,
And hung upon the *Breast*.

4.
To all my weak *Complaints* and *Cries*,
Thy *Mercy* lent an Ear:
Before my feeble Thoughts had learn'd
To form themselves in *Pray'r*.

5.
Unnumber'd *Comforts*, to my Soul,
Thy tender *Care* bestow'd;
Before my Infant Heart conceiv'd
From whom those *Comforts* flow'd.

6.
When in the slipp'ry Paths of *Youth*
With heedless Steps I ran,
Thy ARM (unseen) convey'd me safe
Until I was a *Man*.

7.
Thro' hidden *Dangers*, *Toils*, and *Deaths*,
It gently clear'd the Way:
And from the pleasing Snares of *Vice*,
More to be fear'd than they.

8.
When worn with *Sickness*, oft Thou hast
With *Health* renew'd my Face:
And when, in *Sins*, and *Sorrows*, sunk
Reviv'dst my Soul with GRACE.

9.
Thy bounteous Hand with *worldly Bliss*
Hath made my *Cup* run o'er:
And, as a kind, and faithful, *Friend*,
Hath doubled all my Store.

10.
Ten Thousand Thousand precious *Gifts*,
My daily *Thanks* employ:
And, for the least, a *thankful* Heart
Should taste Thy *Gifts*, with Joy.

11.
Thro' ev'ry *Period* of my Life
Thy *Goodness* I'll pursue;
And, after Death, in distant Worlds,
The glorious *Theme* renew.

12.
When *Nature* fails, and Day and Night
Divide Thy WORKS no more:
My ever-grateful *Heart*, O LORD,
Thy *Mercy* shall adore.

13.
Thro' all *Eternity* to Thee
A joyful SONG I'll raise:
But, ah!—*Eternity*'s too short,
To utter all Thy PRAISE.——

DOXOLOGY.

To Father, Son, *and* Holy Ghost,
The undivided Three:
The one, *sole Giver of all* Life,
GLORY *for ever be.*

To PSALM LXXXVI, *New Verſion.* For *Three Voices.* W. 1

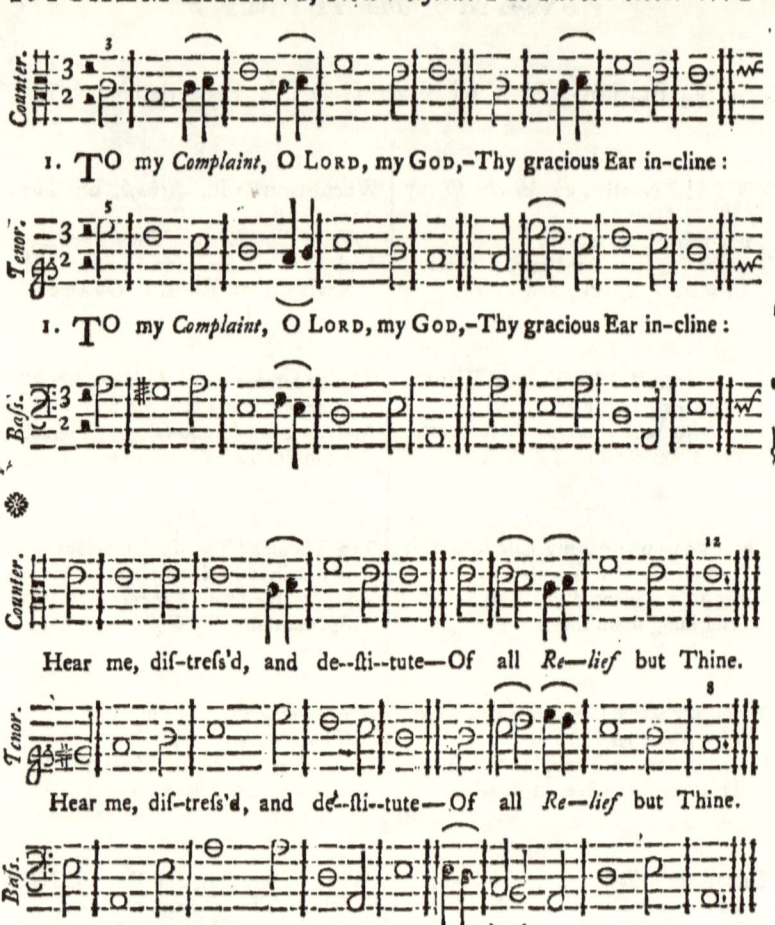

1. TO my *Complaint,* O LORD, my GOD,—Thy gracious Ear in-cline:

1. TO my *Complaint,* O LORD, my GOD,—Thy gracious Ear in-cline:

Hear me, dif-trefs'd, and de--ſti--tute—Of all Re—*lief* but Thine.

Hear me, dif-trefs'd, and de--ſti--tute—Of all Re—*lief* but Thine.

New Verſion.

2.
Do Thou, O GOD, preſerve my Soul,—That does Thy *Name* adore:
Thy *Servant* keep, and him, whoſe *Truſt*—Lies on Thee evermore.

3.
To me, who daily Thee invoke,—Thy *Mercy,* LORD, extend:
Refreſh Thy Servant's Soul, whoſe *Hopes*—On Thee alone depend.

4.
Thou, LORD, art *good,* not only good,—But prompt to *pardon* too:
And ſheweth *Mercy* to all thoſe—As for Thy *Mercy* ſue.

A Me-

A Meditational HYMN, *on a* Future State.

1.

MY Soul, come *meditate* the Day,
    And think how near it stands;
When thou muſt leave this *Houſe* of Clay,
    And fly to unknown Lands.

2.

And ye, mine Eyes, look down and view
    The hollow gaping *Tomb*:
This gloomy *Priſon* waits for you,
    Whene'er the *Summons* come.

3.

O, could we go with thoſe that die,
    And lie there in their Stead:
How would our Spirits learn to fly!
    And converſe with the *Dead!*

7.

Then ſhould we ſee the *Saints* above,
    In all their *glorious* Forms:
And wonder why our Souls ſhould love
    To dwell below with Worms.

5.

We then ſhould ſcorn our Cloaths of *Fleſh*,
    And hate our earthly *Load:*
And long for *Evening*, to undreſs,
    To reſt, in *Heav'n*, with G̦O̦D.

6.

We ſure ſhould long to leave our *Clay*,
    Before our *Summons* come:
And *pray* and *wiſh* our Souls away
    To *CHRIST's* eternal Home.

DOXOLOGY.

To *Father*, *Son*, and *Holy Ghoſt*,
    The undivided *Three:*
The *One*, ſole *Giver* of all *Life*,
    GLORY for ever be.

218 PSALMS and HYMNS.

To PSALM XCIII, New Version. In Four Parts. W.T.

1. WIth *Glory* clad, with Strength array'd,--The LORD, that o'er all *Nature* reigns:

1. WIth *Glory* clad, with Strength array'd,--The LORD, that o'er all *Nature* reigns:

1. WIth *Glory* clad, with Strength array'd,--The LORD, that o'er all *Nature* reigns:

The *World*'s Foundation strongly laid,--And its vast *Fabrick* still sustains.

The *World*'s Foundation strongly laid,--And its vast *Fabrick* still sustains.

The *World*'s Foundation strongly laid,--And its vast *Fabrick* still sustains.

2 How surely 'stablish'd is Thy *Throne!*—Which shall no Change of Period see:
For Thou, O LORD, and Thou alone,—Art GOD for all *Eternity*. [high:
3 Tho' *Floods*, O LORD, lift up their Voice, — And toss the troubled *Waves* on
Yet thou alone canst still their Noise,—And make the raging *Sea* comply.
4 Thy *Promise*, LORD, is ever sure.—And they that in Thy *House* would dwell,
That happy *Station* to secure,—Must all in *Holiness* excel.

—*To Father, Son, &c.*—

An

PSALMS and HYMNS.

An HYMN, *on* CHRIST'*s* Command *to* HIS Difciples, &c. Or, HIS GOSPEL *Minifters*' *Divine* Commiffion.

1.

(C H R I S T.)

Matt. x. 7. GO forth, ye *Heralds*, in MY *Name*,
　　　　　　 Sweetly the *Gofpel-Trumpet* found:
The glorious *Jubilee* proclaim,
Wherever *human Race* is found.

2.

　　　　　Preach to a World of Sinners, blind,
　　　　　And fhew them were their *Danger* lies:
Verfe 8.　 The *Broken-hearted* careful bind,
　　　　　And wipe all *Tears* from weeping *Eyes*.

3.

Verfe 16. Be *wife* as *Serpents* where you go,
And *harmlefs* as the peaceful *Dove*:
And let your whole *Deportment* fhow
That ye 're *commiffion'd* from ABOVE.

4.

Verfe 8.　 And, as ye freely have *receiv'd*,
Do ye to others freely *give*:
Then fhall your DOCTRINE be believ'd,
And, by ye, many Sinners live.

5.

(MINISTERS.)

Dear MASTER! *we'll Thy* WORD *obey*,
And be Thy Meffengers *of* Peace:
At Us *fhall* Devils *flee away*,
And tremble, *where we fhew Our Face*.

6.

O, happy *Servants* of the LORD!
Who thus their MASTER's *Will* obey:
Immenfely *great* is the REWARD
That they'll enjoy another Day.

AMEN.

PSALMS and HYMNS.
To PSALM XCIX. In Four Parts. W. T.

2 The Lord that doth in *Sion* dwell,—Is *high*, and wond'rous great:
 Above all *Gods* He doth excel,—And lofty is His *Seat*.
3 Let all Men *praise* God's mighty Name,—For it is *fearful* sure:
 And let all *magnify* the same,—That *holy* is and *pure*
9 So *praise* our God, and Lord therefore,—Upon his holy Hill:
 For why? our God, whom we *adore*,—He is most *holy* still.

An HYMN for Easter-Day.

1.

1 Cor. xv. 20.   CHRIST from the *Dead* is *rais'd*, and made
The *First-Fruits* of the *Tomb*:
For, as by Man came *Sin*, by Man
Did *Resurrection* come.

2.

Verse 21.   For, as in *Adam*, all Mankind
Did *Guilt* and *Death* derive:
So, by the *Righteousness* of CHRIST
Shall all be made *Alive*.

3.

Colof. iii. 1.   If then ye *risen* are with CHRIST,
Seek only how to get
The Things that are Above, where CHRIST
At GOD's Right-Hand is set.

—To *Father*, *Son*, &c.—

An HYMN for Trinity-Sunday.   W. TANS'UR.

Pfalm li.   LORD, tune our Souls with one Accord,
To *praise* Thy Name above:
And fix our *Faith* in Thee, O LORD,
Pfalm cxxv.   That nothing can it move.

Increase our *Faith*, we Thee desire,
Jude 20.   In Truth to worship *Thee*:
O *Holy Ghost!* our Souls inspire
With *Faith* of *Trinity*.

O LORD, *convert* each wand'ring Soul,
To Thy most heav'nly *Light*:
Eph ii. 5.   And let Thy GRACE our Sins controul,
And guide our *Paths* aright.

DOXOLOGY.

Now, to the bless'd eternal *Three*,
That bear *Record* above:
All highest *Praise* for ever be,
All *Glory*, *Thanks*, and *Love*.

PSALMS and HYMNS.

To PSALM CIII, *New Version.* In *Four Parts.* W. T.

Treble.

1. MY Soul, inspir'd with sacred Love,—GOD's holy Name for ever bless:

Counter.

1. MY Soul, inspir'd with sacred Love,—GOD's holy Name for ever bless:

Tenor.

1. MY Soul, inspir'd with sacred Love,—GOD's holy Name for ever bless:

Bass.

Of all His *Favours* mindful prove,—And still thy grateful *Thanks* express.

Of all His *Favours* mindful prove,—And still thy grateful *Thanks* express.

Of all His *Favours* mindful prove,—And still thy grateful *Thanks* express.

2 'Tis He that all thy *Sins* forgives,—And after *Sickness* makes thee sound:
From Danger He thy *Life* retrieves,—By Him with Grace and *Mercy* crown'd.
3 He with good Things my Mouth supplies,—Thy Vigour, *Eagle*-like, renews:
He, when the guiltless Suff'rer cries,—His Foes with just Revenge pursues.
4 GOD made, of Old, his righteous Ways—To *Moses*, and our Fathers, known:
His *Works*, to his eternal *Praise*,—Were to the Sons of *Jacob* shown.

An

An HYMN, *on* CHRIST's *glorious* Person, &c.

1.

NOW to the LORD a noble *Song!*
Awake my *Soul,* awake my *Tongue:*
Hosanna to His mighty *Name,*
And all His boundless LOVE proclaim.

2.

See! where it shines in JESU's Face,
The brightest *Image* of His *Grace!*
GOD in the *Person* of His SON
Has all His greatest *Works* out-done.

3.

The spacious *Earth,* and spreading *Flood,*
Proclaim a *wise* and *pow'rful* GOD:
And all His *Glories* from afar
Sparkle in ev'ry rolling *Star.*

4.

But, in CHRIST's Looks GOD's Glory stands,
The noblest *Labour* of His Hands:
The pleasing *Lustre* of His Eyes
Out-shines the *Wonders* of the *Skies.*

5.

GRACE! 'tis a sweet and charming *Theme!*
Rejoice, my Thoughts, at JESU's Name:
Ye Angels, dwell upon the Sound,
Ye Heav'ns reflect it to the Ground.

6.

LORD, may we live to reach the Place,
Where CHRIST unveils His glorious Face:
And there His Beauty to behold,
And sing His Name to Harps of Gold.

DOXOLOGY.

O *Holy, Holy, Holy* LORD,
As *Angels* sing, with one Accord:
So may we *sing* with CHRIST most High,
And *glory* in GOD's *Majesty.*

AMEN.

PSALMS and HYMNS.

To PSALM CV, *New Version.* In *Four Parts.* W. T.

1. O Render *Thanks* and *bless* the LORD,—Invoke His sacred Name:

1. O Render *Thanks* and *bless* the LORD,—Invoke His sacred Name:

1. O Render *Thanks* and *bless* the LORD,—Invoke His sacred Name:

1. O Render *Thanks* and *bless* the LORD,—Invoke His sacred Name:

Acquaint the Nations with His *Deeds,*—His matchless *Deeds* proclaim.

Acquaint the Nations with His *Deeds,*—His matchless *Deeds* proclaim.

Acquaint the Nations with His *Deeds,*—His matchless *Deeds* proclaim.

2 Sing to His *Praise* in lofty Hymns,—His wond'rous *Works* rehearse:
Make Them the *Theme* of your Discourse,—And *Subject* of your *Verse.*
3 Rejoice in His Almighty Name,—Alone to be ador'd:
And let their Hearts o'erflow with Joy,—That humbly seek the LORD.
4 Seek ye the LORD, his saving Strength—Devoutly still implore:
And where He's ever present, seek—His Face for evermore.

An HYMN for WHITSUNDAY.

John xiv. 10.
HE's come, let ev'ry Knee be bent,
　All Hearts new *Joy* resume:
Let Nations *sing*, with one Consent,
　The COMFORTER is come!

Ephes. i. 3.
What greater *Gift*, what greater *LOVE*
　Can *GOD* on *Man* bestow?
The Angels JOY in *Heav'n* above,
　And all our *Heav'n* below.

Ibid. i. 17.
Hail, *blessed Spir't!* each pious Soul
　Doth thy Influence feel:
Thou dost our darling Sins controul,
　And fix our wav'ring Zeal.

Ibid.
Thou to the *Conscience* dost convey
　The Checks that all must know:
Thy *Motions* point to us the Way;
　Thou giv'st us Strength to go.

Ibid. i. 26.
As *Pilots* by their *Compass* steer,
　Till they their *Harbours* find:
So, LORD, Thy *Inspirations* here,
　Guide ev'ry wand'ring Mind.

Prov. xi. 6.
'Though *Winds* and *Waves* our Course obstruct,
　And foaming Billows roar:
Thou, LORD, wilt righteous Men conduct
　Safe to Thy *Heav'nly Shore.*

— To *Father*, &c. —

A FUNERAL HYMN; to the 146th Psalm Tune.

1.

I Heard a *Voice* from Heav'n to say,
　" *Write, Blest* eternally
" Are those dead Men, and only they,
　" That in the LORD do die.

2.

" For, from their *Labour* and their Pain
　" They shall for ever cease:
" Their *Works* shall cause them to remain
　" In everlasting *Peace.*"

— To *Father, Son,* &c. —

226   PSALMS and HYMNS.

To PSALM CXII, *New Version.* In *Four Parts.* W.T.

1. THAT Man is blest who stands in Awe—Of God, and loves His sacred *Law*:

1. THAT Man is blest who stands in Awe—Of God, and loves His sacred *Law*:

1. THAT Man is blest who stands in Awe—Of God, and loves His sacred *Law*:

His *Seed* on Earth shall be renown'd,—And with suc--cef--five Honours crown'd.

His *Seed* on Earth shall be renown'd,—And with suc--cef--five Honours crown'd.

His *Seed* on Earth shall be renown'd,—And with suc--cef--five Honours crown'd.

2 His House the Seat of Wealth shall be,—An inexhausted *Treasury*:
  His Justice, free from all Decay,—Shall *Blessings* to his *Heirs* convey.
3 The Soul that's fill'd with Virtue's Light,—Shines brightest in Affliction's Night:
  To *pity* the Distress'd inclin'd—As well as just to all Mankind.
4 His lib'ral Favours he extends,—To some he gives, to others lends:
  Yet what his *Charity* impairs,—He gives, by Prudence, in Affairs, &c.

An

PSALMS *and* HYMNS.

An HYMN, *from the* XXIIId PSALM.

1.

THE LORD my *Pasture* does prepare,
And feeds me with a *Shepherd*'s Care;
His *Presence* does my *Wants* supply,
And *guards* me with a watchful Eye:
 My *Noon-day* Walks He does attend,
 And all my *midnight* Hours defend.

2.

When on the sultry *Glebe* I faint,
Or, on the thirsty *Mountains* pant;
To fertile *Vales*, and dewy *Meads*,
My weary wand'ring Steps He leads:
 Where peaceful *Rivers*, soft and slow,
 Amidst the verdant *Landskip* flow.

3.

Tho' in the Paths of *Death* I tread,
With gloomy *Horrors* overspread;
My stedfast *Heart* shall fear no Ill,
For, Thou, O LORD, art with me still:
 Thy friendly *Crook* shall give me Aid,
 And guide me thro' *Death*'s dismal Shade.

4.

Tho' in a bare and rugged Way,
Thro' various lonely *Wilds* I stray;
GOD's *Presence* shall my *Pains* beguile,
The barren *Wilderness* shall smile;
 With sudden *Greens*, and *Herbage* crown'd,
 The *Streams* shall murmur all around.

DOXOLOGY.

To GOD *Almighty*, Father, Son,
Be Honour, Praise, *and* Worship *done*;
By Saints, *and* Angels *sacred Host*,
To Comforter, *the* Holy Ghost:
 As 'twas in Ages heretofore,
 Be now, *and henceforth evermore.*

228   PSALMS and HYMNS.

To PSALM CXXVIII, *Old Version.* In *Four Parts.* W. T.

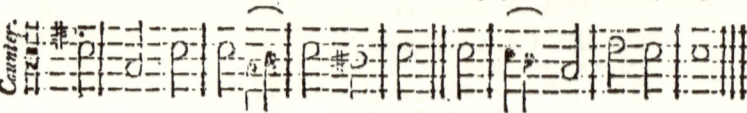

1. Blessed art thou that fear-est God,—And walkest in His Ways:

1. Blessed art thou that fear-est God,—And walkest in His Ways:

1. Blessed art thou that fear-est God,—And walkest in His Ways:

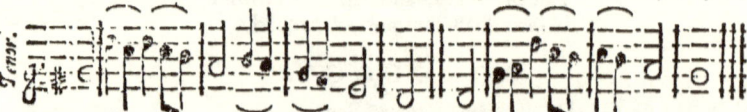

For of thy La-bour thou shalt eat,—Hap-py shall be thy Days.

For of thy La-bour thou shalt eat,—Hap-py shall be thy Days.

For of thy La-bour thou shalt eat,—Hap-py shall be thy Days.

2 Like fruitful *Vines* on thy House-side,—So doth thy *Wife* spring out:
Thy *Children* stand like Olive-plants—Thy Table round about.
3 Thus thou art bless'd that fearest God,—And he shall let thee see
The promised *Jerusalem*,—And her Felicity.
4 Thou shalt thy Childrens Children see,—To thy great Joy, increase:
And likewise Grace on *Israel*,—Prosperity and Peace, &c.

ADVICE

PSALMS and HYMNS.

ADVICE to YOUTH: Or, An HYMN from Eccles. xii.
By W. T. *(To the foregoing Tune.)*

1.

Verse 1.   **K**NOW well thy MAKER in thy *Youth*,
And *godly* be inclin'd:
And early seek GOD's Ways of *Truth*,
That thou may'st GLORY find.

2.

Verse 3.   For, in *Old-Age*, each tott'ring Limb
Will strive, alas! in vain:
Verse 2.   Our Sun-bright *Eyes* will then wax dim,
And Days be full of Pain.

3.

Verse 4.   We, restless, then shall early rise,
And tremble as we go:
Our Ears be *deaf* to ev'ry Noise,
Verse 6.   And ev'ry *Pulse* beat low.

4.

Verse 5.   Then will each Almond hoary Head
Be flourishing and gay:
Concupiscence will then be fled,
And *Vigour* fade away.

5.

Death then strikes ev'ry *Motion* dumb,
Verse 7.   And *Bodies* turn to Dust:
Verse 14.   But Souls must sure to *Judgment* come,
The Wicked, and the Just.

6.

Then happy they! who, in their *Youth*,
Psalm xxiv. 4.   Did *Godliness* regard:
They surely, from the GOD of *Truth*,
Will have a just *Reward*.

7.

Psalm cxlv.   Hence, let GOD's great and sacred *Name*
Be ever on your Tongue:
Psalm ii. 12.   And let CHRIST be (with equal Flame)
The *Close* of ev'ry SONG.

AMEN.

PSALMS and HYMNS.

To PSALM CXXXIV, *New Version*. In *Four Parts*. W.T.

1. Bless God, ye Servants that attend — Up-on His so-lemn State:

1. Bless God, ye Servants that attend — Up-on His so-lemn State:

1. Bless God, ye Servants that at-tend — Up-on His solemn State:

That in His Tem-ple Night by Night — With humble Rev'rence wait.

That in His Tem-ple Night by Night — With humble Rev'rence wait.

That in His Tem-ple Night by Night — With humble Rev'rence wait.

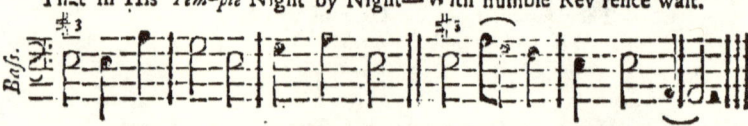

2 Within His House lift up your Hands, — And bless His holy Name:
From *Sion* bless thy *Isr'el*, Lord, — Who Heav'n and Earth didst frame.

DOXOLOGY.

To Father, Son, *and* Holy Ghost, *the undivided* Three:
The One, *sole* Giver *of all* Life, Glory *for ever be.*

PSALMS and HYMNS.

GOD our only SAFEGUARD, by Sea and Land,
A Meditational HYMN; by W. TANS'UR.

1 LORD, for the *Just* Thou doft provide,
How fure is their *Defence!*
Eternal WISDOM is their Guide,
And Help Omnipotence.

2 Though I in foreign Lands remote
Should breathe in tainted Air:
Through burning *Climes*, Thou'rt my Support,
By LOVE, and tender Care.

3 Thy *Mercy* fweet'ned ev'ry Soil,
Made ev'ry *Country* pleafe:
Thou on the fnowy Hills didft fmile,
And fmooth'd'ft the rugged Seas.

4 Think, O my Soul, devoutly think,
How, with amazing Eyes,
When, on the Sea, juft at Life's Brink,
What Horrors did arife.

5 Confufion in each Face appear'd,
And *Fear* in ev'ry Heart:
When Waves on Waves fo lofty rear'd,
As fhock'd the *Pilot*'s Art.

6 Yet, from all Grief, LORD, Thy *Defence*,
And Mercy, fet me free:
When, with an humble Confidence,
My Soul took Hold on Thee.

7 For, though in dreadful *Storms*, with Fear,
We hung on broken Wave;
I know, Thou waft not flow to hear,
Nor impotent to fave.

8 The *Storms* were laid, the Winds did ceafe,
Obedient to Thy Will:
The *Sea* did from its Rage decreafe,
And ev'ry *Wave* lay ftill.

9 Through ev'ry *Scene*, while Life does laft,
Thy Goodnefs I'll adore:
And praife Thee for all Mercies paft,
Thee love—and hope for more.

10 My Life (whilft here, in ev'ry State,)
A *Sacrifice* fhall be:
And Death (when Death fhall be my Fate)
Shall join my Soul to Thee.

AMEN.

232 PSALMS and HYMNS.

To PSALM CXLVI, *New Version.* In *Four Parts.* W. T.

Treble.

1. O Praise the LORD, and thou my Soul—For e--ver *bless* His Name:

Counter.

1. O Praise the LORD, and thou my Soul—For e--ver *bless* His Name:

Tenor.

1. O Praise the LORD, and thou my Soul—For e--ver *bless* His Name:

Bass.

Treble.

His wond'rous LOVE whilst Life shall last—My constant *Praise* shall claim.

Counter.

His wond'rous LOVE whilst Life shall last—My constant *Praise* shall claim.

Tenor.

His wond'rous LOVE whilst Life shall last—My constant *Praise* shall claim.

Bass.

2 On *Kings*, the greatest Sons of Men,—Let none for Aid rely:
They cannot save, In dang'rous Times,—Nor timely Help apply.
3 Depriv'd of Breath, to *Dust* they turn,—And there neglected lie:
And, all their Thoughts and vain *Designs*,—Together with them die.
4 Then happy he! who *Jacob's* GOD—For his *Protector* takes:
Who still, with well-plac'd *Hope*, the LORD—His constant *Refuge* makes.

A Funeral

A Funeral HYMN.

1 Job. ii. 10.   AS now our *Brother*, here deceas'd,
                   Is hasting to the *Grave*:
Tit. ii. 13.   We hope *his* Soul's among the *Bless'd*;
                Let fruitless Sorrow wave.

Phil. i. 21.   Our Loss is now *his* greatest Gain,
                Let no rude Hand annoy:
Psalm civ. 29. Whose *Dust* now sleeps, exempt from Pain,
                In Hopes of future *Joy*.

2 Cor. iii. 18. We at the great *Tribunal-day*
                Must all together meet:
                And there Our grateful Homage pay
                At Our kind MASTER's Feet.

Rom. vi. 13.   Then the great JUDGE, from His high *Throne*,
                Bright *Crowns* of Gold will give
Acts xvii. 31. To such as have His *Precepts* known,
                And study'd well to live.

2 Chron. xxx.   Oh! let Us then Our Souls prepare
18, 19.   For that uncertain *Hour*:
Acts xxvi. 18. Lest *Death* should end our Pain and Care,
                In Sin, by *Satan*'s Pow'r.

Prov. xiv. 18. LORD, give Us *Grace*, Our Times to spend,
                In *Virtue*'s prudent Way:
                That, when Our mortal Lives shall end,
                No Guilt may Us disway. — *Amen*.

A FUNERAL HYMN; by W. TANS'UR.

Rev. xiv. 13.   HOW *bless'd* are they, in CHRIST who die!
                  What LIFE attends their Death!
1 Cor. xv. 20. They *rise*, (scarce fallen) and *revive*
                With their last dying Breath.

Job xix. 26.   And, tho' their *Bodies*, lodg'd in *Dust*,
                Do foul *Corruption* see;
Col. iii. 4.   At the *last* DAY They'll *rise*, as *just*,
                And *shine* t'Eternity.

1 Cor. xv. 55. Bless'd DAY!—Then they loud *Songs* shall *sing*
                Of Mirth, *triumphantly*:
                "O *Death! Where is thy deadly Sting*?
                "O *Grave! thy Victory*?

                O *JESUS*, Who did'st conquer *Death*,
                In *Us* all Sin subdue:
                Thou, rais'd to *Life*, so give Us Birth,
                And JOYS for ever *new*.

                ——*To Father, Son, &c.* ——

PSALMS and HYMNS.

To PSALM CL, *New Version.* In *Four Parts.* W. T.

2 Praife Him for all the mighty *Acts*—Which He in our Behalf has done:
His *Kindnefs* this Return exacts,—With which our *Praife* fhould equal run.
3 Let the fhrill *Trumpet*'s warlike Voice-Make Rocks and Hills His *Praife* rebound:
Praife Him with *Harp*'s melodious Noife,—And gentle *Pfalt'ry*'s filver Sound.

4. Let

PSALMS and HYMNS.

4.

Let Virgin *Troops* foft *Timbrels* bring,
And fome with graceful *Motions* dance:
Let *Inftruments* of various Strings,
With ORGANS join'd, His *Praife* advance.

5.

Let them who joyful HYMNS compofe,
To *Cymbals* fet their SONGS of *Praife*:
Cymbals of common Ufe, and thofe
That loudly found on folemn *Days*.

6.

Let all that vital *Breath* enjoy,
Which GOD does, hourly, them afford:
In juft Returns His *Praife* employ;
And let all Creatures *praife the* LORD.

DOXOLOGY.

John v. 7. GLORY *to* GOD, *our Heav'nly* KING!
Rev. i. 6. *Thy* Name *be* prais'd *in* Perfons THREE:
May we in Heav'n *for ever* fing
Eternal PRAISES *unto* THEE.

---

2 Cor. xiii. 11. { In *Fine*, my *Friends*, I bid ye all *farewel*,
In perfect LOVE may all ftrive to excel:
Be of *good Comfort*, of one godly Mind,
For fuch, in *CHRIST*, will *Peace* and GLORY find. }

AMEN.

Bofton, March 12, 1761.   W. TANS'UR.

FINIS.

ERRATA.

PREFACE, Page ix. Line ult. for *Eccluf.* xxxiv. read xliv. For *Ofterwald*, read *Ofterwald*—Page 3, Pfal. iii. for *Fright*, read *Flight*.—Page 7, make the *Date* 1062.—Page 11, Line 2, read, *with many Weapons.*—Page 35, Line 12, read, *though wicked* Achitophel.—Page 37, Pfal. xlvi. read, *hint what Griefs.*—Page 43, Pfal. li. fet the *Date* 2969 before the large Capital O.—Page 44, Pfal. lii. Line 4, read *Ahimelech*; and the fame on Page 45, Line 11.—Page 131, Col 2, for *Joab*, read DAVID.—Page 153, Line 9, read, DAVID *made fuch Mufic.*—Page 158, Line 24, for 16, read 27.—Page 168, § xvii. for *Beroneth*, read *Beeroth*.—Page 172, § xx. Line 16, read, *if he, and they, walked.*—Page 189, § xxxvi. for *Exod.* read *Deut.* and read, *Iron Bedftead.*—Page 193, § xxxviii. Lines 15 and 17, make the 28, 13; and the 13, 28.—Page 200, fet the 7th *Note* of the loweft Bafs in the lower Space, and the 8th *Note* in the Space above the middle Line; or A. and E. The Mood fhould be $\frac{3}{2}$ Tripla Time.

BOOKS lately published, by WILLIAM TANS'UR, *senior.*

I. THE *New Royal* MELODY *Compleat :* Or, *The New Harmony of* SION. In Three BOOKS. Containing, I. A *New* and *Correct* INTRODUCTION to CHURCH-MUSICK in General, in all its Parts; *Rudimental, Practical,* and *Technical.*---II. A New and Compleat Body of CHURCH-MUSICK, adapted to the most select *Portions* of the BOOK of PSALMS, of either *Versions*; with many *Fuging Chorus*'s and *Gloria Patri*'s to the Whole.---III. A New and Select Number of *Services, Chants, Hymns, Anthems,* and *Canons*; suited to several *Occasions*; and many never before printed : Set by the greatest Masters in the World ; according to the *present* Practice of PSALMODY.

The Whole are Composed in *Two, Three, Four, Five, Six, Seven,* and *Eight* Musical *Parts,* according to the nicest *Rules*; consisting of *Solo*'s, *Fuges,* and *Chorus*'s, for Voices, or Organ ; and fitted for all *Teachers, Learners,* and Musical *Societies,* &c. With a PREFACE on *Church-Musick,* and a TABLE to the Whole in general, &c. &c. &c. The SECOND EDITION, *Octavo.*

II. A New *Musical* GRAMMAR and DICTIONARY : Or, A General INTRODUCTION to the Whole ART of MUSICK ; both *Vocal* and *Instrumental*; *Rudimental, Practical, Philosophical, Technical,* and *Historical*; from the Earliest Times, down to these Present : With all Kinds of LESSONS in great Variety, &c. &c. The THIRD EDITION, in *Octavo.*

☞ The above Books are correctly printed in *Score* for *Voices* or *Organ*; and Sold by the AUTHOR ; Who *Teacheth* the same, after the *Newest* and *Best* Method : Together with all other *Grounds* and *Principles* of MUSICK, &c. &c. &c.

www.ingramcontent.com/pod-product-compliance
Lightning Source LLC
Chambersburg PA
CBHW021401230426
43666CB00006B/600